Douglas B. Miller and Loren L. Johns, Editors

BELIEVERS CHURCH BIBLE COMMENTARY

Old Testament

Genesis, by Eugene F. Roop, 1987
Exodus, by Waldemar Janzen, 2000
Leviticus, by Perry B. Yoder, *forthcoming*
Deuteronomy, by Gerald Gerbrandt, 2015
Joshua, by Gordon H. Matties, 2012
Judges, by Terry L. Brensinger, 1999
Ruth, Jonah, Esther, by Eugene F. Roop, 2002
1–2 Samuel, by David Baker, *forthcoming*
1–2 Kings, by Lynn Jost, *forthcoming*
1–2 Chronicles, by Gus Konkel, 2016
Ezra-Nehemiah, by Steven Schweitzer, *forthcoming*
Job, by Paul Keim, *forthcoming*
Psalms, by James H. Waltner, 2006
Proverbs, by John W. Miller, 2004
Ecclesiastes, by Douglas B. Miller, 2010
Isaiah, by Ivan D. Friesen, 2009
Jeremiah, by Elmer A. Martens, 1986
Lamentations, Song of Songs, by Wilma Ann Bailey and Christina A. Bucher, 2014
Ezekiel, by Millard C. Lind, 1996
Daniel, by Paul M. Lederach, 1994
Hosea, Amos, by Allen R. Guenther, 1998
Joel, Obadiah, Nahum, by James Brenneman, *forthcoming*
Micah, Habakkuk, Zephaniah, by Dan Epp-Tiessen and Derek Suderman, *forthcoming*
Haggai, Zechariah, Malachi, by Patricia Shelly, *forthcoming*

New Testament

Matthew, by Richard B. Gardner, 1991
Mark, by Timothy J. Geddert, 2001
Luke, by Mary H. Schertz, *forthcoming*
John, by Willard M. Swartley, 2012
Acts, by Chalmer E. Faw, 1993
Romans, by John E. Toews, 2004
1 Corinthians, by Dan Nighswander, *forthcoming*
2 Corinthians, by V. George Shillington, 1998
Galatians, by George R. Brunk III, 2015
Ephesians, by Thomas R. Yoder Neufeld, 2002
Philippians, by Gordon Zerbe, 2016
Colossians, Philemon, by Ernest D. Martin, 1993
1–2 Thessalonians, by Jacob W. Elias, 1995
1–2 Timothy, Titus, by Paul M. Zehr, 2009
Hebrews, by Estella Horning, *forthcoming*
James, by Sheila Klassen-Wiebe, *forthcoming*

1–2 Peter, Jude, by Erland Waltner and J. Daryl Charles, 1999
1, 2, 3 John, by Jay McDermott, 2011
Revelation, by John R. Yeatts, 2003

Philippians

Gordon Zerbe

HERALD PRESS
Harrisonburg, Virginia
Kitchener, Ontario

Library of Congress Cataloging-in-Publication Data

Names: Zerbe, Gordon, author.
Title: Philippians / Gordon Zerbe.
Description: Harrisonburg, VA : Herald Press, 2016. | Series: Believers church Bible commentary
Identifiers: LCCN 2016026927 | ISBN 9781513800332 (pbk. : alk. paper)
Subjects: LCSH: Bible. Philippians--Commentaries.
Classification: LCC BS2705.53 .Z47 2016 | DDC 227/.607--dc23 LC record available at https://lccn.loc.gov/2016026927

Library of Congress Control Number: 2016026927
International Standard Book Number: 978-1-5138-0033-2
Printed in the United States of America
Cover by Merrill R. Miller
Interior design by Merrill R. Miller and Alice Shetler

For orders or information, call 800-245-7894 or visit HeraldPress.com.

20 19 18 17 16 10 9 8 7 6 5 4 3 2 1

To my colleagues and students
at the Divinity School of Silliman University,
Dumaguete City, Philippines,
from whom I have learned so much about Philippians

Abbreviations

*	Text in Biblical Context (TBC)
+	Text in the Life of the Church (TLC)
/	alternative to, or; and (as required by context)
//	parallel to
alt.	slight alteration of a quotation
AT	author's translation
BCE	before the Common Era
BDAG	Bauer, W., F. W. Danker, W. F. Arndt, and F. W. Gingrich, eds. *Greek-English Lexicon of the New Testament and Other Early Christian Literature*. 3rd ed. Chicago: University of Chicago Press, 2000.
[bracketed title]	cross-reference to an entry in the appended Essays
c.	century
ca.	circa, approximately
CE	Common Era
CEB	Common English Bible
CEV	Contemporary English Version
cf.	*confer*, compare
ch(s).	chapter(s)
d.	died
DSS	Dead Sea Scrolls
e.g.,	*exempli gratia*, for example
EN	Explanatory Notes (on a section of Philippians)
esp.	especially
ESV	English Standard Version
et al.	*et alia*, and others
etc.	*et cetera*, and the rest
Gk.	Greek
Heb.	Hebrew
i.e.	*id est*, that is
ISV	International Standard Version
JB	Jerusalem Bible
KJV	King James Version
km	kilometer
Lat.	Latin
lit.	literally
LSJ	Liddell, H. G., R. Scott, and H. S. Jones, eds., *A Greek-English Lexicon*. 9th ed. with revised supplement. Oxford: Clarendon, 1996
LXX	Septuagint (the Greek Old Testament, ca. 200 BCE)

mg.	marginal note
NABRE	New American Bible, Revised Edition, 2011
NASB	New American Standard Bible
NET	New English Translation
NIV	New International Version, 2011
NIV 1984	New International Version, 1984
NJB	New Jerusalem Bible
NLT	New Living Translation
NRSV	New Revised Standard Version
NT	New Testament
OT	Old Testament
RSV	Revised Standard Version
sq.	square
TBC	Text in Biblical Context
TDNT	*Theological Dictionary of the New Testament*
TEV	Today's English Version [Good News Bible]
TLC	Text in the Life of the Church
TNIV	Today's New International Version
v(v).	verse(s)
x	times a term occurs

Contents

Series Foreword

The Believers Church Bible Commentary series makes available a new tool for basic Bible study. It is published for all who seek more fully to understand the original message of Scripture and its meaning for today—Sunday school teachers, members of Bible study groups, students, pastors, and others. The series is based on the conviction that God is still speaking to all who will listen, and that the Holy Spirit makes the Word a living and authoritative guide for all who want to know and do God's will.

The desire to help as wide a range of readers as possible has determined the approach of the writers. Since no blocks of biblical text are provided, readers may continue to use the translation with which they are most familiar. The writers of the series use the New Revised Standard Version and the New International Version on a comparative basis. They indicate which text they follow most closely and where they make their own translations. The writers have not worked alone, but in consultation with select counselors, the series' editors, and the Editorial Council.

Every volume illuminates the Scriptures; provides necessary theological, sociological, and ethical meanings; and in general makes "the rough places plain." Critical issues are not avoided, but neither are they moved into the foreground as debates among scholars. Each section offers "Explanatory Notes," followed by focused articles, "The Text in Biblical Context" and "The Text in the Life of the Church." This commentary aids the interpretive process but does not try to supersede the authority of the Word and Spirit as discerned in the gathered church.

The term *believers church* emerged in the mid-twentieth century to define Christian groups with direct or indirect connections to the Radical Reformation, a distinctive faith expression that arose in Europe during the sixteenth century. These believers were concerned that the church be voluntary and not be aligned with political government. *Believers church* has come to represent an identifiable tradition of beliefs and practices that includes believers (adult) baptism; a voluntary fellowship that practices church discipline, mutual aid, and service; belief in the power of love in all relationships; and a willingness to follow Christ by embracing his cross as a way of life. In recent decades the term has sometimes been applied to church communities informed by Anabaptism, evangelicalism, or pietism, such as Brethren Church, Brethren in Christ, Church of the Brethren, Mennonite Brethren, and Mennonites, as well as similar groups. The writers chosen for the series speak from within this tradition.

Believers church people have always been known for their emphasis on obedience to the simple meaning of Scripture. Because of this, they do not have a long history of deep historical-critical biblical scholarship. This series attempts to be faithful to the Scriptures while also taking archaeology and current biblical studies seriously. Doing this means that at many points the writers will not differ greatly from interpretations that can be found in many other good commentaries. Yet these writers share basic convictions about Christ, the church and its mission, God and history, human nature, the Christian life, and other doctrines. These presuppositions do shape a writer's interpretation of Scripture. Thus this series, like all other commentaries, stands within a specific historical church tradition.

Many in this stream of the church have expressed a need for help in Bible study. This is justification enough to produce the Believers Church Bible Commentary. Nevertheless, the Holy Spirit is not bound to any tradition. May this series be an instrument in breaking down walls between Christians in North America and around the world, bringing new joy in obedience through a fuller understanding of the Word.

—*The Editorial Council*

Author's Preface: Philippi, Philippians, Philippines

My assignment to write this commentary on Philippians came when I was serving with Mennonite Central Committee in a second term as a visiting professor at Silliman University Divinity School, Dumaguete City, Philippines. My experience in the Philippines (1996–98, 2002–4) has decisively shaped my interaction with Philippians. Even the terms *Philippians* and *Philippines* have a deep historical connection. A similar colonial history was responsible for the naming of both Philippi and the Philippines. The designation Philippines for a country comes from Spanish conquerors, referring to the islands claimed on behalf of King Philip of Spain, whose name legacy also goes back to the same Philip II who conquered and named Philippi.

I discovered that Paul is not always a popular figure among Filipino Christians and theologians—at least without some significant clarification—because of his apparent "political" perspective. Paul's writings had been used by the ruling elite in their system of domination to recommend passive acceptance, if not direct support, of the prevailing oppressive political structures as "ordained" by God. In reaction, one of my Filipino students explained with an assertion that interrupted my lecture: "The problem with Paul is that he never renounced his Roman citizenship." This remark put me in an awkward position as a holder of both Canadian and American citizenship, among the most privileged in the world. In that way, I myself am aligned with new forms of imperial extension, evident not so much in territorial terms, but certainly in economic terms (see further Zerbe 2003, 2005).

So my students, colleagues, and I together explored alternative ways, other than the received viewpoint, to understand and draw inspiration from Paul. Quite apart from quietist acceptance of unjust political rule, Paul in Philippians promotes a more critical posture toward unjust global rule, in solidarity with the underside of history. He is thus especially relevant for the Philippines and other places of similar experience. Indeed, we might even wonder whether Paul eventually made a personal commitment—even if not a formal, public one—to let go of his Roman citizenship, along with its impressive status and privileges, as a consequence of his declaration that he has let go of all his worldly credentials and privileges in favor of his sole loyalty to Christ (1:27; 3:3-11, 20-21). This commentary is thus dedicated to my colleagues and students from the Divinity School of Silliman University.

There are many people to acknowledge for their work and support during the writing and publication of this commentary. Thanks go to Loren Johns, NT editor of this series, for his tireless work and patient advice along the way. Thanks to Michael Gorman for some helpful feedback on some fine points of exegesis. Thanks to Canadian Mennonite University for granting me a sabbatical during the months of September to December 2015, which I spent mostly on editorial cleanup of the commentary. During most of that time I was privileged to be a guest in the home of Joji and Dann Pantoja, Mennonite Church Canada Witness workers based in Davao City, Philippines. They have developed a visionary and holistic ministry of peace and reconciliation (including social entrepreneurship) in the context of multiply colonized, war-torn, and impoverished Mindanao. They articulate peace as multidimensional: "harmony with the Creator (spiritual transformation); harmony with our being (psychosocial transformation); harmony with others (sociopolitical transformation); and harmony with the creation (economic-ecological transformation)." And in their context of multilateral turmoil among people-groups, they see reconciliation as a way "to address, to integrate, and to embrace the painful past, and the necessary shared future as a means of dealing with the present" (quoted from website of PeaceBuilders Community Incorporated). Their vision and work has been a constant source of inspiration in the final stages of this commentary project.

—Gordon Zerbe
Winnipeg, Manitoba

Introduction to Philippians

The First Reception of Philippians

Imagine the anticipation as a small group of loyal adherents of Lord Jesus Messiah in Philippi gathers to hear a letter just received from Paul. He is not only their founder and leader, as "special envoy" (apostle) of Messiah Jesus to the nations, but also their friend, partner, and brother. The time of writing is most likely in the middle or latter part of the year 55 CE. Paul founded this "assembly" (congregation) of Messiah's faithful about five years earlier, and even though he has not visited them since that time, they have enjoyed a warm and close relationship in the interval, during both good and hard times for each. Right from the start, this community entered into a close "partnership" arrangement with Paul, something no other assembly could claim, probably because of their zealous commitment to work out in practice the ideals of mutual aid and equity that they recognized to be central to the gospel.

Although this relationship of practical mutualism had become dormant in recent years, the congregation had earlier supported Paul and his ministry financially on more than one occasion, despite their relative poverty. But recently, perhaps a month earlier, they had heard of his imprisonment by Roman imperial authorities in Ephesus, the commercial hub and administrative capital of the Roman province of Asia (modern western Turkey). In response, and no doubt in recognition of their earlier "partnership" with Paul, they sent Epaphroditus, one of their own members, to assist Paul in his need and to deliver some financial support. But a week or two earlier, they heard a traveler from Ephesus, at least a week's journey away, report that Epaphroditus had turned severely ill.

It is perhaps evening, and expectancy has mounted, as earlier in the day the news of the letter's arrival has passed around through their informal network. What news will they hear? Will they learn more of the status of Paul's current trial and imprisonment in Ephesus? They fear the worst and hope for the best. What will Paul say about their assistance during this crisis? What will he say about their own Epaphroditus, who is now reported to have returned with the letter? Did he complete the mission they assigned to him and represent them well? What advice will Paul have for their problems and struggles? Paul will surely have heard about their own circumstances by now: on the one hand, mounting pressure and persecution from the Roman elite, including the ruling authorities in Philippi; but on the other hand, signs of conflict within their own ranks. This internal tension likely reflects existing status and social hierarchies internal to the community itself, but now it is exacerbated by debates as to how to understand or to respond to their own ordeal of persecution, harassment, or social exclusion.

So once gathered in a home or a workshop, discreetly and quietly so as not to generate more suspicion from neighbors, perhaps Epaphroditus or a leader of the assembly reads Paul's letter slowly and deliberately, trying to enunciate in a way to best bring out his message to them. The oral reader (lector) knows that the letter is substituting for Paul's own presence among them.

What do they hear? Not just news. What they hear in the short twenty minutes of deliberate reading is a wide-ranging combination of consolation and encouragement, congratulations and support, advice and challenge, resilience and hope. And through the words, their hearts are stirred as they are drawn into a triangular relational bond that joins them, Paul, and Messiah (Christ) Jesus himself. But there are also awkward moments: two individuals at odds within the leadership team are specifically named in the letter, while a designated mediator is advised to assist them toward reaching a shared vision and strategy for the beleaguered community (4:2-3).

After the initial reading, Epaphroditus probably also relays an oral message, perhaps including information or advice too sensitive to be transcribed in writing. Indeed, the presence of coded references that to us modern readers seem deliberately vague leaves the impression that Paul was concerned about possible harsh repercussions if the imperial authorities intercept the letter. Even so, the letter was probably smuggled out of prison, away from the watchful eye of the imperial authorities.

Guided by the local leaders, the assembly engages in further discussion and reflection, perhaps even rereading certain sections. They also ask Epaphroditus or another accompanying coworker what Paul really means by this or that ambiguous, elliptical, or coded phrase (e.g., 1:28; 2:15; 3:2, 18-19). For instance, who and what specifically are the *dogs*, *evildoers*, and *butchery* that Paul asks them to observe or beware? They probably ask for even more news of Paul and his circumstances than what is given in the letter or related orally. What are his chances of surviving this ordeal? Paul seems to have regularly sent a coworker and oral spokesperson to accompany his letters and to explain anything that seemed unclear to the readers (e.g., Tychicus and Onesimus to Colossae, Col 4:7-9; Phoebe to Rome, Rom 16:1-2).

Once they have digested the letter's contents and supplementary oral messages, they go on to discuss among themselves the implications of Paul's written and oral advice and how they might proceed in working out some of his instructions. And perhaps the two women leaders at odds, Euodia and Syntyche, after being so directly named in the letter, make a commitment in the gathered assembly to work out their differences around vision and strategy for the community. Perhaps other renewed commitments are made. The assembly experiences a time of critical solidarity.

Finally, they undoubtedly engage in intercessory prayer, as Paul himself encourages (1:19), as they contemplate the crisis facing Paul. But they also offer prayers of thanksgiving as they reflect on their triumphs in the midst of trials. They conclude with praise, assured of the imminent victory of Messiah Jesus over all forces in creation hostile to God, including the visible ones lined against them right now. We can imagine them going their separate ways after joining in a hymn in honor of Lord Jesus Messiah, exulting (magnifying, boasting) and rejoicing in the Lord *[Circumstances of the Messianic Assembly, p. 277; Date and Place of Writing, p. 290; History of the Messianic Assembly, p. 295; Profile of the Assembly, p. 305]*.

Receiving Philippians Today

Paul's letter to the assembly in Philippians was received on a particular occasion by the specific community to which it was first addressed *[Literary Integrity, p. 298]*. Still, this letter continues to be received dynamically by readers far distant in time, space, and culture. What is required when other and more distant readers pick up this letter is an analogical receptivity and imagination. This commentator hopes that Paul's message can continue to be received, but not merely by importing isolated phrases into a neat theological system, or applying a particular directive to a problem experienced today without regard for context, ancient or modern. My hope instead is that through this commentary, readers of Philippians today will be better able to imagine themselves into Paul's world and the world of the assembly in Philippi, so that they can reciprocally imagine Paul's letter or the congregation's experience into their own world. By entering the letter's own strange world, we become able to see a world and reality beyond ourselves. And in that resulting liminal (in-between) space, we can invite the text to read us and to be received by us.

One choice in translation that might seem initially jarring to many readers is the use of *Messiah* instead of *Christ*. The reason for this is to emphasize that Paul uses the Greek word *Christos* (anointed) not as a name, but as a royal title for Israel's coming deliverer. This translation decision, designed to help transport ourselves into Paul's own time, is explained below (TBC on 1:1-2, "*Christos* [Messiah] as Theopolitical Title").

In some ways we will find that the social, religious, and political context of Paul and the Philippians, along with their particular circumstances, are far different from ours (see below, "Translating Philippians"). We will realize that Paul carefully crafted his letter to meet their very specific need. Still, Paul no doubt would have affirmed a continued recontextualization of the message toward its reception today in diverse and ever-changing settings.

Letter from Prison: A Shared Struggle

At the time of dictation to a secretary, Paul himself was probably imprisoned in the Roman imperial headquarters (*praetōrium*, 1:13) in Ephesus, the leading city and administrative capital of the Roman *provincia* of Asia. In Latin, a *provincia* is literally a "charge," a military term that first designated the mandate of an appointed military governor, and then the "jurisdiction" under that governor's domain. The term applied only to conquered territories; Italy was never labeled a *provincia*. Paul was in prison as he awaited trial on the capital charge of treason. He was thus a kind of "political prisoner" (see TLC on 1:12-26, "Letters from Prison as Genre"). The Roman imperial government imprisoned people not to punish nor to rehabilitate, but only to secure them until a verdict could be rendered. The most serious penalties for guilty verdicts were execution or banishment (e.g., the penal colony on the island of Patmos, Rev 1:9; see also TBC on 1:12-26, "Paul's Imprisonment"; "Factionalism and Rivalry").

At a crucial point in his letter, Paul reminds his beloved congregation that he and they are both engaged in "the same sort of struggle." Moreover, the struggle they are both experiencing is of the same kind that they earlier witnessed Paul go through and now hear Paul to be experiencing again (1:30). This struggle includes "suffering" at the hands of *adversaries* who are bent on their *destruction*, resulting in significant *fear* (1:27-28). Paul mentions this to emphasize that they share a solidarity of circumstances as *partners*. Still, this comment provides a critical clue to appreciating both Paul's circumstances and those of the Philippian assembly. Further indications from the letter suggest that the struggle they are both experiencing is with the Roman imperial authority and the Roman culture it represents. It is a specifically theopolitical struggle—one in which what we would call "religion" and "politics" are inseparably intertwined. The ancient world did not conceptualize religion and politics as properly separate domains, as is typical in modern Western societies. The book of Acts confirms that the believing community in Philippi was engaged in a conflict with Roman imperial power over alternative citizenship claims from its beginnings. A full appreciation of Paul's letter thus requires a general understanding of (1) the dynamics of the Roman imperial world and the specific challenges it gave the earliest cell groups of Messiah's faithful; and (2) the particular character of Roman Philippi (cf. TBC for 1:1-2, "*Christos* (Messiah) as Theopolitical Title") *[Roman Imperial Cult, p. 307; Love of Honor, p. 299; Roman Imperial Propaganda, p. 312]*.

Roman Philippi

The socioeconomic, religious, and political fabric of Philippi in the middle of the first century was the result of at least five hundred years of colonization. Although its first known occupants were the Thracians (ancestors of modern Bulgarians), the region was successively colonized by Athenian Greeks (360 BCE), then by the Macedonians (355 BCE), and finally by the Romans (beginning in 168 BCE). By Paul's time this led to a mixed population culturally, linguistically, and religiously. It included native Thracians and varied Greek-speaking immigrants, all under the thumb of the newest colonial elite, the Romans. This history of colonization does not appear directly in the letter, but it certainly provides an occasion for careful reflection in relation to the text of Philippians.

The city received its name from the famed King Philip II of Macedon (382–336 BCE), the first ruler to absorb all the Greek city-states into a single kingdom, and the father of the world-conquering Alexander the Great. Philip II took the city in 355 BCE because of its strategic location, which offered control of local gold mines and the vast fertile agricultural land around it. The settlement, earlier known for its consistent water source, was dubbed "the springs" and named Krenides. Philip II renamed it after himself and made it the chief city of his kingdom. In the year 338, Philip II became the master of Greece after he defeated an alliance of Greek city-states in the Battle of Chaeronea. While preparing to invade the Persian Empire in 336, he was assassinated by Macedonian rivals. His plans for conquest were to be realized by his son Alexander "the Great," who became the world-conquering icon that Roman generals and rulers—especially Caesar Augustus—later sought to emulate.

Philippi and the entire region of Macedonia were absorbed into the Roman Empire in 168 BCE as part of Rome's steady conquest of territory, which reached its height in the first and second centuries CE. At first the Romans sought to rule the *provincia* of Macedonia through native Thracian overlords as client kings (much in the same way that they used Herod the Great in Judea). But all that changed in 42 BCE after the Battle of Philippi, when Mark Antony and the twenty-one-year-old Octavian (the heir and namesake of Julius Caesar who later became Caesar Augustus) defeated the forces of Brutus and Cassius in one of history's most decisive clashes of power. This battle, fought on the plains just outside Philippi by a hundred thousand combatants on each side, determined control over the extensive conquered territories of Rome—from Spain and Britain to Syria and Egypt.

From that time onward, Philippi became a specially designated *colonia* of Rome. With Philippi as the urban center, the surrounding region of approximately 700 square miles (1,800 sq. km) was designated as Colonia Victrix Philippensium (Colony of the Philippian Victory). This prime agricultural land was expropriated from traditional native inhabitants and doled out to Antony's and Octavian's war veterans as a reward for their military service. As one of the Roman colonies set aside for war veterans, Philippi was given the *ius Latinum* (Latin law; Latin rights), the legal standing of Roman territory in Italy, the highest possible status for a territory outside of Italy. The ruling Roman colonists were granted special rights as Romans—notably, exemptions from the poll tax and land tax. Octavian later renamed the colony as Colonia Julia Philippensis in honor of his own tribe Julia (and that of Gaius "Julius" Caesar), after his defeat of his rival Mark Antony in the Battle of Actium in 31 BCE. When he received from the Roman Senate in 27 BCE the honorific title Augustus ("the revered one" who is worthy of devotion), the newly minted Gaius Julius Caesar Augustus renamed it Colonia Augusta Julia Philippensis (Koukouli-Chrysantaki).

The military victory at Philippi had a profound and lasting impact on the city. By the time of Paul, Philippi was a city with a population of some 10,000 to 15,000 inhabitants in a magnificent 120-acre urban area that exhibited a wealth disproportionate to its size. Probably less than half enjoyed the privileged Roman citizenship. The city was dominated by a small Roman elite descended from original veteran settlers, who controlled a mini-empire of at least 40,000 subjects in its surrounding territory. Much of the colony's rich agricultural land was held in large agricultural estates in the surrounding countryside, owned by elite Romans living in urban villas, and operated by slaves or tenant renters, many of whom could claim to be the native inhabitants.

The diverse and yet highly stratified population of the colony and city included the following, from top to bottom: (1) the Roman core of the urban population, both the small elite group of decurions (the third legal rank of Roman upper-class "patricians," next to the senators and equestrians, who could serve as magistrates) and other free Romans descended from the original settlers or more recent colonists; (2) ethnic Greeks descended from the colonizers of the third century BCE; (3) native Thracians, who had become foreigners on their own native soil; (4) recent immigrants (metics, migrants), whether Greek, Judean (Jewish), Egyptian, or other; and (5) slaves from a variety of conquered territories. Roman rule and culture dominated the city, as evident in its political administration and law, architecture, and public spaces (including the forum, gymnasium, and theater), local military garrison, economy, and civic-political-religious festivities, and temples and altars. Even the dress code displayed its social and political hierarchy: the law allowed only Roman citizens to wear the toga in public, and only those of the highest senatorial rank were allowed to display the purple sash across their toga.

While Thracian inscriptions were more common in the surrounding farming countryside of greater Philippi, the Latin language reigned supreme in the public spaces of urban Philippi. Philippi cultivated a proud and patriotic Roman identity, while cities such as Corinth (also formally a *colonia*) and Ephesus maintained their predominantly Greek character. For the elite Roman magistrates and gentry of the city, the full name of the colony itself—Colonia Augusta Julia Philippensis—broadcast its proud history of military glories and magnificent conquests by reference to its notable founders and benefactors: *Philip*, and indirectly Alexander the Great; Gaius *Julius* Caesar; and most important as the savior of Rome and the world, Imperator Caesar *Augustus*, the renamed Octavian. Both Julius Caesar and Caesar Augustus had been formally "divinized"—granted divine status in the company of the heavenly deities—by the Roman Senate. And in the forum at the city center, at least two magnificent buildings were erected as imperial temples. These temples heralded the virtues and glories of Rome and honored the Roman gods and its rulers, some of whom were given honors "equal to the gods" (cf. Phil 2:6). Just a year previously, Philippi would also have celebrated the divinization (apotheosis) of the late emperor Claudius in solemn Senate assembly in Rome (cf. 2:9), and the investiture of the young Nero as the new "son of the divine" and expected "savior" in the pattern of Caesar Augustus *[Citizenship, p. 279; Roman Imperial Cult, p. 307; Roman Imperial Propaganda, p. 312]*.

Profile and Circumstances of the Assembly

The beleaguered congregation in Philippi was small, perhaps no more than thirty to fifty individuals. Its core members were probably from a Judean (Jewish) heritage, while including some from other ethnic communities, both Greek and immigrant. Women were prominent among its leaders. It was not particularly wealthy ("poor" in comparison to the Corinthians; 2 Cor 8). Few, if any, held the coveted Roman citizenship, although some were certainly striving for social advancement through Roman citizenship *[Profile of the Assembly, p. 305]*.

The primary challenge of the assembly of Messiah (Christ) loyalists in Philippi, then, was a monumental "struggle" that involved suffering and fear. The struggle most certainly had to do with tensions with Roman imperial power and culture in the city. Paul makes four references to those who oppose the community:

1. Certain *adversaries* are bent on the community's destruction (1:27-28).

2. They represent a *crooked and twisted nation* in which the congregation lives as witnessing agents (2:15-16).

3. There are persecuting *dogs, evildoers, butcherers* (3:2).

4. Those who *walk as enemies of the cross of Messiah* will meet their own demise when their regime gives way, when Messiah's gracious regime becomes triumphant throughout the world (3:18-21) *[Opponents in Philippians, p. 300]*.

The seeds of the conflict were evident as soon as Paul stepped into the city five years earlier (Acts 16:11-40). Perhaps the situation became worse for the assembly after messianic adherents disengaged from festivals in honor of the civic and imperial gods. Perhaps their meeting on a regular basis—gatherings not formally sanctioned by the civic rulers—generated suspicion. Or perhaps their alienation from the emperor cult was having a negative economic impact as those who held their messianic allegiance to be primary found it difficult to work or participate in guilds, typically devoted to the honor of Roman virtues and gods. Both jobs and commercial connections or opportunities were probably lost, whether by deliberate conviction or by persecution.

Meanwhile, the assembly was beset by some form of internal disintegration and turmoil (1:27; 2:1-2, 14; 4:2-3). The impression we gather from Paul's exhortation is that this internal conflict had less to do with narrowly theological-ethical disputes or merely interpersonal tensions than with status-and-rank hierarchies based on socioeconomic factors or ethnopolitical identities (2:3-8; 3:4-17). The deeply ingrained preoccupation with rank and status in the surrounding culture was no doubt insidious. The assembly itself likely reflected the stratified, rank-conscious Philippian society, though without the presence of the higher elements of Philippian society. The pressure from the outside was not likely experienced the same by all members. Views on how to respond to the crisis probably diverged widely within the congregation. Some likely favored a more accommodating or assimilationist posture, even striving for higher status and privilege. Others favored a stance of resistance to the regime and its moral and cultural order *[Circumstances of the Messianic Assembly, p. 277; History of the Messianic Assembly, p. 295; Love of Honor, p. 299]*.

Contents: Deeply Spiritual, Warmly Communal, Profoundly Political

This prized letter of Paul reveals a remarkable combination of spiritual resilience, personal pathos, relational closeness, communal dynamism, and political boldness. In some ways it has an edge as a kind of underground political tract. On the other hand, it exhibits Paul's deep piety in extreme hardship and the intimate relational bonds he shares with his separated partners in Philippi. Paul's letter to the Philippians is thus at the same time both a letter of friendship and a letter of bold exhortation and challenge. As a letter of friendship, it seeks both to celebrate and to solidify relational bonds through, for instance, conveying personal information and sharing feelings of separation, longing, mutuality, distress, pain, and joy. As a letter of exhortation, it has features typical of deliberative rhetoric, designed to effect a change among hearers (on letter writing in the ancient world, see Stowers).

Immediate practical concerns provide the occasion for the letter, following Paul's decision to send Epaphroditus back to Philippi along with a letter:

1. Paul needs to acknowledge their assistance formally (4:10-18; cf. 1:5-7; 2:25-30).

2. He desires to explain the situation regarding Epaphroditus, offering words of commendation and gratitude (2:25-30).

3. He wishes to provide an update on his own circumstances, especially regarding his own mental-emotional disposition (1:12-26; 2:17-18).

4. Finally, Paul aims to set the stage for the imminent visit by Timothy (2:19-23) and indeed for his own reunion with his partners (1:25-26; 2:24).

But these immediate purposes are subordinate to Paul's chief persuasive concern: that the assembly remain steadfast and united in the context of a massive assault against them by the powers of Rome in Philippi. Most fundamentally, then, Philippians is a forceful challenge for the "practice of messianic citizenship" (1:27–2:16; 3:1–4:9; see below, "The Structure of Philippians"). Paul's key interest is to enliven patriotic loyalty to Lord Jesus Messiah alone. To this end, Paul engages in both consolation and reassurance in light of Messiah's imminent, final, and global victory (2:9-11; 3:20-21). And he directly addresses the internal, common "political" life of the assembly. He warmly urges it to retain the messianic citizenship virtues of lowliness, neighborliness, and unity, and in so doing to resist the contrasting Roman patterns of consumerism, status-pursuit, and self-promoting glory, along with the general immorality (2:14-16; 3:2-3, 18-21).

But in Paul's theopolitical perspective, the political is never separated from the spiritual, even though Paul's striking and deep personal and relational expressions have often blinded Western readers to the profoundly political and even subversive dimensions of his rhetoric. The expressions of Paul's deep piety and personal relationship with Christ are everywhere apparent, and claimed by many throughout the centuries:

> *Even if I am being poured out as a libation over the sacrifice and ministry of your faith, I rejoice and rejoice together with all of you.* (2:17 NIV)
>
> *I regard everything as loss because of the surpassing value of knowing Christ Jesus my Lord.* (3:8 NRSV)
>
> *For to me, to live is Christ and to die is gain.* (1:21 NIV)
>
> *My desire is to depart and to be with Christ, for that is far better.* (1:23 NRSV)
>
> *I want to know Christ, both the power of his resurrection and the partnership in his sufferings.* (3:10 AT)
>
> *I can do all things through him who strengthens me.* (4:13 NRSV)

Corresponding exhortations also promote an intense piety:

> *Rejoice in the Lord always; again I will say, Rejoice!* (4:4 NRSV)
>
> *In everything by prayer and supplication with thanksgiving let your requests be made known to God.* (4:6 NRSV)

Punctuating the exhortations are powerful words of assurance:

> *The peace of God, which surpasses all comprehension, will guard your hearts and thoughts in Christ Jesus.* (4:7 AT)
>
> *My God will supply every need of yours according to his abundance in splendorous renown in Christ Jesus.* (4:19 AT)

And at the climax, there is resounding doxology:

> *To our God and Father be glory into the ages of the ages. Amen.* (4:20 AT)

Still, in the midst of his resilience and optimism, there is also a foreboding anxiety (1:19-24; 2:17, 23-24) and acknowledgment of deep pain (2:27). Most strikingly, Paul consoles when he is the one who himself should be consoled (Holloway), and he draws attention to unfailing divine resources in suffering that he himself no doubt has relied upon (2:1; cf. 2 Cor 1:3-11).

Central Themes

Four interrelated themes recur in a profound way in the letter and deserve careful attention by any reader: citizenship, partnership, high-low inversion, and joy-gladness.

Citizenship. Drawing on the language and imagery of Greek political theory, the body of the letter (1:27–4:9) is carefully developed around the theme of a devoted, singular messianic citizenship. Messiah's assembly is presented as a kind of *polis* (citizen body, city-state) that has both a social form and distinctive practice (1:27, *politeuomai*), in alignment with a regime (*politeuma*) that is now secured in heaven but to be realized soon throughout the whole world (1:9-11; 3:20-21). As soon as this citizenship theme is put forward in the thesis statement of 1:27, Paul elaborates by employing the military imagery of a citizen-state (*polis*, city-state) that is defending itself against a siege:

- "standing firm as one" in military alignment;
- "contending/fighting in concert, with a unified zeal," oriented to loyalty to the city constitution proclaimed by Messiah; and
- refusing to be affected by the "terror" waged by adversaries.

The centerpiece of the letter takes the form of a political encomium (public tribute) to the savior and deliverer of this regime of citizens, whose leadership pathway of humiliation will one day be victorious throughout the whole world, and whose self-sacrificing pattern of life poses a model for all who will claim allegiance to this Savior (2:5-11).

When the main exhortation comes to a close, Paul comes back to these same themes: Messiah's saving work has inaugurated a new regime of citizens now secured in heaven, along with a corresponding alternative citizenship (3:20-21). The notion of a "regime-citizenship in heaven" clarifies the security of Messiah's regime (for now, in a kind of exile) and the source of Messiah's reclaiming the entire world. It does *not* indicate the ultimate location of Messiah's regime or the final destination of the faithful. Paul's theological vision consistently focuses on the arrival of the age to come, a transformed world under Christ's lordship, not on a retreat or escape to heaven. The repeated call to *stand firm* is the primary implication of the declaration of Messiah's final global victory, involving the subjection of all things, including the Roman regime (4:1). Thus the faithful must *contend* or *fight together* in a posture of unified messianic disposition (4:2-3). Still, merciful forbearance (nonretaliation) even to hostile opponents can and must be displayed, because final vindication through Messiah is near, to whom claims for justice can be deferred. And *anxiety* (4:6; cf. *fear* or *terror* of 1:14, 28) can be abandoned in recognition of *guarding hearts and minds* by the *peace of God* (4:6-7), another military image, a parody-like wordplay on both the imperial Pax Romana (peace of Rome) and the Roman military garrison guarding the city itself. Finally, the pursuit of civic virtues must continue through a discernment ever aware of their messianic redefinition, as mediated by Paul (4:8-9).

Partnership. Drawing further on Greek political imagery, Messiah's assembly is characterized as a partnership (*koinōnia*). Major Greek political thinkers, including Plato (*Republic* 449c–470e) and Aristotle (*Politics* 1.252b), similarly stress that *koinōnia*, or "that which is in common," is one of the primary features of any worthy *polis*, citizen community. But Paul takes this even one notch forward in explaining what this means concretely in the practical mutual aid of nonhierarchical *generosity* (grace), and that this *partnership* extends to solidarity amid suffering (1:30–2:1; 2:17-18), and indeed specifically to partnership in the very suffering of Messiah (3:10). Paul's vision of partnership is posed as a direct challenge to the prevailing sociocultural system of "patronage" (see EN on 1:5-7; 4:10-20).

High-Low Inversion. Images of social inversion are scattered throughout the letter and explain the distinctive feature of Messiah's community as both a *polis* (citizen-community) and a *koinōnia* (partnership). We see this in the language of high status and low rank, honor and shame, lowliness and glory, humiliation and exaltation, losses (divestment) and gains (achievements), selfish ambition versus watching out for others, destruction and defeat versus prizes and victory wreaths, and slaves and lords. At the center of this motif is the humiliation/exaltation drama of Messiah himself, both Lord-Deliverer and model hero of God's ever-expanding *polis* in the world (2:5-11). Paul is carefully deconstructing and reconstructing prevailing norms for honor, status, virtue, victory, and the good life in Roman Philippi, a society deeply preoccupied with status, honor, and rank (Hellerman). (See TBC on 2:1-5, "Status Inversion") *[Love of Honor, p. 299]*.

Joy-Gladness. Words for joy and rejoicing are so common in Philippians that this letter is often described as the letter of joy. But even this repeated motif is closely tied to the call to singular and devoted allegiance to Lord Messiah Jesus alone. Paul's language of *joy* or *gladness* (*chara*) is best understood in light of the long-standing discussion about civic happiness (*eudaimonia*) in Greek political discourse, in the same way that the notion of the pursuit of happiness has become a key political ideal in American consciousness. Where one might have expected Paul to say (with Greek theorists) that the core political ideals are justice, peace, and civic happiness, he instead highlights justice, peace, and joy in the Holy Spirit as the markers of the kingdom of God (Rom 14:17). Paul uses the language of joy as a way to stress the distinctive feature of "the pursuit of happiness" in Messiah's political community. The pursuit of happiness in the community of Christ is not determined by the prevailing measures of success and upward mobility, whether in politics or in business, but in an inversion of those standard notions of value. For this reason there can even be joy in suffering. In Philippians, the practice of citizenship specifically takes the posture of celebrative rejoicing "in Messiah"—that is, in the deliverance that Messiah has secured and will secure—in direct contrast to the celebratory rejoicing in civic imperial festivals that proclaim the glories of Caesar and the "salvation" that Rome has given the world. In Philippians, "rejoicing in Messiah" is parallel to "boasting in Messiah" (1:26; 3:3) or "putting one's confidence in Messiah" (1:14; 3:3), and it has a strong theopolitical edge.

Paul's Rhetoric: The Primacy of Exemplary Models

A striking feature of Paul's persuasive (rhetorical) strategy in Philippians becomes more apparent when it is compared with his other letters. According to Aristotle, deliberative rhetoric is designed to persuade an audience to take some action (in contrast to judicial or epideictic [praising or blaming] rhetoric). It has three main components: *logos*, logical argument, for which there are many types of proofs; *ēthos*, by which the speaker or author appeals—however directly, indirectly, or subtly—to his own credibility or example; and *pathos*, where the author seeks a solidarity of feeling with his audience, pulling on heartstrings (Aristotle, *Rhetoric* 2.1–9). In Romans, Paul's deliberative rhetoric primarily takes the form of *logos* through sustained theological and scriptural argument, with a modest amount of *ēthos* (e.g., Rom 1:9-16; 15:14-32), and negligible *pathos* (yet see Rom 9:1-5; 16:3-4). Philippians, by contrast, offers *logos* of a different sort, supported with a strong dose of both *ēthos* and *pathos*. Paul barely alludes to Scripture in Philippians, while Romans is steeped in Scripture quotation and allusion. In Philippians, Paul exhorts and argues mainly through paradigmatic example, following a long-standing pattern of using exemplary models (*paradeigma*) as proofs for *logos* in persuasive rhetoric (e.g., Aristotle).

Paul makes his case for the "practice of messianic citizenship" by referring primarily to two exemplary models: Messiah (2:5-11, the centerpiece of the letter) and Paul (3:4-17; 4:9). Even where not explicit, Paul's explanation of his own disposition or conduct is clearly intended as a model for others to follow (1:12-26; 2:16-18; 4:10-13). Of course, Messiah as exalted slave is in his own special category as both model and deliverer (2:5-11; 3:10-11, 18-21; 4:5). Even lesser figures, such as Timothy and Epaphroditus, are presented and commended in such as a way as to provide further examples of these two primary models (2:19-22, 25-30; cf. 3:17). In this way, the *pathos* and *ēthos* of the letter are closely correlated to its *logos*. As it is today, patriotic loyalty is best enlivened not by abstract, logical argument, but by the celebration and honoring of exemplary heroes.

The Structure of Philippians

Paul's letter to the Philippians is carefully crafted in word and structure:

A Salutation, 1:1-2
- B Thanksgiving, Longing, and Prayer, 1:3-11
  Theme: Partnership in the Gospel
  - C Disclosure of Paul's Circumstances, 1:12-26
    Theme: Imprisonment on Behalf of Messiah
    - D Exhortation, Part I, 1:27–2:18
      Theme: Being Messiah's Citizen Body
      - E Centerpiece: Messiah as Model and Deliverer (2:6-11)
  - C′ Disclosure of Travel Plans, 2:19-30
    Commendations: Timothy and Epaphroditus as Model Citizens
    - D′ Exhortation, Part II, 3:1–4:9
      Theme 1: Being Messiah's Citizen Body, Continued, 3:1–4:1
      - E′ Core Theme: Paul as Citizenship Model (3:4-17)
        Climax: Messiah's Global Victory (3:20-21)

      Theme 2: Related Concluding Exhortations, 4:2-9
- B′ Receipt and Thanksgiving, 4:10-20
  Theme: Celebrating Partnership and God's Rich Provision

A′ Closing, 4:21-23

Noteworthy is how the themes of the first two segments (A, 1:1-2; and B, 1:3-11) are recapitulated at the end (B′, 4:10-20; and A′, 4:21-23), enclosing the entire letter. Most prominent in these bracketing sections is the theme of mutual *partnership* and God's assured completion of the work and rich provision in the process. In the main body, we find two segments of disclosure and information sharing (C, 1:12-26; C′, 2:19-30), overlapping with two main sections of sustained exhortation (D, 1:27–2:18; D′, 3:1–4:9). These latter sections of exhortations are coordinated around the theme of *citizenship* (1:27; 3:20) and focus on two crucial declarations of Messiah's global supremacy (2:6-11; 3:20-21). The former sections of disclosure and sharing indirectly commend, among other things, citizenship models in the pathway of Messiah and on behalf of Messiah.

Translating Philippians

In liturgy, we strive to transport an ancient text into the present, seeking to contemporize it into our own idiom. But in serious biblical study, our first task is to transport ourselves into the strange and foreign world of the ancient scriptural text by being attentive to its historical, linguistic, and cultural particularity. Scripture study, as a kind of cross-cultural study, requires the discipline of seeking to hear voices from the perspective of a cultural framework often quite unlike our own. Otherwise, all we receive is what we already expect to hear. I am convinced, therefore, that it is necessary to understand Paul first in his foreignness before and as we try to bring his letters into our present. Sometimes a biblical text needs to be made strange so that it can have a new power for us, made foreign so that it can be read afresh. In monolingual English-speaking North America, we are used to having others speak our language, and so this requires a distinct mental commitment.

While nonspecialist Bible readers regularly weary at the ever-increasing number of translations of the Bible that are available, those who work with biblical languages weary that no translation can quite capture it all. As a colleague once put it, when you read the Bible in its original language, you get to see in color; translations only offer a grayscale black and white. For this reason, I have included discussion of crucial Greek words in this commentary, not because readers are supposed to know Greek, but to help the reader appreciate the colorfully rich texture of Paul's own linguistic world. Paul's language is far more metaphorically rich than our abstract use of words. He says "my chains," while we translate "my imprisonment." For the nonspecialist, the best procedure for serious study is to compare multiple translations. (One resource with multiple translations is the Bible Gateway website.) My modest hope is that the few references to Greek words in this commentary may spark an interest in the study of biblical Greek itself.

Meanwhile, any reader of the Bible must continually be aware of the challenges that accompany reading only in translation and the limits that accompany *any* translation. There are at least three challenges. First, there is always something lost in translation. When there is a cultural gap between the speakers of two languages (as is the case between biblical Greek and modern English), the possibility of loss is considerably heightened, especially because there are fewer word equivalences. Resonances or connotations of words in one language especially do not translate readily into another language.

Second, although translations provide the crucial basis for communication across cultural and language divides, standardized versions can sometimes leave the impression that biblical writers speak our language and use our concepts. They do not. Moreover, over the years many of the words used in biblical translation have become specifically church words, not regularly used in common speech. As a result, standard translations give the impression that Paul used a special, narrowly religious vocabulary (*sin, salvation, church, righteousness, glory, gospel, apostle, Christ, Savior, Lord*, etc.). When Paul is placed in his own linguistic environment, however, it becomes clear that he used words that were regularly used in ordinary discourse, often with a variety of deliberate political and social resonances. For instance, *ekklēsia* is properly not "church," but "assembly," a word regularly used, among various senses, for the body and gathering of the citizens of a *polis* (citizen-state) to enact citizen business. An "apostle" is simply an "envoy" (e.g., in politics or business) with an authorized message and task. The word *hamartia*, usually translated *sin* in Bibles, is the ordinary word for "error." And *Christos* in Paul is always a theopolitical title as Israel's royal deliverer, not a name, and thus better captured by the translation *Messiah* than the transliteration *Christ*, whose meaning as "the Anointed One" has been lost. A *doulos* is a "chattel slave," not a household or indentured servant. *Fellowship* is a misleading translation of *koinōnia*, since it conjures up the notion of social interaction, not the reality of partnership or having things in common, which are intrinsic to the Greek word. *Euangelion*, typically translated *gospel* in Bibles, in Greek does not refer specifically to a religious doctrine but denotes a "public proclamation of well-being."

Since many words in the Greek NT cannot be adequately translated with a one-word equivalent, a translator is often compelled to use hyphens or new word combinations. "Loving-kindness" for the Hebrew *ḥesed* is a classic case now normalized. Thus in this commentary I use *loyalty-faith* for *pistis* (instead of *faith* or *belief*); *justice-righteousness* for *dikaiosynē*; *deliverance-salvation* for *sōtēria*; or *government-citizenship* for *politeuma*. Translating prepositions with a one-word equivalent is especially difficult in any combination of languages. Thus, I have sometimes used awkward constructions with a slash to try to convey the breadth of Paul's meaning (e.g., in/among you; in/for Christ).

A third problem with our translations or labels is that we often imprison Paul and other biblical writers within a set of anachronisms. The later conclusions and assumptions of Christendom or our own theological conceptions are retrojected back onto Paul. The most obvious example involves the use of *Christian* or *Christianity*, in contrast to *Jew* and *Judaism*. Yet Paul lived and ministered before Christianity (Toews 2004: 35–36; Shillington 2011), that is, before "Christianity" came to be understood as a movement and a set of doctrines and practices exclusively distinct and separate from "Judaism." Judaism itself evolved dramatically during the first few centuries of the Common Era. The term *Jew* is misleading because it conjures up historical biases and especially implies the polar opposite to *Christian* in narrowly religious terms. Moreover, it does not adequately render the historical sense of *Ioudaios* in Paul's time, which literally means "belonging to Judah," identifying those who belong to or affiliate in some sense with the land, people, religion-philosophy, and polity-citizenship of Judea. The term does not simply connote a religious-philosophical practice or faith but implies a nationality (ethnicity), statehood (citizenship), and homeland all at the same time. A "Jew" in Paul's day was defined especially in terms of being part of the Judean nation. Thus *Judean-Jewish* as a translation would be better, even if cumbersome. Historically, Paul is best regarded as both a self-identified Judean and as a committed Jesus-Messianist, with all the tensions that entailed (Rom 9–11; Phil 3:2-11). Similarly problematic are the terms *Jewish-Christian* or *Judaizing/Judaizers*, since they conjure up categories foreign to Paul's thinking (see Eisenbaum; Nanos 2011, 2012; Boyarin 1994, 2004). Related to this challenge is the fact that all translations, even committee-based standard versions, are beset with some level of deliberate or unconscious bias, whether cultural, socioeconomic, or theological. The quest must continually be for the bias of the text itself to come through.

In this commentary all translations of Philippians are my own, unless otherwise indicated (and translations from the rest of the Bible are from the NRSV unless otherwise indicated). I regularly refer to standard versions, on which I am dependent in multiple ways: NRSV (New Revised Standard Version); RSV (Revised Standard Version); NIV (New International Version, both the 1984 and 2011 editions); TNIV (Today's New International Version [UK, 2001]); TEV (Today's English Version); NABRE (New American Bible, Revised Edition); NET (New English Translation); ISV (International Standard Version); and CEB (Common English Bible). These are listed with the abbreviations at the front of this volume.

Philippians 1:1-2

Address and Grace-Peace Blessing

PREVIEW

Take note of the beginning! Opening words of an exchange are always vital. In any communication, whether formal or informal, whether verbally or nonverbally, how one presents oneself or characterizes the conversation partner makes a huge impact. Paul follows the customary form of a letter prescript: A, to B, greeting. But in every letter, he inserts varied content into these fields to suit the occasion, relationship, and theme.

This prescript is distinctive among Paul's letters in three ways, each requiring some explanation: (1) Paul identifies both himself and his cosender Timothy as *slaves of Messiah Jesus*; (2) Paul characterizes the recipients as *those who are consecrated* (saints), emphasizing that this depiction applies to *all* of them and that they have that identity *in Messiah Jesus*; and (3) Paul specifically addresses a leadership group within the assembly as a subset of *all* of them.

The depth of meaning of Paul's formulaic grace-peace blessing that follows must not be overlooked.

OUTLINE

Sender and Addressee, 1:1
Grace and Peace Blessing, 1:2

EXPLANATORY NOTES

What might an opening prescript communicate directly or indirectly? In what way, for instance, are matters of status or role differences acknowledged or emphasized? Might the self-presentation of the sender be designed to evoke an aura of status or power to enhance a letter's authority or significance? Or does the characterization of an addressee include multiple honorific characterizations to ingratiate the sender with the addressee? What relational bonds are assumed or invoked by seemingly incidental comments? Does the prescript highlight horizontal relational connections or imbalanced ones? These are some of the things carefully considered in prescripts in both formal and informal letters of the ancient world (see, e.g., Klauck).

Senders: Slaves of Messiah Jesus

Paul's self-presentation is brief and provocative. Both he and his cosender Timothy are *slaves of Messiah Jesus*. This depiction is crucial for Paul's persuasive purposes in Philippians. A pivotal theme to come is how, in the realm of Christ, Paul inverts prevailing social assumptions about what counts for real status in Roman Philippi, and thus what constitutes grounds for either shame or boasting (esp. 2:2-11; 3:2-14, 18-21; cf. *shame* and *boasting* in 1:20, 26). Not accidentally, the word *slave* (*doulos*) will occur one more time in the letter: in the letter's shocking centerpiece, which declares the exemplary pathway of Messiah (2:5-11). Jesus is the one who has deliberately taken the *form of a slave* (2:7) as the necessary self-humbling course that precedes his own exaltation and acclamation from all humankind (2:9-11; 3:19-21). Moreover, that messianic example will be modeled both in the life and ministry of Paul (3:2-17; 4:9) and in the ministry of Timothy (2:19-23), who *as a son with a father has served as a slave* [*douleuō*] *with me for the gospel* (v. 22). Both Paul and Timothy, then, display the way of lowly status divestment (2:20-22; 3:3-11) instead of selfish, rivalrous ambition (1:15-17; 2:3-4, 20-21), thereby embracing Messiah's cause and pathway.

The decision of the NRSV translation committee to translate *doulos* (slave) with the softer word *servant* is unfortunate. Slavery in the ancient world of Paul, from Judea to Rome, was chattel slavery, in which slaves were treated as the personal property of the owners. In the social world of Paul and of the congregation in Philippi, the most immediate and obvious meaning of *slave* (*doulos*) would be a person who is owned by, subservient to, completely responsible to, and without identity apart from a master (lord) of a household. The actual status or circumstances of a slave could vary greatly, from those who labored in chain gangs in the mines or on large agricultural estates to those who worked in small manufacturing businesses or in domestic settings, to those educated slaves who were the business managers, accountants, or even physicians of the aristocracy. Slaves of this last type could often anticipate manumission (the technical term for buying someone out of slavery) and could leave slavery with a considerable fortune after a significant period of service. Business management, for instance, was a domain largely staffed by legal slaves in the Roman world (as in the parable of the talents, Matt 25:14-30).

Paul's remarkable identity claim cuts in more than one way and holds plenty of irony. First, it signifies his deliberate dispossession of rank and status in his embrace of weakness and lowliness. It implies a solidarity with the "humiliated" (from Latin *humiliores*, "lowered"), in marked contrast to those whose pursuit is simply for "selfish ambition" and "vainglory" (cf. 1:15-16; 2:3-8; 3:7-11, 18-19; cf. Paul's shaming irony in 1 Cor 4:6-14). While the name *Paul* was usually associated with a relatively high social status, here Paul associates with the rank of slaves (see TBC, "The Name Paul"). Second, it expresses his utter dependency on and complete obligation to a master with whom he nevertheless enjoys a deep relational bond more valuable than any other measure of status (*my Lord*, 3:8)—the term translated *Lord* (*kyrios*) also denotes a "master." The image signals that he has indeed been "seized" by another (Phil 3:12), against his will (1 Cor 9:16-17). Third, Paul's claim of identity as a slave also invokes a role of privilege and status. Many of those in the imperial civil service (*Caesar's household*, Phil 4:22) were designated "slaves of Caesar." Just as they could claim significant status within the Roman imperial administration, Paul as "slave of Messiah" in effect likewise claims a key role in the administrative service of world-ruler-to-come, Messiah Jesus. Indeed, being a "slave of Jesus" means that he is actually a "slave of all" (1 Cor 9:19; 2 Cor 4:5)—under obligation to all people.

Curiously, Paul does not refer to himself as "special envoy" (*apostolos*, apostle) in Philippians. Nor does Paul appeal to any formal apostolic authority later in the letter. This silence may reflect the atmosphere of mutuality in the letter and his warm relationship with the assembly in Philippi (similarly to 1–2 Thessalonians; Philemon). The only occurrence of the word *apostolos* actually applies to the ministry of Epaphroditus (*your envoy* [*apostolos*] *and public servant for my need*, 2:25), and perhaps implies an ironic reversal of "apostolicity" in the immediate circumstances: the apostle receives apostolic ministry from a nonapostle. Nevertheless, Paul's apostolic role is certainly implicit throughout the letter (e.g., 1:20-26; 2:16-17; 4:1), and this framework provides the basis for his specific and direct exhortation in the letter (1:27–2:18; 3:1–4:9), including his call that they follow his example (3:15-17; 4:9). His role as apostle also provides the context for understanding his acknowledgment of their assistance (2:25-30; 4:10-20). In the remainder of the letter, Paul's language shows a kind of midpoint between formal and informal, public and personal, apostolic and mutual. (Similarly, Paul's authority as apostle is also operative in the semipersonal letter to Philemon, even as he highlights his mutual relationship with Philemon as "partner" and avoids the title *apostolos*; Philem 8, 19-21.)

Paul includes Timothy as cosender, thereby testifying to Timothy's close working relationship with Paul, yet also acknowledging his role in the founding of the congregation (Acts 16) and endorsing his anticipated ministry among the Philippian congregation on Paul's behalf (2:19-24; see TBC on 2:19-30, "Timothy"). Although he names Timothy as a cosender, Paul remains the actual author of the letter as the one addressing the Philippian community, as the one composing the letter, and as the primary one with a crucial relationship with the Philippian assembly (e.g., 1:25, 27; 2:12, 19; 4:10-20). Paul takes the role of the sole writer in 1:3, communicating in the first-person singular ("I," not "we"). Later he shares information about Timothy, providing a character reference in the third person ("he") while continuing to speak of himself in the first person (2:19-24).

Addressees: To All Those Who Are Consecrated in Messiah Jesus

In his address, Paul characterizes the entire community with the honorific plural term *hagioi*, which is impossible to render into English with a good one-word equivalent (NABRE: *holy ones*; NIV: *God's holy people*; NRSV: *saints*). The singular word *hagios* in Greek (and the Hebrew *kadoš* that it translates) commonly describes those things (e.g., temples, rites) or persons (e.g., priests) that are "devoted," "consecrated" (lit. "deemed sacred"), or "specially dedicated" to the cultic (ritual) service of God (or the gods). They are "sacred" or "holy" by virtue of being distinct from what is common, ordinary, or unclean. Already in the Hebrew Bible, the word designated the distinctive, set-apart identity, conduct, and mission of the people as a whole, as a "priestly kingdom and holy nation" (Exod 19:6; cf. Lev 11:44-45; 19:2; 20:7, 26; Num 16:3).

Drawing on this biblical tradition, Paul adopts this plural designation *hagioi* (*consecrated ones*) as a key term for the community of those loyal to Messiah. It implies (1) a special status, identity, and belonging (as "consecrated"); (2) an alternative character and manner of life ("holiness"); and (3) a distinctive vocation and mission (as "devoted"). When one considers the force of this simple designation in the context of Greco-Roman conceptions and practices, it appears that Paul is using *those who are consecrated* to highlight a special sense of priestly honor that all adherents of Messiah Jesus share. Civic citizen communities in Paul's world were also liturgical communities devoted to the service of a city's patron god or goddess (with the religious and the political intertwined). In the same way, Paul begins with the sacral, priestly dimension of devotion and dedication to Christ and later will emphasize its communal, sociopolitical aspects (1:27–4:9).

For Paul, this distinctive identity, ethos, and mission is established and enabled only by incorporation, calling, election, and rebirth *in Messiah Jesus* (cf. 1 Cor 1:2). Just as Paul and Timothy's identity and mission are tied specifically to Messiah Jesus as *slaves of Messiah Jesus*, so also is the identity and mission of the entire congregation as *those who are consecrated in Messiah Jesus*. Paul uses the word *hagios* again only at the close of the letter (4:21, 22; another theme by which the whole letter is enclosed). But imagery closely associated with the biblical notion of a sacred, consecrated people reappears a few times in the letter: in his prayer that they might be *pure and blameless* (1:10); in his hopes that they are *blameless and innocent, children of God without blemish in the midst of a crooked generation, in which you shine like stars in the world* (2:15); in his hopes for their quest for *maturity* (3:12) toward receiving the *prize of the upward call* (3:14); in his assertion of the coming *conformity to the body of his glory* (3:21); in his call that they do an audit of the things that pertain to *virtue* (4:8); and in his congratulations for their performance of a *sacrifice pleasing and acceptable to God* (4:18).

The phrase *who are in Philippi* specifies a particular location of *saints* while also implying that this local group is part of a broader, global sacred citizen community *in Messiah Jesus*. Their identity as *consecrated* is far more important than their residential identity as

Philippians (4:15), in the same way that being known as Canadian or American, or in relation to any other nation-state, pales in relation to one's fundamental identity as a Christian.

Both to All and Specifically to Leaders

Paul emphasizes that he is speaking to *all* those who are specially consecrated in Messiah. This emphatic *all* will recur (1:4, 7 [2x], 8, 25; 2:17; 4:21), expressing Paul's consistent concern for unity and inclusion in the letter.

But while addressing *all*, Paul also makes special reference to the leaders among them: *together with the overseers and ministers*. The translation *bishops and deacons* (NRSV) is misleading, freighted with modern assumptions about what those terms mean; better is *supervisors and servants* (CEB). Paul uses two terms (*episkopoi, diakonoi*) that refer to leaders in general. These terms do not imply formal offices with sharp role differentiation at this stage in the emerging structure of communities devoted in allegiance to Christ. Although singled out, these leaders are part of the *all*, not separate from the rest. Paul specifically addresses the leaders both as a way to recognize the special role of leaders in their current situation and as a way to promote unity and mutuality between leaders and the rest. Paul also seems interested in singling out leaders specifically to heed his exhortation on divestment of status and rank (e.g., 2:1-5; 3:2-21), anticipating his words directed to particular leaders (his "coworkers"), including the feuding women Euodia and Syntyche and the designated mediator (4:2-3).

Greeting: Grace and Peace Blessing

The salutation ("wish of good health") is the most consistent in all of Paul's letters, and the most distinctive in relation to letters from that world. The standard salutation in a Greek letter was "be glad" (*chairō*; see Acts 15:23; 23:26; James 1:1), the very same verb regularly translated "rejoice" in the NT. In other words, the letter writer sends his "Be glad," that is, "May you be in good spirits, may you be joyful." This was the normal greeting on the street. In Latin contexts, the standard greeting was *saluto* (health, well-being, safety, salvation!), from which we get the term "salutation."

Paul, however, greets with the traditional Middle Eastern blessing. The blessing *Grace and peace to you* is from the standard words of greeting in Aramaic, the common language of the region of Syria-Palestine, closely related to Hebrew. Paul's greeting is not a blend of

Greek and Aramaic-Hebrew patterns, as regularly asserted. While the most common Aramaic greeting was *šalom* (shalom, peace, well-being, good health) by itself, the combination of *šalom* along with *ḥin* (grace, favor, prosperity; Heb. *ḥen*), in either order, is also attested (Alexander).

More significantly, Paul's blessing echoes the priestly blessing of Aaron (Num 6:24-26): "May the Lord . . . be gracious to you . . . and give you peace" (Martens). This stereotyped blessing is not just a literary device. Rather, it was undoubtedly used in the exchanging of blessings in face-to-face meeting or leave-taking in the context of messianic (Christian) communal gatherings. Paul's letter form most likely reflects actual in-person exchanges.

A regular feature of Paul's blessing is the stress on its divine source: *from God our Father and Lord Jesus Messiah*, again drawing on the theology of the Aaronic blessing. But Paul elaborates christologically, encapsulating the substance of an early creedal affirmation: "For us there is one God, the Father, from whom are all things and for [unto] whom we exist, and one Lord Jesus Messiah, through whom are all things and through whom we exist" (1 Cor 8:6). Here at the outset, then, Paul specifies the full titles of both God and Messiah, something he will do again at the end of the letter (4:20, 23) and at major points along the way (of God, 2:11; of Messiah, 2:11; 3:20; cf. 3:8).

Messiah Jesus is emphatically the central reference point of all three elements of the opening prescript. Paul's opening thereby conjures up a triangulated relational dynamic: a mutual relationship of sender and recipients, intimately correlated in and through Christ Jesus. They are more than dearly beloved friends. Messiah Jesus is pronounced at the outset as the fundamental premise and relational bond of the letter. Jesus is referred to a total of 90 times in this 104-verse letter (if one adds up particular uses of the name [in whole or part], pronominal references to Jesus, and clauses where Jesus is the subject). By contrast, God is referred to only 23 times in the letter. The word *Christos* (Anointed, Messiah, Christ) occurs more frequently (as a ratio of total words) in Philippians than in any other letter of Paul.

THE TEXT IN BIBLICAL CONTEXT

Christos (Messiah) as Theopolitical Title

In the Hebrew Bible, the word *mašiaḥ* (Messiah) means "anointed," referring to a ceremonial anointing of a prophet, priest, or king for office or task, and used most commonly as an honorific title for the Davidic king (1–2 Samuel; Psalms). After the exile, the term came to be used to designate a future deliverer (e.g., Dan 9:25). While Judean (Jewish) hopes for a coming deliverer varied considerably in the first century, the notion of the "Anointed One" was crucial in most cases. For instance, the Essene covenanters of the Dead Sea Scrolls of the same period (2nd c. BCE to 1st c. CE) looked forward to both a royal "Messiah of David" and a priestly "Messiah of Aaron," sometimes combining them in one figure (Collins 1997: 77–87).

When the Hebrew Bible was translated into Greek a few centuries before Paul, translators consistently rendered this word *mašiaḥ* with *christos* (derived from the root *chriō*, "to rub lightly, spread over," for instance, with oil, poison, paint, or whitewash). As a result, by the time of Paul, this Greek word became the preferred way to refer to the coming liberator-deliverer in Greek-speaking Judean environments (e.g., Psalms of Solomon 17:32; 18:1, 6, 8; in 70–45 BCE). In some contexts, the Hebrew word *mašiaḥ* was transliterated into Greek as *messias* (e.g., John 1:41; 4:25; where its Greek translation *christos* is immediately offered).

In accordance with this usage among Greek-speaking Judeans, *christos* in Paul's writings is preeminently a royal designation, along with "Lord," not a name (Jonge). As an honorific label comparable to Augustus (Novenson), the term designates the one who is destined to rule, coming in the line of King David, and who has acted as the liberator-deliverer (e.g., Rom 1:3-4; 15:12; 1 Cor 15:24-28; Phil 2:9-11; 3:20-21; see also Acts 2:36). It indicates theopolitical messiahship, that is, spiritual-political messiahship, an alternative form of politics. It is inaccurate to suppose that Jews hoped for a "political" messiah, whereas Jesus became a "spiritual" Messiah, on both sides of the comparison. Jewish hopes were not exclusively "political," and Paul's vision of Messiah's status and work was not narrowly "spiritual." For that reason, I have translated *christos* as *Messiah* in this commentary, because for the modern reader *Messiah* evokes Paul's notion of the future spiritual-political deliverer of Israelite hopes (similarly Markus Barth in his commentary on Ephesians; the recent ISV translation; and John Toews's commentary on Romans in the BCBC series).

The original theopolitical sense of *christos* specifically as God's royal "anointed one" was soon lost among early Christians, as new non-Jewish converts did not fully appreciate its full significance as a title. Instead, the word was transliterated into other languages (not translated with an equivalent in meaning), beginning with the Latin

Christus, understood as a name. *Christos* thus came to be used and understood primarily as a name even as it was forgotten as a royal role and title.

The title *Augustus* provides a suitable comparison. For many Western readers, *Augustus* by now is simply the name of the first Roman emperor. But the term *Augustus* was known by all Romans at the time as an honorific title meaning "revered, majestic, manifest, sacred, increaser," with semidivine connotations as one worthy of devotion. In Greek-speaking contexts, the meaning-equivalent word *sebastos* (reverenced, sacred) was used to ensure that people understood the meaning and did not just recognize the Latin term. The title *Augustus* was granted by the Roman Senate in 27 BCE to the man born in 63 BCE as Gaius Octavius Thurinus (Octavian in modern history books), but who by 42 BCE had taken on the name Gaius Julius Caesar as the appointed heir of his namesake, the assassinated Julius Caesar. After the divinization of Julius Caesar by decree of the Roman Senate and through solemn ceremony in 42 BCE, the new Caesar took on and broadcasted the title *divi filius* (son of a divinity, son of god), for example, by imprinting that title on coins he minted in his own honor. The Senate in 27 BCE awarded him the title *Princeps* ("first one, chief," avoiding the more offensive designation *Dictator* that Julius Caesar had earlier claimed); and later *Tribunicia Potestas* and *Consul*, the highest political and military designations; and then *Pontifex Maximus* ("high priest," as the head of all religion) in 12 BCE; and also *Pater Patriae* (father of the fatherland) in 2 BCE. Once he had consolidated rule over the entire Roman dominion after defeating his rivals, he effectively renamed himself *Imperator Caesar Augustus*, having the Roman Senate decree that these titles were to be reserved only for him. (*Imperator* has come to mean "emperor," but it originally meant military "commander," equivalent to "commander-in-chief.") While he was increasingly referred to simply as Augustus, everyone knew that term to be an honorific title. The designation was also used for others in the imperial family, or for the entire imperial family dynasty, the *divi augusti*, "the divine venerables" (*sebastoi* in Greek). All subsequent Roman emperors also took on the title Augustus (Gk. *Sebastos*), along with Caesar (which by contrast to Augustus was once a personal or clan name, but after Caesar Augustus also became an imperial title; thus, Kaiser, Tsar).

For Paul, *Christos* (Anointed One) was the counterpart title of *Augustus* (revered, majestic one), and *Kyrios Iēsous Christos* (Lord Jesus Anointed), Son of God, was in direct competition with the successors of *Imperator Caesar Augustus*, *divi filius*, for the hearts, minds, and allegiance of the inhabitants of the Roman Empire (e.g., Acts 17:7) *[Roman Imperial Cult, p. 307; Roman Imperial Propaganda, p. 312].*

God as Father

God is rarely addressed or described as Father in the Hebrew Scriptures (OT). By the time of Paul, however, *Father* was becoming a common title for God in synagogue prayers. This usage certainly reflects the patriarchal context of the biblical and Greco-Roman world. For Paul, however, this title carries the following main significations: (1) It metaphorically connotes the idea of God as the one source, progenitor, and creator of all things (e.g., 1 Cor 8:6). (2) It accordingly provides the framework for familial imagery pertaining to the people of God as "children." Accordingly, Paul can describe Messiah Jesus as *the firstborn of many brothers and sisters* (Rom 8:29 AT). Similarly, Paul can describe Messiah as the new Adam (that is, "firstborn"). As eponymous ancestor, Messiah in effect begins a new genealogical line of those incorporated into him through baptism and their declaration of loyalty to him, a lineage that is at the same time equivalent to descent from Abraham (Rom 5:12-21; Gal 3:26-28; 1 Cor 15:21-22, 45-48). (3) Finally, the claim of God as true father poses a direct counterassertion to Roman imperial claims: *Pater Patriae* (father of the fatherland) was one of the coveted honorific titles taken up by Roman emperors, defining supreme power and authority (Toews 2009).

The Name Paul

From the book of Acts we know that Paul could be identified with one of two names. It is incorrect to suppose that *Paul* was his Christian name, and that he left his Jewish name *Saul* behind. Instead, *Saul* was the name used in Hebrew- or Aramaic-speaking contexts, and *Paul* was his regular name in Greek- or Latin-speaking contexts. Such dual naming practice is common in immigrant situations around the world today: a name within a minority culture is retained in traditional or family settings, while a name for use in a dominant cultural setting is also chosen. This is especially so when an original name would be hard to pronounce, or if it might suggest strange associations (the Greek verb *sauloomai* means "to stagger as if drunk"). When Paul's second name *Paul* is introduced in Acts, it is evident that Paul is another name, not a new name (Acts 13:9). Acts switches from *Saul* to *Paul* once he embarks on his empire-wide mission to the "nations," to Greek-speaking non-Judean peoples.

Paul's two names, therefore, represent his dual citizenship and cultural hybridity.

Paul received a Roman-Greek name, however, not just to avoid strange associations with *Saul*. Paul's parents must have registered his birth as a Roman citizen in the municipal offices of Tarsus (Acts 21:39; 22:3), and he would have received the standard three names (*tria nomina*) for a male Roman: *praenomen*, *nomen*, and *cognomen*. Only Roman citizens were permitted to have and to use the three names. Strict penalties were imposed during the reign of Claudius (41–54 CE) for those who sought to pass themselves off as Romans by using three names. The praenomen was a name reserved for only intimate family or friendship situations and rarely used; indeed, a limited list of possible personal names was available. The nomen was the name of the *gens*, the "tribe" within the official Roman genealogical system (e.g., "Julius" was a tribal name). To be a citizen was to be incorporated into the system of Roman tribes; there were thirty-five official tribes by the end of the Republic (1st c. BCE). The cognomen was sometimes a further surname (to distinguish subclans within a tribe), but it could also be a nickname. Examples of the three-name system include Gaius Julius Caesar and Marcus Tullius Cicero. A case similar to Paul would have been the Jewish historian now known as Josephus. His Jewish name was Yosef ben Matityahu (anglicized to Josephus son of Matthias [Matthew]); his Roman name was Titus Flavius Iosephus, which indicates his incorporation into the Flavian tribe (*gens*) of his patron, Titus Flavius Vespanianus (known in history as Emperor Vespasian) when he became a Roman citizen, after he defected to the Roman side in the Roman-Judean war of 66–70 CE *[Citizenship, p. 279]*.

Paul(l)us, which means "the small" or "little" in Latin, was a common cognomen and a rare praenomen of the Amelius and Fabius tribes. The name is also attested as a cognomen of the *gens* Sergius in Acts 13:7, as in the Roman proconsul (Lucius) Sergius Paulus. While *Paul* was most likely the name given him at birth, its literal meaning no doubt also resonated significantly with his sense of calling later in life—to messianic lowliness (Agamben 2005: 7–12). In his letters, Paul nowhere refers to his Roman citizenship and nowhere hints that he has the coveted three names. In fact, he probably avoided using them, considering them along with his Roman citizenship as more a burden than a blessing, even if part of a set of privileges he did not formally renounce. Still, simply bearing the single Roman name *Paul* betrayed a level of privilege and status. (On the importance of names, see the essays *[Profile of the Assembly, p. 305]*).

THE TEXT IN THE LIFE OF THE CHURCH

The Figure of Saul/Paul: Assumptions and Perspectives

In every meaning-bearing interaction, we bring a set of varied preconceptions and assessments of those with whom we are interacting, based on our prior experience of them or their supposed reputation. These preunderstandings have a huge impact on how we interpret and respond to the message. Paul himself was aware of how varying estimates of his own leadership and message might impact how a particular appeal was received by his hearers.

Since our preunderstanding of a messenger has a crucial impact on our understanding of the message, it is appropriate for us to reflect on and discuss our own various impressions and prior assessments of the figure of Paul, whether we are preaching from Paul or engaging in group or personal study on this writing of Paul. Above all, it is crucial that we remain open, whatever our prior experience and perspective, to receiving new insight into not only the message but also the messenger, so that we can read the letter in a fresh way and experience Paul the person in a new way.

To disclose some of my own perspectives, let me outline what for me have become crucial aspects of thinking about Paul, his message, and his relevance.

1. Saul/Paul was born into an immigrant experience as a member of a colonized and dispersed people. Retaining a name for each of his two main social and language contexts, Paul is best understood as a cultural hybrid and thus well equipped to embark on a mission as a bridge builder and boundary crosser for the sake of Christ. As a missionary from a marginalized nation, his work is unlike the missionary movement associated with the colonial enterprise in the past five hundred years.

2. Saul/Paul is a child of his own cultures. This is something to acknowledge and appreciate. Many aspects of Paul's style that we as Western readers sometimes find difficult were received very differently in his original cultural context: his supposed manipulative rhetoric, his direct authoritarianism in some settings (1 Cor 4:21), his patriarchalism, his sarcastic shaming or sharp cursing of theological opponents (Gal 5:12; 2 Cor 11), or his charged invective against outside adversaries (Phil 3:2). Paul is committed to radical inclusion for the sake of Christ, but he does not always display the polite niceness that we often associate with inclusion. Sometimes we must measure his own seemingly violent words (2 Cor 11:1-15;

Gal 1:8-9) against his own stated beliefs or claims (1 Cor 4:12-13; Rom 12:14; Phil 1:15-18). I am convinced that if Paul knew his passionate words in the moment were to become sacred Scripture, he would ask for the chance to rephrase some things.

3. Paul sees himself as a person transformed and energized by God's radical generosity, by "grace" (1 Cor 15:9-11). Deeply transformed by Christ, likened to being "seized" as a slave might be captured (Phil 3:12; 1 Cor 9:16-17), he experiences this as a close personal relationship with his Lord (Phil 1:23; 3:8). Crucial to Paul's understanding of grace is that all of life is pure gift (1 Cor 4:7). Indeed, the generosity (grace) received through Jesus Christ, by virtue of Christ's own loyal trust, trumps any other framework for community and personal formation. In Christ, human beings are released not only from the regime of Sin (Error), but also from any regime of Law, having been incorporated into the regime of radical Mercy and Grace. Only radical mercy and grace can solve the twin problems of social exclusivity and alienation *and* of human moral inability (Rom 1–8). Still, for Paul, divine grace and empowerment are the flip side of deliberate human agency and effort-filled striving (1 Cor 15:9-10; Phil 2:12; 3:12-14).

4. Paul's theology and core convictions are not focused narrowly on how individuals get right with God so that they can avoid eternal damnation and instead find eternal bliss in heaven. Instead, Paul's theology coalesces around God's gracious and holistic program to reclaim and restore the whole of the universe through God's work in Christ to overcome powers that have corrupted and keep in bondage a creation that is good. Holistic and final restoration, salvation, and re-creation are grandly inclusive, pertaining to both personal and social transformation. Paul envisions the future as involving the reconciliation of all peoples in the context of a restored creation. (See TBC and TLC on 3:18–4:1; on the scholarly debate about construals of Paul's core convictions, see Toews 2004: 29–36; Campbell; Borg and Crossan.)

5. Paul's redemptive vision is expressed in the language and framework of what scholars call Jewish apocalyptic thought. This conceptuality emerged at least three hundred years before Paul's time and took on many forms and functions, especially as a theology of resistance to imperial domination (Portier-Young). Jewish apocalyptic thought was the primary framework also for many in the Pharisaic movement, thus a central part of Paul's heritage. The core concept is the notion of a radical disjunction between "the present age" and "the age to come." The age to come (kingdom of God and

other synonyms) will emerge soon only through a radical intervention by God to bring the whole created order to its intended design. Resurrection is a key sign of the age to come. The conflict between the two ages is being played out in the present as a moral battle within each individual, but it is also played out cosmically as a battle between divine forces (e.g., Satan, demons) and sociopolitically as a battle among human agents and institutions. As a result of his encounter with the risen Jesus, this framework was transformed, even as it became the main vehicle for Paul's theological articulation of the meaning of Jesus in his death, resurrection, and final victory. In Paul's understanding, the reality of the resurrection of Jesus (as the "firstfruits," 1 Cor 15:20) was the critical evidence that the age to come has dawned and will be fully realized just around the corner. (For Paul's theology as a reframing of Jewish apocalyptic perspectives, see esp. Beker.)

6. Saul/Paul is both a radical visionary and a practical pastor at the same time. He values both disruptive charisma (as a sign of the dawn of the age to come) and peaceful orderliness (as a concession that the fullness of the age to come is not yet here). When these come into tension, Paul makes strategic compromises (arguably, for instance, on slavery and gender, or in the exercise of gifts in the assembly).

7. Paul's letters represent the *contingent* (situationally adapted) expression of a *coherent* set of commitments (the truth of the gospel; cf. Beker). Paul always seeks a word-on-target, taking the particular needs of each situation or perspectives of his audience seriously. His letters are marked by a persistent "audience adaptation," and he claims that even his conduct is shaped by a contextualization (1 Cor 9). Thus no one text gives us the final picture of the core of his theology and commitments. Sometimes we find that the practical reasons for a given directive are distinct from the rhetorical arguments that he offers; and even these may not fully represent his underlying convictions. Sometimes Paul argues against two fronts, seeking a middle path in ways that we may not fully grasp but that his original hearers-readers probably did. In many cases, Paul's letters show that his own audiences were diverse. Sometimes he takes a one-sided view on an issue (Galatians); other times he seeks to cut between and reconcile two extremes (Romans). Sometimes he uses what for us seems like an ambiguous shorthand, referring to things he may have discussed or taught earlier, which are not immediately clear to us. Without careful deliberation, therefore, we cannot lift verses out of context as representing the core of his theology or

ethical convictions. Rather, we must weigh his words in one letter carefully in relation to other letters (e.g., Phil 3:8-9 in relation to Romans; Phil 2:12 in relation to other texts). For this reason, the TBC sections in this commentary regularly draw other Pauline texts into the conversation.

8. Paul's success in founding and nurturing small cell groups of Jesus loyalists reflects his gift for interpersonal networking and relationship building, his ability to understand people and to meet them where they are, and his strategic thinking. His success is not necessarily to be found in spellbinding public oratory, an area some consider to be a weakness for him, as he admits (2 Cor 10).

9. Paul is deeply committed to the "spirit" of the gospel and the Scriptures—that is, its inner meaning and intention—not just its "letter," its outward form (2 Cor 3). This is a profoundly significant notion, one that sometimes Paul would no doubt want to have applied to his own words. This suggests that we today should welcome the wrestling (in dialogue) with Paul on some of his particular conclusions or specific directives in light of his own premises and core convictions, and in light of the overall substance of biblical revelation.

10. Paul does not always come across the same way in all his letters. Each of his letters gives us a distinctive window into his person, character, and message/theology. In Philippians, we meet especially the relational Paul as we catch a glimpse of his deep inner life. At the same time, we become acquainted with a politically provocative Paul not always evident elsewhere.

11. Paul acknowledges that his wisdom is second to that of "the Lord." Yet he does not concede that his own wisdom is unreliable (1 Cor 7:10, 12, 25, 35, 40).

12. While the vocabulary of faith in Paul is different from that of the Gospels, Paul's theology displays a remarkable coherence with the teaching and vision of Jesus, especially as a particular contextualization of it in new urban, culturally diverse, and educated settings (see also TBC on 2:6-11, "Paul and the Earthly Life of Jesus").

13. Taken out of context, some of Paul's words are more easily used by systems of domination than most other parts of the Bible. For instance, Paul's words have helped to support the marginalization of many (e.g., women, slaves) through the centuries. Serious questions must be faced: How can we take Paul constructively when his words have served to keep some "in their place," instead of freeing them for ministry, or at worst contributed oppression to abuse and harm? Is this result to be blamed on Paul's interpreters, or do

we regard Paul also as complicit in this history? It is often a pastoral challenge to bring some people into a new appreciation of Paul when his words have been a source of pain and alienation. (For a feminist, postcolonial reading of Philippians, see Marchal 2006, 2008, 2011.)

14. Modern biblical scholarship forces us to face the question "Which Paul?" Do we orient ourselves to the Paul of historians (working only with letters considered to be authored by Paul), or the canonical Paul (including all the letters attributed to Paul in the NT), or both? A strong case can be made that the pastoral epistles (1–2 Timothy and Titus, in which we find a more strident patriarchal perspective) are not authored by Paul but by a disciple or admirer sometime after his death, following a practice not uncommon in the ancient world. Also questioned by most mainstream scholars are Ephesians (fairly strongly), Colossians (less strongly), and 2 Thessalonians (even less strongly), leaving a list of seven "undisputed" letters. My own view of the "historical Paul" includes Colossians and 2 Thessalonians, but not the pastoral epistles or Ephesians (cf. Yoder Neufeld 2002). At the same time, I recognize that questions of authorship are not decisive for reading the Bible in the believing community.

My hope is that this commentary will assist the interactive process by which we claim Paul as a dialogue partner whose wisdom and leadership in the cause of Christ are highly prized through the guidance of the Spirit, not simplistically accepted or rejected as an authoritarian bishop whose every word must remain unquestioned.

Slavery as Institution and Metaphor

The language of slavery resonates differently in different contexts. There are reasons why this language might be avoided today, since it can be demeaning, oppressive, alienating, or foreign. Thus some contemporary translations regularly translate the word for *slaves* as *servants* (NRSV, NIV). But there are also reasons why it is best to name it as it is in the Bible, especially in translation. Paul often appropriates the language of slavery metaphorically (as in Philippians), and usually positively (but see 2 Cor 11:19-20). Precisely because of this, it is crucial to acknowledge that for Paul, slavery—as a primarily birth-based social reality—is an oppressive institution that ultimately will be eradicated in the realm of Christ.

The negation of the institution of slavery "in Messiah" can be observed in the following texts. The charters of freedom pronounce the ending of the social duality of slave and free (1 Cor 12:13; Gal 3:28; Col 3:11). Slavery for Paul is inherently degrading (2 Cor 11:19-21), a status far inferior to that of childship (Gal 4:1-7; Rom 8:15) and freedom (Gal 4:8-9, 24; 5:1, 13). Thus bondage in general is something to be overcome (Rom 8:21). While believers become enslaved to God through Messiah, in no way should they become "slaves of humans" (1 Cor 7:23). Yet true freedom in Messiah is to become "enslaved to one another" (Gal 5:13).

Nevertheless, slavery still exists in the world ("in the flesh"), and Paul assumes that most slaves will remain as slaves (1 Cor 7:21a, 24) and that slaves should obey their masters (Col 3:22–4:1; cf. Eph 6:5-9). Precisely here, however, Paul proclaims an inversion of status perceptions and conduct "in Messiah," even in the present order of time. Every free person must be regarded as a slave, and every slave must be regarded as a freed person (1 Cor 7:22). In Messiah's assembly, to the extent that one still lives with worldly statuses ascribed from birth, greater honor is to be given to those of lower status (1 Cor 12:20-26). Accordingly, Paul advises that slaves should take advantage of any opportunity for manumission (purchase out of slavery; 1 Cor 7:21, 23), and he works hard for the manumission of Onesimus, one of his coworkers (Philemon; Col 4:9).

Although Paul questions the institution of slavery at various points, he often uses the metaphor of slavery positively in his letters. Believers in general "serve as slaves" toward God (Rom 7:6; 12:11; 1 Thess 1:9; 1 Cor 7:23) or toward Messiah (Rom 14:18; 16:18; 1 Cor 7:22). Paul considers it an ironic honor to be a "slave of Christ" (Phil 1:1; Rom 1:1), drawing on the use of the term "servant of God" for special leaders of old (e.g., Moses, Joshua). On the premise that humans are "slaves of the one whom you obey," Paul exhorts against enslavement to sin while embracing enslavement to justice-righteousness (Rom 6:6-22; 7:7, 25). He invites his readers to think of freedom as "serving as a slave to one another" (Gal 5:13). Being "slaves of Messiah" especially applies to apostolic service, whether that of Paul or his coworkers (Rom 1:1; Gal 1:10; Phil 1:1; 2:22; Col 4:12). Moreover, Paul argues that his calling is not to demand apostolic rights, but to be a "slave to all for the sake of the gospel" (1 Cor 9:19). To the Corinthians he somewhat ironically claims that he and Timothy are "your slaves for Jesus' sake" (2 Cor 4:5). On the other hand, Paul also negates any enslavement or the status of slavery in favor of freedom and full inheritance ("childship") in Messiah (Rom 8:15; Gal 4:1-9, 24; 5:1, 13).

Also requiring careful consideration are the many parables in the Gospels, where Jesus uses the master-slave image to illustrate some aspect of discipleship, but without endorsing slavery as such (e.g., Mark 13:34-36; Luke 12:35-38; 17:7-10; Matt 18:23-35; Matt 25:14-30; most English versions use the less-offensive term *servant*). At the core of Paul's understanding of the gospel is Jesus' teaching on social inversion: "Whoever wishes to be first [prominent, leader] among you must be the slave of all" (Mark 10:44).

In the early church after Paul, two directions developed: one worked against the institution of slavery; the other slowly accepted it fully, accommodating to prevailing Roman social values. Paul himself carefully balances exhortations to slaves and those to masters in his "household codes" (Col 3:18–4:1; Eph 6:5-9). But in 1 Peter, where slaves are exhorted to submit even to abusive masters, there is no corresponding exhortation to masters, indicating either that masters were not typically members of the community, or that their behavior was not thought to be a problem. In the pastoral epistles, the household codes only address slaves, who are asked to submit, even to believing masters (1 Tim 6:1-2; Titus 2:9-10). But masters are also not explicitly cautioned, even though it is clear that masters are included in the Christian community. Overall, the pastoral epistles seem to endorse the Roman institution of the patriarchal household and Christianize it by claiming that the church and the Christian family are to mirror the ideal patriarchal household. Nevertheless, in one text "slave traders" are included in a list of those who will not enter the kingdom of God (1 Tim 1:9-11). Similarly, Revelation (18:13) includes an implicit prophetic denunciation of the slave trade by humanizing the "cargo of bodies" as representing "souls of humans." In the postapostolic period, some texts show the church struggling against slavery (Harrill). In 1 Clement 55.2 (96 CE) and in Shepherd of Hermas (*Similitude* 1.8; *Mandate* 8.10; mid-2nd c.), we see the church financing manumission for its members and proposing that members free their own slaves. However, a different trend became the norm in Roman Christianity. Ignatius (120s CE) advises against using the church's common fund for this purpose, seemingly moving to retain slavery in opposition to these liberating measures (*To Polycarp* 4.3). In the Apostolic Constitutions (4th c.), former slaves are not permitted ordination.

Philippians 1:3-11

Thanksgiving and Prayer

PREVIEW

You give me joy! Paul establishes a mood of affection and hopeful optimism in the opening thanksgiving and prayer as he recalls unspoken highpoints in his relationship with the congregation. He congratulates them for their overall commitment to Messiah Jesus, and his carefully crafted words make repeated allusions specifically to their recent support of his ministry while in prison, offering an indirect thanksgiving for their assistance. Most important, he identifies their provision as an expression of their *partnership in the gospel*—indeed a *partnership of generosity*—that emphatically involves *all* of them. Most modern English translations miss these key emphases by spiritualizing Paul's repeated references to mutual assistance as a concrete expression of the gospel. Still, while highlighting their own good work, he also draws attention to the God who energizes all good work, the basis for his future confidence. Paul has them recall both the past and present of their relationship with him, yet he also invites them into the future, the day of Messiah Jesus, the goal of history. His confidence in them is matched by his prayer for their continued maturation. Above all, he wishes to communicate his deep affection and longing for them.

OUTLINE

Thanksgiving to God, 1:3-6
Explanation of Paul's Disposition, 1:7-8
Prayer, 1:9-11

EXPLANATORY NOTES

Following a prescript with an address and a greeting, letters in the Greco-Roman world typically proceeded with some kind of thanksgiving or prayer or wish for health on the part of the recipient. Paul follows this practice with one exception (Galatians), using a number of stereotyped expressions. At the same time, he crafts all his thanksgiving formulations to suit each occasion. Paul's opening thanksgivings and prayers especially offer previews of themes that will become clearer as the letter unfolds. This thanksgiving is brimming with affirmation, confidence, and affection. While he establishes a mood of mutual friendship marked by deep emotional bonds, his apostolic role and sense of responsibility for them is not far below the surface. Paul is already laying the groundwork for the disclosure (1:12-26) and exhortation (1:27–4:9) that follow. The comments below on this opening segment are organized around the key themes that unfold in Paul's opening words (1:3-8).

Affirmation: Their Good Work as an Expression of Partnership

The opening words of Paul's thanksgiving *to God* warmly and extravagantly highlight its occasion (*upon every remembrance of you*) and its manner (*always, in my every petition for all of you, making the petition with joy*). Paul then explains the specific basis for his joyful thanksgiving, using words that highlight themes relevant to this particular letter and the relationships that it seeks to deepen (vv. 5-7). With carefully balanced phrases, Paul draws attention to their recent mutual aid on his behalf with three images: their *partnership in the gospel*, the *good work* begun *in and among them*, and their conduct as *fellow partners* with Paul *in generosity* (Gk. *charis*) in the midst of his imprisonment. Paul congratulates them for sending both financial assistance and their own Epaphroditus to assist him in his imprisonment and trial before the Roman imperial authorities.

While the original audience in Philippi would have picked up on these allusions as soon as they were heard, the modern reader can comprehend their meaning only after taking full account of what Paul says later in the letter (1:12-20; 2:25-30; 4:10-20). Indeed, highlighting the theme of partnership by repeating terms from the *koinōnia* word group, the climax in 4:10-20 closely recaps the themes introduced in 1:3-8, and together these passages bracket the letter:

I give thanks to God (1:3)	*I rejoiced in the Lord greatly that now at last you have revived your concern for me* (4:10)
for your partnership [koinōnia] in the gospel (1:5)	*you did well by becoming fellow-partners [syg-koinōneō] with me* (4:14)
from the first day until now (1:5)	*in the beginning of the gospel* (4:15) *you sent [assistance] . . . both once and twice* (4:16)
both in my chains and in the defense and confirmation of the gospel (1:7a)	*. . . in my tribulation* (4:14) *. . . for my need* (4:16)
You are all fellow-partners [syg-koinōnos] with me in generosity (1:7b)	*no assembly partnered [koinōneō] with me in the accounting of giving and receiving except you alone* (4:15)

Unfortunately, these verbal connections and the emphasis specifically on *partnership* in speaking of mutual assistance are missed by modern translations, which usually render these phrases with the words *share* or *participate* (see TBC below).

Paul makes three allusions to their recent mutual aid in a way that anticipates the more formal discussion of their assistance in 4:10-20. Strangely (at least by Western cultural sensibilities), Paul will never offer a direct thank-you, even though he eventually gives them a formal receipt using regular commercial language (4:18). We would expect Paul to effusively thank his supporting donors right up front. Instead, he offers *thanksgiving to God* and expresses *rejoicing in the Lord* in response to their generous acts, in accordance with the principle expressed in 2 Corinthians 9:11-12: "You will be enriched in every way for your great generosity, which will produce thanksgiving to God through us; for the rendering of this [charitable] ministry not only supplies the needs of the saints but also overflows with many thanksgivings to God."

As we shall see, what Paul wants to stress is that assistance of the sort they have offered establishes neither debt (on the part of the receiver) nor patronage (on the part of the donor). Instead, this aid

1. is offered in service *of the gospel* (Phil 1:5; 4:15) and
2. constitutes an expression of *partnership* (1:5, 7; 4:14, 15), so that it
3. accrues to their total "equity" (4:17; cf. 1 Cor 9:12b-23),

4. thus representing what they owe by way of obligation in the context of a true partnership (Phil 2:30) and

5. ultimately comprising an offering to God (4:18), who is the only one who can truly "repay" (4:19).

Paul accordingly avoids naming their assistance as a gift and omits any specific thank-you directly to them. What he highlights instead is the deep bond and affection and the mutual commitments that exist between them. Paul is concerned for partnership in contrast to the prevailing sociocultural practices of patronage in the Roman world (on this further, see EN on 4:10-12).

This persuasive intention helps to explain Paul's repeated and emphatic stress on *all of you*. Even though the initial uses of these words are stereotypical of thanksgiving formulations and salutations (vv. 1, 4; cf. 1 Thess 1:2; Rom 1:8), there is an excess in the piling up of *all* and *every* terms (vv. 3-4; *every* and *all* translate the same Greek word, *pas*). The threefold repetition of *all of you* in verses 7-8 causes the hearer to take special note: Paul's confident regard and heartfelt longing is emphatically for *all of you* (v. 7a, 8), and he claims them *all* as his *fellow partners* (v. 7b). In other words, all members—regular or leaders, wealthy or poor, high status or low status—are equal partners in the assembly. In the Roman world, financial assistance regularly expresses social hierarchy: more than anything else, benefactions by the rich display elite social status. But Paul wishes to highlight that *all* share in the specific work of the financial support of a few. Paul thereby wishes to emphasize *both* the partnership between himself and the assembly *and* the horizontal partnership within the community itself (2:1, again using *koinōnia*). This further anticipates Paul's concern for the unity of the church (2:1-5), a unity that is apparently being strained not only by their own current ordeal (1:27-30) but also by the potential imbalance created by recent acts of support for Paul himself.

While Paul alludes specifically to their mutual financial assistance in the cause of the gospel, the phrase *partnership in the gospel* is sufficiently inclusive to imply more broadly their participation in the realm of God's saving news. This participation includes their support of proclamation and witness, their loyalty to Messiah, and their internal corporate life devoted to practicing the way of Messiah—and even their mutual bond of affection with Paul and their giving and receiving for the sake of the gospel. Accordingly, Paul later congratulates the community for their general *obedience* in his absence (2:12). Paul speaks to a partnership directed toward the fullness of God's work and reality through Messiah Jesus, not merely their concrete mutual aid or partnership in actively proclaiming the gospel. The same breadth of meaning pertains to *good work*. The word regularly denotes specific acts of mutual assistance (2 Cor 9:8; Gal 6:10) and sometimes identifies general moral fiber (Rom 2:7 [cf. 2:10]; 13:3; Col 1:10; cf. Eph 2:10; 1 Tim 2:10; 5:10; 6:18; 2 Tim 2:21; 3:17; Titus 1:16; 3:1).

Finally, the language of being *fellow partners in generosity* (*charis*) seems to evoke a double meaning. On the one hand, the Greek word *charis* regularly refers to concrete acts of generosity in the form of mutual aid. That meaning is primary here. But the term also implies God's foundational, initiating, and saving generosity (*grace*), a meaning also emphasized in 1:2 and 4:23. To translate *charis* here with "God's grace" (NRSV, NIV) misses the breadth and nuance of Paul's meaning and shows a preoccupation with the spiritual to the neglect of the socially concrete. The word *God's* is not in Paul's Greek text. He is referring mainly to *their* act of generosity, as an expression of God's deeper generosity. (For a similar double sense, see 2 Cor 8:1-9, where the word *charis* refers to the generosity of mutual aid, understood as an expression of God's foundational generosity or grace; see TBC below, "Paul's Reconstruction of *Charis*.")

Consummation: Confidence in Divine Energy for the Completion of the Good Work

Paul's thanksgiving to God for their *partnership* both in the past and *until now* (vv. 3-5, 7) evokes a counterpart parallel confession of confidence in God's *good work* in their midst, begun in the past and to be completed in the future, *until the day of Messiah Jesus* (v. 6). Paul's confidence has to do with God's originating work, and thus Paul reminds them indirectly that their own action is a response to God's prior action. Similarly, in the prayer to come, he reminds them that their fruit of righteousness-justice is founded on the work of Messiah Jesus (1:10-11). This balancing of human and divine action anticipates Paul's exhortation in 2:12-13, where he calls them to work actively toward their own deliverance (salvation), but in synergy with God's active working in and among them. The emphasis on final completion (consummation) anticipates Paul's exhortation on striving to reach the final goal, not resting complacent with present arrival (1:9-11; 3:10-15). It may also specifically hint at Paul's hope that their further involvement in mutual aid (*good work*) will soon be completed. A few months after writing to the Philippians, Paul brags to the Corinthians that the Philippians have now contributed to a relief fund for the poor in Judea, despite their relative poverty (see 2 Cor 8:1-7; 9:1-2; see TBC below, "Paul's Reconstruction of *Charis*").

Paul's words also mean to assure. This is only the first of numerous words of assurance of divine assistance for the present and for the future (1:19, 28-29; 2:12-13; 4:5, 7, 9, 13, 19-20). Paul's letter begins and ends with profound words of assurance (1:6; 4:19-20) that have to do with God's eschatological (future, world-transforming) work throughout the world, for which *day of Messiah Jesus* is shorthand. Throughout this letter, Paul regularly reminds his readers that their life together, their mission, and even their distress are intelligible only in light of God's decisive intervention in the future. In that "consummation," God will deliver them wholly—personally and corporately, bodily and socially, morally and politically—as part of God's act of reclaiming dominion throughout the world, restoring it to its intended state (1:6, 10-11, 28; 2:10-11, 16-18; 3:10-14, 20-21; 4:1, 3, 5; cf. 1:23). Paul consistently highlights ultimate salvation as a participation in God's ultimate renewal of all things, a merging of heaven and earth, not a vertical departure of the individual after death to heaven. In Philippians, Paul's reference toward this future climax of salvation functions both as an ethical warrant for their maturation in love and righteousness-justice (1:6, 11) *and* as an assurance of Messiah's ultimate deliverance over against rival claimants to bring peace and security (1:28; 2:9-11; 3:10-11, 14, 20-21; 4:5; see TBC and TLC on 3:18–4:1).

Disposition: Head, Heart, and Bowels

Right from the start, Paul emphasizes his deep emotional bonds with the community. Invoking depth of pathos, he starts with joyful remembering (vv. 3-4) and positive mental regard and confidence (vv. 6-7a), then moves to heartfelt bonding (vv. 7b) and longing affection in the gut (v. 7b).

The thanksgiving proper (vv. 3-5) highlights Paul's joyful thanksgiving, constant intercession, and supreme confidence. Although Paul elsewhere refers to *joy* in connection with thanksgiving and prayer (e.g., 1 Thess 3:9-13; Col 1:11-12), nowhere else does he make this part of a formal thanksgiving in a letter opening. Paul then dramatizes the depth of his regard for them in a manner unlike any other of his letters as he offers a formulaic declaration (v. 7) and invokes an oath (v. 8).

The formulaic *It is just* is unprecedented in Paul's writings and draws attention to what is generally proper or obligatory. What is *just* in this case is *to think* (Gk. *phroneō*) *this way about all of you* (misleading is the NIV: *to feel*). Paul begins with the disposition of his head-mind, picking up on the mental-intellectual nuance of his prior verb *having become convinced [persuaded, confident]* (v. 6). And at the end of the letter he will congratulate them for *thinking* (being mindful) of him (4:10). Customary practice in Paul's social environment can help explain his choice of words. It was only proper and expected, even obligatory, that those involved in a partnership devoted to some common purpose should be committed to the same "mind-set" (Sampley). Accordingly, the point Paul makes is that his particular mental regard for them is grounded not in some fleeting emotional bond, but in their shared commitment within the framework of a partnership with all of them (v. 7), one founded on the reality of Messiah Jesus (v. 8) and his gospel (vv. 5, 7). But Paul quickly moves on to identify a deeper disposition as the cause of his mental outlook: *because I have you in my heart* (v. 7 NIV, NRSV mg.; the NRSV's *You have me in your heart* is less compelling on grammatical and contextual grounds; on being "in someone's heart," see also 2 Cor 3:3; 7:2-4; 8:16; 1 Thess 2:17; for the heart as the seat of relational affection, see Rom 9:2; 10:1; 2 Cor 2:4).

Then, through an unexpected formality of an oath, Paul deepens the rhetoric of his disposition even further (for oaths in Paul, see also Rom 1:9; 2 Cor 1:23; 1 Thess 2:5, 10; cf. 1 Cor 4:1-5). Paul invokes the very testimony of God as a way to attest to his deepest feelings, using the emotionally charged words of relational "longing" (again in 2:26; 4:1), feelings characteristic of the *bowels of Messiah Jesus* himself. *Bowels* (KJV) is a more expressive translation than *compassion* (NRSV; NIV: *affection*). The word in Greek (*splanchna*) is plural, designating "innards," "intestines," and by extension "desires, affections," especially "compassion." His oath highlights his own deep feeling, and that it is for *all* of them. Indirectly he has also implied that all of them are being held in the bosom of Christ (see also 2:1). This longing is expressed later as a desire to be reunited with them in the near future (1:19, 24-26, 27; 2:24).

It is striking how subjective feeling, deep relational bonds, and gospel-oriented priorities come together in this opening. Paul does not just say, "Remember our good times together, I think of you always, thanks for your gift to me," or the like, as would be typical of simple letters of friendship. Rather, his concern throughout is to create a framework for what relationships, corporate behavior, and disposition look like when oriented around *the gospel* and *Messiah* and the experience of divine grace. What drives Paul is concern for how the Philippians express their *partnership in the gospel* (1:5), their status as *copartners in generosity* (1: 7), and ultimately their *practice of citizenship in a manner worthy of the gospel of Messiah* (1:27). While there is indeed deep human feeling and longing expressed in the opening (1:7-8) and throughout the letter (1:24-26; 2:16-18, 19-30; 4:1), such affection is ultimately founded on the *bowels of Messiah Jesus* himself (1:8; cf. 2:1). This is what provides an occasion for thanksgiving to God. In Philippians, Christ Jesus is not only the model for the mind-set and pathway for messianic citizenship (2:5-11), but also the very resource and foundation for the individual and the community's depth of emotional solidarity and consolation.

Situation: Paul's Chains and Trial

Paul refers to his own situation somewhat incidentally as the context for their partnership in mutual aid (v. 7). After all, it was already known to them. In the next unit, Paul will provide further disclosure specifically about that situation (1:12-26). The use of technical legal terms here (*apologia*, "defense," as in Acts 22:1; 25:16; 1 Cor 9:3; 2 Cor 7:11; 2 Tim 4:16; and 1 Pet 3:15; *bebaiōsis*, "confirmation," as in Heb 6:16) confirms that later, in 1:16 and 1:20, Paul is discussing an upcoming trial before Roman imperial authorities.

Surprisingly absent from the opening segment is any reference to *their* distress, whether by way of acknowledgment (e.g., I know that . . .) or by way of prayer for their safety in the face of persecution. That theme will finally come after Paul reviews his own distress (1:12-26), when he invites their petition on his behalf (1:19; cf. 26). Only when he turns back to address their circumstances through exhortation does he speak explicitly to their own plight (1:27-30; and then to their *need* in 2:14-15; 3:2; 4:19). For now, Paul keeps the emphasis on their partnership and progress in the gospel and on his disposition of unfailing affection toward them.

Intercession: Paul's Prayer

Paul next gives content to his claim of constant prayer on their behalf (1:3-4), elaborating his confidence in God's continued work among them toward full maturation (1:6). Many of the themes of this prayer can be matched in prayers for his readers in other letters (e.g., 1 Thess 3:11-13; 2 Thess 1:11-12; 2:16-17; 3:5; Col 1:9-12; Rom

15:5-6, 13; Philem 6; Eph 1:17-19; 3:14-19). Still, Paul shapes this prayer to apply especially to his Philippian partners. The fundamental concern of the prayer here is for their virtue—the ethical life and corresponding mental disposition of adherents of Messiah Jesus. Indeed, packed into this prayer are many key aspects of Pauline ethics.

1. The specific content of this ethic pertains to *love* (*agapē*) and *justice-righteousness* (*dikaiosynē*; Greek does not distinguish lexically between social justice and personal righteousness). The supreme priority of love accords with Paul's exhortation in other letters (e.g., 1 Thess 3:12; Rom 13:8-10; 1 Cor 8:1; 13:1-13; Gal 5:6, 13-14). In Philippians, love is central to the challenge about disunity and rivalry in their ranks and among believers (1:16; 2:1-2). Love is a priority in their needed consolation and solidarity in suffering (2:1) and the virtue to be demonstrated in their life together (2:2). In contrast to selfish ambition, love is a synonym for *goodwill* (*eudokia*, 1:15-16), a term that can also summarize the goal of God's work within the community and the world (2:13). Paul asks that their love *exceed still more and more* (similarly in 1 Thess 3:12), which is both an indirect compliment (in reference to their assistance), yet also a signal of necessary continued intentionality (2:12; 3:12-16).

Justice-righteousness will reappear in the letter as the key hallmark of messianic identity and character (3:9) and as a focal point of practical and mental virtue (*what is just*, 4:8). Justice-righteousness here is not the gift of status before God, but the ethical fruit that comes through the work of Jesus: *the fruit through Jesus that is justice-righteousness* (cf. Rom 5–8, esp. 6:13, 16-20; 7:4-6; 8:4, 10). The imagery of fruit and harvest implies the filling out of the harvest (cf. Rom 7:4; Col 1:6, 10), a maturation toward the goal (cf. 3:11-15). The *fruit/harvest that is justice-righteousness* can refer to ethical maturation in general, but here it alludes specifically to generous mutual aid (as in 2 Cor 9:8; cf. Gal 6:9-10). Paul uses *fruit* (*harvest*) again at the close of his letter to refer to the mutual aid they provided to him (4:17).

2. In addition to the embodiment of love and justice-righteousness, the ethic also involves a closely related mental discipline for the purpose of careful ethical discernment in ever-new and changing circumstances, a crucial concern for Paul (e.g., Rom 2:18; 12:1-2; 14:22; 16:19; Gal 6:4; Eph 5:10; 1 Thess 5:21). Careful discernment and mental rigor are key themes of this letter (2:3-5; 3:7-19; 4:8-9). Paul deliberately balances the cultivation of *full/deep knowledge* (*epignōsis*) itself alongside its practical application, *complete perception* (*perception* translates *aisthēsis*, the root of *aesthetics*, the "assessment of

beauty-good"). This combination of deep knowledge and practical perception is what makes them able *to discern what is best* (NIV; lit. "to test, assess value, and thus approve the things that distinguish"). This theme of discernment anticipates the appeal at the close of the letter to "audit" what counts for true virtue in relation to claims of value in the surrounding world (4:8-9).

3. The ethic's source and pattern is Jesus. This appeal to Jesus as model is stressed throughout the letter (1:8; 2:1, 5-8; 3:7-11, 18-19). At the close, when Paul invites the community to actively audit what counts for virtue, he points to himself as model (4:9; cf. 3:17), but only as one patterned on that of Messiah (3:3-17 in relation to 2:4-11; cf. 1 Cor 11:1).

4. The ethic is oriented to the climax of God's redemptive work: the restoration and reconciliation of all things. This climax includes a final accounting of—and thus accountability for—all deeds, whether for commendation or for censure (Phil 1:6; 2:16-18; 4:1; cf. Rom 2:5-16; 14:10-12; 1 Cor 4:1-5; 2 Cor 5:9-10).

5. Finally, as an embodiment of the way of Messiah Jesus, the ethic is oriented to the glory and praise of God, as opposed to the praise of mere humans and prevailing norms. Paul sounds this theme at the beginning, center, and conclusion of the letter (1:11; 2:11; 4:19-20). It provides the ultimate purpose for their "excessive" growth in love and justice-righteousness, knowledge and perception, discernment and blamelessness.

THE TEXT IN BIBLICAL CONTEXT

The Gospel: A Royal Proclamation of Public Well-Being

The Greek word *euangelion* is one of the most significant terms in Paul's letters and in the entirety of the NT. Interestingly, Paul uses the noun *euangelion* more frequently (as a percentage of length) in Philippians than in any other letter. Moreover, he uses it at crucial moments (1:5, 7, 12, 16, 27 [2x]; 2:22; 4:3, 15). The traditional translation *gospel* comes from the Old English *godspel* (or *goodspel*), originally meaning "good message/story." By now, unfortunately, *gospel* is just a Bible word—one that does not carry the same connotations as *euangelion* did for Paul.

No one-word equivalent in modern English for *euangelion* exists, because the social practice in which it functioned no longer exists. Its original context is the use of a messenger (*angelos*), herald (*kēryx*), or envoy (*apostolos*)—before the advent of rapid and then instant communication—to carry on foot and then to publicly announce "a message" (*angelia, kērygma*) of major consequence. The word *euangelion* (lit. "well-being message, wellness proclamation") was suitable when the message carried and publicly delivered was positive in content or impact, such as the heralding of a decisive military victory, the imminent visit of an emperor, or the accession of a new emperor. By contrast, for a negative message—such as one about a military disaster, an approaching foreign army, the death of a ruler, or a natural disaster—the word *kak-angelia* (bad message) was used. If the message was neutral in content or impact, such as an offer of surrender to the rival army, instructions on a business venture, the simple *angelia* (message) could be used.

There were two main qualifications to be a messenger, herald, or envoy: First, a person needed to be swift of foot. The most renowned of messengers were runners (e.g., the runner from Marathon) and their patron deity was the god Hermes (Mercury), the fastest of the celestial deities in classical mythology. This context of running explains the blessing on the "feet" of the one who brings the "good message" of national well-being and peace in Isaiah 52:7-8. Second, these communicators needed to be capable in public oral speech. Some cities had competitions on the craft of verbal "heralding" (*kēryxis*). Not accidentally, Hermes, the swiftest of the gods, was also known as the "interpreter" of the gods. The practice of heralding in a local setting was much like that of a town crier in British and American history for communicating announcements of major public importance. Even today, the faster the messenger (medium) with the message, the greater the effect on its impact and character.

In Paul's letters, the word *euangelion* has the connotation of a "royal proclamation of public well-being." As such, it is a theopolitical term (see the Introduction; TBC on 1:1-2, "*Christos* (Messiah) as Theopolitical Title"). Two main patterns of usage in Paul's context give it this resonance. The first is the language of "proclaiming a message of public well-being" in Paul's Scripture, especially in Isaiah's "public announcement" of God's coming deliverance-restoration to the nation of Israel and to the whole world (e.g., Isa 40:9; 52:7; 60:6; 61:1). The second is the word's usage in Roman religiopolitical propaganda. The plural *euangelia* regularly appears in connection with the accession, birth, military victories, or virtuous rule of an emperor. The "good messages" focus on the benefits that come through military conquests or imperial benefactions. The focus of these is on the prosperity and security of the empire, made possible through Imperator Caesar Augustus and later emperors. But while Roman rhetoric highlights the multiple "announcements of wellness events" pertaining to the many mighty deeds and benefactions of Imperator Caesar Augustus (using the plural *euangelia*), Paul always speaks of the singular "proclamation of well-being" (*euangelion*) pertaining to the regime inaugurated through Lord Jesus Messiah. In Philippians, this "royal proclamation" pertaining to Messiah accordingly serves simultaneously as the "constitution" for the good life of Messiah's new citizen community (see EN on 1:27-28; TLC on 1:12-26, "Heralding the Gospel") *[Roman Imperial Propaganda, p. 312]*.

Koinōnia as Partnership

The *koinōnia* word group in Paul is best translated with the language of *partnership*. The word does not designate fellowship in a narrowly religious sense, especially as interpersonal "sharing" over tea. Rather, the key notion is "participating together" in something, which is the original meaning of fellowship, "the state of being fellows." It connotes having a share in something, holding in common, and more specifically, partnering with someone in something. In Paul's time, the *koinōnia* word group could variously refer to a political alliance or league, a community or social association, a business or marriage partnership, shared coeducation, property held in common, or a charitable contribution for the common good.

In 1:5 and 1:7 we have the first two of six uses of the *koinōnia* word group in Philippians, referring generally to their "partnership in the gospel" and their "partnership in generosity." Later, Paul will use the word group in three specific senses: (1) to refer to their act of mutual aid (their "partnering" in Paul's troubles, 4:14; their entry into a "partnership" of mutual aid with Paul, 4:15); (2) to refer to their communal solidarity in suffering (the reality of a "partnership in spirit," 2:1, related to the "one spirit" they should display, 1:27); and (3) to refer the model of embracing a "partnership with Messiah's suffering" (3:10; cf. 2:6-8; cf. 2 Cor 1:5; 4:7-12).

These uses correspond with emphases elsewhere in Paul's writings:

1. Partnership in the work of the gospel: Paul describes his coworkers as "partners" (*koinōnos*, *synkoinōnos*: 2 Cor 8:23, Titus; Philem 17, Philemon); Peter and Paul formalize a "partnership" in mission, in going to different fields (Gal 2:9); Paul celebrates Philemon's "partnership in loyalty-faith" (Philem 6); and Paul claims his ultimate motivation is to be a "partner/shareholder" in the gospel, thus sharing in its equity, unlike a laborer simply receiving wages (1 Cor 9:23).

2. Practical mutual aid, expressing and proving a deeper partnership in Messiah: general exhortation to be partner with those in need (Rom 12:13; Gal 6:6); involvement in the "partnership" (relief fund) for Judea (Rom 15:26; 2 Cor 8:4; 9:13).

3. The ecclesial interdependence of poorer Judeans and richer Gentiles-internationals: Gentiles become "partners" in the spiritual blessings of the Judean (Jewish) heritage (Rom 15:27) and in the riches of the olive tree (11:17).

4. The corporate, sacramental union between believer and Messiah: drinking the cup of blessing is a "partnership" (participation, communion) in the blood of Christ; eating the broken bread as a "partnership" in the body of Christ (1 Cor 10:16), indicating both oneness (and exclusivity) with Christ and the oneness of the Christian community. Our word *communion* for the Lord's Supper comes from the translation of *koinōnia* in the King James Bible at 1 Corinthians 10:16. By contrast, Paul likens participation in the ritual meals of the civic assembly (in honor of the city's patron gods) as a partnership with demons (1 Cor 10:18, 20). Accordingly, Paul refers to the partnership of the intimate personal relationship between the believer and the Son, or the believer and the Holy Spirit (1 Cor 1:9; 2 Cor 13:13).

5. Christian partnership (solidarity) in suffering and hardship: a partnership of both suffering and consolation (2 Cor 1:7; cf. 1 Cor 12:26; Rom 12:15).

Paul's Reconstruction of *Charis* (Generosity, Grace)

The Greek word *charis* (= Lat. *gratia*, from which we get the word *grace*) can have a wide range of meanings: favor, generosity, grace, beauty, gracious act of giving, gift or gratuity, or gratitude/thanks (i.e., the acknowledgment of someone else's generosity). Most commonly, *charis* in Greco-Roman contexts is what a social superior might display to an inferior, never the other way around (except when an inferior who is unable to reciprocate concretely grovels with "thanks" in response to undeserved generosity). In that sense, *charis* is always a downward-moving favor that is unmerited: in Paul's social context, inferiors are always undeserving. Paul radically turns prevailing notions of *charis* on their head in two ways. First, God's own grace toward humans is most supremely displayed through an act in which power and position are relinquished. Second, *charis* among humans is most impressively manifested in horizontal, mutual relationships of partnership. For many in Paul's world, the very combination "partnership of *charis*" would have seemed like an oxymoron. But for Paul, especially in Philippians, this combination represents the very heart of the gospel. (See also TBC on 4:21-23, "Words for *Grace* in the Bible.")

In his writings, Paul uses the word *charis* most commonly to refer to God's or Messiah's grace in the work of redemption in general, indicating God's generous, freely given, and undeserved favor in initiating acts of deliverance or granting salvation. But Paul also consistently uses *charis* to refer to concrete acts of horizontal generosity, specifically mutual aid. This is especially so in 2 Corinthians 8–9, where Paul seeks to raise funds for poor Judeans beleaguered by famine and an unjust imperial tributary system through which resources and taxes flowed to Rome. This passage, written soon after Philippians, provides the best commentary on the premises of Paul's words in Philippians 1:5-7 and 4:14-20.

Already in 1 Corinthians, Paul has advised his readers to make preparations so that he can carry "your *charis* [generous gift] to Jerusalem" (16:3). Note further the following expressions in 2 Corinthians: in boasting to the Corinthians about the Macedonians' recent contribution to the relief fund for the poor in Judea, he refers to "the *charis* of God demonstrated in the churches of Macedonia" (8:1). He then mentions how they asked for "the *charis* [favor] and partnership [*koinōnia*] of ministry for the saints" (8:4 AT). He notes how he has now asked Titus "to complete this *charis* [generous undertaking] also among you (8:5), and he invites them to "excel also in this *charis* [generous undertaking]" (8:6). Critically, Paul draws attention to "the *charis* [generosity] of our Lord Jesus Messiah" as a model and prototype: "though he was rich, yet for your sake he became poor, so that by his poverty you might become rich" (8:9), similar to the pattern of Philippians 2:6-11. Only by relinquishing power and position is God's grace truly displayed! Paul then offers "*charis* [gratitude] to God" for putting a special care for them into the heart of Titus (8:16) and refers to "the *charis* [generous undertaking] being administered by us" (8:19). In the next chapter, Paul claims that "God is able to overflow every *charis* [generous act] in/among you . . . so that you will abound in every good work" (9:8; cf. Gal 6:10). Moreover, participation in this generous undertaking is "a glory to God" (8:19), an "obedience to the gospel" (9:13), and an expression of "the surpassing *charis* [generosity] of God in/among you" (9:14). All this culminates in "*charis* [gratitude] to God for his indescribable gift [*dōrea*]" (9:15).

To summarize, Paul regularly uses the word *charis* to refer to the generous contribution of mutual financial aid among congregations

(1 Cor 16:3; 2 Cor 8:4, 6-7, 19), describing this concrete act as an expression of the "*charis* (generosity) of God" (2 Cor 8:1; 9:14), something supremely demonstrated in the self-giving *charis* (generosity) of Messiah (2 Cor 8:9; 9:15). This horizontal generosity is thus an obedience to the gospel (2 Cor 9:13). It expresses a partnership (2 Cor 8:4; 9:13; cf. Rom 12:13; Gal 2:9-10) and aims toward the goal of equality (2 Cor 8:13-15; cf. Phil 1:27–2:5). It represents a "harvest of justice-righteousness" (2 Cor 9:10; cf. Phil 1:11) and causes "an overflow in many thanksgivings to God" (2 Cor 9:11-12). Ultimately, it is reciprocated only by God himself (2 Cor 9:8-10; cf. Phil 4:20; see TBC on 4:10-20, "Patterns of Economic Mutualism"; on Paul's theology of the gift, see Barclay).

Joy and Rejoicing

In this opening section, we find the first of sixteen occurrences of the joy-rejoice word group in Philippians (*chara*, joy, gladness: 1:4, 25; 2:2, 29; 4:1; *chairō*, rejoice, be glad: 1:18 [2x]; 2:17, 18, 28; 3:1; 4:4 [2x], 10; *synchairō*, co-rejoice, rejoice together: 2:17, 18). In circumstances dominated by adversity—both his and theirs (1:30)—Paul carefully interweaves the story of his own joy alongside exhortations that his hearers-readers remain joyful (esp. 2:17-18). Paul is thus the resilient one who advises his hearers to remain steadfastly resilient in their shared adversity.

Paul expresses his joy in remembering his cherished "partners" in Philippi (1:4); his joy in the advance of the gospel despite adversity (1:18a); his joy at the prospect of his release from prison (1:18b–19b); his fullness of joy at their fidelity and steadfastness (2:2); his joy in the midst of suffering and sharing in joy with them (2:17); their very reality as his joy (4:1); and his joy in their assistance toward him (4:10). Paul also hopes for their progress and joy in loyal faith (1:25). He invites them to rejoice and share in his joy precisely amid adversity (2:18). He celebrates their joy at the return (and return to health) of Epaphroditus (2:28-29), and he exhorts them to maintain a posture of rejoicing in Messiah (3:1; 4:4).

Joy and rejoicing (gladness and being glad) operate at more than one level and have the following texture in Philippians. First, Paul notices the overwhelming joy of being drawn into the saving and transforming sphere of Messiah (1:25; cf. 1:30; Rom 14:17). Paul also exhorts the Philippians to remain joyfully resilient in that relationship of hope (3:1; 4:4; cf. Phil 1:20; Rom 15:12). Second, Paul is joyful as special envoy of Messiah at the continued advance of the gospel despite apparent setbacks (1:18a). Third, Paul affirms joy precisely in suffering, a rebellious hope despite frightening appearances (2:17-18). A few months later, referring to this episode, he says he was "continually pained, yet always rejoicing" (2 Cor 6:10; for joy in suffering, see also 1 Thess 5:15-16; James 1:2-4; 1 Pet 1:6; 4:12-19). Fourth, Paul speaks of joy in solidarity, a joy that is necessarily shared and is revitalized precisely in its being shared, while always attentive to the realities of pain and sorrow (2:17-18; cf. 1 Cor 12:25-26; Rom 12:15). Fifth, Paul experiences joy in the bonds of relationship; more specifically, in the maturation, assistance, and continued fidelity of his cherished "partners" (1:4; 2:2; 4:1, 10). Sixth, Paul experiences continued joy at the prospect of his release (1:18b). And finally, his partners experience joy as they anticipate reunion with their beloved and recovered Epaphroditus (2:28-29). For Paul, joy is not primarily the product of circumstances, but a celebration of relationships and, more deeply, the fruit of an investment in the cause of Messiah that will one day prevail.

This repeated concept of joy provides the thematic punctuation of the flow of Paul's appeal and encouragement and recurs at the start and close of major topical sections. It is uniquely prominent in the opening thanksgiving (1:3-4). It appears as the key hinge to Paul's disclosure of his own circumstances (1:18) and at the close of that section where Paul turns to discuss his hearers' circumstances (1:26). It concludes the first major section of formal exhortation (2:17-18), concludes the paragraph detailing travel plans (2:28-29), and headlines the second major section of exhortation (3:1). The theme of joy introduces a concluding series of exhortations (4:4) and opens the closing paragraph, which celebrates Paul's partnership with his beloved colleagues in Messiah (4:10; see also TLC on 2:1-5, "*Ēthos* and *Pathos*").

THE TEXT IN THE LIFE OF THE CHURCH

Letter and Liturgy: Intercessory Prayer

Many features of Paul's letters reflect patterns of actual communal gatherings. In fact, Heil has argued that Paul tried to replicate the liturgy of the gathered community in the very structure of his letters (Heil 2011). There is certainly plenty of liturgy (stereotyped worship forms) embedded in Paul's letters, including expressions of greeting-blessing and farewell, benediction, doxology and praise, thanksgiving, homiletical exhortation, hymnic chant, scriptural reading, words of consolation and assurance, and finally prayers of petition and intercession.

References to prayer are scattered throughout Paul's letters. He expects congregations to be dedicated to prayer (Rom 12:12; 1 Cor 7:5; Phil 1:19; 4:6-7; 1 Thess 5:17; see also 1 Cor 11:4, 5, 13; 14:13-15). Paul regularly refers to prayers by congregations or individuals: the Macedonians for the Corinthians (2 Cor 9:14); Epaphras for the Colossians (Col 4:12); and the Philippians for Paul (Phil 1:19). And he requests prayers of petition for himself: for his success and safety in ministry (Rom 15:30-32), for his release from prison (Phil 1:19; Philem 22), for his well-being (2 Cor 1:11), and for his ministry (1 Thess 5:25; 2 Thess 3:1-2; Col 4:3-4).

Paul also indicates that he and other individuals offer direct petition for themselves: Epaphroditus pleads for his own physical recovery (Phil 2:27). Paul pleads for release from his "thorn in the flesh" (2 Cor 12:7-8) and for strategic travel plans so that the gospel may be fulfilled (Rom 1:9-10). In suffering, he highlights the interceding role of the Holy Spirit in prayer where words fail (Rom 8:26-27), and he clearly identifies with scriptural psalms of lament in his own prayer life (see TBC on 1:12-26, "Echoes of Scripture"). More commonly, he refers to his regular prayer for others, especially his congregations (Phil 1:4; Col 1:3; 1 Thess 1:2; Philem 4). This accords with his claim that there is "daily pressure" on him in connection with his "anxiety for all the churches" (2 Cor 11:28).

Paul's intercessory prayers for others focus on the spiritual and internal well-being of the Christian assembly, not its physical or outward circumstances (Rom 10:1; 15:5-6, 13; 2 Cor 13:7, 9; Phil 1:9-11; Col 1:9-13; 1 Thess 3:10, 11-13; 5:23; 2 Thess 1:11; 2:16-17; 3:5, 16; Philem 6). Indeed, it is surprising that Paul offers no intercessory petition in Philippians for release from the assembly's struggle and ordeal that they share with Paul (Phil 1:28-30), even though he asks for prayer for his own physical circumstances. His emphasis in prayer is on their internal life of maturation and unity even as he draws attention to the divine and communal resources in the midst of their distress (2:1). Paul would no doubt answer that he is of course "remembering" their troubled circumstances in his prayers for them (1:3-4), but he is especially concerned for the spiritual and social health of the congregation, praying that they will find the internal capacity and the unified stamina to live through the ordeal.

Just as Paul hoped that his words of intercession for his beloved congregation would flood their hearts as they gathered in fervent assembly, so also words of intercession in the gathered community today have a power to go to the deepest level of the soul in shared commonality in Christ.

Philippians 1:12-26

Disclosure: The Gospel's Advance and Paul's Confidence despite Adversity

PREVIEW

Paul has his audience at the edge of their seats as he continues with *I want you to know, brothers and sisters . . .* They perhaps expect to hear a harrowing account of torture under Roman detention. Instead, what they hear next is only resilient optimism about the impact and outcome of his ordeal. Paul has no interest in narrating gruesome details of his suffering, even though in a few months he will admit that at the time he "despaired of life itself" (2 Cor 1:8). What Paul wants them to hear is not *what* he is experiencing, but *what kind* of struggle it represents—what positive opportunities have come from it and how he is responding in the midst of it.

OUTLINE

Retrospective: Messiah Is Being Proclaimed
    The Advance of the Gospel, despite Adversity and Rivalry, 1:12-18a
Prospective: Messiah Will Be Magnified
    The Advance of Loyalty-Faith, in Deliverance and Reunion, 1:18b-26

EXPLANATORY NOTES

In the ancient world, letters of friendship typically move to personal disclosure after the opening greeting, thanksgiving, and prayer. This is so also with Paul (cf. Rom 1:13; 2 Cor 1:8; Col 2:1; cf. 1 Thess 2:17–3:13). The disclosure here comes in two parts: the first recounts the recent past and reflects on the present (vv. 12-18a); the second confidently considers the future (vv. 18b-26). The theme of rejoicing provides the hinge that connects the first section to the second: rejoicing in the present tense (v. 18a) continues with rejoicing in the future (v. 18b). The entire section is bracketed by a repetition of the Greek word *advance* (*prokopē*): the *advance* of the gospel (v. 12) and the *advance* of their loyal faith (v. 25). By the end of the section, Paul has coordinated his own rejoicing (1:4, 18) with their rejoicing (1:25-26; cf. 2:15-16).

In his disclosure, Paul stresses the meaning of his imprisonment—its opportunities and outcome—and his own disposition within the experience. As for what kind of trouble he is in, he emphasizes that he is a political prisoner for Messiah's cause and not a common criminal. As for what has been or will be its impact, he highlights the continued proclamation of the gospel of Messiah, precisely because of and in the midst of his ordeal. As for his own disposition, he highlights two things. First, he is unwilling to let the problem of rivalrous preaching, bad as that is, to overwhelm the more crucial matter of the advance of the gospel (vv. 15-18a). Second, he is confidently resilient about how Messiah will be honored in his body, whether by life or by death, and is thus unwilling to capitulate for reasons of shame (vv. 18b-26). Paul puts forward both of these affirmations as a model for his readers in their own turmoil. Whether thinking of the present or contemplating the future, whether seeing adversity or advance, he can do nothing but rejoice (v. 18). His overwhelming conviction is that he will soon be released and so have an opportunity for further ministry (v. 22)—especially with his friends in Philippi—which should be an occasion for their own boastful disposition that brings honor to Messiah (vv. 24-26).

The vocative address *adelphoi* marks Paul's transition to disclosure. This word is masculine in grammatical gender only, not in social reference, and so is best translated *brothers and sisters* (NRSV; NIV). Paul repeats this address several times in the letter for emphasis or to resume an argument (3:1, 13, 17; 4:1, 8). Later in Philippians, Paul's use of this term confirms that he specifically means to include women and men. After this repeated address to his readers in 4:1, he turns specifically to address two women in 4:2-3. Such a way of addressing his readers and friends was a common device to indicate a special relationship of friendship or common association. For Paul, this is a word of special affection and solidarity for the messianic community. It appears frequently in Philippians (1:14; 2:25; 3:1, 13, 17; 4:1, 8, 21), where Paul uses it interchangeably with the word *beloved* (*agapētoi*, 2:12; 4:1). At root, this kinship image points to their mutual relationship "in Christ"—who is not only the "second Adam" and progenitor of a "new humanity" (e.g., Rom 5; 1 Cor 15; Col 3), but also the "firstborn among many brothers and sisters" (Rom 8:29 NIV).

Paul's Circumstances as a Theopolitical Prisoner

Paul neither explains nor emphasizes the details of his circumstances, which his readers must have known through letters and oral messages. What we know is that Paul was in some kind of imprisonment: Paul refers to being *in chains* under Roman imperial authority (1:7, 13, 14, 17; 4:22). He is being held in the provincial *praetorium* (v. 13), the term used for the military headquarters, and perhaps also residence (NIV mg.: *palace*), of the Roman imperial official who resided as the supreme administrator, judge, and military commander of a conquered region (a *provincia*, governing "charge"). The term probably does not refer here to the *palace guard* (NIV; NRSV: *imperial guard*) in Rome *[Date and Place of Writing, p. 290]*.

The Roman regime usually incarcerated individuals only when under investigation or awaiting execution. To keep someone out of circulation, Romans banished individuals to penal colonies, typically islands. Paul is apparently under investigation on charges that could easily result in the sentence of death (1:20-24; 2:17), and he anticipates an imminent trial in which the verdict of life or death will be delivered (1:7, 16, 20). His imprisonment is marked by deprivation (4:10-14), as typical of someone under imperial detention, and he describes the ordeal as one of *struggle* (1:30) and *suffering* (1:29; 3:10). Torture would have been a real possibility, along with its psychological effects (cf. 2 Cor 1:8; 2:14-16; 4:8-12; 6:4-5, 9; 11:23-25; probably written soon after Philippians). We do not know in what precise way he was chained. Despite this restriction, he could apparently receive visitors, among whom would have been a secretary to aid in writing and dispatching his letters.

As to the cause and meaning of his imprisonment, Paul simply draws attention to the fact that it is *in Messiah* (*en christō*, v. 13), using an ambiguous expression instead of an explicit "on behalf of

Messiah" (*hyper christou*, as in 2 Cor 5:20; 12:10; Phil 1:29). What Paul apparently means by this phrase is that his imprisonment is both "for the sake of Messiah" (NRSV; NIV: *for Christ*) and "in the path of Messiah." That is, it is a sharing in the suffering of Messiah himself for the sake of the gospel (1:28-30; 2:5-8; 3:10). A similar ambiguity is expressed in Philemon 13, probably written during the same incarceration: Paul refers literally to his "chains of the gospel," usually translated "chains for the gospel," but clearly implying "chains characteristic of the gospel." By explaining his chains as being *in Messiah* (Phil 1:13), Paul is highlighting his status as a theopolitical prisoner, rather than being investigated as a common criminal. Uppermost for Paul is the kind of citizenship (politics) that the gospel entails, as will become clear in 1:27–4:9. Paul does not mince words: the gospel inevitably has the dimension of involving a citizenship and an allegiance that sometimes brings it into conflict with the ruling authorities and the prevailing sociopolitical order (see further TBC, "Paul's Imprisonment").

The Gospel Advances despite Adversity

In the midst of his adversity, uppermost in Paul's mind is the status of the *gospel*—God's "royal proclamation of well-being" (1:5, 7, 12, 16, 27 [2x], 2:22; 4:3, 15; see TBC above on 1:3-11). Paul repeatedly refers in his disclosure to the active proclamation of the gospel (see TLC below, "Heralding the Gospel"). Paul above all wishes his readers to take the long view of the Messiah's inevitable and eventual victory, not the particulars of anyone's circumstances. The section thus begins by dramatizing the *advance of the gospel* (v. 12) in terms of two critical outcomes. First, the gospel is advancing in the very corridors of imperial power (*the whole [entire] praetorium and all the rest*), as it becomes known that his imprisonment is *in Messiah*. Paul will soon stress that he has been *positioned* (v. 16) in the situation of Roman imprisonment precisely for the *defense of the gospel*, alluding to his upcoming opportunity to provide a verbal defense of the gospel of his activities on its behalf (1:7, 20). At the close of the letter, Paul will stress that the effect is not just an increased awareness, but one of results: messianic adherents can now be found among those who serve at the imperial headquarters or within the imperial civil service (4:22, *Caesar's house[hold]*).

The second crucial effect of his imprisonment is that it has specifically occasioned a new confidence and boldness *to speak the word* on the part of *most* messianic loyalists in the location of his imprisonment. Paul dramatizes this proclamation as a *daring* marked by excess (NIV: *all the more*) and fearlessness (*without fear*; *aphobōs*; anticipating a reference to the readers' own fear in v. 28). He intends his own imprisonment to be an encouraging model for the Philippian hearers-readers, who are also under pressure from imperial authorities. This abounding and fearless daring to proclaim Christ is based crucially on their *having become confident in the Lord*, using a word that signals the persuasion that leads to confidence. This proclamation is emphasized later with further synonyms: *preaching* (*kēryssō*) and *announcing* (*katangellō*) Messiah (vv. 15, 17, 18), which are equivalent in effect also to *magnifying Messiah* (v. 20) or *boasting in Messiah* (1:26; 3:6), and even to *rejoicing in the Lord* (3:1; 4:4; see TLC, "Heralding the Gospel").

Concession: Rivalry in the Proclamation of the Gospel

Paul immediately admits, however, to a serious fracture within the community of believing loyalists where he is imprisoned. He names internal rivalry and envy of a sort that could compromise the effect of the gospel proclamation itself. Paul explains the problem with a balanced parallelism, contrasting two kinds of proclamation.

Some proclaim:	**Others proclaim:**
because of envy and rivalry;	*because of goodwill;*
out of rivalrous striving, insincerely,	*out of love,*
supposing to increase tribulation in my chains;	*knowing that I have been positioned for the defense of the gospel;*
in pretense	*in truth*

Paul uses highly charged terms, and the effect is sharp condemnation of some preachers in his vicinity. Paul uses the combination *envy and rivalry* elsewhere in vice lists to describe those who will not inherit the kingdom of God (Gal 5:20-21; Rom 1:29; cf. 13:13). *Envy* (*phthonos*) implies not just any desire for gain, but also the determination to deprive or put down the other. *Rivalry* (*eris*) connotes the will to promote discord. Paul also uses it to describe Corinthian factionalism (1 Cor 1:11; 3:3; 2 Cor 12:20). *Rivalrous striving* (*eritheia*; NRSV, NIV: *selfish ambition*) also occurs in lists of vices worthy of judgment (Rom 2:8; Gal 5:20). Paul negates it to depict Corinthian partisanship (2 Cor 12:20). In common discourse, the term referred to those who sought by intrigue to gain public office out of desire for fame, honor, and wealth (Murphy-O'Connor: 224). Paul will use the term again in Philippians to describe an attitude that his readers should overcome (2:3).

Finally, Paul charges that these rivals do not preach *sincerely* (with integrity). Instead, they preach *in pretense* (or, *with pretext*), presumably for self-advancement with financial gain. The issue appears to be similar to that of Paul's conflict with apostolic rivals in Corinth. We can surmise that these rivals—like certain "apostles" in Corinth who belittle Paul's status and character—seek and receive remuneration for their preaching and teaching (2 Cor 10–13). For Paul, however, it is a defining commitment that he preaches and teaches "free of charge" even though he has a "right" to be paid for his ministry (1 Cor 9:18). As he puts it in 2 Corinthians 2:17: "We are not peddlers of God's word like so many; but in Christ we speak as persons of sincerity." As a way to protect the integrity of the gospel, Paul is keen to distinguish himself from the many itinerating preachers and teachers for hire throughout Greco-Roman cities. With this financial issue in mind, he describes his own ministry as marked by sincerity (integrity) and speech of truth (2 Cor 6:6-7).

Paul gives only a few clues as to what is at stake: These preachers do not acknowledge that Paul is *positioned for the defense of the gospel.* Thus Paul implies that he is *appointed* (ISV) for this by divine appointment. By their proclamation, the others are *supposing to raise tribulation in my chains,* apparently attempting either to increase Paul's physical or mental hardship while in prison (NRSV: *increase my suffering in my imprisonment*) or to promote general hardship for Paul's partisans in the church who are not in prison (NIV: *stir up trouble for me while I am in chains*). The overall description implies that the preaching by these rivals is wrong in content, not only wrong in motivation and manner. In other words, this is not just about some "personal rivalry," as many commentators propose, who suggest that there were no serious theological, ethical, or ecclesial issues at stake.

Paul's strident language suggests that this rivalry is a grave concern and amounts to disunity and possible disintegration, seemingly the same kind of rivalry that threatened the Corinthian church (1 Cor 1:10-17). Paul perceives these rival preachers in Ephesus to be minimizing the cruciform and socially radical aspects of the gospel while being sympathetic to Roman imperial authority and elite social values. They appear much like the status-seeking preachers evident in Corinth (1 Cor 1:17-31; 2 Cor 10–13). On this topic, Paul's teaching is closely aligned with that of Jesus: Paul seems to be confronting the same kind of social patterns of status pursuit that Jesus addressed in the exchanges preserved in Mark 8–10 (see TBC below, "Factionalism and Rivalry"; TBC on 2:1-5, "Status Inversion").

Resolution: Proclaiming Messiah, Whatever the Manner, an Occasion for Rejoicing

Paul resists a preoccupation with the negative and abruptly returns to his main point about the *advance of the gospel* (v. 12): whatever the manner or motivation of the preaching, *Messiah is proclaimed, and in that I rejoice* (v. 18). How are we to understand this startling combination of serious denunciation and positive outlook—an honest admission that what one might expect would lead to serious sorrow instead leads to the claim of resilient joy (vv. 15-18a)?

Paul is not saying that serious rivalry and faulty proclamation are to be overlooked for some greater good, nor is he simply sanguine in the face of death, nor are his words simply a demonstration of magnanimity toward his rivals. Rather, he seems to have at least two key aims:

1. He introduces a negative model of rivalrous conduct, anticipating a real danger that he wishes also to discourage among his readers in Philippi (see 1:27; 2:3-4, 13; 4:2-3). Thus the indictment of *rivalrous striving* (v. 17, using the same word as in 2:3) and *rivalry* in his own context speaks also to their need to overcome forces of disunity in their own setting.

2. At the same time, Paul wants to communicate his absolute confidence and resolute optimism in the gospel itself, despite the rivalrous heralds. The work of Messiah does not ultimately depend on any human activity alone. Paul emphasizes that Christ is the center of attention and the Lord of his own destiny through a strategic use of the passive voice: *Messiah is being proclaimed.* This grammatical shift also anticipates the way in which an expected active voice, "I will magnify Messiah," becomes *Messiah will be magnified* in verse 20. In effect, the phrases *Messiah is being proclaimed* (v. 17), and *Messiah will be magnified* (v. 20) stand as the keynote claims of the whole unit. The gospel of Christ *advances* and will ultimately triumph regardless of any external opposition or any internal human frailty, or even disintegrating and self-serving rivalry. This confidence—along with the emphasis on *boldness, daring,* and having *no fear* (vv. 14, 20)—reassures his readers as they face their own opposition.

The Challenge of the Upcoming Trial

Paul moves immediately from present-tense rejoicing to future-tense rejoicing as he faces a challenge no less formidable: his impending trial. In the next dramatically short but intense segment (1:18b-26), Paul starts with confident resilience, then goes through the shadow of death, and finally returns to hopeful confidence.

Paul's future joy is first based on his confidence that *this [ordeal, trial] will turn out for my deliverance* (NRSV, NIV). The word rendered *deliverance* (*sōtēria*) has a broad range of uses. It denotes "deliverance, safety, well-being, healing, return to health, or restoration" in a variety of contexts: personal, physical, spiritual, communal, judicial, social, economic, or national. It is usually translated *salvation* in the NT. Here Paul refers primarily to his own *release* (CEB) from custody (1:25; 2:24). But based on what follows (vv. 20-23), his ultimate *salvation* and *vindication* in the arms of Messiah, even in death, may not be far from his mind. In Philippians, Paul wavers (1:20-24; 2:23) between contemplating the worst (death: 2:17; 3:10) and the best (release: 1:25-26; 2:24), even rethinking what is normally best or worst (1:20-24).

His *release and safety* will be accomplished through a combination of *your prayer* (singular, to indicate its entirety) *and the assistance of the Spirit of Messiah Jesus* (v. 19). Paul thereby indirectly requests prayer, so that his prayer for them (1:3-5) can be mutually reciprocated. The *assistance* supplied by the Spirit includes deep inward personal support (Rom 8:26-27), and especially the supply of words for his possibly final speech before the tribunal—not just in its construction but also in its effective power (1 Cor 2:4, 13; Rom 15:19; cf. Acts 4:8; Mark 13:11; Luke 12:11-12; Matt 10:19-20).

In a bold thesis statement (v. 20) that heads his following words (vv. 21-24), Paul announces his *ultimate desire and hope*, using a word that refers to an eager and intense expectation. The word literally indicates "watching with the head stretched forward alertly." This intense word occurs only one more time in the rest of the LXX and NT, referring to the "eager expectation" of "all creation" amid "groaning" for its redemption (Rom 8:19).

Two complementary verbal images express this intense hope: that he will *not be put to shame* (NRSV, CEB); and that through him *Messiah will be magnified* (lit. *made great*). In other words, he will declare the gospel and the supremacy of Messiah Jesus (2:9-11; 3:20-21) without shrinking back (cf. Rom 1:16), without regard for inevitable shame in the eyes of some, especially opponents. Paul is not referring to shame in a psychological sense (NIV: *be ashamed*), but in the public sense of dishonor. Indeed, a negative verdict and execution would by definition be the ultimate shaming in the prevailing Roman milieu. But this prospect will not cause him to waver. For Paul, real victory and real defeat are in the eyes of the one perceiving shame and honor (1:28; cf. 2 Cor 2:14-16). Elsewhere Paul specifically rejects shame in the context of defending his weakness and suffering as his most impressive credentials, against those who would count his suffering and weakness as illegitimacy and shame (2 Cor 7:14; 9:4; 10:8; cf. 6:8; 11:23–12:10).

Paul explains his resolve that *Messiah will be magnified* in a few key phrases: (1) *With all boldness* (NRSV; TNIV: *sufficient courage*) recalls the *fearless daring* of those in Paul's vicinity who are spreading the gospel, even in corridors of opposition (Phil 1:14). He employs a word (*parrēsia*) that indicates not only *boldness* but also frankness, clarity, freedom, and openness of speech. This term will become a regular feature of Christian martyr stories in the second and third centuries. (2) *Now as always* indicates that he will continue as forthrightly as before, as is his normal practice. He will not now, at the moment of greatest challenge and gravest danger, hold back from full disclosure of the gospel and of Messiah's supremacy over all other rule, even that of Rome (cf. 2:5-11; 3:17-21). (3) *In my body* signifies that he will give witness through the whole of his bodily being, his fullest and whole self (cf. Rom 12:1), including the witness of possible martyrdom (cf. 2:17). (4) *Whether by life or by death* takes his readers in a new turn: he now admits that death is a real possibility. But as Paul stresses elsewhere, facing death will not challenge his resolve (see 2 Cor 4:7-12; 6:3-10; 11:23–12:10; Rom 8:31-39, probably written a few months after this episode).

Paul puts all the attention back to Messiah himself. Instead of using the active voice, as one might expect ("I will magnify Messiah"), he uses the passive voice: *Messiah will be magnified* (CEB: *Christ's greatness will be seen*). Messiah must always be the center. Messiah Jesus himself will ironically and assuredly *be magnified*, even in seemingly ignominious death, whether Messiah's own or that of his followers. And the assault against Messiah and Messiah's own will be the very occasion for victory! There is no tension between the confident claim of *deliverance-salvation* through the present circumstances (v. 19) and the real prospect of death (v. 20) in the cruciform theology of Paul. He is assured that God vindicates in and through suffering and adversity, even the most shameful sort, crucifixion. Paul refuses to concede that what was designed to be the most shameful and terrorizing execution possible—public execution by the Roman imperial authorities—could ever really put him to shame. After all, this was the pathway of the coming ruler of the world (2:6-11; 3:10-11, 20-21).

One might think that such an unwavering claim of allegiance to Messiah would surely jeopardize his potential release from imperial custody, especially as he asserts the world supremacy of Messiah over all other rule, including that of Rome and the Caesar (2:6-11; 3:19-21). What is at issue for Paul is the truth of the gospel and fidelity to Christ. These clearly matter more to him than his personal safety. Paul has recognized and affirmed that while he is the one under investigation, it is really the gospel that is on trial: it is all about Messiah and his cause.

Deliberation on the Prospect of Life or Death

Finally conceding indirectly that death is a real possibility (*whether in life or in death,* 1:20), Paul continues with what one might call a soliloquy. Paul admits to having a deep inner struggle even as we hear mainly resolve and confidence. These words have resounded through Christian history, providing comfort, courage, and assurance to people in diverse circumstances of adversity, especially those directly facing death.

Paul initially places the prospect and opportunities of life or death in the starkest of terms: *For to me, living is Messiah, and dying is gain.* Immediately Paul clarifies the former: *living* is more precisely *life in the flesh* (cf. *to remain in the flesh,* v. 24), implying that that there is also a new mode of "life" that is victorious over death (3:10-11, 21). Moreover, the simple equation of earthly *living* and Messiah means the *fruit of labor for me* (CEB: *results from my work*).

Paul admits that he is *hard-pressed* between a rock and a hard place. He is unsure which he might *choose* (NIV) in the sense of *prefer* (NRSV). As a way to work toward a resolution, he poses a contrast between his own immediate *desire* and *what is more necessary* on their account. On the one hand, his *desire is to depart and to be with Messiah, for that is far better.* Paul has now explained the *gain* that death would bring: it is better both in the sense of a release from pain and torture, but also in terms of relational union with Messiah. Paul thus anticipates how he will describe his "gain" in 3:7-8. On the other hand, what matters *more* than his own immediate desire are their needs. This practical, immediate concern for others now causes him to make the nod in favor of continued mortal life. He is *persuaded* and thus *confident* (using the same term as in 1:6, 14; 2:24; 3:3-4) that continued life in the flesh will be his ordained path. The inner struggle remains, however. Later in the letter, he will again express both confidence in his release (2:24) and considerable doubt as he faces the real possibility of martyrdom (2:17, 23).

Paul is unwavering about hope beyond death. At the same time, he is restrained. Thus Paul does not speculate about spatial geography or any human partitioning after death (e.g., the separation of soul from body). Instead, he emphasizes the unbreakable relational bond with Messiah: *to be with Messiah* is the reality and goal (cf. Rom 8:35-39). The union between Paul and Messiah is assured, both in the present (cf. Gal 2:20) and in the future renewal of all things (3:10-11, 20-21). Even death before Messiah's return cannot undo the bond between Messiah and his people, those who are already *in Messiah.* The verb *to depart* renders a common euphemism for death and does not specifically entail the Greek notion of a soul departing from a body (see TBC below, "What Happens after Death?").

In sum, these words do not indicate an escapist posture or a negation of things earthly and physical. Paul is not focused on some death wish; this is not the expression of a suicidal personality. Instead, these are expressions of the kind of resilience many who have suffered as political prisoners have shown (TLC below, "Letters from Prison"). Two things must be remembered: (1) These are the reflections of someone undergoing serious physical deprivation, and probably torture, with its accompanying mental anguish and uncertainty (cf. 2 Cor 1:8-11). (2) The key of this section is verse 20: *Christ will be magnified in my body whether through life or through death.* Ultimately, everything is about Messiah and serving Messiah, not about the supreme benefits of either life or death. Christ defines both life and death (cf. 1:20): to live *is Messiah*, to die is to be *with Messiah.*

Confidence in Release and Reunion, for the Sake of Their Advance in Loyal Trust

Having passed through the shadow of death, Paul comes back to confidence in his release, focusing on renewed ministry with the Philippians in person, for their own *advance and joy in loyalty-faith*, and their own *boasting in Messiah.* This is the first reference in the letter specifically to their joy (*chara*) and their loyalty-faith (*pistis*), even though he has already highlighted their partnership and good work in generosity and the gospel (1:5-7).

Paul is not referring to "the faith" in the sense of a system of belief and conduct, but to their active loyalty to Messiah (cf. NIV:

progress and joy in the faith; NRSV: *progress and joy in faith*). The word *pistis* in Paul blends *loyalty* (faithfulness) toward, *reliance* (trust, faith) upon, and *conviction* (belief, persuasion) in Lord Messiah Jesus (Zerbe 2012: 26–46). Here the emphasis is on strength of loyalty, practice, and able discernment (cf. 1:9-11), not on mastery of some content of teaching or doctrine. Sometimes used synonymously with "obedience," *loyalty-faith* (*pistis*) is another way to refer to their standing firm (1:27; 4:1) and their confidence (1:14; 3:3-4) in Messiah, as expressed in boasting, glorying, and rejoicing in Messiah (1:26; 2:13, 17-18; 3:1, 3-4; 4:4; note also the close correspondence between loyalty-faith and standing firm under adversity in 1 Thess 3:2, 5, 7, 8, 10).

Their *joy in loyalty-faith* (*faithful trust*) is closely tied to their *boasting in Messiah.* The Greek word group translated as "boasting" (NRSV, NIV) generally denotes being loud-tongued or speaking loudly, and connotes "vaunting oneself." It reflects a preoccupation with status and honor in the Greco-Roman world. The word implies having bragging rights. Paul does not thereby mean conceit. Elsewhere Paul says that when boasting is groundless, it is mere deceit and self-promotion (2 Cor 10:8-17; 11:10-21). The term is roughly synonymous with magnifying, exulting, glorifying, or giving honor (see TBC on 3:1-3, "Boasting and Being Confident").

THE TEXT IN BIBLICAL CONTEXT

Paul's Imprisonment: Accusers and Accusations

In this passage Paul's purpose is to emphasize the effects and outcome of his adversity. His interest is not merely informational. He omits detail about the causes or conditions of the imprisonment, some of which his readers may have known. But the modern reader begs to know more about Paul's actual circumstances as a way to understand how he got there and what was at stake for the first readers.

What charges were being leveled against Paul, and who were his accusers? Paul had admitted to the Corinthians previously that in Ephesus he was "in peril every hour," had "fought wild beasts" (metaphorically speaking), and was confronted by "many adversaries" (1 Cor 15:30, 32; 16:8-9). Paul's accusers then and now were probably members of the civic elite in Ephesus, possibly encouraged by socially high-ranking leaders of the Jewish community. The book of Acts, written thirty years or so after these events, regularly indicates that Paul's trouble with the authorities was caused entirely by rival "Judeans" (cf. Acts 13:50; 14:2, 5, 19; 17:5-9; 19:33; 20:19; 21:21, 27), but the historical situation must certainly have been more complex than this.

As for specific charges, the matter had to do with Paul's proclamation of the gospel of Messiah Jesus (Phil 1:13, 20; cf. 2:9-11; 3:20-21). Paul had earlier experienced trouble with Roman imperial officials in Philippi and Thessalonica over his proclamation, which was seen as subversive and destabilizing for the Roman order (Acts 16:20-21; 18:12). Now his proclamation and work in founding of assemblies loyal only to Messiah Jesus had come to the attention of civic and Roman officials in Ephesus. Given the pro-Roman orientation of Ephesus, the charges brought against him are not surprising. Since 27 BCE, Ephesus was the center of Roman imperial power and propaganda in the jurisdiction (province) of Asia. Its elite citizens had ingratiated themselves with Augustus, leading to the establishment of a local imperial cult. In 29 BCE, sacred precincts were dedicated to the goddess Roma and the divinity Julius Caesar. Later a temple in honor of Augustus was erected, as were royal precincts in honor the Augustus and his family. In 26 CE, the city's magistrates competed with other cities for Ephesus to be officially designated a "temple warden" of the Sebastoi (Augusti, "the Venerables," meaning the imperial family, living and deceased), an honor finally granted in 89 CE. The honor of being a *neōkoros* (temple warden) of the Sebastoi implied that the whole urban area was to be devoted to the service of the Augustan divine rulers, offered on the assumption that the city would in return enjoy special favor of the Augustan gods and rulers, enhancing its status as a city. (Acts 19:35 also uses this term, *neōkoros*, for Ephesus as the temple keeper of the great Artemis *[Roman Imperial Cult, p. 307]*.)

Given that Paul is facing a capital charge, the accusations leveled against him were probably that his proclamation of Messiah was directly counter to loyalty to Caesar and Rome (cf. Acts 17:6-7; John 19:12, 15). At issue was whether one could declare allegiance to Messiah Jesus and still recognize Caesar as Lord—that is, give ultimate homage to the Roman imperial order. Given that Paul was a Roman citizen, the charges thus probably involved *seditio* (sedition, treason), technically that of *maiestas* (majesty), acting against the "majesty" (greatness, honor) of Rome and its people, and especially the emperor as the focal point of allegiance (Sherwin-White 1978). In this case his formal citizenship offered little protection. In fact, it made his plight even more dangerous, since he was under suspicion as a traitor. Oaths of loyalty to Rome (and its divinities and rulers) were a core feature in the induction of new citizens or of civic magistrates *[Citizenship, p. 279].*

Factionalism and Rivalry Where Paul Is Imprisoned

Paul's letters and other NT writings point to various degrees of intramural rivalry and friction in the emerging messianic movement, owing to the ethnic, socioeconomic, and educational diversity of local groups and to the impact of dynamic leaders. For instance, we know of groups oriented around the leadership of Cephas (Peter; 1 Cor 1:12; 3:22; 9:5; Gal 1:18–2:14); Apollos (1 Cor 1:12; 3:5, 22; 4:6; 16:12; Acts 18:24–19:7); "men from James" and agitators in Galatia, who Paul says preach a different gospel (Gal 1:7-9; 2:1-14); and apostles who have made inroads within the Corinthian assembly and who Paul says preach a different Jesus and a different gospel (2 Cor 10–13; esp. 10:12; 11:4-5, 12-15, 19). The relationship between Paul and these others leaders can be described as ranging from cordial despite some tensions and strain (Apollos) to sharply conflictual (Galatians; 2 Cor 10–13) to both cordial and conflictual (Cephas/ Peter). A nonencroachment policy of respecting geographical domains of ministry became important to minimize direct conflict (cf. Gal 2:1-10; 2 Cor 10:13-16; Rom 15:18-21).

Immediate causes of factionalism in Ephesus (the likely place of Paul's imprisonment *[Date and Place of Writing]*) can be attributed to multiple leaders involved in the emergence of the assembly (e.g., Apollos and Paul; Acts 18:19–19:41) and the dynamics of separation from the main synagogue, which may also have created fractures within the group of Jesus loyalists (Acts 19:9) over issues of Torah observance. Later testimony also attests to rival leadership (Acts 20:29-30, "wolves from among your own selves"; Rev 2:1-7, self-appointed "apostles" who are not really apostles).

We can suppose, however, that the rivals identified in Philippians 1:15-18 are not of the same sort mentioned in Galatians, where the agitators proclaim a "Judaizing" gospel (Gal 2:14), requiring all non-Jewish adherents to undergo circumcision (Gal 2:3, 7-9; 2:12; 5:2, 3, 10-12; 6:12-13). Instead, these rivals probably come from the other side of the spectrum, closer in perspective to Paul's rivals in Corinth, who similarly exhibit the temptation to accommodate to elite Greco-Roman culture (e.g., 1 Cor 1–4, 15; 2 Cor 10–13). By analogy to Paul's attack on rivals in 2 Corinthians 10–13, Paul's rivals in this case probably consider defeat or weakness as inappropriate to true apostles. Their refusal to grant that Paul has been *positioned* in prison *for the defense of the gospel* and their desire to increase trouble for him and his faction while he is in prison (1:16-17) suggest that they think Paul has imperiled the social legitimacy of the gospel. Paul seems to think that they are soft-pedaling the cruciform character of the gospel that he preaches (as also the case in Corinth; 1 Cor 1–2; 2 Cor 11–12).

Paul's exhortation in Philippians 3 also implies a potential group of detractors who prefer a more accommodating posture to Greco-Roman political sensibilities and status-preoccupied social values. They are uncomfortable with Paul's emphatic cruciform paradigm for the messianic pathway of lowliness. Probably they are embarrassed by Paul's conflict with the authorities, or perhaps his forthright preaching of a Lord counter to Caesar. The Ephesian detractors likely also consider Paul's imprisonment as a discrediting of his gospel and his apostolic legitimacy, perhaps under fear of social exclusion or harassment for their new faith. (A similar continuum from resistance or accommodation to Roman culture and power can also be seen in the broader Judean synagogue experience more generally during the period of the Roman Empire; see Goodman.)

A Retrospective Allusion to Paul's Trial in Romans

In this section of Philippians, Paul looks ahead with uncertainty yet resilience toward his upcoming trial (1:19-24; cf. 1:7). In Romans, written up to a half year later *[Date and Place of Writing, p. 290]*, we find distinct allusions to this experience as he refers both to prosecutors or accusers (Rom 8:33) and the judge who has the power to condemn to death (8:34). Paul does not draw attention to his own earlier ordeal and its temporary reprieve. In a series of four rhetorical questions, he continues to proclaim confidence in God's final victory through Messiah (Rom 8:31-39): Who is against us? Who will shall bring any charge against God's elect? Who is the one to condemn (pass judgment of death)? Who shall separate us from the love of Messiah? The answers are resoundingly bold. All human and worldly dominion, including the Roman imperium, shrinks in comparison to the executive power and judicial authority of God and to the intercessory agency and love of his Messiah. Paul has not been put to shame (Phil 1:20), and he continues to be unashamed of the gospel (Rom 1:16).

Echoes of Scripture

As elsewhere in his letters, Paul reflects and speaks with the language of Scripture. The words *This will turn out for my deliverance* (1:19

NRSV) are found verbatim in the Greek translation (LXX) of Job 13:16. Similarly, his stress on *not being put to shame* and *magnifying Messiah* recall expressions in the psalms of petition or confidence that a supplicant will be vindicated and not put to shame and that the Lord will be magnified, a consistent feature of prayers of the oppressed and suffering righteous in biblical and postbiblical Jewish writings (Pss 25:2-3; 34:2-6; 35:24-28; 40:15-17; 69:6-7, 30-33; 119:78-80, 116; cf. 1QH 12.23–24 [formerly 4.23–24]; note also the echo of Ps 22:16 in Phil 3:2). Paul has self-consciously identified with these biblical patterns and has sought consolation and courage from them, as also demonstrated in the life of Messiah (2:5-11; 3:10-11). The trial imagery in the context of the allusion to Job's experience (Job 13:16, 18-19) would especially suit Paul's present circumstances. This imagery appears to be drawn out also in Romans 8:31-34 (where Job 34:29 is alluded to). The chosen and suffering servant of Isaiah may also be a significant paradigm and source of comfort for Paul. Set also in a lawcourt scene, the servant refuses to retaliate and to be put to shame (Isa 50:6-7) but rests secure in the knowledge that his deliverance is near because the Lord is his helper and his opponents will ultimately wither away (Isa 50:8-9). Paul may not have expected his readers to notice these resonances (see Hays: 21–24). Yet (later) in Philippians 3:2, Paul may well have intended his readers to notice his allusion to Psalm 22:16, in another psalm of lament—or at least to hear an explanation by the designated interpreter accompanying the letter.

What Happens after Death?

When it comes to the conquest of Death, Paul's consistent and persistent hope is for the general resurrection, when God's reign will be fully established—that is, for the "redemption of bodies" that accompanies the renewal of the entire world on *the day of Messiah/the Lord* (e.g., 1 Cor 15; Rom 8:18-39; 1 Thess 4:13-18; 5:23; Phil 3:9-10, 20-21), not for the departure of a separated soul to heaven after death. Messiah's resurrection stands as proof that the final days have arrived, the first installment of the general resurrection that accompanies the renewal of the whole world (Rom 8:29; 1 Cor 15:21-23; Phil 3:20-21; Wright 2003).

But further questions are naturally raised: What about the interim? What happens to persons who have died? Where are they? Do they have consciousness? In what sense do they exist? Paul gives no formal doctrine about this, but he does offer ad hoc comments pertaining to this issue in connection with other questions.

The notion of an intermediate state of consciousness, in which the dead (or those who sleep in Christ) enjoy full communion with Jesus already, was first explicitly propounded by the theologian Irenaeus in the late second century. For many Christian thinkers, this idea in turn provides proof that Paul believed in the separate, disembodied existence of an eternal soul. Some Jewish writings from around this time express some hope for a reality of existence between death and the final arrival of the reign of God. By contrast, Paul shows significant reserve in relation to this kind of speculation.

What Paul emphasizes is that God's redeeming power is so comprehensive (Rom 8:17-34) that nothing—not even death—can ever constitute a "separation" from the love of Christ (8:35-39). In 1 Thessalonians and 1 Corinthians, where one might expect Paul to expound on the status of those who have died, all he says is that the dead (or those who "sleep in Christ") will surely be included in the final resurrection of the dead when the age to come finally arrives (1 Thess 4:13-18; 1 Cor 15:18, 23). Elsewhere, all Paul says is that death means being "with Christ," so death is never to be feared (Phil 1:23; 1 Thess 5:10; 2 Cor 5:6-8).

Paul is uncompromising when it comes to the primacy of the ultimate goal of resurrection of the dead, especially in controversy with those who sought to emphasize either a spiritual resurrection already in the present or the immortal existence of a disembodied soul as all that mattered. Indeed, he hints that the believers now dead have no existence apart from the resurrection, and apart from resurrection they have "perished" (1 Cor 15:18). This suggests that Paul refused to grant the existence of bodiless immortality. In a similar way, although he grants that to die and thus "be with the Lord" in anticipation of final resurrection is to be preferred (2 Cor 5:8; cf. Phil 1:23), he rejects the notion of any form of soulish "nakedness" (2 Cor 5:3; for a treatment of 2 Cor 4:16–5:10 along these lines, see Shillington 1998: 105–12; similarly Wright 2003: 361–71). Thus it cannot be said that Paul explicitly teaches an intermediate state of consciousness from which can be derived a doctrine of the soul's immortality separate from the body.

Markus Bockmuehl (1998: 91–93) helpfully explains that to seek a final answer to this question of an intermediate state is to demand the impossible—to describe transcendence and eternity in immanent and temporal terms. Paul, he argues, does not directly address this question, and to focus on it misses the point of the passages in which hints are found. N. T. Wright similarly suggests that all we can gather is that Paul posits some experience of "consciousness" in the presence of the triune God who loves us (Wright 2003: 226–27, 267). Appropriately, the *Confession of Faith in a Mennonite Perspective* (1995) and the *Confession of Faith of the General Conference of Mennonite Brethren Churches* (1999) express reserve in this area. The former does not refer to what happens at death, while the latter confesses simply that "Christ's followers go to be with the Lord when they die" (Article 18). It does not suggest the precise location or the separate existence of a disembodied, immortal soul. In death, one moves out of historical time and into transcendent time. The continued existence of a person after death can be posited only on the basis of the future resurrection, not on the basis of the soul's immortality. As J. D. G. Dunn puts it: for Paul, everything short of final redemption is incompleteness, whether in an interim state or in the proleptic (already-experienced) benefits of salvation in the present (Dunn: 489–90; see also Zerbe 2008).

THE TEXT IN THE LIFE OF THE CHURCH

Heralding the Gospel

This opening section of disclosure displays Paul's all-consuming passion for "heralding" the gospel (see TBC on 1:3-11, "The Gospel"). He uses a variety of expressions for it: speaking the word, heralding, announcing, magnifying, and boasting. Those engaged in it are boldly daring and fearless. For Paul, the active heralding of the gospel (message of well-being) has a crucial verbal component, a *logos* (word, reason, argument, discourse). As such, it has a legal defense and confirmation, involving a persuasion (Phil 1:7, 14, 16; see also 2 Cor 5:11; Gal 5:7; 1 Thess 1:5; Col 2:2). Still, this verbal dimension does not stand alone but is closely tied to deeds, demonstrations of power, and the reliability of the messenger (see Rom 1:16; 15:18-19; 1 Cor 2:4-5; 2 Cor 6:7; 12:12; 1 Thess 1:5; 2:4-12). The verbal proclamation stands alongside the assembly's radiation of light as a distinctive community (see EN on 2:15).

Interestingly, however, Paul's letters do not contain specific exhortations for all members of congregations to become active in verbal heralding (for the few verses that might imply this, but are actually quite ambiguous, see 1 Thess 1:8; Phil 1:14; 2:15-16; Eph 6:15; Col 4:6; Rom 1:8; see Yinger). Paul's letters seem to indicate that a group of specially gifted envoys (apostles) are specifically tasked with this aspect of the mission, while others are in various roles of partnership with it (e.g., Phil 1:5). Still, Paul assumes that the church as a body is involved in mission (Ware).

This passage in Philippians invites the church today to reflect on its own heralding of the gospel concerning the Lord Messiah Jesus—its various audiences and contexts, its appropriate medium and form, its specific messages, and its particular goals. The church today is divided over these matters, perhaps still in rivalry over the meaning and manner of proclaiming the gospel (Phil 1:15-18a). I offer the following questions for engaging this conversation.

What are the imperatives and urgencies for daring proclamation of the good news of Jesus Christ today, whether in word or deed? How should the particular content and form of the gospel message be correlated with varied contexts, audiences, and particular crises? What are the core messages about Lord Messiah Jesus that are especially needed today? How should they be articulated or contextualized today? How does a commitment to the uniqueness of Jesus Christ engage with religious pluralism, especially when religious factionalism functions to drive global conflict? How does a commitment to the supremacy of Jesus over all other rule affect a Christian witness to the powers that be? What form of the gospel would we be willing to go to death for? What areas of the gospel message of Jesus are we unsure of, whether intellectually or otherwise? In what ways do these hesitations or uncertainties cause us to shrink from disclosing the good news of Jesus, whether to our neighbors and friends or to our communities and nations? How do we keep the gospel proclamation holistic—encompassing spirit and body, word and deed, personal and political? What are the formal and informal, institutional and neighborly ways in which the proclamation of Lord Messiah Jesus advances? How can the church maintain a commitment to the active heralding of the gospel, inviting transforming loyalty-faith among hearers while avoiding the pitfalls of some forms of Christian evangelism (e.g., paternalism associated with the colonial enterprise)? In what ways is the active, bold, and fearless proclamation of the gospel essential to the transformative renewal of individuals, the building of the church, and ultimately the dawning of the age to come, the destiny of the world toward justice, peace, and the integrity of creation?

Letters from Prison as Genre

Considering the meaning of Philippians is significantly enhanced by reading it alongside not just Paul's other letters from prison, but also other letters from (theo)political prisoners in the course of history. To name just a small sampling, from classical antiquity we have Cicero and John of Patmos (the Revelator). From Reformation

Europe we have Martin Luther, numerous Anabaptists and English dissidents, and Sir Thomas More. By one count, from the beginning of the English Reformation to the end of the seventeenth century, "nearly 3,000 letters from prison had been printed and circulated as acts of conscience and political resistance" (Gilpin). From the last hundred years, we have Antonio Gramsci, Dietrich Bonhoeffer, Corrie ten Boom, Aleksandr Solzhenitsyn, Bouck White, Adam Michnik, Dorothy Day, Martin Luther King Jr., and Nelson Mandela. Indeed, the letter from prison has become a genre of specialized study (Larson). According to Ioan Davies, "It is impossible to understand [Western] thought without recognizing the central significance of prison and banishment in its theoretical and literary composition" (Davies: 3). Even in the East, letters from prison play a significant role (Baraheni): for instance, Imam Ali's letters from prison in the collection Nahj al-Balagha are central for Shi'ite Muslim understanding and faith (Naficy).

Two examples of letters by "political detainees" in more recent experience are especially provocative for reflection on Paul's Philippians: Martin Luther King Jr.'s "Letter from a Birmingham Jail" (1963) and Dietrich Bonhoeffer's *Letters and Papers from Prison* (1972).

Exhortation 1

Practicing Messianic Citizenship, Part 1

Philippians 1:27–2:18

OVERVIEW

Philippians 1:27–2:18 is a single coherent unit, the first of two major installments of exhortation. Unfortunately, the units comprising this larger section are often quoted or treated independently. To fully appreciate the rhetorical significance of each unit individually, it is critical to observe how each unit contributes to the overall argument and appeal and how their themes are closely tied together. Most important, the full meaning and force of Paul's words in the entire segment can only be properly understood in light of the forceful opening thesis statement: *Be a citizen body and practice citizenship in a manner worthy of the gospel of Messiah* (1:27a).

A striking feature of this section is that much of it is imagistic, elliptical, and grammatically rough. We do not have smooth, flowing prose where every idea is carefully explained, where clear transitions alert us to how one thing is meant to follow from what precedes, or where what is really at issue is carefully clarified. A good bit of this has to do with the particular circumstances in which it was written—in the heat of the moment. Paul most certainly does not have the same leisure time as he does when writing Romans a few months later, in the comfortable guest room or library of a well-to-do home in Corinth.

Of course the original readers had a distinct advantage over us: many of the clues to the background, meaning, and force of Paul's words could be left unspoken as part of the "tacit dimension." Things going on with and between them, things that gave full meaning to his words, are implicit and could be assumed. Thus it takes time and work for any modern reader to move beyond what is only on the surface toward a deeper understanding of Paul's concerns.

In many ways, the pattern of thought must be seen beyond its surface grammar. The flow of ideas can be sketched and paraphrased as follows, somewhat differently from the grammatical structure of the section:

Thesis (1:27a)

- "Politicize" in a manner worthy of the gospel of Messiah!

Elaboration (1:27b-28a)

- As Christ's citizen community, put up a vigorous and unified defense and have no fear!

Their Distress (1:28b–2:1)

- Yes, some adversaries desire your destruction, but God will ensure your ultimate deliverance.
- Suffering on behalf of Messiah is also a grace, as much as declaring allegiance to him is.
- We are all in it together; we are facing the same forces lined up against us (1:30).
- In suffering, special resources and virtues keep the community whole and resilient (2:1).

Their Solidarity (2:2-8)

- Mutual love must be displayed by letting go of hierarchies and rivalries that divide.
- Unity must show true concern for the other, while letting go of questing for one's own betterment over others.
- Christ is the supreme example of this mind-set.

Their Victory (2:9-11)

- The story of Christ shows that the pathway of self-giving for others is the way that leads to ultimate victory: the whole world will one day pledge allegiance to Christ, the lowered divinity and exalted slave.

Their Striving, Unity, Character, and Mission (2:12-16)

- Never be passive; just stay on board, because God is making it happen.
- Do not implode internally despite pressure from the outside.

- Make good on your special character in Christ, always knowing you are partners in God's mission of redeeming the world.

Their Resilient Joy in Mutual Solidarity (2:17-18)

- Never give in to doubts and fear; stay strong and rejoice in Christ's love and victory.

OUTLINE

Being a Citizen Body Worthy of the Gospel of Messiah, 1:27-30
A Citizen Body Marked by Unity and Status Inversion, 2:1-5
Tribute to Messiah: Self-Emptied Divinity and Exalted Slave, 2:6-11
The Citizen Community's Agency in the Drama of Salvation, 2:12-18

Philippians 1:27-30

Being a Citizen Body Worthy of the Gospel of Messiah

PREVIEW

Paul finally admits it: they are under siege! Of course, he knows that they know that he knows of their plight. There is no need to state the obvious. We as later readers are unfortunately clued out and rely on almost imperceptible allusions to help us appreciate the nature and depth of the crisis at hand. For the first time he refers to their own *struggle* in which there is *suffering* at the hands of *adversaries* who are bent on their *destruction*, resulting in considerable *fear*.

How then will Paul bolster this community under siege, threatened with external pressure that is fueling internal tensions? He has just signaled his hopes for their own *advance and joy in faithful loyalty* and their *boasting in Messiah* as a result of his imminent release and reunion with them. But soberly he now challenges them to face the crisis regardless of whether he will be with them.

So he cuts to the heart of the matter through an appeal that reverberates through the rest of the letter. This first formal exhortation in the "imperative mood" functions as the thesis statement not only for this first unit of exhortation (1:27–2:18), but also for the entire body of the letter: *Above all else, be a citizen body and practice your citizenship in a manner worthy of the gospel of Messiah*. This compact and bold challenge takes only seven words in Greek.

OUTLINE

The Singular Imperative of Messianic Citizenship, 1:27a
The Unified Alignment of the Citizen Community under Siege, 1:27b-28a
Clarifying the Nature and Outcome of the Struggle, 1:28b-30
1:28b Facing Destruction or Deliverance
1:29 The Graces of Both Loyal Devotion and Suffering
1:30 A Shared Struggle

EXPLANATORY NOTES

The Singular Imperative of Messianic Citizenship 1:27a

This unit opens with an attention-getting adverb (NRSV: *only*; Gk. *monon*), which here functions as an interjection, "Just one thing!" To paraphrase, "As pertains to your advance and joy in loyalty-faith and your boasting in Messiah [1:25-26], *what I turn to next is of singular importance!*"

Paul follows this interjection with a succinct and loaded exhortation, one that does not translate easily into English: *politicize [politeuomai] worthily of the gospel of Messiah.* The crucial and striking element of this exhortation is the verb *politeuomai*, a word used only here in all of Paul's writings! Later the cognate *politeuma* (regime, governing administration, citizenship, political body, commonwealth) appears in Philippians 3:20, also the only time in Paul's writings.

The word Paul uses here is related to the wide-ranging vocabulary the Greeks developed to describe things "political": things that pertained specifically to the citizen-state: *polis* (city-state; for the Greeks, especially a citizen body with a formal constitution), *politēs* (citizen, member of a *polis*; different from being a resident of a *polis*), *politeia* (polity, commonwealth, constitution, government, civic-political ethos, citizenship; e.g., Acts 22:28; Eph 2:12), *politeuma* (practice of *polis* administration, regime, citizenship; Phil 3:20), *politikos* (person engaged in citizen-state business; statesman). From these Greek words are derived the English terms -polis, politics, political, and polity, even policy and police.

In Paul's linguistic context, the verb *politeuomai* (politicize) refers to both (1) the social character of a citizen body as a city-state (*polis*), and (2) individual conduct or practice appropriate to membership in a citizen body (e.g. Acts 23:1). In other words, it can describe both (1) the communal ethos and governing affairs of a *polis*, and (2) individual conduct that serves the *polis*, including taking an active part in city-state governance, and holding public office. Paul's meaning focuses on enacting a certain alternative form of politics and requires several words for a proper translation: *Be a citizen body and practice citizenship*. The English word *politicize* is thus inadequate, since it refers to "becoming political, or politically conscious," in a much narrower sense of the term.

Paul used this word strategically to highlight the singular importance and the distinctive practice and ethos of citizenship as members of Messiah's citizen community (*polis*). Paul is not referring to "living as Roman citizens" in a manner worthy of the gospel (contra Brewer; Winter: 85; ISV: *continue to live as good citizens*), nor to "living as dual citizens of Rome and of heaven" in a manner worthy of the gospel (contra Hawthorne; Silva; Lincoln: 100; Fee). The closest parallel in form and theme to this exhortation elsewhere in Paul is 1 Thessalonians 2:12, where Paul's injunction is similarly loaded with the claim of alternative political allegiance: "Walk in a manner worthy of the God who calls you into *his own* kingdom and glory." (See TBC below, "Kingdom Allegiance"; TLC, "The Politics of Translation"; similarly Bockmuehl; Fowl 2005; Flemming; Gorman 2015: 106–41.)

In Western Christianity (beginning with the Latin translation), this citizenship imagery has been lost or covered up until the present: the verb has been translated to apply to conduct in general (NRSV, NIV: *let your manner of life*; similarly NABRE). But in Paul's world, this word always involved some reference point to a particular city-state (citizen-state) identity or practice. Only recently have mainstream English translations reintroduced the citizenship image: *As citizens of heaven live in a manner worthy of the gospel of Christ* (TNIV); *Above all, you must live as citizens of heaven* (NLT; although the phrase "of heaven" is misleading here; see TLC on 3:20).

Paul's call to "politicize" *in a manner worthy of the gospel of Messiah* would have had a decidedly polemical ring for the first listeners, posing a sharp contrast between rival frameworks of citizenship identity and loyalty. In the Greek city-state tradition, the expected appeal would have been to "politicize" according to a proper constitution (*politeia*) and an appropriate set of laws (*nomoi*). In the Judean (Jewish) tradition, the rhetoric of citizenship practice appeals to the normative Mosaic Torah, the founding constitutional legislation, though sometimes in terms of a particular interpretation of it (e.g., "politicizing according to the Pharisaic philosophy," Josephus, *The Life* 1.12). In the Roman imperial period, Roman rhetoric and propaganda called for loyalty to Rome, especially on the basis of the Lord

Savior Caesar's great deeds of virtue, proclaimed in "good tidings." Loyalty to the empire is enjoined specifically as loyalty to the emperor, as loyalty in response to the "good tidings of Augustus." Paul's citizenship language here thus directly counters that of Rome, and the term *gospel* here is also meant as a counter to Rome's gospel (TBC on 1:3-11, "The Gospel") *[Roman Imperial Propaganda, p. 312]*. In the paragraphs to follow, Paul will spell out more precisely what this messianic citizenship means and how it diverges from standard notions and practices of citizenship *[Citizenship, p. 279]*.

Concepts of citizenship in secular democracies typically do not invoke the idea of "worthiness," a framework more common in the ancient world. Nevertheless, we do use the language of worthiness as a basis for receiving honors or rewards or determining whether someone is "deserving." By using the notion of worthiness, Paul is indicating that there is a distinctive honor to holding citizenship in Messiah's new community—as well as a corresponding expectation. Paul is drawing attention to the benefits and privileges of holding messianic citizenship—based on what it took to create the new citizen community in the first place—which in return imply a set of responsibilities and obligations. In this case, the story of the Deliverer Jesus becomes the basis and standard of "worthiness." So in short order we will come to the high point of the letter, which calls attention to the saving deeds and the upside-down valor of Lord Jesus Messiah himself (2:5-11; cf. 3:20-21). Christ both is the means of securing the benefits of new citizenship and models the conduct for fulfilling its norms and responsibilities.

The Unified Alignment of the Citizen Community under Siege 1:27b-28a

Paul first addresses the "worthy" manner in which the Philippian outpost of Messiah's citizen-state must defend itself against a siege by adversaries—an assault by Roman imperial power and culture in the city (in the Introduction, see "Profile and Circumstances") *[Circumstances of the Messianic Assembly, p. 277]*. Paul draws on stereotypical military imagery, painting a picture of a besieged city being called to muster a vigorous and unified defense (Geoffrion: 35–36, 66–67; Krentz; Oakes 2001: 65, 80; Hawthorne: 56; Reimer: 142–50):

that you stand firm in one spirit,
striving side by side, with one soul,
with the fervent loyalty of the gospel,
and not intimidated in any way by your adversaries.

Each of these words is carefully chosen:

1. Their *standing firm* heads the picture and will reappear at a climax of the exhortation (4:1). Paul uses this term regularly for steadfast conduct or readiness in the face of opposition (1 Cor 16:13; 2 Cor 1:24; cf. Phil 4:1; 1 Thess 3:8; 2 Thess 2:15; Gal 5:1; Eph 6:14). "Standing" in Greek often has the connotation of "resisting"—a "standing" (*stasis*) is one word for "rebellion."

2. The more defensive *standing firm* is coordinated with the more active *striving*. To denote their *striving side by side* (lit. *co-striving*, *co-contending*, or *cobattling*), Paul uses a compound word (*syn-athleō*, "strive together") that is regularly used for both military combat and athletic contest (Pfitzner). A dual military-athletic sense is characteristic of the word *struggle* (*agōn*) in 1:30. This military-athletic imagery will continue in Philippians, applied later to Epaphroditus (2:25-30) and to Paul's coworkers, including Euodia, Syntyche, Clement, and others (4:2-3). As with the Arabic word *jihad*, this word can denote general "striving, struggling," but also "fighting."

3. They hold rank in unified formation, alluding to the necessity of a phalanx to act as one. Paul highlights their solidarity in three ways. They stand firm *in one spirit* (*en heni pneumati*); they strive *in/with one soul* (*mia psychē*; or, "with one inner being, as one person"); and they engage in *joint striving* or *striving side by side* (*syn-athleō*). Later, in 3:16, Paul will employ the military metaphor of "holding the line" as a way to refer to their regulated conduct (*stoicheō*, 3:16). The emphasis on solidarity at the core of their life together will be repeated in 2:1 (*partnership in spirit*) and 2:2 (*being joined in soul*), along with having one and the same mind-set (2:2).

4. Their primary manner of attire or defensive weapon in their standing and striving is the *fervent loyalty* (*pistis*) *of the gospel* (1:27). This imagery is evident in another cry for "rallying troops" from Paul: "Be vigilant, stand firm in loyalty, be courageous (lit. "be manly"), be strong" (1 Cor 16:13; cf. 2 Cor 1:24). Elsewhere, Paul calls *loyalty* along with love the "breastplate" of Messiah's soldiers (1 Thess 5:8-9). Paul's language evokes the notion of the virtues (faith-loyalty, hope, love, justice-righteousness) as constituting the nonviolent attire and weaponry for "battle" (1 Thess 5:8-9; 2 Cor 6:7; Rom 6:3; 12:21; 13:13-14; Eph 6:15; see Zerbe 2012: 123–40). Moreover, this notion is consonant with Paul's stress on the display of *loyalty* (*pistis*) as the supreme virtue displayed by Messiah himself (Phil 3:9; see TBC on 3:4-17, "The Fidelity of Messiah"). Most English translations and commentators suppose that this phrase clarifies the object of their contending (1:27 NRSV, NIV: *for the faith of the gospel*)—namely, that

they are to contend "for the doctrine and convictions espoused in the gospel." Paul rather intends this phrase to highlight the manner or means of the contending: *with* [by means of] *the fidelity appropriate to the gospel* (similarly CEB: *to remain faithful to the gospel*). In this respect the text ironically plays on the Roman imperial rhetoric of patriotic loyalty to the commander-in-chief in warfare (Reimer: 149–50).

5. "Fear not!" is a common feature of speeches mustering troops for battle, both in the Bible and beyond (e.g. Num 14:9; Deut 1:29; 3:22; Ps 27:3; Isa 41:10). Still, Paul's words of muster here are an acknowledgment of the depth of their distress and of the potential for paralysis and capitulation on account of fear. As already noted in 1:14, the work of proclaiming and living out the gospel must proceed without succumbing to intimidation or terror tactics.

Why does not Paul enjoin prayer and blessing on persecutors here, as he does elsewhere (Rom 12:14-21) in alignment with the teachings of Jesus? The answer is that that theme will indeed come later, although in shorthand form (4:5). At this point, his concern is for their basic firmness of loyalty to the gospel of Messiah.

Facing Destruction or Deliverance

Having noticed the presence of intimidating adversaries around them, Paul turns to explain the crisis in which the Philippian assembly finds itself, all while reassuring them in the struggle (1:28b–2:1). He begins by indicating that there are differing ways to perceive the struggle. Paul's words are elliptical, literally rendered as follows: *which is to them a sign of destruction, but of your deliverance-salvation, and this from God*. What precisely is the *sign* that signals destruction or deliverance? Grammatically, *sign* refers back to their *loyalty*, referring to their *faithfulness and courage* (CEB), the community's steadfast loyalty to Messiah (not to Rome and Caesar), and their fearless persistence in the face of pressure.

To whom and about whom is this *loyalty* a sign of *destruction*? The traditional interpretation is that Paul is here pronouncing doom on the adversaries as a way to satisfy the community's thirst for justice, vindication, or vengeance (cf. Phil 3:19; 2 Thess 2:5-10). To make this view explicit, translations typically add words to Paul's text: *evidence of <u>their</u> destruction* (NRSV), *sign . . . that <u>they will be</u> destroyed* (NIV). But Paul can hardly be referring to the destruction of the oppressors: how could any of the conceivable signs implied in the context convince the opponents (*a sign to/for them*) that their own demise was certain or imminent (Fowl 2005)?

Paul rather focuses on alternative perceptions of the situation and its outcome: *which is to them a sign of [your] destruction, but [it is really a sign] of your deliverance.* In effect, continuing the imagery of a city-state under siege in 1:27-28a, Paul is acknowledging that the adversaries are seeking or awaiting the imminent demise of the messianic community as a *polis.* Thus their patriotic loyalty to Messiah constitutes the sign to the adversaries that they are worthy of destruction. But in Paul's comeback, these signals of loyalty are actually that Messiah's own citizen community will find *deliverance* through direct divine intervention.

Deliverance translates a word (*sōtēria*) that has various possible senses (well-being, vindication, deliverance, safety, security, rescue, return to health, salvation) and in its three occurrences in Philippians is used in a dual sense (1:18, 28; 2:12). First, it refers to Paul's release from prison and the community's anticipated well-being and rescue already in the present order of time. But it also refers to the final salvation, when very soon the regime of Christ becomes fully victorious throughout the world (2:9-11; 3:20-21; 4:5), on *the day of Messiah* (1:6, 10).

A paraphrase of Paul's elliptical words might go something like this: "For although your opponents see your loyalty to the gospel as worthy of and inevitably leading to your demise as a *polis* [city-state], your loyalty in the face of opposition is really a sign of your eventual deliverance" (similarly Hawthorne; Fowl 2005; Hansen). Later Paul will return to this contrast when asserting that it is actually these very adversaries who will meet their demise and destruction (3:19) when Messiah reigns supreme (2:9-11; 3:20-21).

This reading is consonant with Paul's ironic reflections in 2 Corinthians 2:14-16 (probably penned soon after writing to the Philippians and after his release from prison). There he likens his own victorious ministry to that of a train of captives in one of Rome's triumphal military parades. The captives are being led on their way to execution, while the pungent smell of burning sacrificial animal meat fills the air: "But thanks be to God, who in Christ always leads us in triumphal procession, and through us spreads in every place the fragrance that comes from knowing him. For we are the aroma of Christ to God among those who are being saved and among those who are perishing: to one a fragrance from death to death, to the other a fragrance from life to life." A similar contrast of perceptions appears in 1 Corinthians 1:18. "For the word of the cross is folly to those who are perishing, but to us who are being saved it is the power of God." In these texts, the Greek word for *perishing* comes from the verb form of the noun translated *destruction* in Philippians 1:28; 3:19.

This phrase then offers reassurance in the midst of their ordeal, whose outcome is secured, as clarified by the concluding remark: *and this from God.* In a similar way, Paul knows that the question of his own demise or deliverance stands in God's hands (1:18b-26). Soon he will proclaim that their salvation in general is secure (2:9-11; 3:20-21). But the comment *and this from God* implies even more; it also refers to God's providence in the whole ordeal, as Paul immediately suggests in the next sentence.

The Graces of Both Loyal Devotion and Suffering

Having drawn attention to their ordeal, he now begins to explain it. It is not simply *suffering on behalf of Messiah.* Rather, it is a kind of grace, indeed on par with "being graciously given" the opportunity to have a relationship of loyal devotion (believing) toward the Messiah (1:25-26). The phrase *it has been graciously granted to you* uses the verbal form (*charizomai*) of the word *charis* (grace, generous giving) that is sounded at the beginning of the letter (1:2, 7) and will be repeated at the end (4:23). By using the passive voice, Paul hints at the indirect way in which God ordains things: God does not *will* suffering, but God is still sovereign and can *use* suffering (cf. Rom 5:3; 8:18-30). Grace is indeed what energizes the human response of loyalty-faith toward the Messiah (cf. 1 Cor 15:8-10; Eph 2:8-9) and is the effective power by which they have become the Messiah's citizen-community (*polis*). In effect their "partnership in grace" now includes a partnership in the Messiah's own suffering (3:10-11), and it will mean sharing mutually in suffering (1:30; 2:17-18). That suffering is the inevitable and ordained pathway toward deliverance is also expressed in Paul's exhortation to the Thessalonians "that no one be moved by these afflictions. You yourselves know that we are positioned for this. For when we were with you, we told you beforehand that we were to suffer affliction" (1 Thess 3:3-4 AT). (See TBC below, "Paul's Theology of Suffering"; EN on 2:10-11; Bloomquist on suffering in Philippians.)

A Shared Struggle

Having clarified that the suffering of the Philippian community is for Messiah's sake, and thus a kind of grace, Paul closes this opening unit of exhortation by naming their circumstances as one of "struggle," which they now share mutually with Paul himself. It now becomes obvious to the contemporary reader that Paul writes about himself in 1:12-26 not just to make his readers aware of his own circumstances. Instead, he presents his resolve and disposition to the ordeal as a model for them to follow and as an example of how God uses apparent defeat for the greater good of the gospel. The focus on Paul as a model for the readers becomes explicit later, in 3:4-17 and in 4:9, but it is implicit even in 2:17-18 and 4:10-13.

Paul has no need to clarify the precise details or causes of their struggle or the identity of adversaries who wish for their destruction: this was already mutually known. What Paul stresses is that they are now all in it together, mutually experiencing *the same struggle, of the sort that you saw I had and now hear that I still have* (similarly 2 Cor 1:6-7: he and the Corinthians experience "the same suffering"). *Of the same sort* of struggle, though not necessarily involving the same precise conditions, suggests the broader issues that led to Paul's first imprisonment and abuse in Philippi (cf. 1 Thess 2:2; Acts 16:11-40) and then his current imprisonment in Ephesus at the hands of the Roman authorities (Phil 1:13). The natural interpretation is that the suffering in all these cases is similarly at the hands of Roman imperial power and Roman society more generally. They are involved in an epic conflict between Messiah and Caesar (Phil 2:9-11; 3:20-21).

The Greek word that Paul uses here for *struggle* (*agōn*; cf. English: agony, agonistic) can refer to any trial, danger, or ordeal, but is especially at home in the context of athletic contest, military battle, or legal trial. The Philippians' own suffering, no less potentially grave than Paul's, probably included economic factors. This might have involved loss of employment or loss of opportunity to engage in trade or commerce (Oakes 2001), if not overt pressure and accusations before the Roman magistrates of the colony. The analogy with Paul's own struggle (1:12-15) and indirect hints (1:27-28) suggest that it is the very proclamation of the "gospel of Messiah" and their fervent loyalty (*pistis*) to this "gospel" that has generated the opposition. In particular, it was likely the proclamation of this new gospel or a refusal to participate in the civic festivities and oaths in honor of the emperor and the empire (in the imperial cult) that caused a reaction from the privileged Roman populace (not from all residents) and the authorities. This gospel proclamation and the readers' commitment to its practice were seen as subversive threats to the harmony and stability of this imperial Roman outpost *[Circumstances of the Messianic Assembly, p. 277; History of the Assembly, p. 295]*.

THE TEXT IN BIBLICAL CONTEXT

Kingdom Allegiance and Messianic Citizenship

Jesus' words of invitation to kingdom commitment provide the best biblical parallel to Paul's words in this paragraph. Consider, for instance, two summary statements of Jesus' proclamation (my paraphrase):

> But first and foremost seek God's reign [kingdom] and its justice-righteousness, for in that commitment and community all the mundane anxieties of life—even those of food, clothing, and shelter—will be more than minimally met. (Matt 6:33)
>
> The fullness of God's reign is near—so near, in fact, that it is already impacting the world as it is and requiring a response from all human beings. So change your ways of thinking and turn your lives around as you entrust yourself in loyalty to God's newly revealed royal proclamation of well-being for the world. (Mark 1:14b-15)

Though not frequent in Paul's writings, the language of the kingdom occurs in key places, showing that it is central also to his theology (e.g., 1 Thess 2:12; 1 Cor 15:24-28; Rom 14:17). Always careful to adapt his language to the circumstances, in Philippians Paul draws on the citizenship language of the Greek political tradition to express the kingdom proclamation of Jesus. What is especially of interest here is the convergence of topics in these two gospel texts with themes from Philippians: nearness of God's reign (Phil 4:5); letting go of the cares and anxieties of life (4:6-7); mental and behavioral transformation (2:2-5; 3:4-17); needs more than adequately supplied through Christ (4:10-20); a focus on the gospel as God's royal proclamation (1:27); faith/belief and trust as fidelity and loyalty (1:26, 27; 3:9); singularity and priority of commitment to God's reign (1:27); and the centrality of justice-righteousness (1:9; 3:9).

Paul's Theology of Suffering in Biblical Perspective

While Paul sometimes addresses the issues of personal, physical suffering through illness or disease (e.g., Phil 2:26-27; 2 Cor 12:7-10), his references to suffering pertain more to what could be termed socio-political suffering: distress and hardship (from physical to economic) because of social and political forces at work.

In the heat of momentary trial, Paul's reflections in Philippians on the experience of suffering remain brief. But there are crucial hints as to how he understands the suffering that he and his beloved partners are experiencing. On the one hand, for Paul, the pain of suffering is real (Phil 1:17; 2:27), making the prospect of death look like a gain (1:21). But insofar as it is on behalf of Messiah (1:29; cf. 1:13, 16; 2:30), it is an inherent part of the grace of becoming a loyal follower of Messiah (1:29). Moreover, the supreme act of Christ's loyal obedience for the sake of the "other" culminated in his suffering unto death (2:4, 8), providing the paradigm for those who continue the work of Messiah, as a "partnership in his suffering" (3:10). In the same mode, then, Paul's own suffering has a vicarious significance for Messiah's community (2:17). Even in suffering, there are new opportunities and advances (1:12-15), even if it is through death that Messiah is thus magnified (1:20). The experience of suffering requires and nurtures a total reliance on God and his Messiah, who strengthens in the midst of distress (4:13) and provides the resources for compassion and consolation (1:19; 2:1; 3:1; 4:4). And because suffering is a moment along the pathway to victory (1:28; 2:8-11; 3:20), even joy can be expressed precisely amid suffering. Indeed, the partnership of being loyal followers of Messiah means that they must always show the solidarity of joy in the Lord in the midst of struggle (1:30; 2:17-18; 3:1; 4:4).

In his next letters, written shortly after Philippians, Paul will elaborate more fully on the meaning of suffering as he reflects retrospectively on his ordeal, unpacking many of the perspectives mentioned only elliptically in Philippians. In the opening blessing of 2 Corinthians (1:3-11), Paul again highlights the themes of God's resources in consolation, solidarity in Messiah's sufferings, solidarity with each other in suffering, suffering on behalf of others, and suffering as drawing people to rely more fully on God, putting confidence in the one who brings the dead to life (cf. Rom 4:17; 2 Cor 4:7–5:10). Pain and suffering, he observes, can be differently perceived, either as a pathway to destruction or a moment on the way to salvation (2:14-16; cf. Phil 1:28). Paul elaborates on the appropriate posture and conduct in the midst of suffering (4:7-9; 6:4-10) and clarifies its meaning as a solidarity with both the death and resurrection power of Jesus, with a vicarious impact for his beloved congregation (4:10-12; cf. Phil 2:17). He asserts that the love of Messiah was displayed precisely in his redemptive suffering (2 Cor 5:14-15), whose ministry of reconciliation still drives Paul's own sense of mission (2 Cor 5:16-21). Paul forcefully testifies to the truth that in his own experience: "God is the one who encourages-consoles the [afflicted] lowly" (2 Cor 7:4-6 AT). The core thesis of his concluding "fool's speech" is clear: precisely weakness and suffering provide the opportunity for God's power to be displayed and, as a consequence, his ground for boasting (2 Cor 11:16–12:11). In a similar vein are Paul's reflections in Colossians, perhaps written in the context of the same imprisonment: "I am now rejoicing in my sufferings for your sake, and in my flesh I am completing what is lacking in Christ's afflictions for the sake of his body, that is, the assembly" (Col 1:24 AT).

Romans, though written in the context of greater comfort (a few months later), continues to wrestle with the topic of suffering (Rom 5:1-11; 8:17-39). "Boasting in the hope of the glory of God" allows one thereby to "boast in our sufferings," especially insofar as it produces the virtues along the pathway to salvation (Rom 5:2-4). Indeed, suffering is the necessary prelude to glory, for both humanity and all creation in solidarity (8:17-25). And the Spirit provides inner resources in the midst of pain (8:26-27). In the context of suffering, God's people are invited to work in "synergy" with God toward the goal of "the good" (for the whole of creation, 8:28). And Paul resoundingly proclaims that no enmity, hostile power, or suffering will ever be able to separate us from the overwhelming victory to come through the "love of God in Messiah Jesus" (8:31-39).

Though Paul finds meaning in suffering, Paul does not glorify suffering or consider it inherently virtuous. Suffering is a messianic pathway, not a masochism (the quest to derive pleasure from pain). Suffering is survived through divine resources working through communal solidarity (Phil 2:1) and resolved eschatologically (in light of the "final outcome"). (See also EN on 3:10-11.)

Paul's understanding derives from a rich biblical and theological heritage while also being decisively shaped in light of Christ. Paul's Scriptures deal extensively with both personal-physical suffering and sociopolitical suffering. In one trajectory of his Scripture (our OT), human suffering of both types is interpreted as a consequence of infidelity to the covenant or misbehavior of some kind. This easily leads to the conclusion that we are to blame for our own misfortune, because of an emphasis on rewards or reprisals for fidelity or infidelity to the covenant. This is sometimes called the "Deuteronomistic" perspective, since it is articulated most clearly in Deuteronomy and the Deuteronomistic History (Joshua–2 Kings). Thus Judah's historical epic (the Deuteronomistic History) explains that Israel's and Judah's eventual demise as nations was caused by their own persistent and extensive disregard of the covenant.

The duration and extent of national suffering caused many faithful to eventually question this simplistic view. The book of Job questions the Deuteronomistic perspective most profoundly, arguing that the righteous also suffer. And the sixth-century-BCE prophet of the exile now known as Second Isaiah (Isa 40–55) argues that suffering as an individual or as a nation can have a redemptive or vicarious outcome (the suffering of one can serve the healing of another). This is stated most impressively in Isaiah 53.

This new perspective later came to have a dramatic impact on reflection on suffering in the Judean (Jewish) tradition between the two Testaments (the period of Early Judaism). At the height of the experience of horrific persecution and oppression at the hands of a Syrian-Greek empire two centuries before Christ, Jewish theologians did not interpret their national suffering as caused by their own fault. They understood suffering increasingly as a consequence of malevolent "satanic" or "demonic" powers in the world, often embodied in earthly regimes (cf. 1 Thess 2:18). Jesus himself accommodates to these two prevailing explanations of distress (human sins; powers of evil) as he heals physical illness by forgiving sins and casting out demons.

During the centuries before Christ, Judean (Jewish) theologians began to understand that the blood of the martyrs could atone for the sins of the nation, something that would lead God to pay attention to their plight (e.g., 2 Macc 6–7; 4 Macc 16–17; cf. Rev 6:9-11). This theology of redemptive or vicarious suffering, reaching back to Isaiah and further developed in the period of Second Temple Judaism, and then demonstrated in the life and death of Jesus, is a crucial backdrop to Paul's own theology of suffering (J. Williams 2010).

THE TEXT IN THE LIFE OF THE CHURCH

Christian Practice and Identity as "Citizenship" in Early Christianity

In the first few centuries of Christianity, before church and imperial state were wedded in fourth-century Christendom, Paul's language of citizenship as expressed especially in Philippians 1:27 and 3:20 was regularly taken up in Christian vocabulary. Early Christians explicitly drew on Paul's claim that Christ established a new political community, with a citizenship that cuts across established identities and loyalties—that Christians were a kind of alternative society or nationality with a distinctive loyalty and manner of life. In a writing now known as 1 Clement, dating in the 90s CE, Clement, bishop of Rome, addresses the Corinthians, first congratulating them on their internal unity and their high moral conduct, summarizing this as "being adorned by a fully virtuous and honorable citizenship [*politeia*], fulfilling all things in the fear of God" (2.8). He goes on, however, to confront the dissidents "who do not practice citizenship [*politeuomai*] according what is fitting to Christ," by living in infidelity (3.4). Drawing specifically on Philippians 1:27, he warns of judgment "if we do not practice citizenship worthily of him and do not practice in unity what is the good and the pleasing before him" (21.1; see also 44.6; 51.2).

Polycarp, the bishop of Smyrna (ca. 69–155), suffered a martyr's death at the hands of the Roman Empire. He recalls Paul's words to the Philippians as he is writing his own *To the Philippians*:

> If we please him [the servant Christ] in this present world, we shall receive also the future world, according as he has promised to us that he will raise us again from the dead [Phil 3:21]. . . . If we practice citizenship worthy of him [*politeusōmetha axiōs autou*, or "if we are worthy citizens of his community," citing Phil 1:27], we shall also reign together with him [2 Tim 2:12], provided only we remain loyal [*pisteuō*]." (Polycarp, *To the Philippians* 5.2 AT)

The citizen imagery for Christian identity and conduct is explicit in the anonymous Letter to Diognetus, a Christian "apology" (defense of the faith) from the second half of the second century:

> For the distinction between Christians and the rest of humanity is neither in land nor language nor customs. For they do not dwell in cities in some place of their own, nor do they use any strange variety of dialect, nor practice an unusual livelihood. . . . Yet while living in Greek and barbarian cities [*poleis*] according as each obtained his lot, and following the local customs, both in clothing and food and in the rest of life, they show forth the admirable and confessedly paradoxical condition of their own polity-citizenship [*politeias*]. They dwell in their own fatherlands [*patridas*], but as resident aliens [*paroikoi*]; they share all things as citizens [*politai*], and endure all things as foreigners. Every foreign country is their fatherland [*patris*] and every fatherland [*patris*] is a foreign country. . . . They pass their time upon the earth, but they have their citizenship [*politeuontai*] in heaven [Phil 3:20]. . . . To put it shortly, what the soul is in the body—that is what Christians are in the world. The soul is spread through all members of the body and Christians throughout the cities [*poleis*] of the world. (Diognetus 5.1–2, 4–5, 9; 6.1–2)

In the same manner, Apollinarius, bishop of Hierapolis (ca. 170s) describes Christians as those "determined to be a citizen body and to practice citizenship [*politeuomai*] according to the gospel itself" (quoted in Eusebius, *Ecclesiastical History* 3.28.2). Polycrates of Ephesus, writing between 160 and 196, characterizes martyrs of the past as "those who practiced citizenship in the Holy Spirit." He describes himself as having "always practiced citizenship in Christ Jesus," drawing attention to the apostolic exhortation "We must obey God rather than men [human regimes]" (Acts 5:29; *Ecclesiastical History* 3.31.3; 5.24.2-8).

Even early in the fourth century, Eusebius uses *politeia* (polity; constitution; manner of life of a citizen community) in a range of senses, referring to standard types of governments and to regular civic and political involvement (*Ecclesiastical History* 1.2.19; 1.6.6; 6.19.7; 8.9.7; 8.14.9; 9.4.2). But he also uses the term to refer to the distinctively Christian "manner of citizen life": he draws attention to "the antiquity of the Christian polity-citizenship [*politeia*] according to the gospel" (2.praef.) and the "distinctive polity-citizenship [*politeia*] according to the gospel" (2.17.15); and he refers to "the pure light of the church's inspired citizenship/polity [*politeia*] and philosophy" shed on every nation, Greek and non-Greek (4.7.13). Summarizing the letter of Dionysius to the Athenians (ca. 171), he calls it "a rousing call to loyalty [*pistis*] and to citizenship [*politeia*] according to the gospel" (4.23.2), and he draws attention to Theonas, bishop of Alexandria, who "demonstrated the genuine manner of gospel-oriented citizenship [*politeia*]" (8.9.7). Accordingly, he describes the general "mode of life" of individuals also as a *politeia* (polity-citizenship, 4.15.30; 5.13.2; 5.1.9), including that of Christ (1.4.4).

It is time to recover the notion of Christian practice and identity specifically as a "citizenship," both in its corporate dimensions (in contrast to individualistic notions of "discipleship") and in its theo-political aspects (over against claims to our loyalty, practice, and identity by the modern state).

The Politics of Translation

Philippians 1:27 is an interesting case of how something is lost in translation, then solidified through political and theological bias. As indicated above, it is hard to capture the full significance of Paul's choice of a single word without translating with multiple words: "be a citizen body and practice your citizenship," longhand for Paul's verb *politeuomai*, "politicize." The traditional rendering of Philippians 1:27 in English as *conduct yourselves* [or, *live your life*] *in a manner worthy of the gospel of Christ* (e.g., NIV, NRSV) is both unfortunate and misleading. This translation reflects the tendency in Constantinian Western Christianity to soften the nature of the church as a "contrast society," a church that earlier (before Constantine tied church and state together in Christendom) claimed an alternative and ultimate allegiance to Christ alone. This translation, in turn, is dependent on the King James Version of 1611 (and prior English translations), which were influenced by the Latin Vulgate (common) version of the Bible, the most influential translation in the history of the Western church, translated by Jerome (347–420).

When Latin translators encountered Paul's Greek verb *politeuomai*, they recognized that Latin had no equivalent verb. While *civitas* (state, commonwealth, citizenship) constituted a rough equivalent to the Greek *polis* or *politeuma*, Latin never developed a corresponding verb; it used expressions pertaining to *res publica* ("affairs of state, the public," whence "republic") to describe political activity. Jerome translated this passage when Christianity had become the official religion of the Roman Empire and Christians believed that their Christian and Roman citizenships could coexist quite naturally and easily. Christian faith no longer constituted an alternative citizenship that put limits on standard political loyalty, nor could it challenge established rule in the name of God, as in the first three hundred years of the Christian church. Whether consciously or unconsciously, Jerome avoided any rendering that might put political (earthly) and spiritual (heavenly) loyalties into any conflict. When he came to Philippians 1:27, he choose to translate *politeuomai* with the Latin verb *conversamini*, which means "to have interactions with," and by extension simply "to live, conduct oneself." When he came to the word *politeuma* (commonwealth, regime, citizenship) in Philippians 3:20, he translated with *conversatio*, in the sense of (1) frequent use or activity, and by extension (2) interactions with persons. In this case, he avoided the words *civitas*, or *res publica*, which would have been the most obvious Latin equivalents to Paul's *politeuma*.

When the translators of the King James Version came to this verse in the early 1600s, they had both Paul's Greek and Jerome's Latin in hand. Moreover, at this time the word *conversation* in English, based on its Latin roots, denoted "keeping company with, conduct, behavior." Only much later did it come to have the meaning "speech interactions," as it has today. Thus they translated Philippians 1:27 as *Only let your conversation be as it becometh the gospel of Christ*; and Philippians 3:20 as *For our conversation is in heaven.* Wherever they found the Latin *conversatio* or related words in the NT, they simply translated with English *conversation.*

Thereby an interpretive and translation tradition emerged in Latin and then English that both individualized Paul's exhortation and robbed it of its original theopolitical implications. Little would the readers of the KJV realize that Paul was countering Roman citizenship identity and commitments with messianic citizenship allegiance. Subsequent English translations have followed this lead, translating Paul's politically loaded verb with terms such as *live your life, conduct yourselves*, and the like. Although biblical scholars for some time have been arguing that these translations miss the depth of Paul's original meaning, not until the recent TNIV and NLT (*live as citizens of heaven*) has any mainstream version of the NT attempted anything else.

The 1999 *Confession of Faith of the General Conference of Mennonite Brethren Churches* rightly appeals to Philippians 1:27 (along with Phil 3:20 and other NT passages) as a text supporting the conviction that "the primary allegiance of all Christians is to Christ's kingdom, not the state or society. Because their citizenship is in heaven, Christians are called to resist the idolatrous temptation to give to the state the devotion that is owed to God."

Philippians in Anabaptist Writings: Suffering and Letters from Prison

Reflection on suffering is a regular theme in Anabaptist writings from the sixteenth century, given their experience of persecution for their role in the Radical Reformation (Klaassen 1981: 85–100; 2001: 28–29). Perhaps not surprisingly, an index survey of collections of Anabaptist writings (Classics of the Radical Reformation series) reveals that Philippians 1:29 is the most frequently cited passage from Philippians. In addition to this text, also cited from Philippians in connection with the theme of suffering are 1:21, dying is gain; 2:5-10, Christ as model in suffering; 2:17, ministers being "poured out" for the work of Christ; and 3:10, becoming like Christ in his suffering. Meanwhile, many Anabaptist letters from prison display a self-conscious awareness of following in the pathway of Paul, drawing on patterns and themes from Philippians and his other prison letters. In this respect, Anabaptists are not unique (see also TLC on 1:12-26, "Letters from Prison").

Philippians 2:1-5

A Citizen Body Marked by Unity and Status Inversion

PREVIEW

Is it possible to console and to confront at the same time? Amazingly, Paul attempts to do exactly that in one long Greek sentence (2:1-4). He first draws attention to the givens of divine and communal consolation, love, compassion, and partnership, thereby continuing to support and encourage his friends in their distress (2:1). Paul draws attention to both the resources that support a community in struggle and the virtues they exhibit in that solidarity. But where one might expect Paul to continue with words of consolation, he redirects, coming back to the issue of maintaining unity within the ordeal, thereby resisting fracture and even defeat (2:2-3a).

But how do you destabilize the prevailing vertical hierarchy in a rank-preoccupied society, the most significant threat to the community's future as a truly messianic citizen body? The disunity problem of the assembly in Philippi appears to be more a matter of vertical divisions (pertaining to social class, rank, and status) than merely horizontal interpersonal differences.

Paul thus begins this unit by highlighting the resources and virtues available through Messiah to sustain a community specifically in the context of suffering (2:1). This immediately leads to an emphasis on nonrivalrous, nonhierarchical unity (2:2-4). Up to this point in the letter, everything has focused around "Messiah" and the "gospel" about Messiah. But the substantive content of the *good tidings of Messiah* that was emphasized as the keynote and framework for Paul's exhortation (1:27) has still not been proclaimed and explained. Paul calls for their steadfastness in trial and for the unifying virtues of deliberate concern both for the lowly and for the other. He does so by asserting that Messiah himself has demonstrated this model (2:5), leading directly to a world-shattering encomium (public tribute) to Messiah that inverts prevailing values and expectations (2:6-11).

OUTLINE

Premises: Resources and Virtues in the Context of Suffering, 2:1
The Soul and Mind-Set of Messianic Communal Politics, 2:2-5
- 2:2 Common Bond and Purpose
- 2:3-4 Common Status: Striving for the Other
- 2:5 Embracing the Mentality of Messiah

EXPLANATORY NOTES

Premises: Resources and Virtues in the Context of Suffering 2:1

In Greek, 2:1-4 is one long sentence with an "if-then" structure, grammatically a "true-to-fact" conditional sentence construction, such that the *if* here has the sense of "because." The flow of 2:1-2a, is thus: *Because there are, in fact, virtues and supports that flow in the saving sphere and committed community of Messiah Jesus, therefore, make my joy complete by enacting these bonds and mental patterns in practice.*

Paul makes a grouping of four, each marked by an introductory *since there is a certain* (or, *since there is a measure of*): (1) *consolation* (*paraklēsis*; NRSV, NIV: *encouragement*) *in Messiah*, (2) *comfort* (NIV; NRSV: *consolation*) *of love*, (3) *partnership in spirit*, and (4) *compassions and mercies*. Earlier, Paul has stressed that his own yearnings for them are like the very *bowels [compassions] of Messiah* (1:8). Now he emphasizes first that all consolation in suffering is also founded and demonstrated *in Messiah*—that is, in the sphere of Messiah's character, power, and community. The crucial *in Messiah* framework made at the outset applies to the whole list. The flow of 1:29–2:1 is roughly the same as that of 2 Corinthians 1:5: "For just as the sufferings of Christ are abundant for us, so also our consolation is abundant through Christ."

The phrase *comfort of love* expands on the first phrase (using a near synonym; similarly 1 Thess 2:12; 1 Cor 14:3) yet dramatically identifies love as the key virtue of Messiah's character and community. The phrase also anticipates what Paul will stress in the next segment: that they have *the same love* (2:2) with each other, a love without rivalry and hierarchy, a love not constrained by social position (2:3-4). Recall that love is the chief virtue in Paul's intercessory prayer for them (1:9). The third phrase, *partnership of spirit*, is roughly equivalent to the notion of being "joined in soul" (2:2), evoking the notion of a committed solidarity, as already pronounced at the beginning of the letter (1:5, 7). Paul reemphasizes that they *stand firm in one spirit* and *strive together with one soul* (1:27). The vital theme of partnership (*koinōnia*) in Philippians is now tied to solidarity in suffering (cf. 3:10; note also 2 Cor 1:7, where "partnership [*koinōnia*] in suffering" corresponds to "partnership in consolation"). The last grouping shifts to two synonymous words: *compassions* (lit. "bowels," as in Phil 1:8) and *mercies*. Both can refer either to virtues or affections and feelings (NRSV: *compassion and sympathy*; NIV: *tenderness and compassion*). Altogether, these virtues and affections—images of deep personal and social bonds—represent the necessary resources and supports that are available *in Messiah*, and thus what the community can and must display in the context of suffering.

Related passages confirm that for Paul, these resources for consolation in suffering have a divine source and foundation. Alluding to the ordeal that he has just endured (2 Cor 1:8-11), and using the same terminology as here, Paul affirms God as "the Father of mercies and the God of all consolation, who consoles us in all our affliction so we may be able to console those who are in any affliction with the consolation with which we ourselves are consoled by God" (2 Cor 1:3-4). He later repeats that even more recently he himself has been consoled by "the God who consoles the [afflicted] lowly" (2 Cor 7:6 AT). Similarly, Paul draws attention in Romans to the intercessory role of the Spirit in the crisis of suffering (Rom 8:26-27; cf. Phil 1:19).

The Soul and Mind-Set of Messianic Communal Politics 2:2-5

Just as Paul inserted his own relational bond with them as a motivating factor for his readers' compliance earlier in 1:26 and 1:27, so now he again stresses that the fullness of his joy will be realized as a result of their good conduct (similarly, 2:16). Paul uses one long clause (three verses) of parallel and contrasting images to lay out the ideal profile of their communal practice, their "politics," elaborating the unity theme announced already in 1:27:

> *that you are mindful of [mentally focused on] the same thing*
> *having the same love*
> *[being] joined in soul*
> *being mindful of [mentally focused on] the one thing,* (2:2)
> *not according to rivalrous striving nor according to empty glory*
> *but in low-mindedness regarding one another as superior to yourselves,* (2:3)
> *not each watching out for their own interests*
> *but each for the interests of the others.* (2:4)

Just as Paul earlier drew attention to his own bond with his listeners at the levels of head, heart, and guts (1:7-8), so also now he highlights the various levels of the community's own fabric: its deep pathos, bonds of feeling (2:1-2), and its mentality and practice (2:2-5). Using a chiasmus (X structure), Paul explains their common bond and purpose (2:2). And then, with two parallel contrasts (not this—but that), Paul goes on to stress their common status and common concern for each other (2:3-4).

Common Purpose. Paul stresses their common purpose and communal singularity with the idiomatic phrases *thinking the same thing* (NIV: *being like-minded*; NRSV: *being of the same mind*) and *thinking the one thing* (NRSV, NIV: *being of one mind*). These expressions do not translate easily into English. In Paul's world, these phrases were used to characterize friendship relations (White: 210). More significantly for Paul's appeal, these words are used in business and communal relationships, both formal or informal, where they denote being committed to a common purpose (Sampley). Moreover, Paul regularly uses this terminology to denote "regarding each other to be of the same status," challenging the prevailing status and honor system (Oakes 2001: 181; Hellerman; see Rom 12:3, 16). In other words, Paul is not calling his readers to a unity marked by unanimity of opinion or sameness of thought, but to a solidarity around a *common purpose* and a regard for each other as having *the same status.* The idiom *thinking the same thing in the Lord* has the meaning of "coming to common purpose and equal status in the Lord." It will recur in Paul's exhortation to two women leaders in 4:2-3.

Common Bond. Paul emphasizes their deep common bond with the phrases *having the same love* and being *joined together in soul* (NIV: *being one in spirit*; NRSV: *being in full accord*). The point in this context is that love knows no social or status boundaries, and so is without rivalry (Phil 1:15-16), in contrast to love that is measured according to social position or level of friendship. Recall that love was the chief desire for them in his opening prayer (1:9-11). The compound term *joined together in soul* (Gk. *sym-psychoi*) picks up the image of 1:27, *co-striving together with one soul* (*psychē*). Paul does not use soul (*psychē*) in the sense of the immortal "soul" of later Christian theology, but in the Hebraic sense of the "inner life" and "essential life-force" (Heb. *nepeš*) of living beings.

Common Status: Striving for the Other. In the first of two contrasts, Paul directly challenges the rank-preoccupied, status-striving, honor-oriented, and glory-seeking patterns of Greco-Roman society *[Love of Honor, p. 299]*. Paul undermines a communal practice based on one's own social advantage (*eritheia*, rivalrous striving, selfish ambition; cf. 1:17) or according to one's high social position (*keno-doxos*, empty honor, *vain glory* [KJV]; Oakes 2001: 182–83). The word *kenodoxos* is particularly striking. Throughout the Greco-Roman world it was commonly used for claiming honor beyond what is properly due. The use of the word assumes that boasting in honor and status is entirely legitimate, but never beyond what is appropriate to one's rank, position, or accomplishments. It is a compound word: *kenos* (empty, vain) and *doxos* (honor, glory = Latin *dignitas*, dignity, honor, worth). Paul plays on the two parts of this word in 2:6-11, where he describes Messiah's "emptying" (*kenoō*), and then his path to "glory" (*doxa*). The irony is that whereas some people boast in their emptiness beyond appropriate limits, Messiah truly emptied himself, though he had the full credential or power to do otherwise. The translation *conceit* (NRSV, ISV; NET: *vanity*) or *vain conceit* (NIV) overly psychologizes the social quest for glory that is at issue here.

Paul encourages his readers instead to *regard others as higher in rank than themselves* (NIV: *value others above yourselves*; NABRE: *regard others as more important than yourselves*). The translation that they are to regard others as *better than oneself* (NRSV) misses the point. Paul's imagery has to do with regarding others to be "higher" or "above" in social rank and value and only in *that* sense as "better" (the word *hyperechō* reappears in 3:8 and 4:7 for things that "surpass"). The virtue with which this is expressed is *humility*, literally *low-mindedness* (KJV, *lowliness of mind*; Gk. *tapeinophrosynē*, compounding the noun form *phrosynē* of the verb *phroneō*, "to think," used in 2:2, 5), a word also used in Colossians 2:23; 3:22 (cf. Eph 4:2). This word does not suggest merely an attitude. For Paul it specifically involves "solidarity with the lowly" (cf. Rom 12:16). In some Greco-Roman texts, this mental framework itself is ridiculed as inappropriate for those of high standing. In conventional morality, the word designates the pattern of life and mental framework suitable only for the lower classes. It is associated with shame and servility (Wengst 1989; Oakes 2001). The unity problem in Philippi seems to be constituted as a social and economic hierarchy issue (see also TBC below, "Status Inversion") *[Love of Honor, p. 299]*.

Paul continues the exhortation on communal relations by stressing a commitment of each person to the concerns of the others, not to one's own interests. The contrast is categorical (not this, but that; NRSV, NIV), which should not be softened (not only this, but also that: NIV 1984; RSV). Moreover, it is best not to psychologize Paul's thought here: he is not dealing with the imperatives of a positive self-concept or saying that we should not take care of ourselves. He is stressing a primary interest in (*watching out for*) the other person as one of the imperatives for the community (similarly 1 Cor 12:22-26). In effect, this is no different from the imperative of love (2:2). Indeed, Paul elsewhere describes love as "not seeking one's own affairs" (1 Cor 13:5). The idea is similar to that expressed in 1 Corinthians in the context of challenging divisions based on a social hierarchy: "Have the same care for one another," shown through being in solidarity in both pain and success (1 Cor 12:25-26). (For the notion of "not seeking one's own affairs, but that of the other," see also 1 Cor 10:24, 33; Phil 2:21.)

A Mental Habit in the Manner of Messiah

Paul now plays his trump card, claiming that the "thinking" (that is, the "life-orienting mental disposition or discipline") that he has just presented in 2:3-4 is the very mentality that Messiah himself displayed.

Paul's somewhat elliptical Greek text literally reads: *This [mindset] think in/among you, which also [was] in Messiah Jesus.* The emphatic initial word *this* draws attention to the communal disposition and pattern that Paul has just identified: the *you* here is plural. It also anticipates the next forceful claim—that this pattern is the very one demonstrated in the life of Messiah himself. The NIV renders the sense well: *In your relationships with one another, have the same mindset as Christ Jesus* (similarly NRSV: *Let the same mind be in you that was in Christ Jesus*). Some translations emphasize the saving aspects of what follows (2:9-11) by understanding "in Christ" as not narrowly ethical in meaning: *Have this mind in you, as is fitting for those in Messiah Jesus* (RSV: *which is yours in Christ Jesus*). Michael Gorman emphasizes both the communal and participatory dimension in his proposed translation: *Cultivate this mind-set within your community, which is in fact a community in Christ Jesus* (Gorman 2015: 118). The emphasis is thereby placed on the communal sphere of life in which messianic conduct takes place, specifically as a participation "in Christ." Such a participatory and communal dimension is crucial to this text, but it should not be understood as minimizing the specifically ethical aspect. Paul clearly puts the emphasis squarely on the model that Messiah displays without suggesting that the declaration of salvation in Messiah (2:9-11) is insignificant. In other places as well, when Paul presents Messiah as a model for behavior, his language spills over to include the saving effects of Messiah's conduct (e.g., Rom 15:7-12; 1 Cor 10:32–11:1; 2 Cor 8:9).

THE TEXT IN BIBLICAL CONTEXT

Habits of the Mind in Philippians

Philippians has a high frequency of words pertaining to thinking and regarding (*phroneō,* being mentally focused on, occurs 10x in Philippians, 13x in the other letters of Paul, and 3x in the rest of the NT; *hēgeomai*, "considering, esteeming, counting," occurs 6x in Philippians and another 5x in the rest of the NT). This frequency, along with the manner in which these words and related synonyms are used, suggests that, here in Philippians, Paul is specifically seeking to foster particular "habits of the mind" among his hearers (e.g., Fowl 2005: 6, 28–29, 82–83; Silva: 21–22; Smith: 44–49; for another passage emphasizing the mind and mindfulness in Paul, see Rom 8:5-8). Closely related to this emphasis is Paul's prayer that they grow in *full knowledge* and *complete perception* (1:9).

The emphasis on mindfulness (being mentally focused on Christ, others, and the common good) occurs both in direct exhortations (2:2, 3, 5; 3:2, 15, 17; 4:8) and through descriptions of models or commendations of others (1:6, 14, 25; 2:6, 20, 21, 24; 3:3, 4, 7, 8, 13, 19; 4:10). Paul's emphasis is on mental commitment to unity and common purpose, a mentality that rejects social and status hierarchies along with consumerist selfish ambition and that deeply cares for the good of the neighbor or other. In other words, Paul emphasizes a mentality most profoundly modeled by Messiah Jesus himself.

At the same time, however, Paul stresses that a proper mentality in Christ is integrally related to matters of the heart (e.g., 1:3-8; 2:1-2, 19-20), of relationship (1:23; 3:8, 10), and of practice (1:9, 27; 2:2-4, 12-14; 3:15-17; 4:4-9), both communally and individually. That is, having a certain mind-set is inseparably linked with a certain feeling and action (Fowl 2005).

Status Inversion: The Reconstruction of Honor and Shame

What Paul attempts in Philippians is a critical destabilizing and reconstruction of prevailing notions and values of honor and shame (Hellerman). The imagery of status inversion appears throughout Philippians, especially in core passages (1:19-20; 2:2-11; 3:3-21), using a variety of images—low/high, loss/gain, lower/elevate, shame/honor, be ashamed/be magnified, destruction/salvation, and humiliation/exaltation. This sustained emphasis must be understood in light of the Roman preoccupation with the struggle for reputation/glory *[Love of Honor, p. 299]*. The unity problem that Paul confronts appears to be especially a social rank problem (2:2-9; 3:3-14). Instead of embracing the prevailing culture's preoccupation with "rivalrous striving (selfish ambition)" and "empty glory," Paul advises that each regard the other as "higher in rank" to oneself according to the pattern of "low-mindedness," a mind-set ridiculed by Roman society's elite as appropriate only for those of low degree (Wengst 1989). At this point Paul introduces the supreme manifestation of the ironic, destabilizing pattern of Messiah's deliberate humiliation (self-emptying, self-lowering, obedience unto death, cross) and resulting exaltation (2:6-11): before him the rest of the world (including Rome and those of high degree) will ultimately lower themselves in obeisance.

When Paul later goes on to stress that the messianic assembly is defined by those who simply *boast in Christ* and claim no *confidence in the flesh* (3:3; cf. 1:26), he immediately draws attention again to the path of social inversion in his own story—first loss and humiliation, then anticipated exaltation (3:4-14). Paul's financial imagery of losses and gains is closely related to this emphasis: everything is reassessed in light of the *surpassing value* (using the same Greek word as in 2:3) of *gaining* or *knowing* Messiah. While the present holds the path of solidarity with Messiah's suffering, the future holds the prospect of experiencing exaltation with Jesus along with the prize and victory wreath (2:16; 3:10-14; 4:1). His embrace of the status of slave (1:1; 2:22) is a further example of his solidarity with Messiah (2:7). Accordingly, while he might be shamed in the eyes of many, his entire life is devoted to *making Messiah great* (1:20). Moreover, he understands that his own utter impoverishment and *lowering*

(4:11-13) can be approached not simply by stoic resignation, but by the prospect of knowing that the God of all wealth and glory will ultimately supply what is lacking (4:19-20). And the *God of peace* (4:9) will be victorious over the powers of violence (cf. Rom 16:20).

Finally, the theme of humiliation leading to exaltation, as being experienced by Messiah, Paul, and the messianic assembly (2:6-11; 3:4-14, 3:20-21), finds its counterpart drama of exaltation leading to humiliation, to be faced by the adversaries of the assembly (2:11; 3:18-19; 4:5). While the adversaries desire the destruction of Messiah's faithful (1:28), the high and mighty who are preoccupied with glory and are thus *enemies of the cross* (3:18), will in fact ultimately meet *destruction* (3:19). The final result is that all glory and praise will go to God (1:11; 2:11; 4:20). Even praise in Philippians is part of the rhetoric of social inversion (cf. 4:8, the need to *assess* what is praiseworthy).

The emphasis on social inversion in Philippians appears in Paul's other letters, especially alongside the theme of economic mutuality (see Zerbe 2012: 67–72, 75–92). Most dramatically, for instance, Paul confronts many status-preoccupied Corinthian believers in their own stratified setting with these words:

> The members of the body that seem to be weaker are indispensable, and those members of the body that we think less honorable we clothe with greater honor, and our less respectable members are treated with greater respect; whereas our more respectable members do not need this. But God has so arranged the body, giving the greater honor to the [supposedly] inferior member, that there may be no dissension within the body, but the members may have the same care for one another. (1 Cor 12:22-25; cf. 1:26-31)

The disunity problem in Corinth also had largely to do with vertical issues of status and rank.

On this matter, Paul is in complete sympathy with the teachings of Jesus (even though he does not quote them directly). In one of the most crucial sections of Mark, for instance, each time Jesus makes a passion prediction (8:27-31; 9:30-31; 10:32-34), the disciples show misunderstanding pertaining especially to status (8:32-33; 9:32-34; 10:35-40), only to be met with clarification as to the real meaning of following Jesus (8:34-37; 9:35-37; 10:41-45):

> For those who want to save their life will lose it, and those who lose their life for my sake, and for the sake of the gospel, will save it. (Mark 8:35)
>
> Whoever wants to be first [leader] must be last of all and servant of all. (Mark 9:35)

> Whoever wishes to become great among you must be your servant, and whoever wishes to be first among you must be slave of all. (Mark 10:43-44)

In the same context, Jesus makes his decisive assertion that in the age to come, "Many who are first [a common term for the "upper class"] will be last [a term for the "lowest class"], and the last will be first" (Mark 10:30-31; see further, TBC on 2:6-11, "The Biblical Pattern of Humiliation/Exaltation"; TBC on 3:1-3, "Boasting and Being Confident").

THE TEXT IN THE LIFE OF THE CHURCH

Servant Leadership

"Servant leadership" is now mainstream, reaching back especially to two influential essays in 1958 and 1970 by Robert Greenleaf (2002), a corporate CEO who reflected carefully on the dynamics of leadership. By now there are multiple institutes and centers of servant leadership, and the *International Journal of Servant-Leadership*. Servant leadership is promoted as a new theory, and for some leadership gurus, the key to improving the corporate bottom line. This interest is fueled by the ever-expanding field of leadership studies, both in scholarship and in how-to books, and demonstrates the widespread belief that autocratic, nonconsultative, noncollaborative, absolute power-wielding leadership does not work in most contexts, especially in business organizations (where it is perhaps harder to get mere wage-earning employees to buy into the mission). Interestingly, Greenleaf's initial inspiration drew from the "Eastern" perspective of Hermann Hesse (1877–1962).

The embrace of the term "servant leadership" in the church is certainly welcome, since it draws especially on the Gospels and Pauline texts just cited. In church contexts, this notion has its own distinctive history, especially since it signals that leadership does not serve itself nor the bottom line, but serves only a divinely inspired mission and a group of people committed to that mission. This term is actually a reminder that leadership roles should be taken on only cautiously, with trepidation, since leadership faces inevitable contradictions when it espouses the apparent oxymoron "servant leadership." In what ways or contexts, for instance, can leaders truly divest themselves of power, decision-making responsibility, salary, stock portfolios, or status? In advanced industrialized societies, one difficulty with embracing both sides of the concept—servant and leader—is that we do not actually use the label *servant* for specific roles or "stations" in our social or institutional hierarchies. Moreover, slavery is now formally illegal in most jurisdictions. Thus the gap and distance we have from "servanthood" (or *serving as a slave*, Phil 2:22) is actually only in our minds, not socially experienced in the stark way it was for Paul and is for many people in the modern world. Furthermore, there are some contexts in which the claim to servant leadership can be made in a way that privileges leaders and avoids true transformation of social hierarchies. (See TLC on 3:4-17, "Preaching Downward Mobility.")

In a significant way, servant leadership is an aspirational and dynamic concept. There are no perfect models out there except the one to be narrated in the next verses (Phil 2:6-11). But the result of this particular downward pathway is martyrdom—not a road most leaders today are prepared to take, literally or figuratively. Thus, when Paul claims to follow the pathway of radical messianic divestment in his own apostolic leadership, we ask: What all could or did he give up (see EN on 3:4-17)? On what issues did he consult? What power did he share? What team did he draw into the circle of leadership? What process of discernment did he follow? No doubt he would have said that there are certain burdens of holding divine appointment as "special envoy" (apostle) of God's new citizen society. Part of the challenge of servant leadership is coping with differing cultural assumptions about what it is to be led—not just to lead—in different institutional or social contexts. To be effective in leading a community or organization in fulfillment of its mission, the would-be leader must be attentive to the often unspoken assumptions.

Ēthos and *Pathos* in Persuasive Strategies

Scholars continue to debate whether or not Paul formally studied the art of rhetoric (spoken persuasion; see Schellenberg). It is clear that Paul was exceedingly aware of the complex dynamics involved in persuasion, both in bringing people to initial loyalty-faith, but also in persuading his converts to embrace particular standards of behavior and patterns of thinking. We can identify one of the crucial elements of persuasion that Paul demonstrates: it is not simply about the what (e.g., specific content and logical reasoning), but even more so about the how (manner) and the why (goals), and how these goals require flexible, varied performances to suit disparate cultures and audiences ("become all things to all people," 1 Cor 9:19-27, esp. v. 22). Persuasion is not just about the rational *logos* (and using proper verbal techniques) but also about the character of the herald (*ēthos*) and the relational and emotional bonds (*pathos*) that are assumed or required to effect a desired outcome.

This framework helps us make sense of the culturally and relationally appropriate appeal *make my joy complete* (for Paul's joy as a motivational device, see also Phil 4:1, 10; cf. 2:16-18; 2 Cor 2:3; 7:4, 7, 9, 16; 1 Thess 2:19; 3:8-9). In many contemporary contexts, this sort of warrant strikes us as an inappropriately self-oriented incentive, especially in parenting: if you do the right thing, you will make *me* happy; and the implied flip side, your bad behavior makes *me* unhappy. In Paul's case, this sort of appeal shows his awareness that it is especially the relational and emotional bonds that bring them together and that can make his appeal effective, in contrast to mere logical argument. When Paul appeals to the Romans, the majority of whom he has never met, his letter contains mostly *logos* (verbal argument), with relatively less *pathos* and *ēthos* (though see Rom 8:26-39; 9:1-5; 11:1, 13-14; 15:30-33). Philippians is just the opposite, reminding us that the most effective persuasive techniques lie in the establishment of relational bonds, ultimately that of love. Moreover, what we see again is Paul's rhetorical flexibility (audience adaptation) that dynamically varies to suit the demands of circumstances and situation. Paul has no single, inflexible way to present the invitation and demand of the *good message of Messiah*, providing a model for varied, contextual discourse in our own settings.

Philippians 2:6-11

Tribute to Messiah: Self-Emptied Divinity and Exalted Slave

PREVIEW

We can imagine that the oral reader has paused, taking a breath before proceeding with what is the theological heart of the letter, around which everything else has meaning. What the listeners next hear is a densely packed tribute that declares Messiah as a paradigm of status divestment (for the sake of the other, 2:6-8) and asserts the ultimate redemptive effect of God's work in Messiah: the whole world will declare allegiance to Messiah's dominion (2:9-11). The passage follows a U-shaped plot: starting high, Messiah Jesus moves down, later to be raised to the heights and acclaimed by all beings of the whole world. Indeed, we come to the high point via the lowest point imaginable: a humiliating death on a cross (2:6-8). There are three distinct "actors" in the drama: (1) Messiah is the volitional agent of verses 6-8; (2) God is the ultimate supreme Being, who intervenes decisively (v. 9) and to whom everything ultimately returns (v. 11); and finally (3) all volitional beings of the cosmos ultimately declare their allegiance to Lord Jesus Messiah (vv. 10-11).

In terms of genre, this passage comes closest to what the Greeks would have called an encomium (a public tribute to a worthy citizen or national hero) and is quite unlike typical hymns extolling the acts or character of a god. Drawing on the biblical paradigm of divine

Wisdom, this encomium to Messiah directly counters themes from Roman imperial propaganda that extol the deeds, virtues, and benefits of Roman rulers.

OUTLINE

Humiliation, 2:6-8
- 2:6 A Divine Being Who Rejects Upward Striving
- 2:7-8 Two Stages of Messianic Humiliation
  - 2:7a–c A Divine Being Who Takes the Form of a Slave
  - 2:7d–8 A Human Being Who Lowers Himself to Death on a Cross

Exaltation, 2:9-11
- 2:9 God Responds to Hyperelevate Messiah
- 2:10-11 Goal: The Final Universal Acclaim of Messiah, to the Glory of God

EXPLANATORY NOTES

The Scholarly Discussion of 2:6-11

More ink has been spilled on Philippians 2:6-11 than almost any other text in Paul, focusing around the following key questions *[Critical Questions, p. 284]*. What is its genre? Is it poetry or prose? Hymn, statement of faith (confession), or tribute? Who composed it? Is Paul quoting or adapting an existing piece of liturgy, or did he compose it for this specific audience? If Paul is quoting a pre-Pauline hymn, what was its original form and stanza structure, and how did Paul modify it? What is the main conceptual framework that explains its terms and images? What is the main purpose of the passage: is it hortatory (ethical instruction), kerygmatic (proclaiming salvation in Christ), or some combination of the two? The conclusions of this commentary can be summarized at the outset. (1) This passage, while rhythmic and carefully lined, is not poetic in the manner of other hymnic songs in Paul's environment, nor does it display similarities to standard "hymns" to gods. Rather, it is closest in genre to an honorific tribute (encomium, panegyric) to a renowned public figure, military victor, or national hero. (2) Paul composed this tribute to suit the rhetorical agenda of this particular letter even as he undoubtedly drew from the tradition bequeathed to him and from his own christological reflection. (3) The tribute displays a deliberate structure and flow, though not neatly organized into "stanzas." (4) The primary conceptual framework for the Christology of the passage is Jewish theological reflection on the figure of divine Wisdom, even as allusions are made to the figure of the suffering servant. But most provocative are deliberate counter-resonances to Roman imperial propaganda. (5) The main purpose of this passage in its context is not specifically doctrinal, but hortatory (paradigmatic, explicitly ethical) and kerygmatic (proclamatory, condensing key elements of the foundational salvation story) so as to further ground the loyal allegiance of the readers-hearers to Lord Messiah Jesus. As an encomium, it is designed to "magnify Messiah" (Phil 1:20).

In the humiliation/incarnation drama of 2:6-8, Paul is not interested in precisely defining the "essential being" (ontology) of Christ as a divine or human being or in explaining how these might coalesce. Rather, using somewhat imprecise terms of incarnation (which was not a new idea in the Greco-Roman world), he primarily seeks to highlight the status issues that this particular incarnation drama involves: willing humiliation *for the sake of others*. The closest parallel in form and function is 2 Corinthians 8:9, where Paul also assumes an incarnational drama. For persuasive purposes, he puts it in terms of economic divestment: "You know the generosity of our Lord Jesus Messiah, that though he was rich, yet for your sakes he became poor, so that by his poverty you might become rich" (2 Cor 8:9 AT/NRSV). In Philippians 2:6-8, Paul does not explicitly say that Messiah acted in this particular way "for the sake of others," but the context of his argument (2:3-5) requires us to make this crucial assumption. As such it is the supreme model for human love for the other.

The Structure of the Tribute

The individual lines and the two main parts of this passage are easily identifiable (vv. 6-8, 9-11). Whether the lines can be grouped into "stanzas" is controversial (complicated by theories that Paul edited an already-existing hymn; see below). While verses 6-7c are often treated as a first stanza, followed by verses 7d-8, the interpretation taken here is that each of the main verbs of verses 6-8 (*he did not regard; but he emptied himself*; and *he lowered himself*) represent an integrated flow of thought: thus 2:6 presents Messiah's refusal to engage in seizing a higher status than he was originally given, followed by two steps in his humiliation: in his becoming human (2:7a-c) and in his life as a human (2:7b-8).

A word-for-word rendering of Paul's words yields the following translation:

Existing originally in the form [morphē] of God, (2:6a)
he did not regard being equal to God as a prize to be seized by force [harpagmon], (2:6b)

but he emptied himself, (2:7a)
taking the form [morphē] of a slave, (2:7b)
becoming in the likeness [homoiōma] of humans, (2:7c)

and being found in shape [schēma] as a human, (2:7d)
he lowered [tapeinoō] himself (2:8a)
becoming obedient all the way to death— (2:8b)
even death of a cross. (2:8c)

Therefore indeed God hyperelevated [hyperypsoō] him
and gave him the name that is above [hyper] every name, (2:9)

so that at the name of Jesus
every knee will bend, of beings in heaven and on earth and under the earth, (2:10)
and every tongue will acclaim [swear allegiance to] Lord Jesus Messiah,
to the glory of God the Father. (2:11)

Humiliation 2:6-8

Part 1 of the tribute focuses on Messiah's own mind-set and corresponding conduct in a way that closely parallels the exhortation that Paul has just offered in 2:3-4, thus providing the direct model for that appeal (2:5). The skeletal structure of the narrative is framed as a drama of incarnation and then martyrdom:

originally existing in the form of God . . .
coming to be in the likeness of humans . . .
being found in shape as a human . . .
becoming obedient all the way to death.

But the heart of the drama pertains to the issue of striving for or relinquishing status, with constant images of high and low. This theme, in its correspondence with the immediately preceding exhortation, is best seen schematically:

(2:3-4) What not to do:	What to do instead:
• do nothing from selfish ambition/rivalrous striving or empty glory • do not look out for your own interests	• in low-mindedness regard others as higher in rank than yourselves • look out [only] for the interests of others
(2:6-8) What Christ did not do:	**What Christ chose to do instead:** [all for the sake of others]
• originally endowed with the highest category of status, he did not forcibly strive to go even higher, to the very top of his rank	• he relinquished all power and assets, going all the way to the bottom *Stage 1:* as a divine being, he emptied himself of his supremely high original status, taking the form of a slave *Stage 2:* as a human being, he lowered himself [in service to others], becoming obedient all the way to the most humiliating death possible, on a Roman cross

We should not miss the point that one of most significant features of Messiah's divestment was giving up immortality shared with divine beings. Not only does Christ meet the eventual inevitability of death when he takes on human form; he also meets a premature death as a martyr, refusing to waver in the very face of death.

A Divine Being Who Rejects Upward Striving

Messiah's career begins with his original status as a divine being: *existing originally in the form of God*. The words *existing originally* translate a verb (*hyparchō*) that was regularly used as a synonym for the verb "to be." But this verb could also have the more specific sense of existing originally or coming into existence, or making a beginning. The question of how (or whether) Messiah "comes into being" as the "firstborn of all creation" (Col 1:15; cf. Prov 8:22) does not concern Paul here.

What it means to "originally exist" *in the form of God* specifically is not defined. In this brief passage Paul's use of the Greek term *morphē* can slide between emphasizing status qualities (*form of a slave*) to more substantive characteristics (*form of God*). Interpreters who seek to align the phrase *form of God* with the doctrine of Nicaea (325 CE), where Jesus as Christ was declared to be of "the same essential substance" of the Father (see TLC, "Philippians 2:6-11 in Christian Creeds"), suppose that this phrase refers to God's "characteristic property" or "essential aspect" and thus translate it *in very nature God* (NIV). On the other hand, if this text expresses a second-Adam narrative (with an adoptionist Christology), then *form* could be understood as the "image" of God (Gen 1:27). More likely, however, Messiah is here cast in the figure of divine Wisdom, which assumes the closest of essences, qualities, and status to that of God the Father himself, though he is not absolutely equated with God. Elsewhere Paul conflates the second-Adam motif of the "image of God" and the notion of divine Wisdom as "firstborn of creation" (Col 1:15) *[Critical Questions, p. 284]*.

The term *form* here is best understand as a sphere, structure, or status of existence. The text makes the strongest link possible with the very being and stuff of God without saying precisely that Messiah was God. Elsewhere Paul makes the closest of linkages between Messiah the Son and God the Father, but never in a way that comprises the distinct and unique deity of God (thus even Phil 2:11; e.g., 1 Cor 8:6; 11:3; 15:24-28). Though *in the form of God*, the Son remains subordinate to the Father in the divine economy. The emphasis here is on Messiah as having shared the status, rights, and privileges as a divine being *in the form of God*. As the next clauses make clear, Messiah, though preexisting *in the form of God*, has the status of a subordinate viceroy who refused to usurp or seize by force what was not his, namely, full equality with God.

The natural sense of Paul's next words is that Messiah as viceroy refused to greedily and forcibly seek more power and status than he already had. He did not regard the next step of advancement—that of achieving complete equality with God the Father—as *a prize to be seized by force* (*harpagmon*). Most English translations try to align Paul's words with later trinitarian doctrine, stumbling over the crucial word *harpagmon* *[Harpagmos, p. 293]*. Assuming that Christ, as a member of the Godhead, could not actually strive any higher, the word is taken to mean either something to be retained without letting go (NIV 1984: *something to be grasped*), or something already possessed from which further gain accrues (NRSV: *something to be exploited*; NIV 2011: *something to be used to his advantage*). This latter reading is perhaps the prevailing interpretation in modern scholarship.

In the present context, however, the most natural meaning of Paul's words is that Messiah refused to *regard equality with God as a prize to be seized by force*. The Greek word *harpagmon* is consistently used in Paul's world either for an "act of snatching or seizing" what one does not have or, in the passive sense, for "what is grasped," either negatively as "what is stolen" (prey, plunder, booty) or positively as "prize or gain" *[Harpagmos, p. 293]*. The emphatic contrast between upward striving and willing humiliation in the immediate context (2:3), which the messianic story is designed to exemplify (2:5-8), confirms this interpretation. Paul's subordinationist Christology is also consistent with this reading (1 Cor 8:6; 11:3; 15:24-28). Christ is always God's right-hand agent as the "Son," never absolutely equated with the one Father and Creator of all things (see also EN on 2:11). In the end, the interpretation offered here is not that different from the prevailing view (NRSV: *something to be exploited*): both highlight what might be pursued through some exercise of greed and self-advancement.

What might Messiah have wished to greedily seize (or exploit)? Paul dramatically identifies it as the desire *to be equal to God* (*to einai isa theō*). The original listeners to the letter would have immediately made connections that we modern readers cannot naturally make. This terminology derives not from Paul's biblical-Judean heritage but from his Greco-Roman environment. Phraseology like this is found from the earliest extant Greek literature, beginning with Homer's description of the heroes as "equal to God" (e.g., *Iliad* 2.565), to later designations of great philosophers honored in the same way (LSJ). Most important, in the centuries leading to Paul's time, the language of "honors equal to the gods" was current for the quest by the elite in Greco-Roman societies for all sorts of civic and political-religious honors. Moreover, great military leaders (e.g., Alexander the Great) or powerful Roman military conquerors in the late Republic period were similarly granted "honors equal to the gods" as a way for elites in conquered cities to nurture patronage relationships of benefaction. The late second-century-BCE Jewish writing 2 Maccabees (9:12) illustrates this. The Seleucid (Syrian) overlord of Judea, Antiochus IV, self-nicknamed Epiphanes ([the divine] manifest), repents on his deathbed as he writhes from an agonizing illness: "It is right [for a reign/king] to be subject to God; a mortal [king] should not think that he is equal to God" (cf. Acts 12:21-23). Most important, during the early Roman imperial period in which Paul lived, this language of being "equal to the gods" became regularly used for honors granted to the divine or divinized Roman emperors *[Roman Imperial Cult, p. 307; Roman Imperial Propaganda, p. 312]*.

Paul's hearers in Philippi, this proud outpost of the Roman regime, could hardly have missed the counterresonance. Messiah refused to grasp at or usurp the highest honor available to any human or heavenly being. Quite by contrast, the emperors of Rome were regularly usurping what was not theirs to seize, including divine honors for themselves, mere mortals. The status of being "equal to God" was in effect the highest possible honor to which any being could aspire. But instead of pursuing that status and displaying *rivalrous striving* and *empty glory* (2:3), Messiah embraced the lowest possible honor and status in the universe, *the form of a slave.* The emperor could claim "equal-to-God" honors on the basis of valor and brutality in world conquest, hailed as a demonstration of his virtuous clemency and fidelity. But God's Messiah was elevated to the highest of honors (2:9-11) only and ironically through the path of the lowest possible humiliation that the Romans could produce—crucifixion—thereby displaying his own obedient fidelity to his Father. This is a bold theopolitical assertion.

A Divine Being Who Takes the Form of a Slave 2:7a-c

So instead of violently seizing what was not his to grasp, Messiah *emptied himself* (NRSV; NIV: *made himself nothing*). He relinquished all status, power, rank, and honor, allowing these assets to be "rendered useless" (a synonym for "emptying" in Rom 4:14 AT). The stress is on his own action of self-emptying: quite carefully the text avoids saying that he "allowed himself to be emptied" or that "he was emptied." In the present context, the word for emptying is used in contrast to the term for boasting (Phil 2:16). It implies emptying oneself of "glory/renown/status" (cf. 2:3). When a legitimate "boast" is undermined, it is said to be "emptied" (1 Cor 9:15; 2 Cor 9:3).

A Human Being Who Lowers Himself to Death on a Cross 2:7d-8

Paul now moves to a second stage in Messiah's downward path. The text begins with a recapitulation of the results of the first stage, the new condition in which Messiah finds himself: *and being found in shape [schēma] as a human.* The word *schēma* is roughly synonymous with the word used previously for *form* (*morphē*, Phil 2:6-7), but often emphasizes outward form or visible shape.

Later in this letter the imagery of form resonates in a significant way, in 3:10 (partnership in Messiah's suffering as con*form*ity to his death) and 3:21 (trans*form*ing bodies of lowliness into con*form*ity to the body of Messiah's glory), two critical texts that elaborate on the messianic drama in 2:6-11. The latter text, in effect, reverses the dramatic imagery narrated in 2:6-8 in alignment with the exaltation themes of 2:9-11. Interestingly, just as Paul avoids a direct equivalence of Messiah and God, so also he avoids the simple equivalence of Messiah and rest of humanity (using the imagistic references of *likeness* and *form*).

As in the previous stage, Paul's interest is not with articulating any precise ontological condition (pertaining to "being")—here the relationship between Messiah and humanity—but in narrating his volitional, downward behavior. Paul proclaims that as a human being, Messiah *lowered himself*, highlighting again, by the use of the reflexive *himself*, that Messiah was the actor. It was not that he *was* lowered or humiliated (cf. 2 Cor 12:21, where God lowered or humbled Paul). The text recalls the notion of lowering (low-mindedness) introduced in 2:3. Paul focuses on issues of status. His words have nothing to do with absorbing oneself with downward-spiraling feelings of inadequacy, nothingness, or self-hate. The drama set before the listeners-readers is not merely an attitudinal, inner-looking story. Rather, it is an outwardly behavioral, social, political, and indeed metaphysical-cosmic drama of divestment from position, status, and honor.

Messiah's self-lowering is identified in particular as becoming *obedient all the way to death*. The NIV translates the phrase more ambiguously as *obedient to death*, implying that the obedience of Messiah consisted primarily or exclusively in his willingness to die (apparently to highlight an atonement theme). But the preposition used here (*mechri*) indicates extent of degree or measure (thus, *even unto*)—that is, Messiah was obedient *to the extremity of death*, or as the TEV puts it, *He walked the path of obedience all the way to death*. Paul's understanding of Messiah's career is not simply one of "cradle to cross," even if he does not elaborate here on Messiah's earthly life of obedience. Epaphroditus later becomes the exemplar of this virtue of service to the point of death in that he was so committed to serve *the work of Messiah* that he came near *to the extent of death* (*mechri thanatou*, 2:30), repeating the phrase of 2:8.

Messiah's obedience should not be understood as the slavish virtue regularly expected of slaves, who have a limited scope of self-determination. Rather, *obedience* is here, as elsewhere in Paul, an aspect of "loyalty-faith" (see EN on 1:25-26). Indeed, Paul coordinates obedience and loyalty-faith in Romans 1:5 and 16:26. He appears to use the imagery of "obedience" synonymously with that of "trusting/being loyal/believing" (Rom 10:16; cf. 15:18; 2 Thess 1:8). A crucial text in Romans 5:19 affirms the obedience of Messiah in parallel with Messiah's "act of justice or righteousness" (*dikaiōma*, 5:18) as an explication of Messiah's loyalty-faith (*pistis Christou*, 3:22, 25, 26; Phil 3:9). Messiah's obedience here is thus a display of his fundamental, self-willing, and self-determined loyalty to and dependence upon God. In the present context, it signals especially his persistence under trial (see 2:12; Oakes 2001: 166).

In this tribute the cross is not explicitly correlated with its saving significance or with its motivation for the sake of others. Paul can do that elsewhere (e.g., Gal 1:4; 1 Cor 1:17-18; Col 1:20). The point here, rather, is to show what the crucifixion meant *for him*. That is, it was the outcome of his life of obedient loyalty. Still, in light of the exhortation in Philippians 2:2-4, which this encomium is meant to support, we can surmise that Paul expects his readers to see Messiah's *obedient loyalty all the way to death* as the supreme example of love (2:1-2; cf. Rom 5:5-8) and of "regard for the other" (2:4; cf. Rom 15:1-3; 2 Cor 8:9). In a similar way, Messiah's active work to bring about universal allegiance is only implied in Philippians 2:10-11, though made explicit later, in 3:20-21.

Grammatically, the next words, *even death on a cross*, leap out, seeming to break the pattern of the rhythmically structured prose. We have come shockingly to the nadir (absolute bottom), which is ironically the occasion for the climax to be realized. For Paul's immediate concerns, identifying Messiah's form of death as crucifixion is entirely critical. The remark appallingly disrupts the narrative, just as the cross fundamentally disrupts the grand scheme of things (cf. Gal 5:11; 6:14). Many scholars who are inclined to consider 2:6-11 as a pre-Pauline hymn suppose that this phrase was inserted by Paul and breaks the scheme of the hymn he is quoting.

Paul stresses the disruptive dynamic of the cross for two reasons. First, it indicates the most humiliating (not to mention painful) death possible, thus putting Messiah's loss of status to the extreme. Second, it identifies the agent of death precisely as that of the Roman regime. Crucifixion, simply put, is the key instrument of Roman imperial terror, carried out publicly both as a deterrent and as a visible humiliation of a conquered people. The placarding of Jesus on the cross as "King of the Judeans" (Luke 23:38; John 19:19), for instance, was designed to shame the Judean people as a whole. Execution on a cross was the preferred mode of punishment against the lower classes, those without citizenship, slaves, murderers, and especially unruly insurgents (freedom fighters) in the conquered nations. These two issues will be addressed in the next part of the tribute (2:9-11): (1) the most humiliating of deaths is not outside of

God's power to rescue (cf. 3:10-11, 20-21); and (2) all human institutions of sovereignty, including Roman imperial authority, will ultimately have to acknowledge and submit to the supreme authority of Lord Jesus Messiah (cf. 3:20-21).

God Responds to Hyperelevate Messiah 2:9

Two small, but emphatic transitional words, *dio kai*, provide the hinge to this compressed messianic epic. They are better translated as *therefore indeed*, rather than the softer *therefore also* (NRSV) or just *therefore* (NIV). We have both a scene change and a change in protagonist. Now it is *God* who steps up to the task, described by two parallel clauses that together make a single point: *God highly exalted him, and gave him the name that is above every name. Highly exalted* translates a word found only here in the NT, literally rendered as *hyperelevated* (*hyperhypsoō*). It is the same kind of unique neologism (new-word construction) as found in Romans 8:37, "We hyperconquer [*hypernikaō*, or "more than conquer"] through the one who loved us" (AT). The emphasis in Philippians 2:9 is on excess, an elevation above to the highest possible degree, in direct contrast to the lowest point possible described a moment earlier, humiliation through crucifixion.

What is assumed here is that Messiah has been exalted "to the right hand" (e.g., Rom 8:34; Col 3:1) through God's act of raising Jesus from the dead (Phil 3:10). Throughout his letters, Paul consistently puts the stress on God as raising Jesus, not on Jesus rising on his own (for numerous references to resurrection, see Dunn: 174–77, 235–40). Here the resurrection is presented as an enthronement, as in other texts where Paul refers to God as raising Messiah from the realm of the dead (Rom 1:3-4; 8:34, using Ps 110:1; cf. Eph 1:20-22; Col 3:1; Acts 2:24-25, 32-33, using Ps 110:1; Acts 5:31; 13:13, using Ps 2:7).

The next phrase, *and gave him the name that is above [hyper] every name*, confirms that what we have here is a picture of accession to rule, investiture, or enthronement. Paul again emphasizes the status shift by highlighting the surpassing feature of the name that Messiah receives. God exalts by naming, just as elite in the Roman provinces considered their granting of honors to the emperor a contribution to his divinization. When Caesar Augustus rehearsed his own accomplishments in Roman propaganda, he emphasized the titles and names by which he was honored by the Roman Senate. His great deeds and achievements for the world's benefit were inscribed in bronze tablets in front of his mausoleum, with copies displayed throughout the empire in sacred precincts. These were still plain to see in Paul's day and are now being recovered through archaeology *[Roman Imperial Cult, p. 307; Roman Imperial Propaganda, p. 312]*.

But what is *the name that is above every name*? The beginning of the next phrase (*so that at the name of Jesus*) seems to point to the name *Jesus*, the Greek form of the Hebrew *Yeshua*, an adaptation of *Yehoshua* (Joshua), meaning "Savior" (cf. Phil 3:20; see Matt 1:21 for the play on *Yeshua* and "saving"). The point would be that God made this name in the person of Jesus to be supreme. Alternatively, some propose that Messiah is now given the name *Lord*, reserved in Israel's Scriptures for God alone. Jesus would thus now be receiving an *equality with God* (Phil 2:6). This is perhaps suggested in the way the next verse adapts the language of Isaiah 45:23, where the one and only God says, "To me every knee will bend and every tongue will swear" (Yoder Neufeld 2007: 321). In other words, a scriptural citation about the worthiness of God alone (cf. Rom 14:11) is here applied to the worthiness of God's Messiah. God, via the resurrection, has invested Christ with the name or title that till now has been reserved for God alone (cf. Rom 1:3-4, where the investiture/installation focuses on the title "Son of God"). But since there are indeed acclamations to "many lords" (1 Cor 8:4-6) and especially to "Lord Caesar" in the environment of Paul and his readers, the name or title *Lord* in itself is not above every name.

Yet it is not actually something inherent in a name that makes it the highest. The point is that what makes this name higher than all others is the way it is invoked, by virtue of the way God invests it with power (cf. Rom 1:3-4). The word *name* here thus emphasizes its sense as fame and reputation, expressing the inherent character and social position of the bearer (cf. "Hallowed be your name," Matt 6:9). And so *the name that is above very name* is perhaps best understood as the full name-title, the acclamation *Lord Messiah Jesus* that immediately follows. This full threefold name-title of Jesus is reserved in the letter to the Philippians for crucial moments: at the outset (1:2); here at 2:11; at 3:20-21, which extends the proclamation of 2:9-11; and at the conclusion (4:23). (See TBC on 1:1-2, "*Christos* (Messiah).")

Philippian auditors would immediately have sensed a counter-resonance with the apotheosis (divinization) liturgies of the Roman Empire (Wright 2000; Heen; Hellerman). Since the death of Julius Caesar, deceased Roman rulers were typically proclaimed as a *divus* (divine being), enjoying elevated status and immortal life with the gods. Just a year earlier (in 54 CE), the apotheosis of Claudius (ruled 41–54 CE) was formally proclaimed by the Roman Senate and celebrated throughout the empire. Festivities in his honor were no doubt also held in imperial temples in Philippi. Paul's first listeners surely understand his declaration about Messiah as directly challenging the claims of the emperor's apotheosis in Roman imperial liturgies.

Goal: The Final Universal Acclaim of Messiah, to the Glory of God 2:10-11

Paul now moves the messianic epic into the future, drawing from the words of Isaiah 45:22-23:

> Turn to me and be saved, all the ends of the earth! For I am God, and there is no other. By myself I have sworn, from my mouth has gone forth in righteousness a word that shall not return: "To me every knee shall bow, every tongue shall swear."

Philippians 2:10-11 implies Messiah's achievement in bringing the whole world into his dominion (cf. Phil 3:20-21; 1 Cor 15:24-28; Rom 11:32; 15:12). But what is explicitly narrated is the universal acclamation that results from that work. Paul portrays the grandest possible public liturgy of royal acclamation: all beings of the universe act as the respondents. Lord Messiah Jesus has come to fully reign throughout the world and is now put on public display in formal ceremony. To dramatize the ritual, Paul focuses on *knees bending* and *tongues confessing*. Just as today, formal acts of declaring loyalty to a sovereign are typically both verbal and kinetic (e.g., stand and remove headgear for the singing of a national anthem). Paul uses a standard purpose clause that implies no doubt about the prospect of all knees bending and all tongues confessing, nor does it suggest an "ought." Thus the translation *will* (NET, NASB, CEV, TEV) gives the sense better than *might* (CEB) or *should* (KJV, NRSV, NIV).

All beings in the cosmos will do ritual obeisance *at the name of Jesus* and will acclaim (i.e., make an oath of allegiance to) the name *Lord Jesus Messiah*. The word that is usually translated *confess* (*homologeō*) indicates more than mentally agreeing with a statement. Much more, the word has the sense of swearing, promising, or binding oneself in oath, as in a treaty (Agamben 2011; Zerbe 2012: 40–41). The close correlation of *every knee bending* and *every tongue acclaiming*—two aspects of one action—confirms that *confessing* is tantamount to declaring loyalty or making a pledge of allegiance. For this reason, it is better to take the Greek words *Kyrios Iēsous Christos* as the chanted acclamation *Lord Jesus Messiah!* (cf. 1:2; 3:20;

4:23) instead of a predicative assertion, thus here meaning *Jesus Messiah is Lord* (similarly in Rom 10:9-10).

The implied conquest resulting in the acclamation is absolute and total. No zone of resistance will be found anywhere in the universe. The action of *every knee* and *every tongue* is on the part *of beings in heaven and on earth and under the earth*. By the time of Paul, many educated urban dwellers understood the world to be a sphere, a view popularized by the writings of Plato (*Timaeus* 33; *Phaedo* 108–110; *Republic* 616–617). By 240 BCE, Eratosthenes had calculated the earth's circumference to within 5 percent of what is now known. Accordingly, since the time of Augustus, Rome had regularly minted coins showing an emperor or one of the Roman deities with a foot raised over the globe (a sphere), indicating world conquest and dominion. Paul, however, employs the more archaic and probably more commonly accepted imagery of the entire cosmos as the three-storied universe to indicate the universal scope of Messiah's dominion. This framework thus explicitly includes all human beings: the living (on the earth), the deceased (under the earth), and any divinized humans (the few who enjoy immortal, heavenly existence with the gods). It also includes the heavenly (*ouranian*, in the sky) deities, the below-earth (chthonian) deities, and the earthly spirits (*daimōnia*) of the Greco-Roman worldview. (Paul himself denies the actual reality of these so-called divine beings of popular belief, but he accommodates to this understanding; see 1 Cor 8:4-7. For the theme of Messiah's sovereignty over the whole created order, human and nonhuman, see also Rom 8:31-39; 1 Cor 15:24-28; cf. Eph 1:10, 20-22; cf. Pss 148, 150.) Later in Philippians, Paul uses the abstract term *all things* to designate the entire universe that Messiah will *subject to himself* (3:20-21). In effect, the whole cosmos now lowers itself in obeisance to the exalted slave: the humbled one has been exalted, and the currently exalted rulers (including Rome) will be humbled (see TBC below).

Dramatically compressing the salvation epic, Paul does not elaborate on possible finer details of the picture. For instance, he does not precisely specify (1) how the victory that would result in this universal acclamation will be achieved, or (2) whether those who bend and confess are truly yielding by choice or are somewhat unwillingly constrained to acknowledge supreme honors to Messiah. For contemporary theological reflection on Paul, this text needs to be considered in connection with all his references to Christ's final victory. Paul's language is deeply paradoxical: some texts use the language of rule through conquest and world domination (as here).

Other texts use the language of world reconciliation, presumably by the invitational and transforming power of God's persistent mercy and love (see EN on 3:20-21; TBC on 3:18–4:1, "Messiah's Final Victory").

All this celebration is ultimately *to the glory of God the Father*. Messiah gives everything back to God. The final words of this tribute are not an afterthought. Paul's fundamental monotheism is intact: the messianic drama begins with God, is hinged by God's decisive action, and ends with God (cf. Phil 1:11; 4:20; Rom 11:36). In a similar way, Paul in 1 Corinthians claims that

> the final goal is achieved when Messiah delivers the kingdom to God the Father after neutralizing every rule and every authority and every power. . . . Once the whole world has been subjected to Messiah, then the Son himself will be subjected to the One who put the whole world under him, so that God will be all in all. (1 Cor 15:24, 28 AT)

Summary Reflections

1. In such a short span in Philippians 2:6-11, we have the most complete overview of the career of Messiah Jesus in the writings of Paul (see TBC below, "Messiah's Epic Career"). Yet many details remain ambiguous, and many details or aspects are left out, based on comparison with declarations elsewhere in Paul's writings. For instance, there is no discussion of the restoring benefits of the cross and resurrection (e.g., release from sins; gift of righteousness/justice; cf. Rom 3:21-26; 4:24-25). Only later does Paul specifically highlight the benefits of God's exaltation of Jesus to his final universal dominion (3:11, 20-21). Moreover, there is no discussion of how this drama fulfills God's promises in Scripture (e.g., Rom 1:2-5; 3:1-4, 21-31; 4:1-25; 15:7-13; 1 Cor 15:3-4). There is no explicit correlation of this drama with the conquest of Messiah over cosmic powers (Rom 8:31-39; 1 Cor 15; Col 1–2) or any explication of the role of Messiah in the creation of the universe (1 Cor 8:6; Col 1). There is no explanation as to how and when the universal dominion of Messiah will be realized (cf. Rom 11:25-32; 1 Cor 15:24-28). There is no emphasis on how God's victory delivers Messiah's people from the "wrath to come" (1 Thess 1:10 KJV; 5:9-10).

While elements of the epic story encapsulated in Philippians 2:6-11 can be found scattered throughout Paul's writings, the key features of the messianic career articulated here are closely tied, verbally and thematically, to the rest of the letter to the Philippians. Each element included in this dramatic rehearsal is relevant for the present audience and situation. All of this suggests, along with other evidence, that this declarative tribute (encomium, panegyric) was designed and composed for this particular letter, even if elements were taken from typical formulaic statements of Paul or traditions of the early church more generally. Paul's declarations of the messianic drama elsewhere appear specially designed for the rhetoric and audience at hand, and the same situation appears to be the case here.

2. The counterresonances with themes from Roman imperial claims are so specific that it is appropriate to speak of this messianic proclamation as being a parody of "the gospel of Augustus." This is not to say that the pervasive imperial-theological propaganda is the only target, framework of inspiration, or point of counterresonance. Rather, what we have is a narration of the messianic drama on its own inner logic and consistency. In this case, it unmasks Roman imperial claims as the most obvious counterexample, the actual parody of Messiah's reality. Elements of a Wisdom Christology, a second-Adam Christology, or suffering-servant Christology are deeper in the background. In the foreground of this messianic declaration is a pointed exposé of Roman imperial rule and ideology. Caesar is a mere human pretender whose desire is to grasp honors equal to the gods, especially through violent military conquest (*harpagmon*, a prize seized by force). Messiah, instead, is truly worthy of divine honors, not by original status but by taking the path of weakness and lowliness. The salvation story of Lord Messiah Jesus has overtaken and trumped the salvation story of the Roman regime. It is not that some mere imperial antagonism or resentment provides the reflex point for the emergence of the countering *good tidings of Messiah*. Nevertheless the Roman Empire is implicated here, confirmed by the rest of the coded language in Philippians, as a chief example of a world in bondage to the powers of Death and Sin *[Critical Questions, p. 284]*.

3. This messianic drama is first and foremost designed as a model for a mind-set and its associated conduct. That is, it grounds a call to imitation (2:5). Hearers-readers are thus invited to take their own place in the epic story. That this is the meaning becomes apparent by the exhortation that immediately follows: *Therefore . . . work out your own deliverance/salvation* (2:12). The whole drama—not just the particulars of downward modeling (2:3-4, 6-8)—are crucial as the grounding point of all conduct appropriate to messianic citizenship, whether internal in the assembly (1:27-28; 2:1-4, 14; 4:2-3) or external in relation to outsiders and adversaries (1:27-30; 2:15-16; 4:1, 5). Thus Paul's listeners are:

- assured of their own resurrection to triumph and exaltation with honors (3:11, 13-14, 20-21; cf. 2:15), despite opposition from the Roman imperial authorities or the Rome-dominated society around them;

- assured of the endless supply of God's mercy to comfort, riches to supply, and power to deliver—both now and ultimately (1:28; 2:1, 13, 27; 4:13, 19-20);

- assured that their messianic citizenship trumps any other claim to loyalty and identity, or any pursuit of the benefits of citizenship (1:27), especially that of status-seeking, consumerist, and licentious Roman citizenship (2:15-16; 3:2, 18-21).

- invited to make their own oath of allegiance (1:27-28), which in practical terms means refusing to pursue the great advantages and privileges of Roman citizenship, divesting themselves of Roman citizenship, or refusing to participate in the civic/imperial celebrations in which oaths of allegiances are made to the emperor, empire, and the gods of Rome;

- invited to persist in the "work of Messiah" (2:12-18; 4:1-3);

- invited to identify with Messiah's suffering (3:10), becoming faithful themselves even to the point of death (1:20-24; 2:27);

- invited to refuse the temptation to "selfish ambition" and "empty glory" (2:3; 3:5-17, 18-19);

- invited to give further evidence of divestment from earthly security (3:1; 4:6, 10-18) by resting on the riches of God's endless supply and the security of God's victory (3:1; 4:7, 19-20);

- invited to be blind to social rank, especially any ranking within the messianic assembly, and to maintain communal solidarity within the struggle (1:27-28; 2:2-4; 4:2-3, 5); and

- invited to respond joyfully to the certainty and security of deliverance in Messiah.

We should assume that this text will be heard differently by different readers. In it the poor and suffering will hear hopes of vindication. The rich and the powerful, even within the congregation, may hear it as a challenge to their own status and pattern of life. In it some will hear the political implications of Messiah's universal rule and its challenge of Roman citizenship values (de Vos), while others will hear the socioeconomic inversion that takes place through Messiah (Oakes 2001).

Both parts of this tribute are decisive. As Paul will make clear later, conformity to Messiah's death is the path of conformity to Messiah's resurrection, a resurrection activated by the same power that will ultimately transform the whole cosmos under subjection to Messiah (3:10-11, 21). God's power is always an embrace of the marginal victim, always manifest *through* weakness (1 Cor 1:26-29; 2 Cor 11–13) and *for* the weak (Rom 5). Messianic victory and world dominion ironically occur through humiliation and emptying. This is the heart and essence of the gospel, the good news, the *good message of Messiah*. God's embrace of the humiliated, crucified Messiah—and by extension those who are suffering in Philippi—is what turns the world upside down. Without the downward paradigm, the salvation story is empty. Without the salvation story, the downward paradigm has no purpose or power and degenerates to masochism.

Around this messianic career, then, everything in the letter hangs. Indeed, the further exemplary stories and models of Paul (1:12-26, 30; 2:17-18, 30; 3:4-14; 4:10-13), of Timothy (2:19-24), and of Epaphroditus (2:25-30; 4:18) become a sort of midway point between the story of Messiah and the hearers-readers' own story.

THE TEXT IN BIBLICAL CONTEXT

Take Up Your Cross and Follow Me

The sequence of words from Philippians 2:5-8 can be encapsulated by the call of Jesus: "If any want to become my followers, let them deny themselves and take up their cross and follow me" (Mark 8:34). In its original context, this involved a call to be prepared even for martyrdom in the cause of the kingdom. Cross-shaped existence in Messiah ("cruciformity," Gorman 2001), however, can take more than one profile, and the gospel of Luke appropriately adjusts the call with the small word *daily* ("take up their cross *daily*," Luke 9:23). This slight addition makes it clear that this appeal must be wrestled with in everyday life, even in the small things of life, not just in the big things.

The Biblical Pattern of Humiliation/Exaltation

The pattern of humiliation as a prelude to exaltation (Phil 2:6-11; 3:4-11, 10-11, 21) and the reverse move from exaltation to humiliation (3:19) are themes that run throughout Scripture. The NT writers were especially inspired by this theme in the Hebrew Scriptures. There we find these themes in the Prophets (e.g., Isa 52:13–53:12; Ezek 17:24), wisdom writings (Job 22:29), and the Psalms (e.g., 37:9-15). Exaltation and humiliation are closely correlated. In nearly every use of the verb "to elevate/exalt" in the NT, it relates to a corresponding lowering/humiliation (Matt 11:23 // Luke 10:15; Matt 23:12 // Luke 14:11; Luke 1:52; 18:14; 1 Pet 5:6; James 1:9-10). In the Gospels, especially Luke, this upside-down theme is associated with the message of God's favoritism toward the poor (4:16-30; 6:20-23; 7:18-23; 14:12-14, 15-24) and the proclamations of social reversals that accompany God's reign (e.g., 1:52-53; 6:20-26; 13:30; 14:11 // Matt 23:12; Luke 16:19-26; 18:14; 22:24-27). Elsewhere in Paul, the reversal themes can be found in various forms and contexts, whether pertaining to Paul, Messiah, or God's people (Rom 15:1-7; 1 Cor 1:26-31; 4:10; 10:24–11:1; 2 Cor 4:7-12; 6:10; 8:9; 11:17–12:10; Gal 1:4). A striking text in Paul appears in 2 Corinthians 11:7, "abasing/lowering myself in order that you might be elevated/exalted" (AT). Paul uses verbs for *elevating* and *lowering* that are cognate to those in Philippians 2:8-9, as he ironically challenges the status-conscious Corinthians. The high-low theme also appears significantly in the general epistles, where it applies to situations of social disparity and serves to encourage those in distress (1 Pet 5:5, 10; James 1:9-12; 4:6-10).

Christological Formulas in Paul's Letters

Christological affirmations, acclamations, or declarations can be found throughout Paul's letters (e.g., Rom 1:3-4; 3:22-26; 4:25; 5:6-11; 8:3-4, 31-35; 10:9-10; 15:1-3; 1 Cor 8:6; 15:3-4, 23-28; 2 Cor 4:5; 5:14-15; 8:9; Gal 1:4; 4:4-5; Phil 2:6-11; 3:20-21; Col 1:15-20; 1 Thess 1:10; 5:9-10). They resist easy categorizing. Sometimes they appear quite stereotyped and formulaic, and sometimes they seem to be articulated ad hoc, at the moment. All appear designed or suited for Paul's persuasive or instructional aims. Sometimes they are expansive and rhythmic (as in Phil 2:6-11) and sometimes quite brief. Sometimes the emphasis is on clarifying Messiah's career, status, and character (his person), and sometimes the emphasis is on the saving effects and benefits of his life and career (his work). Sometimes the stress is on Messiah's paradigmatic significance for behavior and disposition (as model). Sometimes Messiah is the key volitional actor (in his incarnation, life, and death; e.g., he "gave himself," and the text speaks of his obedience and fidelity), and sometimes Messiah is the one acted upon (in his life, death and resurrection; e.g., he is sent, handed over, crucified, raised).

Many expansive and formulaic passages seem to reflect actual verbal practices of the assemblies, whether (kerygmatic) patterns of proclamation, didactic (instructional) traditions, or liturgical expressions (doxologies, blessings, grace-wishes, etc.). Paul himself refers to didactic, instructional traditions (e.g., 1 Cor 11:23; 15:1-4), to practices of creedal affirmation and oath declaration (Rom 10:9-10; Phil 2:10-11), and to spoken acclamations in liturgy (1 Cor 12:3; Rom 8:15-16; Gal 4:6). But to confidently call these ad hoc formulations "creeds," "confessions," or "hymns" assumes finalized forms and modern categories not always appropriate to them (cf. Brucker).

Messiah's Epic Career in Paul's Letters

From the various christological references found in Paul's writings, the following main lines of Messiah's epic career can be discerned.

1. *Preexistence.* Paul speaks only rarely and obliquely of the preexistence of Messiah, and in some places he seems to imply an adoptionist Christology (Rom 1:3-4). He affirms his original existence *in the form of God* (Phil 2:6), his prior status as "firstborn of creation" (Col 1:15; cf. Rom 8:29, where the reference to him as firstborn refers to his saving role as second/new Adam). Paul also affirms his role as the agent of creation and thus the sustaining reality that pervades all creation (1 Cor 8:6; Col 1:15; based on the scriptural and developing Jewish reflections on divine Wisdom [*sophia*] and word-rationality [*logos*]).

2. *Incarnation.* Paul does not use the language of "the Word becoming flesh" (cf. John 1:1-14). Paul does refer to Jesus having been "sent" by God (Rom 8:3, 32; Gal 4:4) and his *becoming in the likeness of humans* and *being found as a human* (Phil 2:7; cf. Rom 8:3). At the same time, Paul also refers to his human genealogy from Israel (Rom 9:5; 1 Thess 2:14-15), being "born of a woman" (Gal 4:4), and his "coming into being from the seed of David according to the flesh" (Rom 1:3).

3. *Earthly Life and Ministry.* Though Paul says next to nothing about this in his letters (see TBC below, "Paul and the Earthly Life of Jesus"), he refers generally to Jesus' obedience (especially but not exclusively to his obedience in death; Phil 2:8; Rom 5:19), his righteousness (Rom 5:18), his generosity (2 Cor 8:9), and his fidelity

(Rom 3:22, 26; Phil 3:9; Gal 2:20), especially but not exclusively citing his path to the cross. He also refers to his teaching (1 Cor 7:10-11), his final supper with his disciples (1 Cor 11:23-26), his commitment to inclusive welcome (Rom 15:1-3; presumably in both life and in death), and his becoming poor for the sake of others (2 Cor 8:9).

4. *Crucifixion.* Paul refers to the death of Jesus on a cross perhaps more than any other aspect of Jesus' life, articulating its meaning and effects in a variety of ways in different contexts. Jesus is presented both as acted upon by human actors ("handed over, put to death, crucified," Rom 4:25; 8:32; 1 Cor 2:6-8; 11:23; cf. Eph 5:2, 25) and as volitionally active ("gave himself," Gal 1:4; 2:20; cf. Phil 2:6-8; 2 Cor 8:9). The crucifixion's effects "on behalf of" humans (e.g., Rom 5:6, 8; 14:15) include dealing with Sin/sins (Rom 3:25; 8:3-4; 1 Cor 15:3; Gal 1:4; see Toews 2004: 409–13), "deliverance from the present evil age" (Gal 1:4), reconciliation with God (2 Cor 5:19-21; Rom 5:1-11), and exposing the injustice of the authorities and neutralizing their power (Col 2:14-15).

5. *Resurrection and Enthronement (Investiture).* In the resurrection, Jesus was acted upon (God *raised* him from the dead; he did not *rise* on his own) in an act of vindication, exaltation, and enthronement at the right hand of God (1 Cor 15:3-20; Phil 2:9; Rom 1:4; 8:34; Col 3:1).

6. *Final Victory and Acclamation.* The primary awaited work for Lord Jesus Messiah is as future *Savior* (Phil 3:20), who will soon return to complete the work of world dominion and world reconciliation, resulting in universal victory and acclamation throughout the world (Phil 2:10-11; 3:20-21; 4:5; 1 Cor 15:21-28; Rom 8:18-31; 11:25-32; 15:9-12; 16:20). Paul's shorthand for this is *the day of Messiah* (Phil 1:6, 10; 2:16; cf. 3:14) or the *parousia* of Messiah (1 Cor 15:23; 1 Thess 2:19; 3:13; 4:15; 5:23; 2 Thess 2:1, 8). The Greek term *parousia* (and its Latin equivalent *adventus* [Advent]) was regularly used to describe the royal "arrival" (presence, coming) of a Roman emperor (see TBC and TLC on 3:18–4:1).

7. *Relinquishing Power.* Paul affirms that when his work is completed, Messiah will give the power and rule he was granted back to God, the source and goal of all that is, so that "God will be all in all" (1 Cor 15:24-28; Rom 11:36; 1 Cor 8:6; cf. Phil 2:11b). This parodies the claim of Caesar Augustus that he will give all power back to the Roman Senate and the people of Rome once he achieves worldwide dominion and consolidates his power in Rome, "restoring the republic" (Res gestae divi Augusti 34).

Paul and the Earthly Life of Jesus

Paul's letters are surprisingly silent on the earthly life and ministry of Jesus. About all that his letters reveal is that Jesus was born of a woman (Gal 4:4), that he belonged to the people of Israel/Judah (1 Thess 2:14-15; Rom 9:5, "according to the flesh"), that he was of David's line "according to the flesh" (Rom 1:3), that he was poor (2 Cor 8:9), that he had a final supper with his disciples commemorating the beginning of a new covenant (1 Cor 11:23-26), and that he died on a cross (e.g., Phil 2:8). In addition, Paul cites "words of the Lord" that correspond with Jesus' teachings as recorded in the Gospels (e.g., 1 Thess 4:1-2, 15; 1 Cor 7:10-11, 25; 11:23-24; 14:37), and sometimes quotes or echoes teaching from the Gospels without indicating its source (e.g., Rom 12:14; 13:8-10). But significant differences in language and conceptuality between the synoptic gospels and the letters of Paul can also be observed (arguably analogous to the differences between the synoptic gospels and the gospel of John). Paul himself refers to "my gospel" (Rom 2:16) or "the gospel that I proclaim among the nations" (Gal 2:2 AT) as way to speak of some differences between his proclamation and that of other apostles, including James and Peter (Gal 2:2, 7). While Paul's theology coheres in a variety of ways with the four Gospels, the gospel perhaps in closest theological and ethical alignment with Paul's letters is the cross-oriented gospel of Mark. Still, Paul nowhere talks about "following Jesus" or being "disciples." Instead, he speaks mainly about participating "*in* Messiah Jesus," "imitating Messiah," or "entrusting oneself in loyalty to (believing in) Messiah" (e.g., Rom 3:22; 6:3, 23; 1 Cor 1:30; 11:1; 2 Cor 5:17; Gal 2:16; 3:26-28).

To explain this evidence, some interpreters argue that Paul was simply ignorant of the traditions about Jesus that would later be included in the Gospels. This is unlikely. Paul refers specifically to reliable authorities that passed on the traditions about Jesus to him (1 Cor 11:23; 15:1-3), which no doubt included the leaders Peter and James (the brother of Jesus; Gal 1:15-18; 2:1-10), and perhaps others. Scholars who stress discontinuity between Jesus and Paul propose that Paul was theologically disinterested in Jesus' earthly life and ministry, focusing only on his cross, resurrection, and future victory (*parousia*, royal "arrival"). Some go so far as to argue that Paul's gospel is so distinctive (and his ministry so significant in its results) that he should be regarded as the "second founder" of Christianity.

It is true that Paul points especially to the cross, resurrection, and future victory of Jesus as most decisive for salvation and ethics. Much less frequently, Paul refers to the notions of preexistence and incarnation, let alone to details of his earthly ministry. This does not mean, however, that Paul considers the earthly ministry of Jesus to be theologically irrelevant. For instance, Paul's claim not to regard Messiah "according to the flesh" (2 Cor 5:16-17) means that he no longer regards Messiah "from a human point of view," that is, from the standpoint of preoccupations with status and power, not that he has no regard for the "fleshly-earthly Jesus." Besides the continued regard for the special, authoritative value of Jesus' teaching, Paul's interest in the earthly Jesus is most apparent in the notion of "imitating Messiah," which does focus especially on the cross, in alignment with the gospel theme ("Take up your cross and follow me"), but not exclusively so (see TBC below, "Imitating Messiah").

Others properly propose a fundamental continuity between Jesus and Paul, observing that the character of Paul's letters simply does not provide sufficient opportunity to cite details from Jesus' ministry, or that Paul takes for granted a familiarity with the story of Jesus on the part of his readers-hearers, or that his commitment to audience-oriented contextualization of the gospel causes him simply not to quote stories and teaching from the life of Jesus (Schoberg; Stanley). On a whole range of topics, significant continuity can be seen between Jesus and Paul, such as on the issues of peace and nonretaliation and of social inversion that accompanies the arrival of God's reign (see TBC on 2:1-5, "Status Inversion"; TBC on 2:6-11, "The Biblical Pattern of Humiliation/Exaltation").

Imitating Messiah: Messiah as Model in Paul

Paul nowhere uses the language of "following Jesus" found so frequently in the synoptic gospels. He does occasionally draw attention to "imitating Messiah" in a number of crucial texts. In Philippians 2:5, Paul's exhortation to take the mind-set and behavior of Messiah as a concrete model for faithful messianic citizenship is one of these, and it adds a significant dimension to Paul's understanding of the importance of the earthly Jesus. When Paul asks the Corinthians to "be imitators of me, as I am of Messiah," he emphasizes the virtues of seeking not one's own advantage but that of the other. And he speaks of seeking to please everyone in everything one does for the sake of their well-being and salvation (1 Cor 10:24–11:1). Paul also points to Messiah as model in Romans when promoting the virtue of pleasing one's neighbor instead of oneself, for the good purpose of building up the neighbor, especially through vicarious suffering (Rom 15:1-3). Paul further highlights Messiah as model exhibiting a desire to welcome diverse peoples (Rom 15:7-9) and as the model of forgiveness toward the establishment of peace (Col 3:13-15). Moreover, the voluntary embrace of poverty for the sake of equity with the neighbor is also demonstrated by Messiah (2 Cor 8:6-13). These texts emphasize the same kinds of virtues as Paul promotes in Philippians 2:2-8.

In addition to these explicit texts, we can observe other notions in which Messiah provides a model prototype of those joined to him as the "second Adam," insofar as he is the "firstborn of many brothers and sisters" (Rom 8:29 AT). This is evident in the shared human experience of moving from suffering to glory, then from humiliation to exaltation (Rom 8:17-31). More specifically, Messiah's own conduct of obedience, faithfulness, and righteousness is both salvific and prototypical. Jesus is the "righteous One," who becomes both the agent and the model for all others to be made righteous in him (Rom 1:16-17; see Toews 2004: 54–57). Moreover, the embrace of suffering, especially obedience in suffering as far as death, is something that one does in solidarity with and in the pattern of Messiah (Phil 2:8; 3:10-11; Rom 5:18-19; 2 Cor 1:5; 4:8-12; 6:8-10; 11:30–12:10; Col 1:24). Messiah's manner of suffering unto death as a model for those experiencing abuse or hostility, alongside the declaration of his exaltation and saving benefits, is a thematic combination that can also be seen in 1 Peter 2:21-24 and Hebrews 12:1-11.

THE TEXT IN THE LIFE OF THE CHURCH

Philippians 2:6-11 in Christian Creeds and Confessions

Paul's tribute (encomium) to magnify Christ (Phil 1:20), even over Caesar, is designed to be both hortatory and kerygmatic. As hortatory, it provides an ethical model or paradigm of relinquishing status and power. As kerygmatic, it proclaims a message of deliverance, an assurance of victorious hope. It further grounds loyal allegiance to Lord Jesus Christ. Its purposes are not specifically doctrinal, to clarify precisely what must be believed about Christ. When it comes to creed-like formulations, Paul keeps it simple: declare allegiance to Lord Jesus Messiah, convinced that God raised him from the dead (Rom 10:9). Indeed, many of the tribute's assertions in Philippians 2:6-11 are periphrastically ambiguous, lacking precise definitions of both Christ's relationship with God (also the exact nature of preexistence) and relationship with humanity, or about how the divine and human dimensions intersect in the person of Jesus. Some contemporary readers assume that Paul simply says, "Christ was God but became human," importing concepts of trinitarian doctrine resolved a few centuries later. But Paul is careful to nuance his words more cautiously. The emphasis throughout is on Christ as a model in refusing to overreach and in divesting himself of status, not on his precise ontological relationship with God or his exact nature as a human ("ontological" is that which pertains to "essential being"), even as Paul assumes that Christ shares the closest of relationship with both God and humans.

In the following Christian history, however, Philippians 2:6-11 became a crucial text in the endeavor, involving massive debates and serious schisms, to provide doctrinally (philosophically) precise terminology and accounts of these aspects of Christ. The most important ecumenical councils were held at Nicaea (325), Ephesus (431), and Chalcedon (451). These councils, led by the most powerful bishops of the churches in the Roman Empire, established the exact contours of trinitarian doctrine in the Latin West and the Greek East, concluding in sequence that Jesus was of the "same [not 'like'] substance" of the Father, being "begotten, not made" (Nicaea); that Mary should be affirmed not just as "birth-giver of Christ" (*christotokos*) but also as "birth-giver of God" (*theotokos*; Ephesus); and that in the human Jesus the two natures (divine and human) coalesced as a union "in one manifestation [*prosōpon*, face] and reality [*hypostasis*, foundation, structure]" without compromising the distinctive "properties" of each (Chalcedon). Those who could not affirm the details of these creeds were formally excluded and cursed (under the *anathema*). These councils were not entirely ecumenical (worldwide), since they did not involve Christians from Rome's rival to the east, the Zoroastrian Persian-Parthian Empire. The spiritual descendants of these Christians have not always given assent to the creeds produced by these councils.

Philippians 2:5-11 also features significantly in Anabaptist and Mennonite confessions of faith, affirming that God the Son took on human nature, that he was obedient and humbled himself in death for the sake of others, that this provides a discipleship model for Christians, that Christ was exalted in his resurrection as King and Lord of all, and that he will eventually be universally acknowledged as Lord of all (e.g., *Confession of Faith in a Mennonite Perspective*, 1995, Articles 2, 15, 17, 24; *Confession of Faith of the General Conference of Mennonite Brethren Churches*, 1999, Articles 1, 16, 25).

Passion and Struggle

During the Spanish-Catholic colonial period of Philippine history (1565–1898), the passion story of Christ was annually performed publicly before a captive native audience, in the hopes that this might make the natives (Indios) passive and compliant. The irony is that the passion story, as told and retold orally among the indigenous peoples, sowed the seeds of revolution: it celebrated Jesus the (slave) rebel, the one who stood up against imperial power. At the same time, the narrative of Jesus' final victory in the world fueled countless millenarian movements, many of which claimed that by divine assistance they would be protected from the white man's bullets and that their foreign overlords would be pushed back into the sea, during a struggle in which they would not need to bear arms (Ileto).

More recently, in the context of severe hardship and oppression at the hands of the America-supported dictator Ferdinand Marcos, Christians in the Philippines have engaged self-consciously in a distinctive "theology of struggle." This theology is marked by reflection on the meaning of Christ within, about, and for the struggle of the Filipino people toward a truly "abundant life": real social transformation that could provide cultural resilience, spiritual harmony, economic well-being, and political justice (Fernandez; Apilado). Some Christians self-consciously embraced armed struggle toward these goals, while others did not, preferring a nonviolent struggle in alignment with the vision of the NT (Zerbe 2005). The Anabaptist movement of the sixteenth century had strands that took up arms in the name of justice even as the majority eventually took the pathway of nonviolence. The embrace of principled nonviolence itself is a deep personal struggle for many Christians in the Philippines and elsewhere.

Have No Fear (1:28)

It is hard for those of us who live in relative economic well-being and political stability to imagine what economically or politically induced fear is. The closest we come to feeling the emotion is in a movie theater. In a gathering of the Peace Church (supported by Mennonite Church Canada Witness) in Manila, Philippines (October 2015), I witnessed one member recall the struggle with his own fears during the turbulent year 1986, when he faced the military tanks that propped up the dictator Ferdinand Marcos. Marcos had plundered and devastated the country. During his violent regime, more than ten thousand persons disappeared or were "salvaged" (the term for the violent deaths of dissidents who were found on the vast trash heaps of Manila). Ka (Comrade) Boyet shared how, motivated by his faith, he was among the first waves of courageous peaceful marchers in an action that grew into the nonviolent "people power" movement and eventually toppled the dictator (the EDSA Revolution), forcing the dictator Marcos to flee the country under the protection of the American military. Ka Boyet admitted that many fellow Christians had remained fearful. They joined in the nonviolent marches only when it became clear that the dictator was on the defensive and was unable to control the entire military. He soberly mused that it should have been the evangelical Christians (an identity he claimed for himself) on the front lines of the struggle. They, at least, should have had no fear on account of their "assurance of salvation." (Written with the permission of Joseph Astrophel C. Ongkiko [Ka Boyet]; see also the "People Power Revolution" page on the Wikipedia website.)

Philippians 2:12-18

The Citizen Community's Agency in the Drama of Salvation

PREVIEW

The oral reader must have again paused after the stunning tribute to Messiah, letting its power flood over the gathered assembly. Then they hear, in effect: "But do not just sit back and passively wait, content with your own assurance of salvation because of what Messiah will fully accomplish! Stay engaged! Strive even harder to make a difference! Get your own divided house in order! Make the mission of God in Christ your own mission, and take your own place in this continuing epic, now that you are assured of its inevitable outcome! And above all, let's support each other in hopeful resilience, even in the face of death."

OUTLINE

Active Participation in the Drama of Salvation, 2:12-13
A Community of Character and Mission, 2:14-16
Mutual Rejoicing in the Midst of Suffering, 2:17-18

EXPLANATORY NOTES

After the crescendo of the preceding passage, Paul draws attention to the implications with a simple and direct *therefore, my beloved* (2:12). Paul sometimes uses the term *beloved* formally, even to a congregation with whom there is a strained relationship (1 Cor 10:14; 15:58; 2 Cor 7:1; 12:19) and with readers he has never met (Rom 12:19). Here the opening *beloved* indicates the depth of his relationship with them (cf. 4:1) and invites them to ponder the gravity of what he has just declared.

Active Participation in the Drama of Salvation 2:12-13

Before the specific words of exhortation, Paul congratulates them on their persistent and steadfast obedience to date: *just as you have always obeyed* (cf. 1:5-7; 4:14-16), whether he is away or present. The repeated imagery of Paul's absence or presence (2:12a) is a reminder of how their lives have been and continue to be intertwined (1:3-8, 24-26, 27; 2:16-18, 19-30; 4:1). That their obedience to the gospel has been displayed especially (*much more*) in his absence is likely another allusion to their past and recent assistance to him (cf. 1:5-7; 2:25-30; 4:10-16). In Paul's vocabulary, the Greek word usually translated *obedience* is a virtual synonym for the Greek word usually translated *belief* or *faith*, but more fundamentally means "loyalty, faithfulness, fidelity" (*pistis*, a term that includes conviction, trust, and loyalty all in one; see EN on Phil 1:25; 2:8; 3:9; Zerbe 2012: 26–46; on the correlation of obedience and faith, see, e.g., Rom 1:5; 10:16; 15:13 in relation to 15:18). Faith-loyalty and obedience are of the same piece in Paul's vocabulary. The NRSV (*just as you have always obeyed me*) wrongly suggests that they have obeyed Paul in particular, adding the object *me* that is not in Paul's Greek text. Although Paul in one place advises obedience to himself (2 Thess 3:14; cf. Philem 21), he more commonly speaks of obedience in relation to the gospel, to God, or to Messiah (e.g., Rom 1:5; 15:18), limiting his own role to that of modeling (e.g., Phil 3:15-17; 4:9; 1 Cor 4:10; 11:1; 1 Thess 1:6; 2 Thess 3:7, 9). Indeed, the repetition of the language of obedience—just used in the tribute to Messiah (2:8)—shows that they themselves are following in the same pathway that Messiah followed (2:5).

In continuity with their loyalty already demonstrated, Paul invites them as a community—the imperative is plural—to energetically strive in the same direction: *Work out your own salvation*. In the immediate context, this exhortation is based squarely on the victory that Messiah has already secured, paralleling the story of how Messiah's own commitment contributed to God's response of vindication. Taken in isolation, this call has been a source of consternation for many Christian readers, seeming to contradict what Paul says elsewhere (e.g., Rom 4:2-6; Eph 2:8-9; TLC below, "Works and

Grace"). But a careful consideration of this passage indicates that Paul is referring not to working at achieving the gifts and bliss of "personal salvation" that only God can give, but to their active striving alongside God toward the goal of God's redemptive mission in the world (for a similar emphasis on the missional focus of this section, see Gorman 2015; Flemming).

As with the earlier uses of *sōtēria* (deliverance-salvation, 1:19, 28), the precise sense of the term can be determined only by the context since the word can have more than one nuance. It can refer to personal or communal experiences of physical deliverance, rescue, restored health, or survival—or to the fullness of salvation in the age to come (e.g., Rom 1:16; 13:11; 1 Thess 5:8-9). Earlier in Philippians, the word refers to Paul's own "release" from imprisonment and potential death in 1:19, and in 1:28 the term applies to their deliverance and survival as a citizen community. Here Paul seems to use the word again with more than one sense. On the one hand, his exhortation implies that they actively work both toward their communal well-being and solidarity in the immediate struggle. On the other, it reaches toward their full experience of salvation in the age to come (3:20-21).

Paul's piles up words for "working" and "enabling" (built on the Greek root *erg*, from which we get the word *energy* and the scientific term *erg* as a unit of energy):

> *Work out [katergazomai] your own deliverance-salvation,*
> *for it is God who is the enabling power [energōn] in and among you,*
> *both to will and to enable [energeō] for the sake of goodwill.* (2:12b-13)

The verb used in the first line (*katergazomai*) is the common term for laboring or effecting via labor. It draws attention to the content of all the exhortations Paul has already made in 1:27–2:5 and those still to come. The second word (*energeō*) has the sense of "empower, enable, or energize, make effective." Paul typically uses it in reference to God or the Spirit (e.g., 1 Cor 12:6, 11). In 3:21 he employs its related noun form (*energeia*) for the "enabling power" that works in Messiah to reconcile the whole universe to himself. Here in 2:13 Paul grabs our attention by claiming that God enables a human enabling (or empowers an empowering) *for the sake of goodwill.*

Their invitation to work out their own salvation is thus cast in parallel terms to actively striving toward the goal of goodwill (*eudokia*, lit. "regarding well, good repute"). What precisely Paul means by the goal of *goodwill* is itself uncertain (Fee: 239: "perfectly ambiguous"). At least three dimensions seem to be on Paul's mind at the same time. First, Paul is drawing attention to their goodwill as a kind and peaceful disposition toward others, including hostile adversaries (cf. 4:5), but especially to each other in Messiah's new community (cf. 1:27; 2:1-5; 4:2-3). This is suggested by Paul's earlier use of the same word in the sense of goodwill toward others, along with love, in contrast to rivalry, envy, and rivalrous striving (*selfish ambition*; 1:15-17). Similarly indicative of this meaning is his concern that they display positive regard to the "other" in contrast to rivalrous striving and empty glory (2:4), and his call that they desist from divisive disputatious in the immediate context (2:14). Accordingly, the virtue of *eu-dokia* (*eudokia*, good repute) provides a direct verbal contrast with the vice of *keno-doxos* (*kenodoxos, empty repute*) in 2:3. But second and more generally, *eudokia* in 2:13 may also refer to moral and social excellence in general. In this case, the term would be roughly synonymous with *the things that distinguish* (Phil 1:10), "the (morally) beautiful" (Rom 12:17; 2 Cor 8:21), "what is well-pleasing" (*to euareston*, as in Rom 12:2), "the good" (Rom 7:13, 19), or *virtuous excellence* (Phil 4:8). Finally, however, Paul is not simply speaking of a virtue that is one's possession (NRSV, NET: *God's good pleasure*; ISV: *what pleases him*), but communally and theo-politically about the ultimate goal of God's reconciling work, which embraces the whole world (see discussion on 3:18–4:1). In this sense *eudokia* here can also refer to "God's *good purpose*" (NIV; NABRE) for the whole world, as a synonym for *salvation*. As such, it conjures up the notion in Greek political theory of the goal of *eudaimonia*, "abundant happiness" for the whole citizen-community (*polis*). Moreover, the image is thus similar to the notion of working alongside God toward "the good" of the whole world in Rom 8:28 (see TBC below).

In alignment with the story of salvation just pronounced (2:6-11), then, in a narrative whose final conclusion is yet to be fully realized, the readers are thus invited to get on board, actively pursuing a steadfast loyalty and unity as *their own* contribution. Already Paul has implied that if God were not at work, their suffering would be senseless and their loyalty would indeed be a signal of their destruction (1:28-30). But just as they have shown active partnership in the gospel, so also God will bring their good work to completion (1:5-6). Paul is now indicating that the disposition and conduct he has been endorsing (1:27-28; 2:1-5) and the goal of God's worldwide victory that they are sharing will be realized through God's empowerment, overcoming the divide between "willing" and "doing or effecting." As a result, Paul's associates in Philippi will become effective *fellow-contestants* or *combatants*, indeed dedicated *soldiers*, for the *gospel of Messiah, the word of life* (1:27; 2:25; 4:3).

The phrase *with fear and trembling* (v. 12) implies reverent loyalty, not a nervous anxiety to do one's duty or a posture of cowering before some angry God. This phrase was idiomatic for an attitude of obedience (2 Cor 7:15) and humble service (1 Cor 2:3; cf. Eph 6:5; Mark 5:33). Earlier Paul warned against fearing human *adversaries* (1:14, 28), but here Paul advises a posture of loyal allegiance before the appointed world ruler (cf. 2:11) in a manner reminiscent of a psalmist's declaration of God's world dominion:

> Now therefore, O kings, be wise;
>   be warned, O rulers of the earth.
> Serve the Lord with fear,
>   with trembling kiss his feet,
> or he will be angry, and you will perish in the way;
>   for his wrath is quickly kindled.
> Happy are all who take refuge in him. (Ps 2:10-12)

The influence of Psalms 2 and 110 on messianic exaltation texts in the NT suggests that *with fear and trembling* is to be understood in relation to Messiah's emerging world dominion. This is formal language to express the posture of loyalty and homage to the one whose name is above all others, indicating again that in Philippians 2:12-13, the readers are in effect invited to take their place in the epic story of Messiah's worldwide dominion (cf. 3:20–4:1).

A Community of Character and Mission 2:14-16

Immediately moving beyond the general, Paul returns specifically to their life as a community, creating a remarkable and powerful word picture, using images from a variety of scriptural texts.

Their Unity. Paul instructs, *Do everything without murmuring and arguing*. He begins by calling them to desist from divisive *murmuring* (NRSV; NIV 2011: *grumbling*; NIV 1984, TEV: *complaining*) and *arguing*. The first word picks up language from the wilderness experience of Israel, indicating weariness and insubordination against leaders (cf. 1 Cor 10:10; drawing on Exod 16:7, 8, 9, 12; 17:3; Num 11:1; 14:27, 29; 17:5, 10; Ps 106:25 [105:25 LXX]). The second word can denote dialogue or argument more neutrally, but here it signals protracted debate (cf. 1 Cor 3:20; Rom 1:21; 14:1). This is now the third direct exhortation in a short span pertaining to a real or potential disunity that threatens the community (cf. 1:27; 2:2-4; cf. 4:2-3).

Their Character and Identity. The purpose is *so that you may become blameless and untainted, children of God without blemish.* Paul again refers to their distinctive character as a "consecrated community," highlighting the virtues appropriate to their new identity (1:1, 9-11). Their identity and status as *children of God* (cf. Rom 8:16, 17, 21; 9:7, 8, 26; Gal 4:28, 31) poses a sharp contrast to the *crooked and twisted nation* in whose midst they dwell. Both they and their coresidents of Philippi are thereby identified by a genealogical image, the prevailing model for citizenship in that cultural environment *[Citizenship, p. 279].* These images are drawn from Deuteronomy 32:5, where the phrase "crooked and twisted nation" (ESV) denotes degenerate, wayward children in contrast to the worthy and true *children of God.* Paul thus understands the community of Messiah typologically, replaying the story of Israel: though they have already experienced the redeeming grace of God, they are still in the wilderness, surrounded by hostile forces, and on their way to the land of promise (similarly 1 Cor 10:1-13). They are "resident aliens" (cf. Acts 7:6; 1 Pet 2:11), oriented to Messiah's regime, now secured in heaven, which aims to reconcile the world *to himself* (Phil 3:20-21).

Their Context. They are *in the midst of a crooked and twisted nation.* The word *nation* (in its original sense as a "community defined by common descent"; from Latin *natio*, "be born") translates the Greek word *genea*, which refers to that which is generated or defined by birth or pedigree, the root of our word *genea*logy. The word here refers to those descended from a common ancestor (nation, ethnic group, race, clan, ancestors; e.g., Luke 16:8; Acts 2:40; 8:33), not to "contemporaries" (NRSV, NIV: *generation*). Paul is thus naming the dominant citizen body (KJV: nation) that is now hostile to the citizen community of Messiah. The adjectives *crooked and twisted* emphasize its moral perversity. For the first hearers, the overall image would most certainly suggest the Roman citizenry of Philippi, including its leaders, a further take on the adversaries lined up in siege around them (Phil 1:28; 3:2, 18-19).

Their Mission. Paul continues with a challenge: *among whom you shine like bright lights in the world.* Here he immediately moves to emphasize the messianic community's missional vocation precisely in this hostile environment. His words are inspired by the Greek translation of Daniel 12:3, which describes the final victory through tribulation for those "written in the book" (cf. Phil 4:3): "And those who are wise will shine as bright lights [*phōstēres*] of heaven, and those who hold strong to my words [will shine] as the stars [*astra*] of heaven, forever and ever." The imagery of shining as *bright lights in the world* also recalls the imagery of Isaiah in which the people of God are a "light to the nations" (Isa 9:2-7; 42:6-7; 49:6; 58:8-10). Paul adjusts the text in Daniel by identifying their shining, not in heaven (*ouranos*, sky or heaven), but "in the *kosmos*," focusing on the earthly world of humanity. The messianic *polis* has an identity oriented to God's current regime in heaven (Phil 3:20). But its missional vocation is squarely in the midst of the terrestrial world, and its destiny is in this world transformed (3:21; cf. Rom 8:18-25). Outsiders, even enemies, are always potential insiders.

Their Security and Armaments. They are to be *holding on to the word of life* (NET; cf. NRSV, NIV 2011). Paul draws attention to what they hold securely in their hands, connoting both how they maintain their own stability, yet also how they interact with hostile adversaries. In the first case, they are *holding on* in the sense of standing firm in the face of external opposition, continuing with the Greek text of Daniel 12:3 that Paul draws upon ("Hold strong to my words"). The image is roughly synonymous with *standing firm together* and *striving [fighting] together with the loyalty-faith of the gospel* (1:27; 4:1). The word of life is the gospel of Messiah, the sole foundation for their citizenship practice and the only security for their destiny.

But the phrase also seems to imply what armaments are in their hands as they face a hostile *nation.* Instead of taking up arms in the ordeal, they take up the word of life, fighting God's warfare of love with "weapons" appropriate to the gospel of Messiah. The image reminds us of Paul's language of "weapons of warfare" as the virtues that Jesus loyalists display even to adversaries. In particular, Paul refers to struggling "with the weapons of justice-righteousness for the right hand and for the left" (2 Cor 6:7 AT) or "taking the sword of the Spirit, which is the word of God" (Eph 6:17; cf. Rom 6:13; 12:21; 13:12; 1 Thess 5:8-9; 2 Cor 10:4; also Phil 4:5). What they hold in relation to hostile adversaries will later be clarified as simply *forbearing clemency* (4:5; see also EN on 1:27; TLC on 2:19-30, "Paul's Military Imagery").

To impress upon his listeners the seriousness of his appeal, Paul brings himself back into the picture (Phil 1:24-27; 2:2, 12; 4:1). He began by saying that their unity and fidelity would fill him with complete joy (2:1-2). Now he emphasizes that they are also the reason for his *boast on the day of Messiah*. He does not want to have *run* or *worked* on their behalf in vain (lit. *into emptiness*). As he will put it shortly: his dearly beloved are both his *joy* and his *victory wreath* (4:1). He means all this as a display of affection and as a statement of confidence, not pessimism or rebuke (cf. 1:3-6; see TLC on 2:1-5, "*Ēthos* and *Pathos*").

Mutual Rejoicing in the Midst of Suffering 2:17-18

Paul then easily moves into a reminder of their need to mutually support each other in a posture of gladness (rejoicing), despite the crushing circumstances. Returning to his own experience, he dramatically pictures it as sacrificial ministry on their behalf. He is the drink offering of wine "poured out" in conjunction with animal sacrifice (Gen 35:14; Exod 25:29; Num 15:5). Paul's sacrificial language evokes the idea not only of his current suffering (NRSV, NIV: *even if I am being poured out*), but also of possible impending martyrdom (RSV: *even if I am to be poured out*). The libation of wine was regularly understood by Jews to represent blood (Sirach 50:15). Paul may also be alluding to the ministry of the suffering servant of Isaiah, who also "pours out himself unto death" (Isa 53:12), a figure of Messiah himself.

Paul thus understands his own suffering and potential martyrdom as continuing in the pathway of Christ himself, who was willing to go all the way to death for the sake of others (2:4-8). Thus his own ordeal is a *partnership in the suffering of Christ* (Phil 3:10). Elsewhere Paul describes this *partnership* as "completing what is lacking in Christ's afflictions" (Col 1:24, perhaps written during the same ordeal). Soon after his release, he will emphasize to the Corinthians the character of his suffering as vicarious: providing benefit for others (2 Cor 1:3-7; 2:14-16; 4:7-12).

Earlier, Paul has expressed his resolve to rejoice in light of the advance of the gospel precisely because of his chains (1:12-18a) and because of the assured outcome leading toward deliverance-salvation (1:18b-26). But now he is determined that his joy will remain, even through the depth of suffering toward martyrdom. This is not joy instead of sorrow, but joy in the midst of sorrow and pain (cf. 2 Cor 6:10).

There is another new element to Paul's rejoicing: it is a mutual rejoicing in solidarity with each other, emphasized with a verbal redundancy: *I rejoice [chairō] and rejoice together [synchairō, co-rejoice, rejoice mutually] with all of you*. That is, he rejoices doubly, both in his own person and in solidarity together with *all* his beloved in Philippi. As before, *all* emphasizes the inclusive solidarity of the entire group of "saints" in Philippi (1:1, 4, 7 [2x], 8; 1:25; on unity, 2:2-5).

And then Paul emphatically exhorts his readers to display the very same posture (lit. *the same also you*), in effect using himself as the model (cf. 3:15; 4:9). In this first explicit call that they *rejoice*, he repeats the same two verbs he has just used for his own disposition: *rejoice [chairō] and rejoice together [synchairō, co-rejoice] with me*.

The special mutual sense of the second compound verb can be observed in another of its four occurrences in Paul: "If one member suffers [*paschō*], all suffer together [*sympaschō*, cosuffer]; if one member is honored, all members rejoice together [*synchairō*]" (1 Cor 12:26; cf. 13:6).

Paul began this larger section (1:27–2:18) with a note about their mutual participation in the *same ordeal* (1:30), and he closes off the section with an emphasis on their mutual rejoicing in suffering. Paul has stressed how their lives are fully intertwined (1:3-8, 24-26, 27, 30; 2:2, 12, 16). The undercurrent theme is that they are "in it together and bonded together." This then sets the stage for a review of recent and anticipated travels through which their lives are intertwined (2:19-30).

THE TEXT IN BIBLICAL CONTEXT

Divine-Human Synergy

The notion of divine-human synergy is a significant feature of Paul's theology, and expressions of it can be found scattered throughout his letters. For instance, it is a crucial theme in how Paul understands his own ministry: "I worked harder than any of [the other envoys-apostles]—though it was not I, but the grace of God that is with me" (1 Cor 15:10). He writes similarly: "So we are ambassadors for Christ, since God is making his appeal through us; we entreat you on behalf of Christ, be reconciled to God. . . . As we work together [*synergeō*] with him, we urge you also not to accept the grace of God in vain" (2 Cor 5:20; 6:1). Paul summarizes his ministry to the Romans as follows: "In Christ Jesus, then, I have reason to boast of my work for God. For I will not venture to speak of anything except what Christ has accomplished through me to win obedience from the Gentiles, by word and deed, by the power of signs and wonders, by the power of the Spirit of God" (Rom 15:17-19a).

Regarding the drama of salvation more generally, Paul explains: "For we know that together with [alongside] those who love God, together with those called according to purpose, he [God, or the Holy Spirit] coworks [*synergeō*] all things toward the good [of the whole world]" (Rom 8:28, see NIV mg.). Far from being a visionary who invites the faithful to sit back passively and wait for the universal realization of God's reign, Paul encourages them to active participation alongside God, working in alignment with God's purposes.

According to Josephus, this affirmation of God's involvement in the affairs of humans in concert with human deliberation and action is distinctly Pharisaic. Thus it is in contrast to the Sadducees, who put everything (e.g., the course of history) on the side of human action; and in contrast to the Essenes, who put everything on the side of divine intervention (Josephus, *Jewish War* 2.162–65; *Jewish Antiquities* 13.171).

Willing and Doing/Enabling

For Paul, the gap between "willing" and "working, enabling" is a critical feature of the human condition. In Romans, the fissure between willing and doing is diagnosed as a kind of slavery under the power of Error/Sin (Rom 7), a mysterious viral force that operates in the world (Rom 5–6). The antidote comes as the power of Error/Sin in the Flesh (the realm of human weakness) is broken by the act of Christ and through the infusion of power from the Holy Spirit (7:6; 8:1-13). This infusion energizes a mind-set of "life and peace" and thus "life" in "the Spirit" (8:6). As a result of this alone, the "just requirement of the law [is] fulfilled" (cf. Rom 13:8-10) by those who "walk not according to the flesh but according to the Spirit" (8:4).

In Galatians, the gap is diagnosed as a conflict between the powers of Flesh and Spirit: "The Flesh has desire opposed to the Spirit; and the Spirit opposed to the Flesh. These are lined up against one another, so that you are not *doing* what you are *willing*" (Gal 5:17 AT). The antidote, Paul says, is to "walk by [the power of] the Spirit" (an implied synergy! [5:16 AT]). . . . Those who belong to Christ have crucified the Flesh along with its passions and desires. Since we live by the Spirit, let us walk by the Spirit" (5:24-25 AT).

Paul also employs the theme of willing and doing for purposes of exhortation, specifically in his fundraising for relief: "It is best for you now to complete what a year ago you began not only *to do* but also *to will* [or, desire]; but now complete *the doing*, such that your readiness in *willing* [and pledging] will match the completion [in doing] according to what you have" (2 Cor 8:10-11 AT).

THE TEXT IN THE LIFE OF THE CHURCH

Works and Grace in the Salvation Drama: The Anabaptist Perspective

This passage has continued to vex many Protestant Christians. Taken out of context and read as advice to individuals, some take it as promoting works-oriented or works-based personal salvation without the element of grace. But this reading is misplaced on many counts. For one thing, the emphasis in this passage is on the believing community, not narrowly on individual experience: the imperatives are in the plural, as is the reflexive pronoun (*your own*, 2:12). From the beginning of the exhortation in 1:27, Paul has focused on the community's common life together. Certainly a community is composed of individuals. But for Paul, individual and corporate striving is a both/and matter, not either/or. The fundamental issue of this passage has to do with how "saved people" (those within the salvation sphere made possible through Christ) live out this salvation so as to participate in its ultimate destiny (2:11; 3:21). Even the premise of the exhortation indicates that what is at stake is the ongoing "obedience" (loyal steadfastness, 2:12) of the community. This is their human contribution to the journey toward ultimate deliverance-salvation in the day of Christ, in the same way that Christ has contributed to the drama.

Anabaptist writers of the sixteenth century drew on this passage in their theological disputes with Catholics and Protestants (see Klaassen 1981, 2001). Michael Sattler, for instance, explained "works of faith" in a pamphlet "not as what man can do from himself, but what he really can do in the power of faith; which thereby are not man's works but God's, since *the willing and the ability* to turn to God are not of man but the gift of God through Jesus Christ our Lord." He argues for staying on a "middle path" between that of works-righteousness and that of a faith without works ("On the Satisfaction of Christ," emphasis added; alluding to Phil 2:12; Sattler: 116). Balthasar Hubmaier also cites Philippians 2:12 explicitly in his defense of the significant role and freedom of human choice, insofar as it is infused with divine grace, in opposition to those who stressed the complete bondage of the will (Hubmaier: 400, 462, 484). As Walter Klaassen explains, Anabaptists preferred a "synergism": while stressing that the process of salvation begins with God's gracious act in Jesus Christ, they also assigned to humans a contribution in the process of salvation—that of choosing and surrendering; humans are not saved in spite of themselves (Klaassen 1981: 41).

A City Set on a Hill: Mission as Alternative Community Formation

The image of *shining forth as bright lights in the world* (2:15) as a feature of the community's life as a *citizen community* (1:27, *politeuomai*) evokes Matthew's missional image of the "city [*polis*, citizen community] set on a hill" (Matt 5:14-16). There, as in Philippians 2, the emphasis is on the distinctive character ("good works"; cf. Eph 2:10) of the messianic community that is put on display and shines forth, ultimately for the glory of God. Both Paul and Matthew balance mission as "heralding" with mission as "visible witness" through alternative community formation ("doing"). Matthew also balances the image of the "light to the world" with "fertilizing salt for the land," a somewhat different missional metaphor and implying a somewhat different, complementary missional mandate. The light metaphor highlights the church's alternative existence as a witness to God in the world. The salt metaphor implies losing identity in the work of God's renewal of the world, in alignment with the Lord's call through Jeremiah to "seek the welfare [peace, shalom] of the city where I have sent you into exile" (Jer 29:7).

Revelation's new Jerusalem, a realization of the reign of God on earth as in heaven (Rev 21:2, 11), also radiates "light to the nations" (21:24). In this case, God is the light of the sun and the Lamb is the lamp by night so that the city itself never experiences darkness (21:23; 22:5; cf. Isa 60:19-20). As a vision of the future reign of God, the nations bring their glory and honor (tribute) into the reigning world city (21:24, 26), expressing the same idea as Philippians 2:10-11.

Elsewhere in NT, light imagery also functions significantly, inspired especially from Isaiah's image of God's people as light to the nations (Isa 42:6; 49:6; 51:4; 58:10; 60:3; cf. Rom 2:19; Luke 2:32) and as light for those in darkness (Isa 9:2; esp. Matt 4:16; Luke 1:78-79). Paul is described as "the chosen light" (Acts 13:47); Paul exhorts believers to be "of the light" (daytime; Rom 13:11-14; 1 Thess 5:5; Eph 5:8-14); and Jesus is proclaimed by John forcefully as "the light of the world" (1:4-9; 3:19-21; 8:12; 9:5; 11:9-10; 12:35-36, 46; 1 John 1:5–2:10).

Is Paul's Theopolitical Vision Sectarian, Escapist, or Exclusivist?

Throughout Philippians, and arguably all of Paul's letters, the emphasis is on nurturing the citizenship community of Messiah as an alternative community. This community is presented as the avant-garde of a citizen-state in exile. They live in anticipation of and alignment with the worldwide transformation under way through the reconciling work of Lord Jesus Messiah. Paul's emphasis is thus not on being good citizens of Rome, or even of a local city. His main concern here is not on "seeking the welfare [shalom] of the city" in which you live as exiles (Jer 29:7). In Philippians it is quite the contrary: Paul's interest is in resisting the seductive draw of the prevailing norms and ethos of the dominant political community, along with exposing its insidious theopolitical propaganda. He shows no obvious interest in reforming the prevailing system, although he most certainly is committed to "doing good toward all people" (Gal 6:10 AT) and extending love toward all people (1 Thess 3:12). Paul indeed longs for the goal of God's purposes in the world, not the end of the world as such. What he awaits is the imminent ending of the prevailing world system (1 Cor 2:6-8; 7:31; 1 Thess 5:1-6), through the direct intervention of Messiah, so that God will be supreme on earth as in heaven (1 Cor 15:24-28; Phil 3:20-21; similarly Matt 6:10; Rev 21–22). In this sense, we can understand Paul's theological vision as a type of utopianism or "millenarianism"—the term anthropologists use for oppressed communities' persistent visionary aspirations for direct divine intervention that transforms the world (see Zerbe 2003; TBC and TLC on 3:18–4:1).

Some interpreters have concluded that Paul's radical visionary perspective for a transformed world is sectarian and exclusivist insofar as it seems to be so preoccupied with the boundary maintenance of the "consecrated messianic community" and a kind of "politics of othering" (for instance, against the *crooked and twisted nation among whom you shine forth*, Phil 2:15). Paul's universalism and global inclusivism is therefore thought to be just another particularism or narrow exclusivism. Or Paul is faulted for reinscribing the very hierarchies (gender, class, etc.) that he elsewhere proposes are ended in Christ (Gal 3:26-28). Others claim that this redemptive vision is escapist and irrational.

These are crucial issues with which readers of Paul must wrestle. What is required at minimum is a critical analysis of our own situations and contexts. The situation of those of us in the Global North is significantly different from that of Paul, whose context is much closer to that of the Global South *[Citizenship, p. 279]*. He and fellow Messiah Jesus loyalists (and the broader Judean religious-political community from which he came and to which he was committed) were entirely marginalized and alienated from the major centers of political power. By contrast, we live in liberal democratic states (where *liberal* refers to a commitment to individual liberty among the highest goods). In these countries we are invited to take on the responsibilities of citizenship and democratic process for the common good (though typically limited to that of a given state). In this setting, the challenge of maintaining an alternative identity and mission based on the gospel of Messiah is ironically even more difficult since the pressures toward assimilation and accommodation to prevailing norms and values are massive. The claims of Christ have often been reduced to the spiritually private, while held in symbiotic and sympathetic alignment with a patriotic commitment to a particular national identity (nationalism). Thus the challenge, as we reflect on Paul's legacy along with other biblical voices, is to ever discern (1) when is the time to align with the prevailing order and/or to reform it, (2) when is the time to uncouple from the prevailing order and/or to resist and protest, and (3) on what issues and on what grounds do we so act. When does patriotic identification with membership in a particular political (national) community come into conflict with the higher claims of Christ's call to the imperatives of a global citizenship, toward God's redeeming work of peace and justice in this world? Paul puts much of the emphasis on Christ's agency in bringing the world to its appointed destiny, but the need for the church (as the body of Christ) to take on the risks of agency in alignment with God's redeeming purposes is increasingly urgent (see also TLC on 4:2-9, "Nearness and Agency").

Philippians 2:19-30

Travel-Talk Interlude: Timothy and Epaphroditus as Models of Messianic Citizenship

PREVIEW

Who is practicing messianic citizenship? Are there actual living people whom the Philippians know and whose living they can observe? In a word, yes.

Thinking of the mutuality of their joy in the midst of ordeal, Paul interrupts his formal exhortation. He turns to travel activity that has and will bring them together. Timothy, Paul's personal emissary to them, is soon to be sent (2:19-23), while Epaphroditus, their personal emissary to him, is being returned (2:25-30). Sandwiched in between and bringing them all together, Paul confidently affirms that he himself will soon be reunited with them in person (2:24).

Paul continues to exhort and teach indirectly by deliberately foregrounding both Timothy and Epaphroditus as models of the messianic way. Both are held forth as patriotic heroes of the messianic community for the congregation to celebrate and to emulate. Thus Paul adroitly brings travel and networking disclosure into the orbit of his appeal about *practicing messianic citizenship* (1:27).

In the midst of discussing seemingly incidental travel plans, the relational and personal pathos of the letter deepens significantly.

One could call this passage the emotional-relational heart of the letter.

OUTLINE

Plans for Sending Timothy Soon, 2:19-23
- 2:19 The Hope for Timothy's Imminent Visit and Its Purpose
- 2:20-22 Recommendation of Timothy as Model Messianic Envoy
- 2:23 Timing Contingency: Paul's Own Circumstance

Confidence in Paul's Own Imminent Visit, 2:24

Commendation of Epaphroditus as Model Messianic "Soldier," 2:25-30
- 2:25 The Necessity of Sending Epaphroditus
- 2:26-28 The Reasons for Sending Epaphroditus
- 2:29-30 Receiving and Honoring Epaphroditus

EXPLANATORY NOTES

Paul's Anxiety, Pain, and Inner Being

Small cracks in Paul's resilient optimism come through in this section, hinting at the depth of his inner and outer pain. While we do not sense much of this in Philippians, he says that, in a few months of his recent ministry, he was "continually pained [physically and emotionally], yet always rejoicing" (2 Cor 6:10 AT). Speaking of his ordeal while writing Philippians, he later admits that "we despaired even of staying alive" (2 Cor 1:8 AT; cf. 4:7-12). Now in the heat of the moment, and in solidarity with a community itself in turmoil, he remains buoyant, consoling while he himself is in need of consolation (cf. 2 Cor 1:3-8).

Paul remains surprisingly reticent about referring to his physical and psychological pain and pressure. Precisely when admitting the prospect of martyrdom (Phil 2:17a), he immediately moves to rejoicing (2:17b). Now, in the context of travel-talk and shared interaction, he acknowledges his own physical and psychological pain. This appears most obviously when referring to the restoration of Epaphroditus to health: *But God had mercy, and not only on him, but also on me, so that I might not have pain upon pain* (2:27). The Greek word that Paul uses (*lypē*) can refer to both physical and psychological pain (grief, sorrow; cf. the related verb in 1 Thess 4:13; 2 Cor 6:10). Epaphroditus's sickness was a deep emotional pain to Paul, compounding his existing pain, whether the physical pain of privation and torture in imprisonment or the pain of anxiety for his own circumstances and that of his assemblies. Paul also hints at his "pain" of anxiety, sorrow, and grief when he describes why he is returning

Epaphroditus: *so that I might become more free of pain* (*alypoteros*, Phil 2:28; NRSV: *may be less anxious*; ISV: *may feel relieved*). His struggle to maintain resilience is evident in explaining why he is sending Timothy: *so that I may be renewed in spirit by knowing of your affairs* (2:19). Paul uses vivid language in describing his need for *renewal in spirit*, using a form of the word for the deep inner being (*psychē*, soul, inner life force): he hopes that he might *become well-souled* (*eupsycheō*; by contrast, the "fainthearted" are [lit.] the "small souled" [*oligopsychos*], 1 Thess 5:14).

Paul's inner distress did not leave in the months after his release. Though his meeting in Macedonia with Titus a few months later was the cause of considerable rejoicing (2 Cor 7), he still attests to continued hardship, including "fights on the outside and fears on the inside" (2 Cor 7:5) and "the daily pressure of anxiety for all the assemblies" (11:28).

Recommendation of Timothy as Model Messianic Envoy 2:20-22

Paul begins to commend Timothy as soon as he announces his imminent dispatch to Philippi: *I have no one similarly empathic who will be genuinely concerned for your affairs.* It is clear that Timothy is being sent not just to bring news back to Paul (2:19b), but also to provide ministry for the Philippian assembly on Paul's behalf (2:20-22). No one else is *similarly empathic* (*isopsychos*, lit. "same-souled"). The TEV renders the sense well: *He is the only one <u>who shares my feelings</u> and really cares about you* (cf. Fowl 2005: *I do not have anyone else <u>who shares my loves and desires</u>*). Paul is stressing that Timothy has the same emotional and dispositional tie to the Philippians that he has, thereby both recommending Timothy and at the same time reasserting his own deeply felt interest in them (cf. 1:7-8).

The particular virtue of Timothy is that he *will be genuinely concerned* for their welfare. The recommendation continues by way of contrast: *For everyone seeks their own interests, not those of Jesus Messiah.* This comment recalls the exhortation *not to look out for one's own interests but the interests of others* (2:3-4), a perspective notably exemplified by Messiah himself (2:5-11; for this language, cf. 1 Cor 10:21, 33). Later in Philippians, Paul will continue the same focus on the affairs of Messiah as opposed to one's own affairs, using himself as a model (3:4-14). *Everyone* (NIV; misleading is NRSV: *all of them*) is meant as a generalization and rhetorical hyperbole about a common disposition (cf. the *many* in 3:18), mainly to dramatize how

Timothy stands out in relation to a general norm oriented to *selfish ambition* (2:3).

To assert Timothy's proven credentials (*tested worth*), Paul invites his listeners to recall their prior experience with him, during the founding of the congregation, and perhaps visiting while en route to Corinth from Ephesus (1 Cor 4:17; 16:10-11). Paul uses two verbal images to describe Timothy's committed work *for the gospel*: that of filial loyalty (*as a child to a father*) and that of slave service (*He served as a slave with me*). The father-child image indicates not primarily intimacy, but especially loyalty and duty. Timothy is a model of filial loyalty to his father and so exemplifies the ideal virtue of sons' behavior in relation to fathers. Indeed, even though the messianic drama (2:6-11) does not use father-son imagery specifically, Timothy's behavior as a loyal son imitates the filial loyalty of Messiah himself. *Serving as a slave* recalls the imagery of Paul and Timothy's status as *slaves of Messiah* in 1:1 (cf. also Rom 12:11; 14:18; 1 Thess 1:9), but especially the model slave status shown by Messiah himself (2:7). In light of the letter's emphasis on "lowering" for the sake of the neighbor, this notation about Timothy's credential is certainly strategic.

Paul initially says he will send Timothy *soon* (v. 19), but then recognizing considerable uncertainty about himself, clarifies that soon means *at once, whenever I should have full view of my own circumstances* (v. 23).

Confidence in Paul's Own Imminent Visit 2:24

Though Paul is not sending Timothy right away because of uncertainty about the outcome of his upcoming trial, Paul is *confident in the Lord* that a positive resolution of his case is imminent, so he himself will also be able to come *soon* (v. 24). Although this remark appears almost incidentally, it will reassure his distressed readers-hearers. Here Paul's resolute confidence immediately follows and clarifies his earlier sober reflection on the worst-case scenario: his possible martyrdom (2:17-18). This is not vacillation but a head-on facing of an uncertain future. Meanwhile, the hope and confidence that he has is *in the Lord* (2:19, 24), indicating his acknowledgment of divine providence (in the manner of "Lord willing") and thus contingency (cf. 1 Cor 4:19; 16:7, also in regard to travel plans).

Commendation of Epaphroditus as Model Messianic "Soldier" 2:25-30

Paul has delayed explaining why he sent Epaphroditus back to Philippi (presumably along with the letter), perhaps because it is a delicate matter. His return is possibly an embarrassment to the congregation or perhaps an occasion for suspicion about possible negligence. Accordingly, Paul carefully explains Epaphroditus's significant role for both him and them and offers an explanation for his return as a matter of necessity (though full of emotional grief). He recommends that Epaphroditus be received with joy and honored with accolade, and Paul finally commends him for his self-giving service. All of this also indirectly thanks the entire congregation for their ministry through him, as Paul has done already (1:5-7) and will do again at the end of the letter (4:10-20).

Apparently the congregation earlier sent Epaphroditus to Paul with some financial assistance (4:10-18). But Epaphroditus was no doubt also sent with a broader mission. When someone was imprisoned by Rome and awaiting trial, the authorities permitted friends or family members minimal access to the prisoner to take care of basic needs, including the provision of personal safety, food, clothing, even books (Crossan and Reed: 276–77). Thus Paul acknowledges that Epaphroditus became the community's *public welfare service provider* (*leitourgos*) for his *need* (*chreia*, a term that frequently refers to basic "necessities of life"; cf. 4:16, 19). Epaphroditus might also have been sent to be Paul's legal advocate during his ordeal in Roman military custody before a Roman military tribunal. Some have speculated that Epaphroditus was a Roman citizen who had some potential access to the authorities in charge of Paul's custody and trial. That Epaphroditus is more than merely the bearer of financial aid is indicated (1) in the impression that he is not expected to return immediately; (2) in the way Paul names him as a valued colleague in the work of Messiah; and (3) in the way deep emotional bonds of friendship have been established with him. His possible involvement in Paul's trial is suggested by Paul's reference to their partnership, presumably through Epaphroditus, in the *defense and confirmation of the gospel* (1:7). It is probably in this context that *he risked his life*, perhaps intervening with the authorities and/or advocating on Paul's behalf.

As soon as he refers to Epaphroditus, Paul describes him with special titles and roles. The first three epithets highlight Epaphroditus as a valued colleague of Paul (*my brother, coworker, and fellow soldier*), and the second two focus on his special responsibilities to Paul on behalf of the Philippians (*your envoy and minister for my need*).

The first three epithets represent what Epaphroditus has recently come to mean to Paul as a result of his service. The first two collegial terms (*brother, coworker*) are found regularly in Paul's writings to describe his close associates in the work of the gospel. *Fellow soldier*, however, is rare, occurring elsewhere in the NT only of Archippus in Philemon 1:2 (cf. Col 4:17). The designation is consistent with the military imagery of *struggling together* (*synathleō*) in Philippians (1:27; 4:2-3). In the context of Philippi, a Roman colony founded for military veterans, the image is suggestive of a patriotic hero for Messiah and implies a contrast between God's army and Caesar's army (Fowl 2005: 135). His valor is evident most supremely in his willingness to *risk his life* for the cause of Messiah (2:30; see TLC, "Paul's Military Imagery").

The next two epithets extend the honored roles that Epaphroditus has filled on behalf of the Philippian assembly: *your envoy [apostolos] and public servant [leitourgos] for my need.* Paul otherwise uses the title *apostolos* mainly to refer to himself and a fairly small group of leaders, namely, those who were eyewitnesses of the resurrection (1 Cor 15:7, 9). But Paul also uses the role of *apostolos* to characterize an even broader group, including Silas and Timothy (1 Thess 2:6) and Andronicus and Junia (Rom 16:17). Moreover, Paul acknowledges that rivals also claim the role ("false apostles," 2 Cor 11:13; 12:11-12), and he identifies Titus and two unnamed "brothers" as "envoys [apostles] of the assemblies, the glory of Messiah" (2 Cor 8:23 AT). Now Paul turns this title of honor around, claiming Epaphroditus as the Philippians' *apostle* to Paul (*messenger* as a translation is too weak; e.g., NRSV, TNIV). Perhaps this role identification is meant to extend the level of mutual reciprocity between Paul and his Philippian readers by a kind of inversion. Observe that Paul seems to avoid self-identifying himself as formal *envoy* (apostle) in this letter, even though he writes with the voice of one in that role.

The role of *public servant* (*leitourgos*) recalls the language of 2:17 (*leitourgia*, public priestly service) and will be repeated in 2:30 for the obligatory service expected of the entire assembly (see below). The term can refer to any public service for a city. While the word may have the nuance of priestly temple service (LXX; cf. Phil 2:17; 4:18), here the term implies *public welfare service* to Paul during his imprisonment. (Paul also describes the financial contribution to needy Judea as a *leitourgia*; 2 Cor 9:12; Rom 15:27.)

The Reasons for Sending Epaphroditus 2:26-28

Paul eventually explains why it was *necessary* to send Epaphroditus back to Philippi: *for he was longing for all of you and was distressed because you heard that he was ill.* Later, Paul adds to this reason: so that they *might have joy* at seeing him again and so that Paul might be *more free of pain* (Gk. *alypoteros*; TEV: *my own sorrow will disappear*; NRSV: *less anxious*). Paul presumably will be *more free of pain* once Epaphroditus is in better surroundings for his continued return to health and not obligated to serve Paul further.

These explanations in no way imply that a character flaw—such as homesickness, a nervous disorder, emotional instability, or a negligence in duty—is the reason why he is being sent back to Philippi. Paul is not diminishing the legitimacy or significance of Epaphroditus's longing for his loved ones. This comment simply explains Epaphroditus's state of deep anguish (the same term occurs in the Gethsemane story: Mark 14:33; Matt 26:37) and does not really explain why he is being sent back. Epaphroditus's own distress is matched by Paul's: Paul sent him back *with much passion* (*spoudaioterōs*; possibly, *with haste, with great pain*, or *with much zeal*).

Paul stresses the gravity of his illness: *He was indeed so ill that he was a close neighbor to death* (v. 27; cf. v. 30, *He came near to death*, evoking the imagery of Messiah's own pathway in 2:8). Then Paul credits God's *mercy* for his eventual restoration. Paul also acknowledges that his own story is intimately tied to Epaphroditus's story: each of them is a recipient of God's *mercy*. Otherwise the loss of Epaphroditus would mean *pain upon pain* (*lypēn epi lypēn*, or, *sorrow upon sorrow*). Paul shares the deep emotion that accompanies sickness, potential loss of life and friendship, separation, and, of course, incarceration.

Receiving and Honoring Epaphroditus 2:29-30

Paul's exhortation that they properly receive and honor Epaphroditus (v. 29) does not mean that Paul has some doubt about either their joy or the honor they will give to Epaphroditus. With the words *Welcome him therefore in the Lord with all joy*, Paul in effect is simply saying, "Be glad in your reunion; be joyful for his return to health," although with considerable solemnity. It might also strike us as odd that Paul asks them to honor one of their own. But Paul lives in the world of formal social practices of giving and receiving honor, and his language is in large part conventional. (For instructions on proper reception in commendations or recommendations elsewhere in his letters, see 1 Cor 16:10-11, 16-18; 2 Cor 8:24; Rom 16:1-2.)

Paul emphatically puts Epaphroditus into a special class of worthy honorees: *such people* (cf. 1 Cor 16:16, 18). In effect, Paul proposes that he be awarded a special medal of honor appropriate to worthy soldiers. Epaphroditus has come *near up to death* by *risking his life*, specifically *because of the work of Messiah*, and more precisely *to fill up your arrears in service to me* (Phil 2:30).

What risk might Paul be referring to? Certainly more than the normal risks of travel by land and sea and the normal risks of illness. More likely, Paul refers to the risks attached to assisting and being an advocate for a suspect chained on a capital offense, a charge that smacked of disloyal treason. In a similar way, Paul describes Prisca and Aquila as ones "who risked their necks for my life," probably in connection with this same incarceration in Ephesus (Rom 16:3-5). This voluntary risk to the point of death is what marks him out as Paul's *fellow soldier* (2:25) and thus worthy in effect of a medal of honor in God's work of peace (cf. 4:7, 9).

The imagery of *filling arrears in service* (2:30) causes stumbling for Western interpreters, who typically shift the image to refer to "inability" or "lack of opportunity" (NRSV: *to make up for those services that you could not give me*; NIV: *to make up for the help you yourselves could not give me*; NET: *inability to serve me*). But Paul deliberately refers to "unfinished duty," "unpaid debt," or being "behind in the discharge of obligations." The NASB is closest to Paul's meaning: *what was deficient in your service to me* (cf. ISV: *what remained unfinished in your service to me*). The metaphor *arrears* (*hysterēma*, what is behind) makes perfect sense within a cultural framework in which terms of partnership (1:5, 7; 4:10-18) or friendship involve reciprocal mutual assistance as an indebtedness or obligation (Fowl 2005). Later, Paul confirms that earlier they had no opportunity to fulfill that obligation (4:10), not that they had no obligation in connection with their partnership.

The final clause is thus an indirect thank-you. Paul in effect says that through the ministry of Epaphroditus, the Philippians have fulfilled any possible obligation or responsibility that they might have had toward him, based on their friendship and partnership. Paul does not insinuate that they were doing less than they should have. Rather, his words give significant social meaning to their acts within the framework of their mutually obligatory relationship (see further the EN at 4:10-20).

The notion of reciprocal debts of obligation pertaining to partnership or friendship is foreign to individualistic, needs-based responses to assistance based on pleas. But these conceptions were a normal part of the ancient Mediterranean social system. Elsewhere Paul says that Philemon is both his partner but also in debt to him (1:17, 19). And the network of Paul's congregations are sending funds to the poor in Jerusalem both because they are in "partnership" with them and because they "owe" it to them (Rom 15:26-27).

THE TEXT IN BIBLICAL CONTEXT

Networking and Travel-Talk

Paul engages in discussion of travels or visits pertaining to himself or his associates in all but one of his letters. We find retrospectives on previous times with his congregations (1 Thess 1:5–2:13; 2 Thess 3:7; 1 Cor 1:16; 3:5–4:6; 2 Cor 1:19; 2:1; 7:12; 10:14-16; 11:7-9; 12:12; 13:1-2; Gal 4:12-20; Phil 1:3-5; 3:18; 4:15). There are announcements of planned arrivals or visits (1 Cor 4:14-21; 16:5-9; 2 Cor 9:5; 12:14; 13:1, 10; Philem 21-22; Rom 15:14-33; Phil 1:24-26; 2:24). Paul refers to the travels of his associates, whether retrospectively (1 Thess 2:17–3:13; 2 Cor 2:13; 7:5-16; 11:9; Col 1:6-8; 4:12-13) or in process (Rom 16:1-2; 1 Cor 4:17; 16:10-12, 15-18; 2 Cor 8:6, 16-24; 9:3-5; 12:18; Phil 2:19-30; Philem 8-20; Col 4:7-9). We even find Paul defending himself from charges of vacillation, not keeping his promises to visit (2 Cor 1:15–2:13). The impression we get is of an active dynamic social network involving travel and information exchange through personal visits, oral reports, and accompanying letters. Paul engages in travel-talk to provide information on himself or his associates, but especially to ensure proper receptions of those accompanying letters and to prepare for future visits. This all shows that the informal networks among assemblies founded within the sphere of Paul's ministry were maintained and solidified not just by letters, but also by the actual presence of emissaries dispatched by Paul or by others traveling from place to place and given special responsibilities in relation to the life of these assemblies. Sometimes letters and visits succeeded in finding success; sometimes both failed. Clearly the reports by Paul's associates upon their return to him is an occasion for tremendous joy (1 Thess 2–3; 2 Cor 2, 7; cf. Phil 2:29) and also an occasion for consternation. Important in these notices about travels are the commendations and recommendations about Paul's associates on the move.

Timothy

Timothy was one of Paul's most trusted junior associates. More is known of his work than about other close associates of Paul (for instance Titus or Silas/Silvanus). Paul recruited Timothy, a native of Lystra (Acts 14:6-19; 16:1-4), in approximately the year 49, during Paul's missionary described in Acts 15:30–18:21. Since Timothy was Jewish by ancestry (through his mother; for discussion see Cohen: 363–77), Paul had him circumcised to avoid the charge that Paul was inviting Jews to forsake the practice of Torah (cf. Acts 21:20-21).

With a Greek father, Timothy's bicultural heritage was no doubt seen by Paul as a crucial asset.

From that time onward, Timothy accompanied Paul in his travels and joined in his ministry. As a result, Paul included him as cosender (not always coauthor) in a number of his letters (1 Thess 1:2; 2 Thess 1:1; 2 Cor 1:1; Phil 1:1; Philem; Col 1:1). On a few important occasions, Paul dispatched him for special ministry on his behalf: from Athens to visit Thessalonica (ca. 49 CE: 1 Thess 3:1-10; cf. Acts 17:14-15; 18:5) and from Ephesus to Corinth (ca. 54: 1 Cor 4:17; 16:10-11). As envisioned in Philippians 2:19-24, Timothy indeed preceded Paul to Macedonia (Acts 19:22) where they were later reunited (2 Cor 1:1; 7:5). Still later, Timothy was with Paul in Corinth (Acts 20:2-3), sending greetings to the church of Rome (Rom 16:22). And finally Timothy joined the entourage of coworkers who accompanied Paul as he brought the financial gift from the assemblies in Asia and Greece to Judea (2 Cor 8:18-24; Acts 20:4-21:26; 24:17). Later information on Timothy is more sketchy. He serves in Ephesus (1 Timothy) and Rome, where he was imprisoned for the cause of Messiah (Heb 13:23-24; 2 Timothy).

Paul describes Timothy as his "brother" (1 Thess 3:2; 2 Cor 1:1; Philem 1; cf. 2 Cor 8:22) and "coworker in the gospel" (1 Thess 3:2; Rom 16:21), including him in the wider group of "envoys" ("apostles," 1 Thess 2:7). Most impressive are the accolades Paul gives Timothy in writing to the Corinthians: He "is my beloved and faithful child in the Lord, to remind you of my ways in Messiah Jesus" (1 Cor 4:17 AT; cf. 1 Tim 1:2); "he is doing the work of the Lord just as I am" (1 Cor 16:10). Another recommendation might also pertain to Timothy: "our brother whom we have often tested and found eager in many matters, but who is now more eager than ever [to serve you] because of his great confidence in you" (2 Cor 8:22).

THE TEXT IN THE LIFE OF THE CHURCH

Paul's Military Imagery

Paul's letters include an extensive and rich array of military imagery and vocabulary. Drawing on his scriptural and theological heritage, as well as contemporary conventions of speech, Paul employs this language in four major ways. (1) He uses this imagery for the battle of God's Messiah against the "powers" (in the past and present, concluding with the victorious transformation of the universe). (2) Military language is applied to the destructive warfare of Sin (cosmic "Error") against the human being, corrupting it from within

(Rom 5:12; 6:14; 7:7-11; Gal 5:16-17). (3) Battle imagery is used for the struggle of Messiah's community in the world, in which the saints as fellow soldiers take up and put on as their defense attire and offensive "weapons" only the virtues—fidelity, love, hope, justice-righteousness, good, purity, knowledge, forbearance, kindness, truth, prayer (1 Thess 5:8; 2 Cor 6:6-7; Rom 6:13; 12:21; 13:14; 15:30; Eph 6:15). (4) Paul uses military language for the (apostolic) battle for divine wisdom against human pretension even in Messiah's community (2 Cor 10:1-18).

In continuity with this overall usage, Paul depicts the assembly in Philippi as a besieged citizen community needing to muster a unified defense (1:27-28). He names their envoy as Paul's *fellow soldier* (2:25) and himself and their leaders as *fellow contenders [in battle]* (4:2-3). Paul identifies their ethical life with the metaphor of *holding the line [in battle formation]* (3:16), draws attention to the future victory of Messiah over all hostile powers (3:20-21; 4:5), and proclaims *the peace of God* as the supreme power that will prevail, parodying Roman peace propaganda (4:5, 7, 9; cf. 3:20-21).

This military imagery must be carefully considered in relation to the peace theology of Paul (which are closely intertwined; Swartley 1996) and in relation to the modern imperatives for peacemaking. This usage certainly does not mean that Paul endorses Roman imperial militarism or any other kind of earthly use of lethal force. It does not necessarily mean that Paul's rhetoric permits or promotes crusader violence, nor does it legitimize violence in God's name. And it does not mean that we should use military imagery uncritically in our contemporary contexts without reflecting on its violent potentiality. Yet it does mean that Paul lived and worked in a context steeped in military practice and imagery. It does mean that Paul understands peace not as passivity, but as striving in peacemaking toward a peace won through struggle. It allows for Paul's commitment to the God of liberating, transforming justice. And it means that Paul envisioned God's warfare of love as ultimately bringing an end to war and war machinery. Paul thus uses military language while trying to subvert all military violence. (For a fuller treatment, see Zerbe 2012: 123–40.)

Messianic Medals of Honor?

In the United States, the Medal of Honor is the highest military award, given for acts of valor above and beyond the call of duty. Paul advises that envoys and "soldiers" like Epaphroditus should receive special honors in service of Christ (Phil 2:29-30). In what way should the church today honor or recognize significant and bold acts of service, whether far away or near at home? How might one honor some as an inspiration and model for others without setting honorees apart, compromising the mutuality enjoyed in the church, or implicitly inviting people to strive simply for the honor (something Paul also cautions against)?

Exhortation 2

Practicing Messianic Citizenship, Part 2

Philippians 3:1–4:9

OVERVIEW

Which citizenship will you embrace? Which will you claim as your own? This passage contrasts two citizenships, Roman and Israelite-messianic.

Marked by a transitional *as for what remains* and a renewed address (*brothers and sisters*), Paul now moves to the second part of his exhortation. It recasts the agenda of the first part (1:27–2:18), reframing some themes and introducing some new ones. This second appeal comes in two parts: the first refocuses the imperative of a distinctive messianic citizenship and is the longest, most closely argued segment in the letter (3:1–4:1). The second is a looser grouping of closing exhortations (4:2-9), but still closely tied to the concerns expressed earlier in the letter.

At issue in 3:1–4:1 is the establishment of a messianic identity and citizenship, based on a focused and exclusive loyalty to Messiah. Messiah's own fidelity is the ground for new citizenship/identity *in Messiah* (3:9), and he is the intimate of any loyal follower (3:8-12). But Messiah is also above any other, and he will eventually reign supreme in the universe, exalting and redeeming his beloved (3:19-21). This messianic citizenship cuts two ways: first, it clarifies the nature of status and citizenship in Israel (3:3-11); and second, it means the renunciation of imperial Roman claims, and the privileges, statuses, allegiances, practices, and values that accompany that citizenship. The climax contains one of the strongest direct hits against Caesar and the Roman Empire in Paul's writings (3:18-21).

In the previous exhortation (1:27–2:18), Messiah himself was the supreme model of a proper citizen mind-set that embraces downward mobility (2:5-11). Now in this second major section, Paul puts his own citizenship story at the forefront (3:4-14), offering it also specifically as a model mind-set of divestment (3:15-17, corresponding to the mind-set language of 2:5). Paul also draws attention to the final establishment of God's global regime in both major sections, in the first case stressing the ultimate act of God (2:9-11; cf. 1:28), while in the second underlining the powerful agency of Messiah himself (3:20-21). This is the flip side to Messiah's divestment and weakness (2:6-8) and consequence of his exaltation (2:9-11). Paul does admit to the importance of an upward striving (3:12-14), but it is an upward striving of a very different sort than that demonstrated by those who resist the downward claims of the cross (3:18-19).

Once Paul's coded language is understood, it becomes apparent that the passage begins with a contrast between two citizenships, Roman (3:2) and Israelite-messianic (3:3); and it closes with the same contrast, Roman (3:18-19) and messianic (3:20-21). The expression of messianic citizenship *for we are the circumcision* (3:3) corresponds with the assertion *for our government [politeuma] exists in heaven* (3:20). And the caricature of adversarial Roman power and society as *dogs, evildoers,* and *butchery* (3:2) corresponds with the depiction of the *enemies of the cross of Messiah* (3:18-19), a further elaboration of the *corrupt and perverse nation* in which they live (2:15).

Heightening the parallel contrast is the use of threefold imagery for both Roman (3:2, 19) and messianic polities (3:3): messianic citizens positively named as the *circumcised* are *those who serve God in the Spirit, those who boast in Messiah Jesus, and those who do not seek confidence in fleshly credentials* (3:3). In contrast are *those whose God is their belly, whose glory is in their shame, and who are mentally preoccupied with earthly things* (3:19), a further explication of the *dogs, evildoers,* and *butchery* (3:2). As for outcomes: they who are pursuing shameful glory are doomed (3:18-19), but those whose regime is secured in heaven will find deliverance and the highest possible exaltation to glorious status (3:20-21), recalling the doom/deliverance contrast of 1:28.

Between these opening and closing contrasts, we find Paul's own story of citizenship (3:4-14), deliberately patterned on Messiah's model of divestment from any claim to status and offered as an exemplary model (3:15-17). This carefully argued clarification of messianic citizenship and assurance of final messianic victory becomes the basis for the repeated main appeal of the letter: *Therefore, my brothers and sisters, . . . stand firm in the Lord* (4:1; cf. 1:27), the antiphonal counterpart to the initial parallel exhortation, *My brothers and sisters, rejoice in the Lord* (3:1; 4:4).

OUTLINE

Resumed Exhortation on the Priority of Messianic Citizenship, 3:1–4:1
- A Resumption of Exhortation, 3:1
  - B Identity: Israelite-Messianic Citizenship Contrasted with Roman Adversaries, 3:2-3
    - C Paul as Model of Israelite-Messianic Citizenship, 3:4-14
    - C′ Exhortation to Practice This Mind-Set and Pathway, 3:15-17
  - B′ Destiny: Destruction to Those Aligned with Roman Values, Deliverance to Those Loyal to God's Regime Secured in Heaven, 3:18-21
- A′ Concluding Exhortation, 4:1

Closing Exhortations, 4:2-9
- 4:2-3 Mediating a Conflict among Leaders
- 4:4-7 Joy, Clemency, Prayer, and Assurance
- 4:8-9 Assessing and Practicing What Counts for True Virtue

Philippians 3:1-3

Israelite-Messianic Citizenship Contrasted with (Roman) Adversaries

PREVIEW

The sequence in 3:1-3 is dramatically attention-getting. Paul renews his exhortation in summary form (3:1a), takes a clarifying pause (3:1b), and then launches a startling blast in naming a threat to the community (3:2). This is immediately followed by an alternative framework of identity (3:3). In effect, Paul has introduced two rival formulations of identity and conduct (3:2-3), to be clarified and discussed in the passage to follow (3:4-21).

These verses abruptly and dramatically introduce the next major unit of argument and exhortation (3:1–4:1). The opening call to *rejoice in the Lord* (3:1) is repeated with a closing counterpart call to *stand firm in the Lord* (4:1). A sharp contrast between two identities and polities propounded in 3:2-3 will be further explained in 3:18-21. Moreover, the opening sharp contrast sets the stage for a lengthy treatment of Paul's own citizenship story (3:4-14), presented as a model to the readers-hearers (3:15-17; cf. 4:9).

OUTLINE

Transition and Resumption of Exhortation, 3:1a
Hesitation Formula, 3:1b
Israelite-Messianic Citizenship Contrasted with Roman Polity, 3:2-3
3:2 Coded Caricature of Roman Polity
3:3 Israelite-Messianic Citizenship Claimed and Reframed

EXPLANATORY NOTES

The traditional and prevailing interpretation of Philippians 3 is that Paul is suddenly shifting topics, now targeting either the Jewish community or specific theological threats or particular opponents within the "Christian" community, possibly even within the Philippian assembly itself. One common opinion is that Paul is attacking a Judaizing threat within the church. Opponents are supposedly seeking to impose strict law observance onto Gentile converts, including the practice of circumcision (but this perspective imports the agenda and themes of Galatians into the rhetoric of Philippians). Others, however, think that up to three different threats can be discerned in Paul's argument: Judaizing, 3:2-3; perfectionism, 3:12-15; and antinomianism, 3:18-19. Others propose that the threat named is that of Judaism in general, or Jews in the Philippian vicinity opposed to the new messianic community. Some are even convinced that this section comes from a different letter sent to Philippi, later conflated with another letter or two, because it is so different in focus compared to other parts of Philippians. All these proposals are problematic and should be discarded *[Opponents in Philippians, p. 300; Literary Integrity, p. 298]*.

What Paul actually does here is identify in coded language the Roman social and political order and its values as the chief threat to the community's own practice of citizenship. The most natural way of reading Philippians is that the opposing forces to be "observed" in 3:2 and 3:18-19 are the same as those identified in 1:28-30 and 2:15. These forces are the persecuting and yet alluring Roman sociopolitical system and its values, the same forces now holding Paul in chains (1:7, 12-14, 20; 2:17). Thus Philippians 3 in different words recapitulates what has been Paul's consistent concern throughout the letter: to clarify the distinctiveness of messianic identity and practice for a persecuted, suffering, struggling, and fractious community. This chapter then continues the main citizenship-polity agenda of 1:27–2:18 and so represents *the same things* (3:1b).

Transition and Resumption of Exhortation 3:1a

Now for what remains, brothers and sisters: rejoice in the Lord. These words mark a crucial transitional pivot in the letter that is both resumptive and summative. They provide closure to the preceding travel-talk yet also serve as a heading for what is to follow, almost as a piece of punctuation. Though some translations begin with *finally* here (NRSV, NIV 1984), a better rendering of the flexible term *to loipon* (lit. "the remainder," but meaning "henceforth, further, or finally") is *further* (NIV 2011).

While Paul has used the theme of rejoicing repeatedly to this point, he now exhorts his readers to rejoice specifically *in the Lord* (cf. 2:29, *receive him in the Lord with all joy*), a call roughly synonymous to *boast in Messiah* (1:26; 3:3). In the present context, the added clarification is the crucial point. The discussion that follows will focus on the posture and identity of being *in Messiah, in the Lord,* even though Paul will point to himself as the main exemplar through whom identity *in Messiah* will be demonstrated (3:4-14). *Rejoice in the Lord* is the first of a series of parallel statements modified by *in Messiah/the Lord* that will run through and then conclude the unit: *boast in Messiah Jesus* (3:3); *being found in him* (3:9); *the prize in Messiah Jesus* (3:14); and *stand firm in the Lord* (4:1). The phrase *in Messiah* occurs a total of sixteen times in critical places in this letter. Given a range of possible senses of the preposition *en*, the phrase can clarify the sphere *in*, the mode *through*, and/or the instrumentality *by which* the believer lives and acts (see also 1:13, 26; 2:1, 29; 4:3, 4, 7, 10, 13, 19, 21; cf. also 1:14; 2:19, 24). In the unit to come, the focus on Messiah is expressed also in the following ways: all of life has been revaluated *because of Messiah* (3:7-8); new priorities are *to know him* (3:8, 10-11), to be *conformed* to him (3:10), *to gain Messiah* (3:8), and to consider knowing him as *the surpassing value* (3:8). Finally, Messiah's own loyalty is the very foundation for the believers' justice-righteousness (3:9), and Messiah's power and victory will assure final deliverance (3:20-21).

In other words, the stress here is not on rejoicing by itself as a spiritual exercise, important as that is. Rather, the point is for the community to do their joyful celebration *in Messiah*, rather than via some other instrumentality or in some other sphere (as will become most clear by 3:18-21). Only *in Messiah* is there cause for true joy. This exhortation has real consequences for life in Philippi, including the readers' necessary avoidance of celebratory civic festivals, which are filled with rejoicing in the salvation brought by Caesar as his subjects celebrate his and the empire's virtuous military exploits that have brought "peace and security" and the wealth of its citizens (see also TBC on 1:3-11, "Joy and Rejoicing").

Hesitation Formula 3:1b

Paul pauses in an explanatory digression before the attention-getting start to his appeal that follows. A literal rendering would go thus: *To write the same things to you is not a shrinking [oknēron,* thus also *negligence, hesitation] on my part; but for you it is a safeguard [safety, security, stability].* Here Paul uses a well-attested epistolary convention known as a hesitation formula, which serves to remind the recipient that the sender is not being negligent or lazy, whether in business, friendship, or in the mere maintenance of contact (Reed: 257–58). Paul thereby acknowledges that what is to come (and what he has just said in 3:1a) is a continuation of the theme.

Indeed, the repetition serves to assure their stability, security, or safety (*asphales,* lit. *nonfalling).* Destruction or deliverance is at stake (1:28; 3:18-21). Their ultimate security is fully dramatized with the proclamation of Messiah's global rule in 3:20-21. Thus, to *stand firm* in that reality is what will assure their definitive security (4:1). Undoubtedly Paul is also playing ironically on the Roman propaganda of "peace and security" that the Roman Empire has proudly achieved for the world (see 1 Thess 5:1-3) *[Roman Imperial Propaganda, p. 312].*

The *same things* Paul writes include the exhortation to rejoice (2:17-18; cf. 4:4, *again I will say, rejoice*), but cannot be limited to it. Nor is Paul referring primarily to an earlier communication to his listeners (cf. 3:18). Rather, he is indicating that what he will say about messianic citizenship largely restates what he has said in 1:27–2:18. Once the internal coherence of 3:1–4:1 is recognized, along with its close correspondence with 1:27–2:18, this sentence makes perfect sense as a transition and needs no complex theory of a cut-and-paste editing job; or of an interruption, delay, or change of plans; or of some prior written or oral communication (cf. 3:18) that he is now repeating (also Engberg-Pedersen: 84–87) *[Literary Integrity, p. 298].*

Coded Caricature of Roman Polity 3:2

In this chapter, Paul's main purpose is to affirm, clarify, and promote the nature, practice, and salvation of Israelite-messianic citizenship (3:3-14, 15-17, 19b-21). Paul begins with a startling caricature of the threatening alternative (3:2) and later adds to the parody while challenging its claim to bring final salvation (3:18-19a, 19b-21). His rhetoric is imagistic and seems deliberately coded, meant to conceal meanings from anyone (esp. the Roman authorities) who might intercept the letter. We should assume that at this point Epaphroditus advises the listeners orally as to what Paul's oblique words are meant to convey.

Verse 3:2 is attention-getting for its literary repetition, rhythm, and sound (alliteration), but also by its content:

Blepete tous kynas.	*Be(a)ware of the dogs.*
Blepete tous kakous ergatas.	*Be(a)ware of the evil workers.*
Blepete tēn katatomēn.	*Be(a)ware of the butchery [the cutting up].*
Hēmeis gar esmen hē peritomē.	*For we are the circumcision [the cutting around].*

The repeated Greek verb *blepete* (*watch! observe!*) here has the sense of both (1) *Observe and take note!* and (2) *Watch out, danger!* Throughout antiquity the word *dogs* was used for various derogatory associations (e.g., Isa 56:9-11). Dogs are detested as a scourge, as vicious and scavenging lowlife. The metaphor is especially suggestive of uncleanness and moral indecency and of sharp social demarcation. The term is deployed especially to mark off the unclean or despised "outsider" (Rev 22:15; Matt 7:6; Mark 7:27-28 // Matt 15:26-27). The term *evil workers* is similarly generic. It draws attention to immoral and unjust practices (cf. 2:15; 3:18-19). The third term, *katatomē,* was commonly used for various forms of intense physical violence ("cutting up, hacking, butchery, slaughter") against people, or for severe "cutting up" of leather, landscape, or stone.

The prevailing Christian interpretation is that Paul is hurling violent and slanderous invective against a new group of opponents—either Jewish adversaries in general or "Jewish-Christian" (Judaizing) preachers who demand that all male Messiah loyalists be circumcised. Christian commentators routinely claim that *dogs* was a common epithet used by Jews to derogate Gentiles and that Paul is justifiably reversing this invective. But there is no evidence that this was a common (or uniquely used) epithet used by Jews for Gentiles. Ironically, the clearest evidence for this is on the lips of Jesus (Mark 7:27 // Matt 15:26-27). The traditional view also supposes that the *cutting up* (butchery, slaughter) is designed as a mocking attack on the practice of Jewish circumcision. In accordance with this interpretation, the translation *mutilation* has recently prevailed in English versions, though it was unknown before the last hundred years. While *mutilation* is a possible nuance of the Greek *katatomē*, it unnecessarily and misleadingly narrows the scope of Paul's meaning. Paul simply contrasts a violent, forceful *cutting down* or *cutting against* (*katatomē*; KVJ: *concision*) with a refined, surgical "cutting around" (*peritomē*, *circumcision*). The coherence of the argument of this chapter and the entirety of Philippians suggests that the same adversaries are in view here in 3:2 as elsewhere in the letter (1:27-30; 2:14-18; 3:18-19). There is no evidence of any specific threats in the vicinity of Philippi from the Jewish community in general or from "Christian Judaizers."

The most crucial clue to understanding this threefold image of *dogs*, *evildoers*, and *the cutting up* (butchering, slaughtering) is a distinct intertextual resonance with Psalm 22:16, following the textual tradition evident in the Dead Sea Scrolls and the Septuagint (but not the Masoretic Text of later rabbinic tradition; Flint: 43; ISV mg.):

> *Dogs* have surrounded me;
> a gang of *those who practice evil* has encircled me;
> they have *gouged* my hands and my feet. (Ps 22:16 [21:17 LXX] ISV)

Indeed, it appears that the entire psalm of lament is on Paul's mind. This would not be surprising, since it is apparent that Paul has been recalling lament psalms for encouragement and as a way of understanding his own distress (see TBC on 1:12-26, "Echoes of Scripture"). In Psalm 22:12, the threefold image describes a group of violent oppressors with animal imagery:

> Many bulls encircle me;
> strong bulls surround me;
> they open wide their mouths at me,
> like a ravening and roaring lion.

The psalm also describes particular forms of physical violence, which Paul would naturally relate to his own torture. As the psalm finishes its lament, it petitions the Lord in a prayer that correlates the dog with the sword: "Deliver my life from the sword, my life from the power of the dog! Save me from the mouth of the lion!" (22:20-21a). At that point the psalm turns toward its end by expressing hope and confidence in divine deliverance (22:21b-26) and proclaiming the Lord's worldwide dominion (22:27-31; cf. Phil 2:9-11; 3:20-21). The thematic correspondences with Philippians are remarkable. Paul probably thought of this psalm christologically (as having been the experience of Messiah; Mark 15:34) and thus of his own suffering and that of the pressured community in Philippi in light of that paradigm. In the same way, he alluded earlier, in 2:17, to the suffering servant of Isaiah 53, which he likely understood first christologically and then also as a paradigm for his own ministry.

As elsewhere in Philippians, then, the adversaries caricatured are those representing the Roman sociopolitical order: the *crooked and twisted nation* among whom the community lives (Phil 2:15). Scavenging, vicious, and assaulting *dogs* echoes Paul's reference a few years earlier to the struggle with Ephesian forces opposed to him as "fighting against wild beasts" (1 Cor 15:32 AT). The depiction of the opponents as the *butchery-mutilation* (those who cut up, hack, or slaughter) might refer (1) to the general military violence of the Roman regime (Paul's reference to the prospect of Roman military violence ["the sword"] lined up against the messianic assembly in Rom 8:35-36, written a few months after Philippians, lends support to this; for Roman violence in general, see Lintott; Wengst 1987; Wistrand); or more specifically (2) to his own experience of torture in Roman detention (2 Cor 11:23; the image in Ps 22:16 [21:17 LXX] also suggests this). It has also been proposed that Paul is referring (3) to non-Jewish cultic and philosophical alternatives, such as some unknown Roman pagan ritual practice (Nanos 2009, 2013; the cognate verb *katatemnō* is used for the flesh-cutting actions of the prophets of Baal in 1 Kings 18:28 LXX).

Once it becomes clear that Paul is mainly drawing attention to the Roman sociopolitical order, it is understandable why he would avoid a direct reference to it, given the likelihood that his letter could easily be intercepted by the Roman authorities (Cassidy 2001b: 89). His own Roman citizenship is what is keeping him alive by a thread. Thus, to attack Roman imperial violence explicitly or to have renounced his own citizenship directly would have been suicidal (see also TLC below, "Is Paul's Depiction of Adversaries 'Violent'?") *[Opponents in Philippians, p. 300; Literary Integrity, p. 298]*.

Israelite-Messianic Citizenship Claimed and Reframed 3:3

Paul contrasts the caricature of Roman opposition with a claim to an alternative identity formation: Israelite citizenship (marked by circumcision) as practiced in Messiah (3:3). As a contrasting play on the violent image of "those who cut up/hack/slaughter" (*katatomē*), Paul now claims and affirms: *We are those who are cut around* (*peritomē*, circumcision), using again a singular noun for a collective entity (cf. Gal 2:7-9). Paul here appropriates this citizenship marker in Israel positively as the outward sign of the covenant (e.g., Gen 17:10-14, 23-27; Exod 4:25; 12:44, 48; Lev 12:3), as "sign and seal" of Abraham's "righteousness of loyalty-faith" (Rom 4:11 AT). Abraham "received circumcision as a sign or seal of the righteousness of loyalty-faith while he was still in foreskin, so that he might become the father of all who believe through [the condition of] foreskin . . . , and thus the father of circumcision, not only to those who are from the circumcision but also to those who follow the example of the loyalty-faith of our father Abraham while still in foreskin" (4:11 AT). For Paul, being baptized into Messiah essentially incorporates that person in Abraham (Gal 3:23–4:7, esp. 3:29), who is thus to be regarded among the "circumcision." Paul does not qualify circumcision here as true circumcision or spiritual circumcision, as if the actual circumcision is completely negated. Rather, actual circumcision (as both physical *and* symbolic) is affirmed, just as Paul admits elsewhere that there is "considerable advantage" to (the) circumcision (Rom 3:2). This positive appropriation reflects Paul's own affirmative appraisal of his Israelite identity (e.g., Rom 9:1-5; 11:1-32). It also suggests that the core of the messianic assembly in Philippi was drawn from a Judean (Jewish) heritage and that the assembly continued to prize that heritage. Even Acts is aware that the Philippian public construed the struggle in Philippi as that between "Judeans (Jews)" and "Romans" (Acts 16:20-21) *[Profile of the Assembly, p. 305]*.

Here Paul does not debate or criticize the actual value or status of circumcision as a practice (cf. Rom 2:25–3:2; 1 Cor 7:19; Gal 5:6; 6:15). Debates about whether God intended circumcision as a literal or symbolic sign had been going on already for a few hundred years in some diasporic Jewish communities. Yet Paul here simply draws on the language of circumcision as a core image of membership in God's elect people of Israel. In that respect, it is essentially synonymous with declaring the identity of the messianic assembly as *saints [consecrated] in Messiah* (1:1), which also draws on a traditional symbol of Israelite identity ("a priestly kingdom and a holy nation," Exod 19:6). As for actual practice, Paul was vigorously opposed to imposing circumcision on non-Jewish adherents of Messiah, as part of a proselyte ritual of absorption into the Judean (Jewish) people. But nowhere does he argue against those of Jewish ancestry becoming circumcised, and instead he seems to endorse this practice (Nanos and Zetterholm).

Circumcision as the preeminent Israelite citizenship symbol is immediately clarified with three clauses:

those who serve in/by the Spirit,
and who boast in Messiah Jesus,
and who put no confidence in the flesh.

To express the notion of serving, Paul uses a verb (*latreuō*) that does not refer narrowly to *worship* (NRSV, NIV 1984) in the gathered assembly, but to God's people's broader need to *serve* (NIV 2011) as they express their devotion and loyalty to God in all of life (similarly, "essential-substantive-spiritual service," *logikē latreia*, Rom 12:1 AT). This service, Paul says, occurs by the instrumentality of the Spirit (NIV: *by his Spirit*) and/or in the modality of the Spirit (NRSV: *in the Spirit*), echoing themes that he explains at greater length elsewhere (e.g., Rom 7:4-6; 8:1-27; 12:1-2; cf. 2 Cor 3, for the Spirit as a key marker of the new covenant).

The next two descriptors become the focus of attention for the rest of the chapter (3:4-14, 18-21): on the positive side, *boasting in Messiah*; and on the negative side, *not putting confidence in [relying upon] the flesh.* The Greek word translated *boasting* (*kauchaomai*) literally means "to speak loudly," especially "to vaunt, to pride oneself in, to glory in" (cf. 1:26; 2:16). Boasting in Messiah resonates directly with rejoicing in the Lord (3:1) and standing firm in the Lord (4:1). Paul's stress on "boasting in Messiah" emphasizes a contrast with the pervasive quest for public acclaim and glory in Roman society in general and Roman Philippi in particular, addressing again the key issues of status, honor, privilege, and glory running throughout the letter *[Love of Honor, p. 299]*. Not surprisingly, Paul uses similar language when he contests and shames the upwardly seeking, status- and honor-conscious elite of the Corinthian assembly (see TBC, "Boasting and Being Confident"). The notion of "putting confidence *in the flesh*" poses a sharp contrast with "serving *in the Spirit*" and will be repeated twice in the next verse (3:4). The word *flesh*, used earlier in the letter to denote Paul's "physical life" (1:22, 24), here signals things earthly and material generally, especially things of worldly status, power, privilege, and comfort, including things pertaining to polity-citizenship, such as military might. The image is not meant simply (nor even mainly) as a polemic against the significance of physical circumcision. In this verse, then, Paul both affirms circumcision and qualifies it with matters of devotion and practice.

This threefold depiction of the community of Messiah will soon find a contrasting parallel with the threefold depiction of the *many enemies of the cross of Messiah* (3:18-19):

[we] who serve in/by the Spirit	*their god is the belly*
[we] who boast in Messiah Jesus	*their glory is in their shame*
[we] who put no confidence in the flesh	*their minds are set on earthly things.*

THE TEXT IN BIBLICAL CONTEXT

Boasting and Being Confident in Paul's Letters

While the language of boasting occurs only three times in Philippians (1:26; 2:16; 3:3), it is disproportionately found in Paul in relation to the rest of the NT (58 of 64 total occurrences). It appears most frequently in the correspondence addressed to the Corinthian assembly (29x). This terminology has its home in the ancient world's value system and cultural context of pursuing honor and avoiding shame. It overlaps in meaning with "commending oneself" (2 Cor 3:1; 4:2; 5:12; 6:4; 10:12, 18), "being confident" (2 Cor 1:9; 3:4; 10:2, 7), being "aggressively bold" (2 Cor 5:6, 8; 10:2), and "glorifying" or desiring "glory" (Phil 3:19).

In Paul's letters, there is legitimate boasting and improper boasting. Faulty boasting is boasting in the wrong thing, or boasting without basis and truth, which results in disgrace and shame (2 Cor 7:14; cf. *empty glory*, Phil 2:3). He speaks against "boasting" on the part of the Judeans in relation to pedigree, status, identity, or distinctive morality (e.g., Rom 2:17, 23; 3:27; 4:2; cf. Gal 6:13-14; Eph 2:9) or against boasting through body-denying ascetics (1 Cor 13:3). Most extensively, he speaks against boasting on the part of the upwardly mobile elite of Corinth who are vaunting their impressive wisdom and social wisdom while disdaining aspects of Paul's style, ability, and lifestyle (1 Cor 1–4, 9; 2 Cor 3, 5, 10–13). Paul shames (1 Cor 4:14) some in the Corinthian assembly who are apparently boasting of their wisdom and social position (1 Cor 1:17–2:5). In particular, he scolds them for boasting of rival leaders (1 Cor 3:21) and for their economic, intellectual, and moral overconfidence (1 Cor 4:7; 5:6; cf. Phil 3:19, *Their glory is their shame*). Here Paul adapts words from Jeremiah 9:23-24 (9:22-23 LXX): "The one who boasts should boast in the Lord" (1 Cor 1:31 AT; cf. 2 Cor 10:17; Phil 1:26; 3:3; Rom 5:11). When Paul's relationship with some in Corinth grew even more tense, apostolic rivals denigrating Paul are charged with "boasting in face [appearances], not in heart" (2 Cor 5:12 AT), of inappropriately "commending themselves" (10:12), of "boasting in the flesh" (11:18, 21) and "beyond limits" (10:13, 15).

In the face of this opposition, Paul also offers a "boast" ("the fool's speech," 2 Cor 11:16–12:11). Ultimately he claims that his only legitimate grounds of boasting are "the things that show my weakness" (2 Cor 11:30; 12:5, 9; cf. 1 Cor 2:1-5), "so that the power of Christ may dwell in me" (2 Cor 12:9). In Galatians, speaking against those who boast in human pedigree, identity, and status ("flesh"), Paul says that he "will only boast in the cross of Messiah Jesus" (Gal 6:13-14 AT). In Romans, he adds that he boasts in the hope of the "glory of God," yet precisely since this entails "boasting in our sufferings" (Rom 5:2-3), suffering is the path to glorification (8:17-30). Thus, he can reflect this way on his ordeal in Ephesus while he wrote Philippians: "We had received the sentence of death on ourselves, so that we would put our confidence not in ourselves but in the God who raises the dead" (2 Cor 1:9 AT).

At the same time, Paul can offer a "boastful" defense of his ministry and its fruit (Rom 15:17; 1 Cor 9:15-16; 15:10, 31; 2 Cor 1:12-14; 5:12; 10:8; 11:10), and he invites others to boast on his behalf (2 Cor 5:12; 10:12). He also boasts to others about the qualities of a congregation (1 Cor 15:31; 2 Cor 7:4, 14; 8:24; 9:2, 3), and he considers the commitment and maturation of his converts as his ground for boasting at the day of Messiah (1 Thess 2:19-20; Phil 2:16; 4:1; 2 Cor 1:14).

THE TEXT IN THE LIFE OF THE CHURCH

Is Paul's Depiction of Adversaries "Violent" (3:2)?

If Paul is actually warning the congregation in Philippi in 3:2 about "Christian Judaizers" or about the Jewish community in general, as is with rare exception assumed, what we have is a case of sharp, derogatory, and slanderous invective against rival Christian preachers or against the rival Jewish community in general. But rarely is this acknowledged by modern interpreters. Instead, Paul is regularly celebrated as simply throwing insults back at his opponents, premised on the idea that to reverse a verbal attack is somehow legitimate for those in the right. Other interpreters, less inclined to give Paul the benefit of the doubt, have suggested that this is simply one of many "violent" texts in Paul (cf. Gal 5:12; 2 Cor 11:13-15).

As it turns out, this sort of verbal barrage would not measure up to Paul's own stated standards of ethical speech: elsewhere he exhorts that one should conciliate when slandered and bless when reviled (1 Cor 4:12-13; cf. Rom 12:14; 1 Pet 3:9). Moreover, this interpretation of 3:2 is also dangerous. It represents the long legacy of Christian anti-Judaism (Nanos 2009). Indeed, many Christians came to assume that theological attacks on Jews, as the murderers of Jesus, are somehow always legitimate. Even though Paul did not intend this meaning, Christians have lots of explaining and apologizing to do for the ways in which we allowed this and other passages in the NT to generate the long and shameful history of Christian anti-Semitism. (On the issue of possible anti-Judaism in the NT and Paul, see Donaldson.)

The interpretation offered in this commentary is not designed to exonerate all texts in Paul of their actual or potential violence. But it is crucial to distinguish between, on the one hand, religioethnic slander and hostile invective among horizontal rivals, and on the other hand, sharp political critique and caricature by an oppressed or marginalized community (not motivated by mere resentment or rivalry). But when that reactionary critique from the underside is eventually put into the hands of the powerful (as in the period of Christendom), the intent of the original critique is easily lost, and its potential for harm against the marginalized is enhanced. (For a lengthier treatment of the question of potentially violent texts in Paul, see Zerbe 2012: 169–80.)

Philippians 3:4-17

Demonstrating Messianic Citizenship: The Model of Paul

PREVIEW

As Christians, whose are we? What citizenship do we claim? Did Paul "add" a heavenly citizenship and thus invoke a "dual" citizenship? Or did he see his heavenly citizenship as a religious-political *alternative* to his Roman citizenship?

Paul invokes his own story of Israelite citizenship as a way to clarify the two sides of a new citizenship identity that he has just propounded—boasting in Messiah and putting no confidence in the flesh. First he will concretely illustrate what it is to *have confidence in the flesh* (3:4-6), and then what it means instead to *boast in Messiah* (3:7-14). Boasting in Messiah means a fundamental revaluation of and divestment from former assets and achievements (3:7-8), a resocialization into a new personal and social bond (3:9-11), and finally an all-out pursuit on the racetrack (3:12-14). Listeners are then enjoined to follow this example (3:15-17).

OUTLINE

Being Confident in the Flesh: Paul's Israelite Cursus Honorum, 3:4-6
Boasting in Messiah, 3:7-14
- 3:7-8 The Balance Sheet: A Reassessment
- 3:9-11 The Social Register: A Resocialization

3:12-14 The Racetrack: Intense Pursuit toward the Ultimate Prize
Practicing the Mind-Set, 3:15-17

EXPLANATORY NOTES

Being Confident in the Flesh: Paul's Israelite Cursus Honorum 3:4-6

With a sharp adversative conjunction (*kaiper*, even though) and an emphatic self-reference (NRSV: *I, too*; NIV: *I myself*), Paul sets up his own story as paradigmatic, with the claim that he has *basis for confidence [status] in the flesh*—indeed, more than others. *Flesh* here refers to the realm of worldly status, power, privilege, and comfort. Paul's emphasis on *more* anticipates the imagery of the contrasting *surpassing value* of Messiah (3:8).

As Paul itemizes his grounds for confidence in the flesh, there is no hint that he is being defensive or polemical. Although Paul's autobiographical statements serve a mainly apologetic or defensive purpose elsewhere (1 Thess 2:1-12; Gal 1:13–2:14; 2 Cor 11:23–12:12), Paul's purpose here is to present himself as a model or paradigm. Except for the admission that his zeal led him to persecute, Paul expresses pride in this rehearsal, even though he will later claim that Messiah undercuts any confidence in these credentials.

The listing of citizenship credentials and achievements is terse:

Circumcised on the eighth day
Out of the nation of Israel
Of the tribe of Benjamin
A Hebrew of Hebrews
In regard to the law, a Pharisee
In regard to zeal, a persecutor of the assembly
In regard to justice-righteousness in the law, blameless

Honorific inscriptions like this, detailing and celebrating a person's cursus honorum (course of honors), were prevalent in the public spaces of Roman Philippi and have survived on stone pillars. Paul seems to deliberately follow this pattern. Thus Hellerman summarizes:

> The recipients of the letter lived in a social context in which elite claims to ascribed honor (birth status) and acquired honor (virtuous deeds and civic and military posts) were proclaimed in the form of *cursus* inscriptions throughout the colony. . . . These values and practices were replicated in miniature among the members of various cult groups and in other social settings. For Paul to dismiss his indisput-

> ably impressive Jewish *cursus* as "rubbish" (. . . v. 8) would have profoundly challenged the social sensibilities of those steeped in the values of the dominant culture of Roman Philippi. (Hellerman 2005: 127)

In presenting his credentials, Paul first lists items of pedigree pertaining to impressive citizenship givens (ascribed honor). Then he moves to items of achievement (acquired honor), emphasizing (1) higher education and elite party membership, (2) demonstrated zealousness (patriotism) even to the point of persecuting traitors, and (3) moral rigor and reputation. The listing of ascribed honors before achieved honors, along with the emphasis on tribal and genealogical heritage, is characteristic of surviving Roman inscriptions from Philippi.

In naming the honors of citizenship as a matter of family heritage, Paul begins with *circumcised on the eighth day*, recalling the emphasis on circumcision as the key identity marker of covenant membership (3:3) and indicating his family's strictness in matters of cultural-political-religious identity, as required by the Law (cf. Lev 12:3; Luke 1:59; 2:21). Paul continues with *of the nation* (Gk. *genos,* genealogical community) *of Israel*, emphasizing his pureblooded birthright in Israel (cf. Rom 9:4; 11:1; 2 Cor 11:22). *Of the tribe of Benjamin* directly parallels the Roman preoccupation with detailing one's tribal status in Roman honor inscriptions. A person's tribe (*gens*) was included in the three-name convention for Roman citizens (TBC on 1:1-2, "The Name Paul") *[Citizenship, p. 279]*. Here Paul's tribal identity draws attention to his membership in a select, favored tribe from which comes his namesake Saul and in whose territory is the holy city Jerusalem. Benjamin alone joined Judah in loyalty to the Davidic covenant and was granted the designation "the beloved of the LORD . . . [who] rests between his shoulders" (Deut 33:12 NIV). Claiming to be *a Hebrew of Hebrews* puts the emphasis on language and cultural distinctiveness. It is perhaps meant to highlight that he derives from a traditionalist family that worships and speaks Hebrew (or Aramaic) at home and that has close connections with the Judean homeland. That these identity markers are matters of pride for Paul is confirmed by other contexts, where he lets these credentials stand without undermining them: in 2 Corinthians 11:22 he claims his identity as "a Hebrew," "an Israelite," and "seed of Abraham," and in Romans 11:1 he claims the honor that he is "an Israelite, out of the seed of Abraham, of the tribe of Benjamin." Paul perhaps avoids reference to Abraham here as a way to focus on his "national" citizenship through Israel. While Paul elsewhere self-identifies as a "Judean," accommodating to prevailing religioethnopolitical terminology (e.g., 1 Thess 2:14; Gal 2:15; cf. Acts 22:3), his primary orientation is toward "all Israel," the polity of God's historic covenantal relationship and future promise (Rom 11:25-26).

Next, Paul lists three items of achievement (toward acquired status), all introduced by *in regard to.*

1. *In regard to the law, a Pharisee.* This achievement (cf. Acts 22:3; 23:6-9; 26:5; Gal 1:14) identifies membership in an elite religiopolitical party historically involved in the governance of Judea, legislating and adjudicating on the basis of the Torah, the "constitution" of the Israelite nation. Like Paul, the historian Josephus, as a matter of distinction, claims to have begun at the age of nineteen "to practice citizenship [*politeuomai*] according to the Pharisaic doctrine" (*The Life* 1.12). Josephus was born into a high-priestly family in Jerusalem and was involved in governance by the ruling establishment. Later he was a general in the war against Rome, until he defected to the other side, eventually receiving Roman citizenship while also becoming an apologist for his Judean nation. Josephus estimates the numbers of this elite group of Pharisees at around six thousand. Pharisees were not all of one persuasion, and Paul was not the only Pharisee to have joined the early messianic movement (Acts 15:5; cf. Matt 23:15).

2. *In regard to zeal, a persecutor of the assembly.* At issue here is the matter of "patriotism," the fervor of commitment to the people, the state, its constitution, and its symbols. "Zeal," and especially "zeal for the Law" (tantamount to "defending the constitution" in modern oaths), had become a slogan, since the days of the Maccabees, for rigorous, nationalist revitalization in the face of foreign domination and influence, whether by military conquest or insidious cultural-religious pressure. Phinehas, who had taken up arms to violently cleanse the nation of traitors (Num 25), had become the hero and model of "zealousness" for many (25:11, 13), perhaps also for Paul. Paul claims that it was especially his own zeal in persecuting the traitorous messianic assembly that became an established part of his reputation, proof of his loyalty to the Law (the constitution) and to the integrity of the nation (cf. Gal 1:13, 23; cf. Acts 7:58; 8:3; 9:1-2; 22:3-5; 26:9-11). Elsewhere, too, Paul highlights his "zeal" as a mark of his life before Messiah, his "former life in Judaism": "I advanced in Judaism above many of my own age among my nation [*genos*], being so exceedingly zealous for the ancestral/patrimonial traditions" (Gal 1:13-14 AT). Here in Philippians, Paul wants to highlight his unwavering, patriotic, "zealous" commitment to the

people and cause of Israel. He leaves implicit what he says directly elsewhere—that his "persecution of the assembly of God" was a massive error, for which he could be considered "unfit to be called an apostle," and that he is what he is now only by "the grace of God" (1 Cor 15:9).

3. *In regard to justice-righteousness in the law, blameless.* This item brings the catalogue of credentials to a climax. It is not so much a private accomplishment as a social reputation, showing public citizenship. In other words, Paul says, I have the reputation for being scrupulous in Torah (constitutional-legal) observance: blameless in matters of purity, commerce, finance, food, Sabbath, sexuality, and so on. Justice-righteousness is defined relative to the Law, a framework that will undergo significant revision from the vantage point of Messiah (1:11; 3:9; cf. Rom 3:21-31; 7:1-6; 8:1-4; 9:30–10:7). As for performance, then, Paul is *blameless*, the same word used in 2:15 (for the community as a whole) and synonymous with the word *mature* (*perfect, complete*) in 3:15.

The Balance Sheet: A Reassessment 3:7-8

Paul begins the reassessment of these impressive "grounds of confidence in the flesh" through the commercial metaphor of a balance sheet. His former patriotic zeal is likened to the quest for commercial gain. Though these items of status and achievement were once to him "gains"—"income and assets," what we might call "social capital"—now he has come to regard them as "losses, liabilities, or write-offs" (*zēmia*, Lat. *damnum*, loss, damage, penalty). The financial reassessment moves in three steps. Each step expands the breadth of possible assets now put on the deficit side of the ledger.

> *Whatever things were for me gains [assets, income], these things I consider . . . as loss.* (v. 7)
> *More than that, I consider everything [panta] as loss.* (v. 8a)
> *All things [ta panta] I have lost and consider as refuse.* (v. 8b)

This broadening scope is not explicitly explained. Presumably he intends to include anything given special value from a "fleshly" or "earthly" perspective: not just his prior statuses or achievements, but also any material, religious, physical, political, or intellectual advantages that come before or compete with messianic priorities and imperatives. Indeed, the final term *all things* often denotes the universe in Paul's vocabulary. Similar is Galatians 6:14: "Far be it from me to glory except in the cross of our Lord Jesus Messiah, through whom the world [*kosmos*] has been crucified to me, and I to the world" (AT). A close parallel to Paul's words appears in the Gospels. In calling his disciples to take up their cross, Jesus says that those who lose their life will find or save it. And it hardly profits people to "gain the world but lose their very selves" (AT: Matt 16:24-26 // Mark 8:34-36 // Luke 9:23-25).

By the end, all these things are reassessed as "losses." Moreover, they are items of "refuse"—junk that gets in the way and needs to be discarded. Paul uses a well-known vulgarity (*skybalon*), which can refer to "refuse, trash," even "dung" (although Paul does not use the technical term for excrement). The image strikes a resonance with what Paul says elsewhere, when he shames the status-conscious Corinthians: "We have become, and are now, as the refuse [*perikatharmata*] of the world, the off-scouring [*peripsēma*] of all things" (1 Cor 4:13 AT).

Each of the three claims of mental reassessment (*I consider*) gives the same fundamental reason: *because of Messiah* (v. 7); *because of the surpassing value of knowing Messiah Jesus my Lord* (v. 8a); *because of him [Messiah]* (v. 8b). The reference to what is of *surpassing value* (a term also found in 2:3 and 4:7; cf. 4:19) shows that Paul is speaking of a relative, not an absolute change in value. Something of superior value has caused former assets to pale in worth (cf. 2 Cor 3:7-18). It is not as if all things from his past have lost all inherent value (cf. Rom 3:1; 9:1-5; 11:1-2, 28-32). Still, a significant "paradigm shift" has occurred in Messiah. On the one hand, any confidence or pride in ethnic pedigree, moral credentials, or social achievement is completely undercut. Moreover, as we will immediately see, the manner of striving toward the goal of *justice-righteousness* by reference simply to zeal for the Law has been entirely reoriented (3:9). Nevertheless, Paul will continue to promote energetic striving as reoriented in Messiah (3:12-14). And he never categorically rejects the Law nor his prior identity markers (Rom 3–11).

The Social Register: A Resocialization 3:9-11

Gaining Messiah

Paul has let go of all his assets and achievements *in order to gain Messiah and to be found in him*. Now Paul will elaborate on the way in which *the knowledge of Messiah Jesus [as] my Lord* holds *surpassing value*. The image thus shifts from the commercial to the relational, social sphere. The *gain* is a new relationship *with* Messiah, a new identity and solidarity *in* Messiah, and a new social virtue *through* Messiah.

Paul thus uses the image of "gaining" persons, as in friends or patrons, just as he elsewhere describes gaining converts through his ministry (1 Cor 9:19-22). Paul lives in a society organized through networks of patron-client relationships. By highlighting that he has come into a new personal relationship with a new "lord," Paul especially implies the notion of "gaining" a patron, thus gaining a different kind of social capital. Indeed, at the outset he identifies himself as *slave of Messiah Jesus* (1:1). Patrons are crucial in providing for security, status, wealth, identity, and even survival. While Paul rejects the negative social consequences of the pervasive patronage and benefaction of his day as a way to gain honor and status, he nevertheless employs the imagery of gaining a new bond with a patron for persuasive purposes (just as he uses military imagery while subverting the value of the military in real terms).

Being Found in Him

Gaining Messiah is coordinated with *being found in him*, identifying a new place of belonging and home. *Being found in Messiah* suggests images of rebirthing, adoption, and incorporation into Messiah (and his "body"), as Paul explains elsewhere (Gal 3:26-28; 1 Cor 12:12-13; Col 3:1-11; Rom 6; see TBC, "Becoming Messianic Citizens"). At the same time, it implies Paul's radical personal transformation (Gal 1:11-17; 1 Cor 15:7-11). As Paul will soon report, he has been *seized* by Messiah (Phil 3:12) into a new relational, social, and transforming reality. *Being found* in Messiah is more than a statement of a new spiritual state and bond. Rather, it expresses a new political identity: citizenship in Messiah's regime (1:27; 3:20), with all the rights, privileges, and responsibilities thereto.

Having a Justice-Righteousness through the Fidelity of Messiah

Paul proceeds to explain the social gain as involving a corresponding new character: *having a justice-righteousness* (for "being found" in terms of moral character, see 1 Cor 4:2; Gal 2:17; as a condition, cf. 2 Cor 5:3). *Justice-righteousness* (*dikaiosynē*, a word that embraces both personal righteousness and social justice) is the key virtue and value in any citizenship, body politic, or social order, and of God's regime in particular (cf. Rom 14:17). Using the same word as Paul, the philosopher Plato seeks both the justice of the individual and the justice of the citizen community in his classic work the *Republic* (e.g., 368e). *Justice-righteousness* is a crucial mark of membership in the covenant of Israel, including legal, moral, social, personal, and even political aspects. For Paul, justice-righteousness is the supreme God-given, Messiah-established, and Spirit-energized identity marker of God's citizen community (Rom 4:11).

Paul's language in verse 9 is brief and elliptical. What we can discern from other letters of Paul is that *justice-righteousness* is first God's own covenant loyalty and the order of right relationships that will prevail through the faithful loyalty of Messiah (Rom 1:16-17). Yet it is also the gift bestowed on those who respond in faithful trust (Rom 3:21–4:21) as well as the personal and social virtue generated within the believer through the energizing of the Spirit (Phil 1:11; Rom 7:1-6; 8:1-12; 12:1–15:13; see Toews 2004: 54–64, 99–113). The justice-righteousness that Paul now *has* is thus both established as a gift (cf. Rom 3–4) and something being actualized in the life of the believer (cf. Rom 6–8; Phil 1:9-11). Crucial in this context, justice-righteousness is the indispensable mark of covenant membership in Israel, and now for the citizen community of Messiah.

In contrast to his Israelite pedigree just noted, Paul emphasizes that this *justice-righteousness* is no longer oriented only to or established only by the Law (Torah). Nor is it a matter of possessing it as "one's own," as one's own achievement (cf. Rom 9:30–10:7). Rather, he stresses the crucial new act of God through the faithfulness of Messiah in making a new way of justice-righteousness possible. Justice-righteousness comes *through the faithfulness of Messiah [dia pisteōs christou]* (Phil 3:9), though it is ultimately *sourced from God, based on [that] faithfulness.* Paul is not referring here to faith *in* Messiah (the traditional interpretation; NRSV, NIV) but to the faithfulness *of* Messiah (TBC, "The Fidelity of Messiah"). Messiah's own trusting loyalty, already highlighted with reference to his "obedience" in 2:6-8 (cf. Rom 5:19), is the crucial means for God's ultimate victory and the establishment of justice-righteousness in the world. Moreover, it is the prototype that all humans follow to demonstrate that new righteousness within God's emerging order of justice-righteousness (Toews 2004: 54–57).

Paul's first hearers-readers might easily have discerned an implicit counterclaim to Roman imperial ideology in which the "loyalty of divine Augustus" (*fides divi Augusti*) is proclaimed as that which has brought salvation, peace, and security throughout the empire. They would have noticed furthermore that "justice" (Lat. *iustitia*, synonym with *dikaiosynē*, as in Phil 3:9) is one of the cardinal virtues in Roman imperial theology, a gift of the gods. The direct contrast with Roman claims will become explicit by the end of the chapter (3:18-21).

The Ultimate Goal: To Know the Power of Christ's Resurrection

The next two verses (Phil 3:10-11) are grammatically set apart from what precedes as a self-standing "purpose clause," *to know him*, with further content explicated through a chiasmus (X structure).

> *To know him*
> *and the power of his resurrection*
> *and the partnership with his suffering,* (3:10a)
> *becoming conformed to his death,*
> *so that somehow I might attain the resurrection from the realm of the dead.* (3:10b-11)

What the reader must supply are some introductory framing words. The previous purpose clause followed Paul's litany of resolutions: *in order that I might gain Christ and be found in him*. This further purpose clause could be understood as the purpose for his giving up former assets. But it is probably better to assume some appropriate introductory words: *[My greatest aim now in Christ, because knowing him holds surpassing value, is] to know the power of his resurrection*.

The train of thought has been focusing on new gains made possible in Messiah. We would thus expect Paul to go to the ultimate goal and hope of being raised in new life so as to participate fully in the restored world in the age to come. But shockingly, Paul uses an intensive *and* in the first line to indicate that his ultimate desire is to know (in experience) *both* the power of Messiah's resurrection *and* partnership in his suffering. Paul is not suggesting that suffering in solidarity with Messiah is the goal or virtue in itself, but is rather the necessary pathway. Moreover, he indicates that resurrection power is already experienced in the present via the very experience of suffering and yet is something to be fully experienced only in the future. This latter aspect will become the focal point in 3:20-21.

Perhaps the best commentary on Paul's compressed words is his own later reflection in Romans 8:14-39, penned a few months after writing Philippians. Moving to the crescendo of ultimate victory in Messiah, Paul first stresses that those who are in Christ, being led by the Spirit, enjoy a new social registry as "children of God" (Rom 8:14-16; cf. Phil 3:8-9). Then he moves to consider the future, stressing how this means that they are "heirs" of God and fellow heirs with Christ. Recall that what was promised to Abraham and his heirs was "the world" (Rom 4:13). Being heirs includes the prospect of being "glorified with Christ" (8:17). But precisely here, Paul offers a proviso: "If, in fact, we suffer with him so that we may also be glorified with him" (Rom 8:17). Suffering is not a virtue or goal, but it is the ordained pathway—both for Christ and for all who attach themselves in loyalty to him. Indeed, it is the pathway of the whole of creation, which groans in pain as it awaits its transformation and renewal in the age to come. It finds its destiny alongside a transformed and renewed human community (Rom 8:18-25).

As Paul remarks in numerous places, life experienced at its most vulnerable becomes the seed for the establishment of life (e.g., 2 Cor 1:3-11; 2:14-16; 4:7-11; 4:16–5:10; 6:4-10; 11:23-30; 12:5-10; cf. 1 Cor 4:8-13). By the end of this chapter, Paul will move unequivocally to victory and resurrection (Phil 3:20-21). But his concern here is to establish a theological framework for his readers' and his own understanding of their suffering: Messiah's own suffering becomes the "standard of intelligibility" (Fowl 2005: 156) for their suffering (cf. 1:29-30). His suffering and their suffering are both in the pathway of Messiah, in conformity to and in partnership with Messiah. But they are also *on behalf of Messiah* (1:13). Paul says elsewhere that tribulation and suffering are the ordinary lot of believers (1 Thess 1:6; 3:2-3; 2 Cor 1:5; 4:7-18; Rom 8:17; Col 1:24; Phil 1:29). Paul is not here discussing the ethical or theological implications of dying or rising with Messiah (cf. Rom 6; 7:4-6; Col 2–3). Rather, his concern is to make sense of real suffering (see TBC on 1:27-30, "Paul's Theology of Suffering").

The purpose clause ends on a provisional note: *if somehow I may attain* . . . (NRSV). This translation seems to suggest that resurrection is something to be personally "achieved." Better is the CEB: *so that I may perhaps reach the goal* . . . Paul seems to want to prevent any kind of realized eschatology that claims to experience all the blessings of Messiah's resurrection already in the present. Still, this proviso leads directly to his next words that stress goal-oriented pursuit.

The Racetrack: Intense Pursuit toward the Ultimate Prize 3:12-14

There is indeed a synergy of divine and human effort working in concert (2:12; cf. 1 Cor 15:10). Twice Paul negates the idea that the final blessings of salvation are already experienced. Claiming that it is not so much about the arrival as in the striving and moving, Paul introduces a new metaphor: the racetrack. He articulates a set of parallel disclaimers and resolutions. Paul's words are terse and imagistic, somewhat hard to follow precisely.

- Disclaimer 1: *[It is] not that I have already obtained [the prize* or *goal] or have already reached the goal [*or, *been perfected],*

- Resolution 1: *But I race in pursuit so that somehow I might take hold of [the prize],*
- Basis: *just as I have been taken hold of by Messiah.*
- Disclaimer 2: *Brothers and sisters, I do not consider myself to have taken hold [of any prize].*
- Resolution 2: *[I am committed to] just one thing: forgetting the things behind me and straining toward the things ahead, I race in pursuit toward the mark [finishing tape], for the prize of the upward call of God in Messiah Jesus.*

The words that Paul uses for his energetic pursuit are intense. Twice used is *diōkō*, "pursuing, pressing on, catching, racing." It is also the word for "persecuting." *Taking hold of* translates *katalambanō*, "to seize, grasp, take aggressively" (LSJ). The pursuing is clarified as a "stretching, straining forward, reaching out toward" (*epekteinomai*). The overall image adds to the intensity, that of a runner with a singular drive: (1) preoccupied by just *one thing* (cf. the *only thing* of 1:27); (2) focused on the *mark* (*skopos*, lit. "the sight," thus "target, goal"); (3) *forgetting* (in the sense of "neglecting" or "disregarding"; cf. Heb 6:10; 13:2, 16) those *things behind*, whether other runners or circumstances, even previous races in the past; and (4) driven entirely by the quest for the prize and the glory attached to it, *the upward/above call.* (For another extended athletic metaphor, this time emphasizing the discipline of training, see 1 Cor 9:24-27. For racetrack imagery, see also Phil 2:16; Rom 9:16, 30-32.)

This striving pursuit, however, is grounded in *having been seized* (or, *taken hold of*) *by Messiah Jesus* (3:12). Paul does not specify the circumstances of when and how he was *seized.* Most likely he is referring to the dynamics around receiving the transforming "revelation of Messiah" in his person, which turned his life around and gave him his calling (Gal 1:15-16; Rom 1:1; cf. 1 Cor 9:16, "necessity is laid on me").

The ultimate goal of Paul's straining pursuit is *the prize of the upward call of God. Upward* translates the adverb *anō*, which can have either the sense of motion "upward" or rest "above, on high." The phrase conjures the image of receiving honor at pan-Hellenic contests, such as the Olympic games, in which the victor receives public recognition. Following a race, the victor, the father's name, and the victor's country are declared by those presiding over the games from seats on high, and then the victor is invited up to receive the *victory wreath* (*stephanos*, as in Phil 4:1; e.g., Bruce; Martin 1980; Hawthorne). Similar is Paul's image of the quest for the "imperishable victory wreath" instead of merely the "perishable victory wreath" (1 Cor 9:24-27).

What constitutes the actual prize should be identified in the manner already explained: full knowledge of Messiah, union with Messiah, and participation in the resurrection life of the age to come. Paul is not referring to the prize as the call to be with Jesus in heaven (NIV: *the prize for which God has called me heavenward*; TEV: *God's call to the life above*; NRSV: *the prize of the heavenly call of God*). In Paul's writings, heaven is the source, security, and foundation of God's saving work in all creation, not the final destination. Heaven is the place where God's reign is now supreme, where God's regime is in a kind of exile as the whole world awaits its full restoration, when heaven and earth will merge through God's act of re-creation (3:21; cf. Rom 8:18-25). The calling has a *heavenly* origin (cf. Gal 4:26; Col 3:1-2; 1 Thess 2:12), but the destination is not simply heaven (see TBC on 1:12-26, "What Happens after Death?"; TLC on 3:18–4:1, "The Renewal of the World").

Practicing the Mind-Set 3:15-17

As has been implicit from the very beginning (Phil 1:12-26; 2:17-18), Paul now explicitly asserts that his story is exemplary for them, both for their *mind-set* (3:15) and for their *walk* (vv. 16-17). It can hardly be the case, as some argue, that in verse 15 Paul is referring back only to verses 12-14, targeting some specific question of spiritual perfectionism. Rather, Paul wants his readers to consider the proper *viewpoint* in all that he is communicating. Boasting in Messiah (3:3-14) and taking on the mind-set of Messiah (2:5) is exemplified in the letter as (1) reassessing earthly glory and privilege, especially the privileges attached to earthly citizenship and achievement; (2) questing for an intimate relationship with Messiah and desiring to belong primarily to the community of Messiah, showing loyal fidelity to him in response to his initiative; (3) being willing to partner with and conform to the "lowest" forms of life, including suffering and death, instead of one's own achievements; and (4) eager striving toward the goal to which all history is leading: God's sovereign reconciliation of the entire universe, including the prize of their own participation in it (3:10-11, 12-14, 20-21).

Paul indicates that there is a progressive movement in a person's relational attachment to Messiah (1:6, 9-11, 25). As a result, he first addresses those who are *mature* (3:15). In Paul's vocabulary the word *mature* (*teleioi* can also mean "complete, perfect") is applied to acting as adults and not as children (1 Cor 2:6; Eph 4:13). The term *mature* is consistent with the imagery of striving in verses 12-14 and picks up verbally on the image of verse 12 (*teleioō*, "reaching the goal, making complete"; similarly in 1:6, God *will complete [epiteleō] the work*). While the word here has the connotation of maturity (not perfection), it is a provisional maturity that can never be complete until the goal of God's redemptive work has been reached (vv. 12-14; cf. 1:6, 9-11). Paul acknowledges that some *think otherwise*. Still, Paul exudes confidence in their continued maturation through divine enabling (cf. 1:6; 2:12). Inviting all to maintain the level of their progress thus far, Paul moves from the imagery of mind-set to that of the *walk*. He employs a word commonly used in military contexts to refer to staying in battle formation as a body: *go forward according to the rule* (TEV; the verb *stoicheō* means "to stay or walk in line, in a row"; also in Gal 4:25; 6:16; Rom 4:12). (On warfare imagery in Paul, see Zerbe 2012: 123–40.)

With a renewed address, *brothers and sisters*, Paul now puts his own life directly into the foreground, using a newly constructed word unique in Greek literature: *become fellow-imitators* (*symmimētai*, co-imitators) *of me*, emphasizing their mutuality in this practice. The point is repeated with a further clause: *And just as you have us as a model, keep your eyes on those who walk as we do* (v. 17). The wording *keep your eyes on* uses the verb form (*skopeō*) of the word used in 3:14 for the *mark* (*skopos*, sight) that the racer *keeps in view*. The same verb was used in 2:4 to stress the *marked* concern for the other person. Then Paul uses term *walk* to denote manner of life, the most frequent verb in Paul's vocabulary for "conduct" (Rom 6:4; 8:4; 13:13; 14:15; 1 Cor 3:3; 7:17; 2 Cor 4:2; 5:7; 10:2; Gal 5:16; Eph 2:2, 10; 4:1, 17; 5:2, 8; Col 1:10; 2:6; 3:7; 4:5; 1 Thess 2:12; 4:1, 12; 2 Thess 3:6, 11). This vocabulary draws from his Pharisee heritage (Heb. *halakah*: ethics as "the walk"). The word sets up the terms for the next verse, where Paul will consider the negative pattern of those *who walk as enemies of the cross of Messiah*. By contrast, Paul invites his readers to consider his conduct and that of the *mature* generally as a *model* (*typos*, "figure, image, pattern," also used in 1 Cor 10:6; 1 Thess 1:7; 2 Thess 3:9).

THE TEXT IN BIBLICAL CONTEXT

Why Does Paul Use Israelite Citizenship Symbols?

The recurring theme in Paul's exhortation is that members of Messiah's citizen-community must divest themselves of any privileges of status or pursuits toward honor by which people are divided or marginalized. Privilege, status, and honor come from prior identity or earthly citizenship markers, whether Israelite or Roman (2:3-8; 3:4-19). Corresponding to this is the repeated emphasis on the embrace of lowliness as the path to exaltation (2:6-11; 3:4-14, 20-21) and the doom awaiting those who exalt themselves in shame (3:18-19). To highlight this theme of status divestment, Paul uses his own Israelite citizenship story to speak to the issue of residents of Philippi who are pursuing gain or status through Roman citizenship. Paul seeks instead to focus their loyalty and security solely on Messiah (Wright 2000).

If Paul ultimately wants to apply his exhortation to the lure and pursuit of (or boasting in) Roman citizenship, why does he highlight his Israelite story instead of his Roman citizenship story? Could he not score more rhetorical points with the latter? In other words, why didn't he say, "I have more status and achievement than most others by virtue of my Roman pedigree, but I have renounced the value of it all"? The answer is likely in the following: First, Paul's Israelite citizenship actually constitutes his primary personal identity (Rom 9:1-5; 11:1-2; 2 Cor 11:22). Second, it would have been suicidal for him to renounce his Roman citizenship explicitly if such words had reached the eyes or ears of the Roman authorities. Roman citizenship is keeping him alive by a thread (Cassidy 2001b: 89). This also explains why Paul needs to refer to the Roman ruling elite in coded terms. Third, most of the members of the Philippian assembly are probably also Judean citizens by birth or had come to embrace the tradition and identity of God's history in Israel *[Profile of the Assembly, p. 305]*. Finally, Paul is conscious that the Messiah himself was a full-fledged member of the Judean family (Rom 9:1-5; 11:25-29; 15:8), even if his destiny was to "rule the nations" (Rom 15:12 AT; Phil 2:9-11; 3:20-21).

For these reasons, then, Paul positively affirms the community's and his own Judaic circumcision identity, even as it is reframed through Messiah and provides no opportunity for claims to special honor *in the flesh* (3:3). While Paul celebrates his Israelite citizenship in its continuity with Messiah (3:3), he also qualifies its specific significance in light of Messiah (3:4-14). Paul does not introduce his Judean citizenship identity to destroy it or to renounce it completely. Paul is a self-identified Israelite *and* a Jesus-Messianist.

Becoming Messianic Citizens: Rebirthing and Resocialization

Throughout Paul's Greco-Roman world, citizenship was first understood as membership in a genealogically defined "tribal" community.

Second, it was applied hierarchically, excluding slaves and the urban and rural poor, with the "free" also graded in terms of status and privilege. And third, it excluded women formally and practically *[Citizenship, p. 279]*. By contrast, Paul's Israelite-messianic citizenship perspective involves a radical resocialization at various levels, working against these notions in crucial ways:

1. Entry into this new citizen community is via solidarity with and absorption into Messiah as experienced in baptism. This means a rebirthing (dying and rising with Messiah, Rom 6), re-creation (2 Cor 5:16-17), or adoption ("filiation," Rom 4:13-25; 8:15-21, 29; Gal 3:26–4:7). What results is a new humanity. Christ as the "second/new Adam" is the progenitor of the new humanity (Rom 5:12-21; Col 3:10-15). But he is also the firstborn of a large new family of brothers and sisters (Rom 8:29). This new social reality of *knowing Messiah*, *gaining Messiah*, *being found in Messiah*, and *partnering with Messiah* (Phil 3:8-10) radically undercuts prevailing boundary definitions through genealogical arrangements (whether Judaic or Roman). It cuts across the Jew-Gentile divide (Gal 3:28; Eph 2:11-19) and involves a radical "unplugging from the organic community" (Žižek: 123–30).

2. This new social reality undermines prevailing hierarchical socioeconomic conceptions and status divisions: there is "no longer slave or free" (Gal 3:28; 1 Cor 12:13), and the goal includes economic "equality" (2 Cor 8; on Paul's "economic theory," see Zerbe 2012: 75–92). In this regard, Paul's understanding of messianic citizenship is based squarely on the ideals of Mosaic legislation, where all members of the covenant community are equal in standing and value and the weak and poor are specially protected.

3. There is "no longer male and female" in Messiah's citizen community (Gal 3:28), and Paul endorses the leadership role of women. Arguably, the historical Paul is a decisive (but lost) voice in the movement toward universal suffrage.

The Fidelity of Messiah (*pistis Christou*)

This small phrase occurs in a number of crucial passages in Paul's letters (Rom 1:16-17; 3:21-22, 25-26; Gal 2:16, 19-20; 3:22; Phil 3:8-9). It has been the subject of considerable attention and debate among biblical scholars in recent decades. Increasingly, it is recognized that the phrase should be translated as the "faithfulness *of* Christ" (Phil 3:9 ISV: *faithfulness of the Messiah*; NET: *Christ's faithfulness*; CEB, NIV 2011 mg.: *faithfulness of Christ*; KJV, NRSV mg.: *faith of Christ*)—not as "faith *in* Christ," the traditional reading that has prevailed for a hundred years (NRSV, NIV). (For a detailed discussion with bibliography, see Toews 2004: 29–31, 54–57, 108–11; Boer 2011: 148–50, 192–93; for a cautionary view, see Brunk: 305–10.) This interpretation does not take away the crucial human response of loyal faith in response to God's act in Christ, but it does acknowledge Paul's consistent stress on the agency and model of Christ in establishing righteousness-justice both as a gift and as a transformation within the person and throughout the world.

Knowing and Being Known

Paul's language of "knowing" is worthy of attention. In the Corinthian correspondence, Paul writes to those who promote the virtues of (worldly) wisdom and knowledge (1 Cor 1:18–3:23). There, Paul seeks to move attention away from preoccupation with substantive, rational knowledge (even as he affirms both the crucial role and limits of that knowledge). Instead, he draws attention to "being known" personally (1 Cor 8:3; 13:12). When describing the new place of formerly idolatrous Gentiles in the community of faith in Galatians, in contrast to their former ignorance of God, Paul comments: "But now you have come to know God, or rather, have come to be known by God" (Gal 4:8-9 AT). This perspective of being known is expressed in Philippians with terms such as *being found in him* (3:9) and *being seized by Christ* (3:12). These texts illustrate Paul's relational understanding of his bond with Christ (cf. Phil 1:23) and his awareness that Christ has taken the initiative in the personal knowing. While promoting growth in *knowledge and perception/insight* (Phil 1:9-10), Paul also recognizes *the peace of God, which surpasses all understanding* (Phil 4:7) and "the love of Christ that surpasses knowledge" (Eph 3:19).

THE TEXT IN THE LIFE OF THE CHURCH

Preaching Downward Mobility: Are There Limits?

Paul emphatically claims to have divested himself of assets and status in favor of sole dedication to Christ and to have committed himself to a life of moderation and contentment (Phil 4:11-13). He emphatically endorses this *walk* of "cruciformity" (3:18; Gorman 2001) as a model for those loyal to Christ, inviting them to desist from *selfish ambition, rivalrous striving*, and the pursuit of *empty honor* (2:3-8; 3:4-19). This is a call to a hard path—one against the grain, both then and now. It is reminiscent of Jesus' call to radical discipleship (see TBC on 2:1-5, "Status Inversion").

How does one preach this pathway of downward mobility? To whom might it be relevant, and under what circumstances? These words can hardly apply to those among the "lowly" today—the many people in places of desperation around the world who seek betterment through enhanced privilege, for instance, through immigration and citizenship in a place of greater opportunity and prosperity. Many such people are already troubled with a sense of guilt for these very aspirations or for abandoning their own people and their struggles. The same holds for those who are suffering in debilitating and oppressive relationships. In these sorts of circumstances, Paul's call to resilience and solidarity within suffering is not a statement about the virtues of passively accepting suffering.

Paul addresses these words to those already having comfortable means and aspiring to enjoy the status and privileges of the highest echelon of society. He calls them instead to a "solidarity with the lowly" (Phil 2:3; Rom 12:16 AT). Presumably, then, these words apply to similar circumstances today—to those in the Global North or to those on one side of the tracks, inviting them to a true "partnership of generosity" (Phil 1:7) appropriate to messianic citizenship values and aspirations. Still, a preacher can afford to make such a connection only delicately: after all, the *walk* that Paul promotes rubs against prevailing values of upward mobility among the middle class. Paul would not have understood how individual self-interest could be seen as the driver of greater wealth for all, as in "classical" (capitalist) economic theory. Economic thinking was markedly different in his day compared to the modern world. Paul would no doubt agree that more profound than some privatized ascetic morality of self-denial or self-sacrifice is the social posture and virtue of "partnership" as a community and in solidarity with the downtrodden.

Just as Paul was a master of contextually appropriate communication, the church today must be ever conscious of how our best theology and cherished ideas can have vastly different impacts in different settings, requiring appropriate messages and modes of communication, without compromising what it means to *practice citizenship in a manner worthy of the gospel of Christ* (Phil 1:27).

Philippians 3:18–4:1

Contrasting Regimes and Destinies

PREVIEW

You have enemies around you! Take note! This passage brings to a close the unit starting with 3:1-3, where two rival identities are dramatically contrasted. The previous section has clarified the distinctive disposition and walk of Messiah's people by reference to Paul's own story and example (3:4-17; cf. 3:3). This concluding section will (1) unveil the walk, mentality, and destiny of those who resist Messiah and his way (3:18-19; cf. 3:2); (2) proclaim the alternative deliverer and the destiny of those oriented to Messiah's regime now exiled in heaven (3:20-21); and (3) close with the concluding exhortation to maintain loyal commitment to that regime (4:1).

OUTLINE

Enemies of the Cross: Their Walk, Mind-Set, and Destiny, 3:18-19
Messiah's People: Their Awaited Deliverer and Destiny, 3:20-21
Concluding Exhortation: Stand Firm, 4:1

EXPLANATORY NOTES

Enemies of the Cross: Their Walk, Mind-Set, and Destiny 3:18-19

Paul has explained the mind-set and walk of *those who boast in Messiah*, especially in his model of divestment for the sake of others

(2:3-8; 3:3-17); now he identifies a sharp contrast between all that and the mind-set and walk of *many* who *walk as enemies of the cross of Messiah* (3:18-19). *Many* is a term for the majority, general population. "To walk" is a term for conduct appropriate to a body politic (e.g., 1 Thess 2:12), so the statement rings as a direct counterpart to Paul's opening exhortation: *Practice your citizenship singularly according to the good news of Messiah* (1:27).

This is now just the second time the cross has intruded into the letter, in a decisive way once again. At stake is the fundamental messianic imperative of lowering oneself and being in solidarity with the lowly (2:3-8). The enmity or opposition here has to do with a fundamental pathway, indeed, the priorities of a citizenship. This is not simply an in-group theological dispute about circumcision for Gentile converts (as in Galatians) or general moral laxity or spiritual enthusiasm (as in 2 Cor 10–12). Enmity here has a distinctly theo-political sense. Paul does not say *your* enemies. He avoids language that would personalize any enmity. Rather, the enmity has a deeper root than normal social hostility. It has to do with responding to the character, pathway, and reality of God's chosen deliver: Messiah.

The contemporary reader will notice a resonance with Paul's more polemical proclamation of the "cross of Messiah" in 1 Corinthians 1–2 in opposition to "Greek wisdom" and "Jewish signs." There Paul shames "the pretentious elite questing after power, wealth, wisdom, noble birth, and honorific public office" (Horsley 1997: 244), engaging in a parody of the ruling social and political order to which many believers in Corinth were aspiring (Georgi: 52–57). Although the polemic is not as sharp in Philippians, the core issues at stake appear to be familiar.

The original order of Paul's words is noteworthy: *For there are many people walking—of whom I have often told you, but now tell you again as I weep—who are enemies of the cross of Messiah.* Paul in effect pauses with a preface about his comments on the *enemies of the cross.* First, he explains that this is not new information for them (cf. Acts 16:20-21) and that he has deep sorrow over it. Paul's weeping probably refers to his continued grief at the presence of continued hostility to the gospel of love and reconciliation in Messiah, the one destined to rule and reconcile the world (cf. Rom 9:1-5). The presence of hostility conjures up not hatred, but sorrow.

Still, Paul goes on to declare their doom and to dramatize what they affirm by way of mind-set and practice. The abrupt announcement that *their destiny is destruction* anticipates the contrasting image of deliverance in Philippians 3:20-21. It also returns to the contrast between destruction and deliverance-salvation (*sōtēria*) in 1:28. In effect, this pronouncement is the counterpart of the adversaries' hope that the messianic community will meet destruction (1:28). This is strong language, but not unique in Paul (see also 1 Cor 1:18; 15:18; 2 Cor 2:15; 4:3; 11:15; Rom 3:8; 6:21-22; 2 Thess 2:10). *Destiny* here translates *telos* (end, goal), which elsewhere in Paul refers to one's final destiny (Rom 6:21-22; 2 Cor 11:15) and the climax of the ages (1 Cor 10:11) in connection with the "day of Messiah" (1 Cor 1:8; 15:24). Paul's declaration anticipates the arrival of Messiah's ultimate triumph (3:20-21), which will mean humiliation and defeat for some and exaltation and triumph for others. A close analogy to this image is in 1 Thessalonians 5:3, where Paul parodies Roman imperial boasts: "When they say, 'There is peace and security,' then sudden destruction will come upon them." (For images of doom or dissolution on the prevailing world system, including the Roman imperial order, see also 1 Cor 2:6-8; 7:31; Rev 18.)

The three depictions of what these *enemies of the cross* affirm are schematic and oblique. They become fully transparent only when the counterpart declaration of the heavenly regime and the messianic victor is fully presented (3:20-21).

1. *Their god is their stomach.* "Stomach" (*koilia*) in Greco-Roman writings was regularly used as a metaphor for the "appetites" in general, especially for gluttony or sexual excess. The overall picture of this phrase is that of a life oriented to insatiable consumption and excess—to the gratifying of the appetites, including the sexual appetite. It is a metaphor pertaining to the lavish lifestyle of the privileged and wealthy.

2. *Their glory is in their shame.* The quest for *gloria* (fame, praise, and public adulation), along with *dignitas* (reputation, worth, honor, esteem) and *auctoritas* (prestige, respect), was one of the cardinal values of Rome's elite classes (Ward, Heichelheim, and Yeo: 53–54). The phrase picks up the theme of honor and status consistently used in Philippians (TBC on 2:1-5, "Status Inversion"). The depiction is ironic: those who pursue glory will only attain shame. *Shame* appears to be a general castigation of elite Roman society (cf. *the corrupt and perverse nation* in which they live; 2:15). It would be a fair stretch to apply this to some "Judaizing" threat within the community.

3. *Their mind is set on earthly things.* Paul again uses the verb *phroneō* to identify a mental or dispositional focus (cf. 2:2-5; 3:15; cf. Col 3:2). *Earthly things* as a priority is the same as things of the *flesh* (cf. 3:3-11), meaning matters of worldly status, power, and privilege.

Moreover, it anticipates the contrast with the *governing regime* (*politeuma*) of Messiah's people that now exists in heaven, the source of the world's final transformation through Messiah (3:20-21). *Earthly* is used in a metaphorical, ethical sense. Just as Paul's use of the term *flesh* indicates no inherent antagonism to physical life, so also this use of *earthly* does not suggest disregard for the created order that God seeks to transform and redeem (cf. Rom 8:18-25). Paul's vision of redemption is not ultimately an escape to heaven, but the final transformation of "all things" in which heaven and earth merge, so that God will be all in all (see TBC and TLC below).

Who, then, might these *many enemies* be? First, they do not appear to be part of the Philippian assembly. Paul's reference to the generic *many are walking* and reminder of having mentioned this pattern on earlier occasions precludes this (Fee). Second, they are not presented as teachers (as are the opponents in Galatians and 2 Corinthians). Paul highlights, as elsewhere in Philippians, the critical matter of *conduct* (1:27–2:16; 3:17; 4:9), not of *doctrine*. Third, they are not depicted as personal rivals to Paul (cf. 1:15-17). Fourth, they can hardly be identified exclusively as lax or lapsed believers on the grounds that Paul would not shed tears for outsiders (contra O'Brien). To the contrary, just as Paul weeps for the uncommitted among his own people of Israel (Rom 9:1-5), it appears that here Paul is shedding tears for the majority in the non-Jewish, Greco-Roman world, insofar as the goal of universal inclusion and reconciliation in Messiah (e.g., Rom 11:25-32) seems so remote.

The reference is thus primarily to those many who remain antagonistic to Messiah and his regime. Indeed, the palpable counter-Roman rhetoric in the next verses suggests that Paul is depicting the *practice of citizenship* of general Roman society. Their imperatives of earthly glory (including social, economic, political advancement; cf. Phil 2:3), conspicuous consumption, and moral license combine to make it antithetical to Messiah's pathway to the cross. While the humiliated faithful will be exalted (3:20-21), the presently exalted will presumably be humbled (3:18-19). The resumption of the themes of 1:27-30 and 2:14-16 further suggest that in 3:18-21 the same threat and set of adversaries is in view. The first known commentator on Philippians assumed that the *enemies of the cross* referred to Roman persecutors (Polycarp, *To the Philippians* 12.3; 2nd quarter of 2nd c.) *[Opponents in Philippians, p. 300]*.

But the rhetoric actually cuts against any outsider or insider whose *walk* exhibits these characteristics and priorities. Here Paul is sharpening the central priorities of cruciform messianic citizenship.

His appeal is meant both to reassure those whose commitment is sure and who are suffering for it, and to warn those whose walk is affected by the insidious draw of the privileged and corrupt society around them. Paul is less interested in naming (and damning) a precise group than he is in identifying a pattern to be avoided, a pattern inimical to the messianic way that he has just articulated (2:3-11; 3:3-11).

Messiah's People: Their Awaited Deliverer and Destiny 3:20-21

The imagery of the next verses is that the *governing regime* (*politeuma*) of Messiah's citizen community (*polis*) is now secured in heaven, as in a kind of exile, and that Messiah will soon act to reclaim God's rightful worldwide dominion as Creator of the universe (cf. Rom 11:36; 1 Cor 15:28).

The word *politeuma* is found only here in the NT (cognates appear at Phil 1:27; Acts 22:28; 23:1; Eph 2:12). It explicitly takes up the imagery of the citizen-community (*polis*) introduced in 1:27. In regard to a civic-political order, *politeuma* can denote (1) the "business of a government, operations of state, governing regime"; (2) the "state, commonwealth," the "civil polity"; or (3) its "citizenship" (LSJ). The notions of "colony" or "homeland" are not attested meanings. With *politeuma* here, Paul is referring to "the state as a constitutive force regulating its citizens" (Lincoln: 99). Paul is not making the point that heaven is their destination or their homeland, to which they must be striving to reach. Rather, his point is that the *regime* (commonwealth, dominion) and thus *citizenship* of the people of God now exist securely in heaven. That is where God now reigns supreme and where the risen Lord is now at the right hand, to use Paul's imagery from elsewhere (Rom 8:34; Col 3:1). Heaven is thus where their citizenship registry is held securely (4:3, *the book of life*). Also implicit is the notion of the "heavenly Jerusalem," the counterpart to the earthly Jerusalem (Gal 4:25-26; Rom 11:26; cf. Heb 12:22; Rev 20–21; Lincoln). The reality of God's reign now in heaven and their citizenship now securely held in heaven means that they must orient their lives accordingly.

Heaven is not just the foundation of their secure commonwealth and citizenship. It is also the source of their deliverance: *from it we await a Savior*. In the readers' minds, these brief words evoke what Paul has undoubtedly described to them earlier: the drama of the "day of Messiah," the "royal visit" (*parousia*) of Messiah (Rom 11:25-26, "out of Zion"; cf. 1 Thess 1:10; 4:13–5:11; 1 Cor 15:20-28).

Elsewhere, too, Paul identifies heaven specifically as the source of deliverance or judgment (e.g., Rom 1:18; 11:26; 2 Cor 5:2; 1 Thess 1:10; 4:16).

The community of Messiah is thus placed in a position of expectant "waiting." And in a few verses, Paul will assure them, *The Lord is near* (Phil 4:5). Paul regularly highlights the future-oriented character of their salvation (1:6, 10, 20, 21-24, 26; 2:10-11, 16; 3:11, 12-14; 4:5). The posture of waiting certainly does not imply passivity (cf. Rom 8:19, 23, 25; Gal 5:5; 1 Cor 1:7; 1 Thess 1:9-10).

The word *Savior* resounds with significance. Paul gives it special emphasis: *indeed, a Savior* (*kai sōtēra*). *Savior* is not Paul's usual description or title for Jesus; in fact, it occurs only here in the undisputed letters (cf. Eph 4:23; Titus 1:4; 3:6; 2 Tim 1:10). Paul uses it here for the decisive contrast being posed in regard to regimes and citizenship. As commonly employed in the Greco-Roman world, this title does not mean deliverance from sin or from moral or ritual impurity. Rather, it is commonly used for one who has acted to bring any deliverance, protection, or liberation (e.g., in war, commerce, love, or health). This title can be applied to the gods (esp. for Zeus, Apollo, Poseidon, Heracles, Asclepius, and Sarapis) or human figures, especially military conquerors (e.g., Pompey). More significantly for Paul's readers in Roman Philippi, it is a title for the Roman emperors (lit. "commander-in-chief"), going back to the naming of Caesar as the "Savior of the World" and Augustus as the "Savior of Humankind" (Forester). Pausing to heighten the drama, Paul continues with the full title of Jesus: *Lord Jesus Messiah*, as in an acclamation (cf. Phil 1:2; 2:11; 4:23). N. T. Wright puts it bluntly: "These [Savior and Lord] are Caesar titles. The whole verse says: Jesus is Lord, Caesar isn't. Caesar's empire, of which Philippi is the outpost, is the parody; Jesus' empire, of which the Philippian church is the colonial outpost, is the reality" (2000: 173).

3:21 Transformed Bodies and Transformed Universe

After the full acclamation of Jesus' royal identity, the particular deeds by which he deserves the title *Savior* are next enumerated. Two major deeds are named: (1) the transformation of our *bodies of lowliness* to be in conformity with *the body of his glory*; and (2) the subjection of *all things [the universe] to himself*. The former is a subset of the latter. The personal is correlated with and inseparable from the global and political.

The intimate correlation of these two dimensions of future hope in Paul is confirmed through other texts. In 1 Corinthians 15, the proclamation of resurrection is narrated alongside the final subjection of the whole world to Messiah (1 Cor 15:24-28). In Romans 11, the ultimate "reconciliation of the world" is expressed in parallel to the reality of "life from the dead" (Rom 11:15). And in Romans 8, the liberation of "the whole creation" occurs alongside "the redemption of our bodies" (Rom 8:18-23; see TBC and TLC below).

3:21a Transformation of Bodies

Messiah *will transform our body of lowliness to be conformed to his body of glory.* These words resonate closely with the redemptive imagery that Paul uses elsewhere. In 1 Corinthians, Paul asserts that the human being "is sown in dishonor, it is raised in glory [honor, renown]. . . . Just as we have borne the image of the earthly [Adam], we will also bear the image of the heavenly [Messiah]" (1 Cor 15:43, 49 AT). In Romans, Paul declares that God has destined the elect to be "conformed to the image of his [God's] Son" (Rom 8:29). The awaited, final transformation of the world will include "the redemption of our bodies" (8:23). In 2 Corinthians, Paul adds to this theme by declaring that already in the present order of time, "we . . . are being transformed into the same [Messiah's] image from glory unto glory" (3:18 NASB). And in Galatians he writes that already now "Messiah is being formed in you" (Gal 4:19 AT).

In this context, the trans*form*ation of bodies from humiliation to glory recalls the language of resurrection in Philippians 3:10-11, including the notion of "con*form*ity to Messiah's death," to which this text is the ultimate answer. Paul's words also reach back further, to 2:6-8, where he describes Jesus as being in the *form of God* and then the *form of a slave.* The phrase *bodies of lowliness-humiliation* (*tapeinōsis*) implies notions of shame in the ancient world. The image reflects the stance of *mental lowliness* (*tapeinophrosynē*) that Jesus loyalists should undertake (2:3) and the *lowering* (*tapeinoō*) that Messiah himself embarked upon (2:8). Paul will use the same verb for his own pattern of life in 4:12: he knows *what it is to be lowered.* Thus the phrase *body of lowliness* (and similarly the human as "sown in dishonor," 1 Cor 15:44) should not be taken as a commentary on the low inherent value of physical human form, just as 2:7 should not be used to consider *human form* to be essentially "slavish." It is a matter of comparison: relative to *his [Messiah's] body of glory* (cf. 2 Cor 3:18; cf. Rom 8:29; 1 Cor 15:44, 49), the human form is found in a *body of lowliness.* Moreover, it is the present experience of suffering that is the occasion for *humiliation* to be the characterizing feature of physical human life, not humanness itself (cf. Rom 8:17-25, where Paul says the same thing about the whole creation).

In using the language of lowliness in contrast to glory (renown, fame, honor), Paul expresses solidarity with (1) those of low degree and status, (2) those who risk losing status on account of Messiah, and (3) those who are now humiliated (put to shame; cf. Phil 1:20) through suffering on account of Messiah. Here *glory* does not simply refer to some heavenly state of splendor. Rather, *glory* (Gk. *doxa*; Lat. *gloria*) is a social-status term. Here it expresses the matter of status and honor so coveted in the Greco-Roman world (TBC on 2:1-5, "Status Inversion") *[Love of Honor, p. 299]*. Resurrection hope is always a social reality, both in the NT and in Jewish perspective. It is the experience of a corporate people, an experience with Messiah and with the people of Messiah, not merely the private experience of an individual (e.g., Rom 8:28-30).

What Paul in effect claims is that what it means to have honor or dishonor (humiliation, shame) will be completely inverted on the day of Messiah, when the present age gives way to the age to come. In other words, he invites his listeners to disengage from preoccupations with honor in the present order (cf. 3:3, 19). We can presume that some of his listeners are already in positions of honor and are wary of losing it for Messiah, hesitant to walk the downward path of divestment. Others are simply preoccupied with the benefits of glories that coincide with advancement through the coveted Roman citizenship as they strive for that. Still others might already be in the position of having lost all things of honor for the sake of Messiah (cf. 3:3-11). Paul has specifically chosen words to embrace the vulnerability and suffering of the Philippians in their current circumstance.

3:21b Subjection of the Universe

Paul does not say that the transformation of bodies will occur *by* (NRSV, NIV) the power operative in Messiah. Rather, Paul says more precisely that it occurs *in accordance with* (*kata*) that power. As a consequence, Paul puts the two clauses in parallelism, with the former reference to resurrection (3:21a) as a feature of the latter and more comprehensive undertaking of total world dominion and complete renewal (3:21b; cf. Rom 8:18-25; Rev 21–22, "a new heaven and a new earth"). Indeed, this last clause pertaining to Messiah's universal lordship is central to Paul's claim about messianic citizenship and its universal commonwealth. Taking up the declaration of 2:9-11—the universal acclamation of all beings before Messiah, to the glory of God—Paul explains the extent of the power that will assure their own resurrection and attainment of ultimate *honor* (*glory*). It is the same *effective power* (*energeia*; see 2:13 for the related verb) operative in Messiah's ability *even* (an emphatic *kai*) *to subject all things to himself.*

All things here refers to the entire created world (as in Rom 11:36; 1 Cor 8:6; 11:12; 15:27-28; Gal 3:22; Col 1:16, 17, 20). The phrasing is from Psalm 8:6, "You have put all things under his feet" (8:7 LXX), interpreted messianically. Although this psalm identifies God as the one active in securing Messiah's reign, Paul in Philippians 3:21b posits Messiah's own active role in achieving cosmic dominion (as he does in 1 Cor 15:24-25, citing in addition Ps 110:1, declaring that Messiah "will neutralize every rule and every authority and every power," and "will place all enemies under his feet" [AT]).

The *consecrated in Messiah* (1:1) thus recapitulate the path of Messiah: they share his downward path through suffering and lowliness (2:6-8), they share his exaltation to honor and glory in resurrection (2:9; 3:10), and they will thus participate in his worldwide dominion (2:10-11). Similarly, Paul asserts elsewhere that believers will inherit the world (Rom 4:13), that they will be given the universe (Rom 8:31), and that they will even assist in judging the world (1 Cor 6:2-3).

As with 2:6-11, the inspirational background of this declaration is early Christian proclamation based on its own inner logic, as articulated especially on the basis of OT texts (e.g., Pss 2, 8, 110; see also 1 Cor 15:24-28; Eph 1:19-22). Some interpreters claim that Philippians 3:20-21 may be from a piece of pre-Pauline tradition. But the form of the articulation is clearly designed for this audience, who surely hear profound counterresonances in the pervasive imperial rhetoric expressed all around them, through multiple media. In particular, they would have recognized that (1) the titles ascribed to Jesus counter Caesar titles; (2) the future hope of God's exaltation of the humiliated Messiah and his humiliated people poses a direct contrast to the propaganda of Rome's eternal glory (Augustus took control of the prophets and oracles of Rome); and (3) the claim to world dominion provides a direct challenge to the world designs of Rome, as said to be willed by the gods (for the imperial rhetoric, see Wengst 1987: 46–51). For instance, the word Paul uses here for *subjection* (*hypotassomai*) had particular currency as a word for geopolitical control (e.g., Pss 18:47; 47:3; 144:2 [LXX: 17:48; 46:4; 143:2]; Dan 11:39 LXX Theodotion; Wisd of Sol 8:14) and was regularly put on monuments and public displays as part of Roman propaganda celebrating the "subjection" of conquered peoples (regarding Augustus, e.g., Res gestae divi Augusti 26–33; Pliny the Elder, *Natural History* 3.20.136). Roman coins were minted showing a spherical world under the feet of Roman gods or emperors, and Caesar Augustus boasted that he "made the boundaries of the empire equal to the boundaries of the earth" (Diodorus Siculus 40.4; Horsley 2003: 22).

Since the counterresonances with Roman imperial claims are so many and so specific, it becomes clear that Paul is making a direct hit against Roman imperial ideology and propaganda. He challenges his readers to an alternative loyalty. They are asked to give their undivided loyalty to a Savior, Lord, and Benefactor *other than* Caesar (cf. Acts 17:7).

Are they being asked to renounce their Roman citizenship, those few in the messianic community who might have had that privileged status? Perhaps not. They are asked, however, to radically reconsider it in light of Messiah. They are asked to resist compromising their fundamental allegiance to the royal Messiah Jesus, the one true Lord, Savior, and world conqueror-reconciler. Caesar and his empire will be humbled (2:9-11; 3:30-21; cf. 1 Cor 2:6). As for those without the coveted Roman citizenship (probably the majority of the messianic assembly in Philippi), they are invited not to strive for it as the key to their success and security. Thus Paul argues that the people of Messiah claim not just that their citizenship is in heaven, but also that they are world citizens (*kosmos* + *politēs* = cosmopolitan [LSJ]), no longer giving significance and loyalty to their diverse and competing earthly citizenships. Whereas many in Philippi claim citizenship in far-off Rome (where it is recorded), Paul counters this by offering citizenship in heaven (where it is recorded; Phil 4:3).

Concluding Exhortation: Stand Firm 4:1

Paul transitions from the climax of his assertions to the crux of his exhortation with a resounding *therefore* (*hōste*, cf. 2:12). He moves into his final appeal with a resumption of personal address to them, emphasizing his special relationship with and affection for them (Reider): *my brothers and sisters, beloved ones, and longed-for ones, my joy and victor's wreath.*

This flood of affectionate terms comes in two sets of epithets (3 + 2 repeats the pattern used already for Epaphroditus, 2:25). The first set of three terms emphasizes their bond of friendship and its emotional component. *Adelphoi* (*brothers and sisters*) as an address has already occurred at crucial points (1:12; 3:1, 13, 17) and will be repeated in 4:8. *Agapētoi* (*beloved ones*) as a corporate address is less frequent in Paul (elsewhere in Rom 12:19; 1 Cor 10:14; 15:58; 2 Cor 7:1; 12:19). In Philippians it has already occurred in 2:12, the previous place in the letter where a major implication was being drawn from declarations of the salvation that Messiah brings. This term of endearment and address will also be repeated after the brief appeal in 4:1, somewhat awkwardly, but providing a striking transition to his address to two dear coworkers, Euodia and Syntyche (4:2-3). The word *epipothētoi* (*longed-for ones*) is not found otherwise in the NT or LXX. Paul uses the related verb form in 1:8 and 2:26 to emphasize deep emotional bonds of relationship. These three terms together represent Paul's deepest feelings, confirmed earlier with an oath of assurance (1:8).

The second set of two terms, *my joy and victor's wreath [stephanos]*, are honorific and endearing terms for his readers (4:1). They also emphasize his confidence in them. While Paul's *joy* for them is already evident in the present (1:4; 2:2; 4:1), the second term, *stephanos* (*victor's wreath*, not *diadēma*, royal crown), has a decidedly eschatological sense. Picking up the image of the Philippian believers as his *ground for boasting on the day of Messiah* in 2:16, Paul now confidently pictures the moment when, at the final victory celebration, they will stand together with Messiah. The imagery of the future prize in 3:12-14 is close at hand. The use of both images recalls a similar expression of confidence for the Thessalonians: "For what is our hope or joy or victor's wreath [*stephanos*] of boasting before our Lord Jesus at his coming? Is it not you?" (1 Thess 2:19 AT; cf. 3:8-9). The phrase reminds us of Paul's emphasis on the "imperishable victory wreath" for which Messiah's athletes strive (1 Cor 9:25 AT). (Similar also are Paul's comments to the Corinthians, highlighting the high stakes he has in them: "You are my workmanship in the Lord" and "You are the seal of my apostleship in the Lord" 1 Cor 9:1-2 AT; "You yourselves are our letter of recommendation" 2 Cor 3:2-3 AT.)

The crucial implication of Paul's proclamation and appeal boils down to one thing: *stand firm in the Lord in this manner* (cf. a very similar closing exhortation in 1 Cor 15:58; see also 1 Cor 16:13; 2 Cor 1:24; 2 Thess 2:15). This number-one exhortation repeats the main point of Paul's exhortation in 1:27 and thereby "encloses" his exhortation by way of conclusion. Indeed, Paul's reference to the victory wreath indicates that we are still in the framework of struggle: that of a city under siege, with its citizens needing to stand firm in unified defense. Under duress, they must maintain a firm and united stance. Indeed, each of the other remaining final exhortations of 4:2-9 extends this primary exhortation in some specific way. The exhortation in 4:1 is thus the heading for the rest of the concluding exhortations (4:2-9) even as it brings to initial closure the argument begun in 1:27 and resumed in 3:1.

Paul clarifies *stand firm* with a crucial *in this way*. But in what precise manner? Following immediately on the heels of 3:18-21, Paul emphasizes that to *stand firm*, one must be ever aware of the core elements of messianic citizenship—its character, its saving benefits and extent, and its imperatives (1:27; 3:18-21). Paul says it positively, although the negative is assumed: *stand firm* specifically *in the Lord*. By implication, do not give loyalty to Caesar and his order, political, moral, and spiritual. Paul wishes his readers to remember that the manner has been demonstrated by exemplary models, whom the readers must *mark out* (3:17). First and foremost, he emphasizes the model of Messiah himself (2:5-11), the paradigm that makes all other examples intelligible, including his own example (3:2-17; 4:9; cf. 1:12-14, 15b-23; 4:10-13), but also that of Timothy and Epaphroditus (2:19-30). This paradigm is ultimately oriented to the concerns of the neighbor, motivated through love, and committed to the path of lowliness instead of self-promotion (2:2-8, 20-22, 25-30). Paul stresses that they must stand firm *together*. They must show to the world a *united front*, as the first reference to standing firm emphasizes (1:27-30). As a result, Paul immediately turns to the specific case of individuals who, as leaders, must come to a unified frame of reference in their service of the gospel. The discourse on citizenship is thus designed also to solve a unity problem: If Jesus is the Lord of the whole world through the path of the cross and in solidarity with the humiliated, those who give him allegiance must be united in the commitment to this lordship and its pathway. Otherwise the claims of the gospel will be seriously compromised.

THE TEXT IN BIBLICAL CONTEXT

Messiah's Final Victory: Violent Conquest or Merciful Reconciliation?

Throughout the NT, the climax of salvation is realized when God, through the agency of Christ, becomes victorious and reigns supreme throughout the world. Short of the realization of this hope, everything pales in insignificance. This future, world-transforming (eschatological) conclusion is so decisive that it figures as the backward-looking starting point. Thus "eschatology" (discourse on "last things") in the NT is actually a framework of inevitable "first things" that are already impacting the present.

But the depiction of this world-transforming hope is often expressed throughout the NT with violent imagery, sometimes alongside nonviolent themes. In the Gospels, for instance, there are scenes of excruciating pain and terror to be visited on those who are subject to divine retribution. In Revelation we meet both Christ the slain Lamb who "conquers" by his self-giving love in martyrdom and Christ the military conqueror who tramples out the grapes of wrath in the "winepress of God's fury." The same tension can be found in Paul's letters. On the one hand, in some letters the primary image is that of "world subjection" (replete with violent conquest themes), but in others the main image is that of "world reconciliation" (through God's unrelenting mercy and generosity).

What do we make of this seeming contradiction? Neville (2013) describes this as "a discrepancy at the heart of the New Testament"—Jesus's peaceful incarnation ("the nonviolent historic mission of Jesus") in tension with his violent and vengeful return ("Jesus as violent avenger"). In the case both of Paul and of Revelation, we can ask: Which image ultimately "conquers" or "reconciles" the other? Is Paul a believer in final peace through conquest, by which a forced allegiance by all volitional beings is realized, or is he a believer in final peace through the transformative power of divine mercy and grace, by which a willing allegiance to Messiah by all creatures is decisively achieved? With which framework do we interpret Philippians 2:10-11 and 3:20-21? To put it another way: Does divine mercy truly "conquer" all (cf. James 2:13), or does God's mercy finally embrace only some, perhaps a "chosen few"?

This is a subject for careful further study, and space permits only a few comments in response. Johns (2003) has shown that the slain Lamb is the crucial saving figure in Revelation and thus the framework for assessing the imagery of Christ on the white military horse. Neville (2013) has subjected the violent imagery in NT narrative texts to careful scrutiny, sometimes "protesting" it, in light of the core nonviolent perspective of the ministry of Jesus.

What about the tension in Paul between the scenarios of world subjection and world reconciliation? On the one hand, Messiah's final victory involves the universe being brought under "subjection" to Messiah (1 Cor 15:27-28; Phil 3:20-21)—that is, put under his feet (1 Cor 15:27, citing Ps 8:6). Sudden destruction will come upon those who proudly proclaim "peace and security" (playing on Roman imperial propaganda, 1 Thess 5:2-3). Messiah will render useless (or neutralize) every hostile rule, authority, and power (1 Cor 15:24), so that even the rulers of this age are rendered ineffective (1 Cor 2:6) and the structures of this world will come to an end (1 Cor 7:31). Even Satan will be crushed under the feet of the saints (Rom 16:20), and Death, the final enemy, will be vanquished (1 Cor 15:23-26, 51-56; 1 Thess 4:13-18; Phil 3:20-21; Rom 5:12-21; 8:29-39). Ultimately, Messiah will transfer the kingdom back to God, who will then be all in all, and to whom even Messiah will be ultimately subjected (1 Cor 15:27-28). All nations will be brought under the rule of Messiah (Rom 15:11) and all beings of the cosmos will pledge allegiance to Messiah (Phil 2:10-11). Paul can depict this world-transforming cataclysm in vivid militaristic terms. Messiah will descend from heaven (1 Thess 4:16; Phil 3:20), accompanied by angelic, heavenly armies (1 Thess 3:13 NIV, "holy ones [angels]"; 1 Cor 15:23), at the head of which will be the archangel (1 Thess 4:16, presumably Michael). Messiah will lead the battle through the trumpet call and the voice of command (1 Thess 4:16; 1 Cor 15:52) and will meet his newly raised followers in the clouds and air (1 Thess 4:17), who will then escort him in triumphal procession onto the redeemed earth.

On the other hand, this same world transformation is depicted as "the reconciliation of the world" (Rom 11:15). Messiah will reconcile the world to himself, a process already under way (Col 1:20; 2 Cor 5:18-19), with the goal that all things will be reunited in him (Eph 1:10). Thus Messiah will come from Zion—not with the conquering sword, but with a mercy that overcomes human disobedience, thereby eradicating all hostility in the world (Rom 11:25-32). Indeed, all creation will be liberated from its bondage to decay in the same process as the redemption of human bodies (Rom 8:19-23). Ultimately, God's mercy will embrace all humanity as it triumphs over all human infidelity and resistance, overcoming all disobedience, and leading to the interdependent and complete salvation of "all Israel" along with the "fullness of the nations" (Rom 11:25-32 AT). This is because grace and generosity will ultimately reign in justice, toward life for all in the age to come (Rom 5:12-21; 1 Cor 15:22).

A few comments might help explain this two-sided picture. First, violent conquest imagery for understanding Messiah's future work was an integral part of the theological heritage bequeathed to NT writers, even as there were notable nonviolent exceptions to the basic pattern (Zerbe 1993; Crossan 1999). Second, Paul regularly uses military imagery for various purposes without ever endorsing direct military activity itself (see TLC on 2:19-30, "Paul's Military Imagery"). Third, Paul's use of violent-conquest imagery for depicting Messiah's future victory correlates with the persuasive agenda of different letters. This imagery is especially evident in 1–2 Thessalonians and

1 Corinthians. Philippians uses world-subjection imagery without explicitly violent conquest motifs. On the other hand, world-reconciliation imagery predominates in Colossians, 2 Corinthians, and Romans. It is perhaps not insignificant that these latter letters are not only later in chronology, but also framed within a persuasive agenda that emphasizes reconciliation among all people. Fourth, a good case can be made that, despite the use of varied images in different contexts, the scenario and logic of world reconciliation is theologically more fundamental in Paul's basic convictions. What "wins" in Paul's theology is the hope for final peace and reconciliation through the transformative power of divine mercy and grace, by which a willing allegiance to Messiah by all beings in the world is decisively achieved. Short of this, God's own promise to restore the whole creation remains unfulfilled (Zerbe 2012: 108–21; 2015).

THE TEXT IN THE LIFE OF THE CHURCH

The Renewal of the World, Not the End of the World

Paul has traditionally been regarded as the one who transformed Jesus' message of the kingdom into a doctrine of personal, spiritual-heavenly redemption for the soul. On the contrary, over the following centuries this happened as leaders reframed Paul's own theopolitical theology and holistic, sociospiritual vision of redemption.

Paul himself does not speak with anxiety about some apocalyptic "end of the world" or, after death, the release of "soul" from body, for a destination in heaven. Indeed, what he passionately awaits is the return of all creation to its original design—not the *end*, but the *transformation* of all things through God's redeeming work in Christ. What he longs for is the imminent end of the present world order (1 Cor 2:6-8; 7:31) so that God's reign of justice, peace, and well-being (Rom 14:17) will be fully realized, will reach its true end (*telos*, goal). The framework of identity (citizenship) for all of Christ's followers is thus reoriented to that near future (1 Thess 2:12; Phil 3:20; Col 1:4, 12-14) so that they become coworkers and cocreators toward this goal (Phil 2:12; Rom 8:21, 28; 2 Cor 5:17).

Paul's hope is thus no different from that expressed in the Lord's Prayer: that God's reign be established on earth as in heaven (Matt 6:10). The hope for a complete renewal of the world is also evident in other NT texts: "the renewal [*palingenesia*] of all things" (Matt 19:28); "the restoration [*apokatastasis*] of all things" (Acts 3:21 NASB, NLT); the coming of heaven to the terrestrial plane (Rev 21–22).

Transformation of Bodies and Creation: The Site of God's Redemption

Paul does not talk about the departure of souls from bodies but rather the "transformation" of bodies. For Paul, what changes between this age and the next is not the fact of having a body. Rather, what changes is the nature of its animation: the human now is a "soulish body" (*sōma psychikon*) but one day will be a "spiritual body" (*sōma pneumatikon*; 1 Cor 15:44-49; see further Zerbe 2008). Similarly, Paul never talks about a "replacement" of creation or a hope to depart to heaven. Rather, he claims that in Messiah all creation will be transformed (Rom 8:18-25). This has important implications for the Bible's affirmation of the physicality of God's created order (Wright 2003), the site of God's redemptive work.

Paul's redemptive vision is far more terrestrially next-worldly than vertically otherworldly. The goal of redemption is anticipated not as disembodied individual immortality but as a corporate re-embodiment in the context of a restored creation. Final salvation in Paul does not entail the departure of the righteous from earth to heaven, but rather an ultimate merging of heaven and earth, so that God's imperial reign (now only supreme in heaven) will be universally realized throughout the all creation (Phil 2:10-11; 3:20-21).

Christ's Final Victory in Lyric

The third stanza of the hymn "This Is My Father's World," originally the fourteenth and fifteenth stanzas of a sixteen-stanza poem by Presbyterian minister Maltbie Babcock (1858–1901), majestically expresses the theopolitical and ecological dimensions of Paul's grand hope in Philippians 3:20-21:

> This is my Father's world.
> O let me ne'er forget
> That tho' the wrong seems oft so strong,
> God is the ruler yet.
> This is my Father's world.
> The battle is not done.
> Jesus who died shall be satisfied,
> and earth and Heaven be one.

Christian Citizenship as Patriotic Cosmopolitanism

The implication of Paul's words in Philippians 3:20-21 is that, by definition, Christ's people are global citizens since the reconciling work of Christ embraces the whole world. Moreover, Paul suggests that this politics is of a decidedly patriotic kind: Paul expects those welcomed into the saving sphere of Christ to be fervently loyal to it, even to the point of death (Phil 2:8, 17, 30; 3:10). As a result, loyalty to Christ's regime cannot easily coexist with an equivalent zealous loyalty to any other dominion, whether human or spiritual. The notion of a neatly coexisting dual citizenship (spiritual/heavenly and national) is foreign to Paul's thinking. For Paul there is only "citizenship in Christ," secured in heaven, which means that its members from Israel and the nations can only be "world citizens" also in the present. Paul rejects an identity-based particularism, whether statist, national, or ethnic (3:2-6), and thus equally rejects a coercive, universalizing Roman citizenship (3:18-21). The claims of Christ trump all other claims to political sovereignty.

Philippians in Anabaptist-Mennonite Confessions of Faith: Politics

In some Anabaptist circles, Philippians 3:20 became a crux text for concluding that Christians should not serve as magistrates in government, a perspective articulated in the Schleitheim Confession (1527), Article 7, "On the Sword." Following the affirmation that a Christian may not "use the sword against the wicked for the protection and defense of the good, or for the sake of love," the text continues:

> It does not befit a Christian to be a magistrate: the rule of the government is according to the flesh, that of the Christians according to the Spirit. . . . Their citizenship is in this world, that of the Christians is in heaven [Phil 3:20]. The weapons of their battle and warfare are carnal and only against the flesh, but the weapons of Christians are spiritual, against the fortification of the devil [2 Cor 10:3-4]. The worldly are armed with steel and iron, but Christians are armed with the armor of God, with truth, righteousness, peace, faith, salvation, and with the Word of God [Eph 6:10-17; 1 Thess 5:8; 2 Cor 6:7; Rom 6:13].

Although not specifically disallowing participation at some level of government, the *Confession of Faith* (1999) of the Mennonite Brethren churches makes a similar affirmation, based on Philippians (and other texts):

> The primary allegiance of all Christians is to Christ's kingdom, not the state or society. Because their citizenship is in heaven [citing Phil 1:27; 3:20], Christians are called to resist the idolatrous temptation to give to the state the devotion that is owed to God. As ambassadors for Christ, Christians act as agents of reconciliation and seek the well-being of all peoples.

The *Confession of Faith of in a Mennonite Perspective* (1995) puts it this way:

> The church is the spiritual, social, and political body that gives its allegiance to God alone. As citizens of God's kingdom [Phil 3:20; Eph 2:19], we trust in the power of God's love for our defense. The church knows no geographical boundaries and needs no violence for its protection. The only Christian nation is the church of Jesus Christ, made up of people from every tribe and nation [Rev 7:9], called to witness to God's glory.

Philippians 4:2-9

Closing Exhortations

PREVIEW

There is trouble in the church! At its root are disagreements between two of the leaders. What can be done?

This final unit of exhortation brings out further practical implications of the preceding discourse. These concluding exhortations are brief and varied, but all in some way extend the crucial concerns of the letter. Of particular note in the midst of this final appeal is the set of assurances (4:3b, 5b, 7, 9b) that complement and deepen the declaration of victory and security through Messiah that was just sounded in 3:20-21. These reassurances maintain the theopolitical edge that runs throughout the letter and are designed to sustain this persecuted congregation in the face of hostility from the dominant Roman social and political order.

OUTLINE

Reconciliation of Euodia and Syntyche, 4:2-3

Consolation and Encouragement in Suffering, 4:4-7

- 4:4 Rejoice in the Lord Always
- 4:5a Clemency toward All People
- 4:5b Assurance: The Lord Is Near
- 4:6 No Anxiety, Dedication to Prayer with Thanksgiving
- 4:7 Assurance: The Peace of God Will Guard Hearts and Minds

Ethical Discernment and Models, 4:8-9

- 4:8 Auditing Civic Virtues and Public Commendations

4:9a Practicing in Accordance with Paul's Teaching and Modeling
4:9b Assurance: The God of Peace Will Be with You

EXPLANATORY NOTES

Reconciliation of Euodia and Syntyche 4:2-3

To set the stage for addressing a delicate but (potentially) divisive issue in the congregation, Paul repeats the endearing address: *beloved ones* (the last phrase of 4:1, but actually introducing 4:2; CEB). That emphatic endearment leads immediately to the naming of two individuals: *Euodia I urge and Syntyche I urge* (4:2a). Paul takes up a case of internal conflict within the congregation in Philippi, having earlier spoken of the need for unity in more general terms (2:2-5, 14). His judicious and balanced words show that he takes the problem seriously but does not want to blow it out of proportion. He wishes to avert a major crisis while expressing a confidence that the difficulty can be resolved.

This sudden move to address a specific problem by directly identifying persons by name is unique in Paul's letters to assemblies. Yet a similar tactic is in his letter to Philemon, where he includes the whole congregation as addressees (in effect, inviting them to listen in on a personal communication) so that they can be aware of how he is facing the triangulated dynamic of Paul-Onesimus-Philemon and become part of the solution. As in that case, Paul here intends the congregation to overhear what he says to these particular individuals, since they are probably all involved somehow in the dispute and thus can be part of its resolution. Paul may have geared the whole argument of Philippians toward addressing this problem (Kittredge: 93; Agosto 2004: 118).

Paul addresses three individuals directly: two principals in a dispute by name, Euodia and Syntyche, and the proposed mediator by role, *genuine conciliator* (or perhaps by name: *truly named Conciliator*) *[Syzygos, p. 314]*. Euodia and Syntyche are addressed in carefully balanced ways—the same words are applied to both, indicating that Paul wishes to remain neutral in the affair. Paul *urges* (exhorts, encourages) Euodia and Syntyche to come to agreement, but *requests* the *genuine conciliator* to lead in mediating and resolving the dispute. The different words of appeal are used to imply different roles within the case, with the role of the mediator being in many ways the more difficult.

We know nothing about Euodia and Syntyche apart from what is said in these two verses. They have common Greek names, though this does not reveal their actual ethnic background. Euodia means "prosperous journey" and thus "success," while Syntyche means "with fortune, lucky" (named after the goddess of Fortune, Greek *Tychē*, Latin *Fortuna*, a popular goddess). We can infer that these women were probably part of the congregation at its founding (Acts 16) and most likely part of its leadership team. They are commended as being among the elite ranks of Paul's *coworkers* (*synergoi*), acclaimed for having *contended along with* (*synathleō*) him in the past (Dahl). This agrees with the testimony that the Philippian congregation was constituted around a Jewish gathering of women, including at least one Gentile "God-fearing" sympathizer (Lydia; Acts 16:13-15). This is also consistent with evidence that women enjoyed leadership roles in public life more generally in Macedonia compared to other regions (Fee: 391; Abrahamsen; cf. Acts 17:4, 12). As a result, we should consider them as among the group of *overseers and ministers* specially identified at the beginning of the letter (1:1).

Paul deftly identifies a mediator in a way that must have been perfectly understandable to his first readers-hearers. The most likely scenario is that Paul is addressing a recognized but unnamed conciliator in the congregation and addressing that person with a term that dramatizes a role and capability, "one who joins together" (Fee: 392–93, taking *syzygos* in its active sense) *[Syzygos, p. 314]*.

Lost in translation is Paul's play on words, the sequence of words built from the prefix *sy[n]-* (co-, with, together): *I request also you, genuine conciliator [con-joiner, sy-zyge], co-mingle [syl-lambanō] with these women.* Paul regularly creates compounds with this prefix to emphasize mutuality. He did so earlier to dramatize the general unity of the assembly (1:27, *syn-athleō, contending together*; 2:2, *sym-psychos, joined in soul*) and to highlight the mutuality between Paul and the congregation (1:7, *sug-koinōnoi, co-partners*; 2:17-18, *sug-chairō, rejoice together*; 3:17, *symmimētai, fellow-imitators*). The *conciliator* (*Syzygos*) is asked to *bring these women together* in the specific sense of reconciling them. The translation *help these women* (NRSV, NIV) is too weak, missing Paul's vivid language.

What, then, was the nature of the conflict? The common view that this was merely a personality or interpersonal conflict is surely off the mark. Paul asks Euodia and Syntyche *to be mindful of the same thing in the Lord.* This idiom emphasizes commitment to common purpose or to common status. It appeared already in 2:2 to address the overall unity of the assembly. Here the added *in the Lord* specifically indicates (1) that their involvement is in the sphere of the Lord's community and work, and (2) that their agreement must take account of the strategic imperatives of the gospel. When Paul hands the case to the *genuine conciliator*, he immediately offers a comment that implies a character commendation while also indicating the gravity of their conflict (*because they have contended side by side with me in [the work of] the gospel*). Their impressive credentials and significant work are further illustrated by reference to another individual with whom the congregation is no doubt very familiar and who enjoys a positive reputation within the congregation. These two women, with Clement and the rest, are identified as belonging to a special class of coworkers. The seriousness of the case, then, seems to arise particularly on account of their leadership roles; which would be especially so if, as seems most reasonable, this congregation is small, between thirty to one hundred people *[Profile of the Assembly, p. 305]*.

What particular issues of congregational leadership might have been under dispute? Judging from how Paul argues and exhorts in this letter, we can entertain the following possibilities:

1. The conflict might have pertained to how to respond to the external challenge—persecution and suffering. Should one accommodate to the surrounding Roman culture, or should one hold sharp lines of distinction to it? Can a person visit the civic-imperial festivals and remain untainted by the obvious oaths of loyalty implied in those activities (cf. 1 Cor 8–10)?

2. The conflict might have had to do with missional priorities or tactics of the congregation. How should weaker members be assisted? Should they receive assistance or be expected to survive on their own (cf. 1 Thess 5:14; 2 Thess 3:6-15)? What about those who have lost jobs or commercial opportunities because of harassment or exclusion because they have refused to make oaths of allegiance to the city's gods and patrons or a trade guild's patron deities? How should ministries of hospitality be run? Who should preside over the financial management of any shared resources (cf. Phil 4:10-20)?

3. Perhaps social status issues were at stake for these two (and for the congregation in general), especially if their family background and pedigree, education, or economic accomplishments put them into different social ranks. Paul's communities were not immune from issues arising from socially determined rank and status, so crucial in Greco-Roman society (cf. 1 Cor 1–4, 11). The repeated emphasis on virtues of lowliness over against self-achievement suggests a conflict in this direction. Still, if these two women manifest significant differences of approach on questions that Paul has raised in his letter, he makes no hint of this here. Paul remains officially neutral. Readers familiar with the issues would know right away if

Paul is hinting that one needs to change more than another (cf. Rom 14:1–15:6, where Paul seeks to resolve a problem while admitting that theologically he stands on one side of the question, although rejecting its tactics; see TLC below, "Mediators in the Church").

Designed both for the community and for the disputants themselves, Paul's commendation of Euodia and Syntyche introduces two further *syn-* compound words. He reminds his readers that these women have specifically *contended along with* (*syn-athleō*) *him* and that they are among the elite group of his *coworkers* (*syn-ergoi*). The impressiveness of their contribution is enhanced by listing another individual who must have been held in high regard in the congregation: Clement. We know nothing about this Clement. *Clementus* is a Latin name (here found in its Greek form), often indicating the person's generous character or the conditions of "clemency" the person received. It is a common name for "freedmen," a Roman legal classification for those born slaves and later freed, whose children will enjoy full status as free citizens. He probably is and was a member of the congregation, no doubt part of the leadership team, although he might also be an itinerant in Paul's larger network.

As soon as Paul identifies Clement, however, he recognizes the hazard of naming and so speaks simply of *the rest* of those in the same impressive category of *coworkers*. While unnamed, the rest are given the status of being "named" more importantly in the *book of life*. The notion of the *book of life* occurs only here in Paul, but it represents a fairly widespread notion of a heavenly registry of God's truly righteous (e.g., Exod 32:32-33; Ps 69:28; Dan 12:1; 1 Enoch 47:3; Rev 3:5; 13:8; 17:8; 20:12, 15; 21:27; 22:19; Luke 10:20; Heb 12:23). While this final reference to those *whose names are in the book of life* allows Paul to leave other coworkers unnamed, it more importantly highlights to all his readers that all their names are secure in the heavenly registry of citizens (Phil 3:20) in contrast to the registry of Roman citizens in the administrative buildings of Colonia Julia Augusta Philippensis (Philippi) and in Rome. Paul has employed yet another image of alternative identity and citizenship.

Consolation and Encouragement in Suffering 4:4-7

The next three exhortations (4:4, 5a, 6) are brief and appear to be similar to the staccato-like imperatives that Paul uses elsewhere to close his letters (cf. 1 Thess 5:12-22; 1 Cor 16:13-14; 2 Cor 13:11; Rom 12:9-21). The closing in 1 Thessalonians 5 in particular covers many of the same topics as in Philippians 4:1-9, illustrating issues considered crucial by Paul: (1) concern for leadership and peace within the community (1 Thess 5:12-13; Phil 4:2-3); (2) showing forbearance and nonretaliation to all people (1 Thess 5:14b-15; Phil 4:5); (3) rejoicing always (1 Thess 5:16; Phil 4:4); (4) praying without ceasing (1 Thess 5:17; Phil 4:6-7); (5) giving thanks in all circumstances (1 Thess 5:18; Phil 4:6); (6) testing all things, holding to the good (1 Thess 5:21-22; Phil 4:8-9). The insertion of assurance into closing exhortations is part of Paul's repertoire (cf. 2 Cor 13:11). The series of exhortations to rejoice, demonstrate forbearing clemency, and to pray is also found in Romans 12:12: "Rejoice in your hope, be patient in tribulation, be constant in prayer" (RSV). While the exhortations that Paul selects may be standard topics for his letter closings, Paul adapts them to suit the particular purposes and contexts of each letter. Here the next three exhortations are designed to encourage and console a community in suffering.

4:4 Rejoice in the Lord Always

Paul adds yet another command to rejoice "in the Lord" (see on 3:1), this time with the added qualifier *always* and with a balanced repetition to drive home the point (see TBC on 1:3-11, "Joy and Rejoicing").

4:5 Clemency toward All People

Paul next draws attention to the community's relationship with a hostile and persecuting environment. The reference to conduct becoming *known to everyone* (NRSV; NIV, *all*) is meant to refer especially to outsiders, as parallel expressions elsewhere in Paul's letters suggest (1 Thess 2:14-15; 3:12; 5:14-15; 2 Cor 3:2; Rom 5:18; 12:17-18).

The word that Paul uses for the virtue to display in relation to all people is hard to express with just one English word: *gentleness* (Phil 4:5 NRSV, NIV), *kindness* (NABRE), or even *forbearance* (RSV; Fowl 2005). The word has the sense of *forbearing clemency*, as refusing to seek injury in kind, instead responding to evil with graciousness and goodness. This exhortation is thus a shorthand expression of Paul's usual teaching on nonretaliation and peace (1 Thess 3:12; 5:14-15; Rom 12:12, 14, 17-21; 1 Cor 4:12-13; 13:4-7; 2 Cor 6:4, 6; Col 3:12-15; Gal 5:22; Zerbe 1992). Paul's choice of this word here might have been occasioned by his recent reference to Clement (Phil 4:3, *clemency*), a Latin name equivalent in meaning to the Greek word that Paul uses here. In effect we have a play on words: I urge you all to be *clemency* in relation to all people.

This brief exhortation has an importance in inverse relationship to its length. Paul has challenged them to be wary of the insidious dangers of the culture and political system around them (1:28; 2:15; 3:18-19). He has identified their adversaries in strong terms (3:2, 19) while emphasizing their solidarity as Messiah's alternative citizen body (1:27; 2:15; 3:3, 20-21). The community could easily develop a triumphalist or isolationist mentality with a strong desire for revenge, even in the present order of time. It is precisely such a temptation that Paul seeks to avert. Every presently hostile outsider is to be treated with forbearance. For Paul, every outsider is always a potential insider and fellow participant in the regime of Grace.

In this framework, the immediately following assurance *The Lord is near* makes sense. The logic of Paul's exhortations not to retaliate but to respond to injury with blessing and goodness is fundamentally based on deferring justice to God, waiting for God to vindicate and reconcile (Rom 12:17-21). Thus the assurance that *The Lord is near* (Phil 4:5), referring back to what he has just said in 3:20-21, is meant as a general assurance of God's deliverance for a suffering community. It provides grounding warrant for their *clemency*, assuring them that justice will someday prevail and that they can leave their own quests for justice in God's hand.

4:6 No Anxiety, Dedication to Prayer with Thanksgiving

Continuing to draw attention to their fundamental hope and security *in the Lord* (3:20–4:1; 4:4), Paul advises them to desist from any *worry about anything*, recalling the earlier calls not to fear (1:14, 28). Instead, the appropriate posture *in everything*, especially in their suffering, is to *make requests known to God with prayer and petition accompanied by thanksgiving*. Thanksgiving and petition are closely tied together in Paul's writings (Phil 1:3-4; 1 Thess 5:17-18; Col 4:2; cf. 1 Tim 2:1). The posture of thanksgiving is a recurring theme in Paul's letters and a central aspect of corporate worship (1 Cor 14:16-17). Thanksgiving is not a thank-you in advance for the receipt of a particular request, but an overall posture of gratitude for God's deliverance and sustaining power available through Messiah—a gratitude and conviction that ground any act of service (cf. Phil 4:10-20; see TLC on 1:3-11, "Letter and Liturgy").

4:7 Assurance: The Peace of God Will Guard Hearts and Minds

That Paul is advising a posture of prayerful dependency on God in the specific context of their suffering is confirmed by the reassurance that follows: *The peace of God surpasses all comprehension* (Gk. *nous*, "mind," and thus *understanding*, NRSV) regarding what truly counts for peace. It *will guard your hearts and minds in Messiah Jesus.* Paul knows that peace is a contested term and that there are competing claimants as to who can truly bring peace. Thus as soon as he refers to *the peace of God*, he adds that it is a kind of peace beyond what one could ever imagine. Moreover, the *peace of God* will be the true *guard* to bring deliverance and security in the battle, which is to be won at the level of *hearts and minds* (lit. *deliberations of the mind, noēmata*). Here we have another military image, a parody and a wordplay on both the imperial Pax Romana (peace of Rome) and the Roman garrison guarding the city of Philippi itself. "Peace" was a crucial element of Roman imperial propaganda *[Roman Imperial Propaganda, p. 312]*. Here Paul counters it with his claim about the *peace of God*. He knows that in Roman imperial propaganda, "peace" is the primary legitimation and code word for military conquest.

Here, in contrasting parallelism, *God's peace will guard* the security of Messiah's people *in and through Messiah* (the preposition *en* could have the sense of either location as "in" or instrument as "through"). As a result, we can see the close relationship between the exhortation to nonviolent, nondefensive, and nonretaliatory clemency (4:5) and the promise of a true peace that is of God and that will truly make them secure (4:7). Although the peace of God here secures the community in relation to an external threat that can be destabilizing on the inside, in a counterpart text in Colossians 3:15, the peace of Christ establishes interpersonal peace within the community: "Let the peace of Christ function as arbitrator among your hearts, to which indeed you were called in the one body" (AT). Paul consistently emphasizes the mental disposition characteristic of messianic citizenship and the practice that coordinates with that mentality. His stress here on *hearts and minds* is consistent with that accent (see TBC on 2:1-5, "Habits of the Mind").

Ethical Discernment and Models 4:8-9

Taking up the imagery of *guard[ing] hearts and minds* and following his usual pattern of emphasizing moral discernment at the end of a letter (see 1 Thess 5:21-22; Rom 12:1-2; 16:19), Paul concludes this final set of exhortations by taking up a specific matter of mental engagement: the need to carefully test claims on moral criteria. Paul is not exhorting his hearers-readers to "contemplate" the things that have self-evident or inherent virtue. Instead, Paul's exhortation is literally to *do a reckoning*, or *an accounting* (*logizomai*) of the things claimed to be virtuous or worthy of commendation in the surrounding society.

Some translations suggest that Paul is here calling his readers simply to a form of contemplation. They do not properly capture Paul's meaning (e.g., Phil 4:8 NRSV, NIV: *think about*; TEV: *fill your minds with*). The verb that Paul uses has the primary sense of "reckon, calculate, do an accounting, perform an audit," and is used especially in commercial settings (cf. Rom 4:4; used earlier, in Phil 3:13). "Considering" and thus "reasoning" is a secondary sense, the consequence or feature of careful scrutiny, evaluation through deliberation (e.g., Rom 14:14). "Contemplating" is not an attested meaning of this verb. What they are to *assess* is the extent to which things may indeed be true, revered, just, and lovely. Paul uses the correlative pronoun (*hosos*), a word with no direct counterpart in English. The idea entails "the degree to which, as much as, as far as" something might be the case. The translation *whatever* (NRSV, NIV: *whatever is true*) is thus misleading. Paul's point is that his readers must investigate the precise content of the terms used in common social, moral, and aesthetic discourse. The whole point of Philippians is that matters of virtue and commendation appropriate to divergent citizenships are not self-evident, but rather must be carefully assessed.

Paul's listing of the areas of virtue and commendation come from the common vocabulary of Greek ethics, civic virtue, and public honor. Although there are similarities to Greco-Roman listings of virtue, no list corresponds precisely to this one. Paul knows that this terminology of values is socially constructed and has much to do with differing definitions of civic duty and public honor. Morality in Paul's world (as now) was self-consciously oriented to what is virtuous or honorable in the public eye.

Paul begins with (1) the notion of what is *true* (*alēthēs*, Phil 4:8), a basic term for various applications of truth—in science, art, philosophy, the family, and in law, including what counts to be true in a court proceeding. (2) The next word (*semnos*) has the sacred connotation of what is "revered" or "hallowed," yet it can also have a generic sense of what is *noble* (NIV) or *worthy of respect* (NRSV: *honorable*). The intermingling of "religious" devotion and of "ethical" conduct is important for much of Greco-Roman moralism, as for the biblical tradition. These are not separate issues in Jewish *or* in Greco-Roman society. (3) The question of what is *just* (*dikaios*) is a crucial matter for civic virtue (cf. 3:9), the subject of vigorous debate in the Greek philosophical tradition. (4) The next term (*hagnos*, 4:8) highlights the issue as to what counts for being "full of religious awe" (LSJ), thus also *pure* (NRSV, NIV) and *hallowed* in a moral sense. (5) The term *lovely* (NIV) or *loveable, dear* (*prosphilos*; NRSV: *pleasing*) applies to the world of personal disposition and admiration, and to interpersonal relations, even to consumer interest or to aesthetic appreciation, not so much to formal ethics. (6) Similarly, the adjective *well-spoken of* (*euphēmos*, from which we get *euphemism*) is not an inherent virtue in a strict sense, but denotes conduct that is *commendable* (NRSV) or *admirable* (NIV) by people in general.

The vague content of such value-laden terms continues with the final two words, generic terms for civic virtue or public honor. A term for "prowess" or "valor" in war (*arētē*) had become by this time the overall term for *civic virtue* (or general *excellence*) whether personal, social, military, or political virtue. The final term, *commendation* (*epainos*; NRSV: *something worthy of praise*), is a term most at home in the area of receiving public honor for practiced virtue or for successful accomplishment or benefaction.

While Paul uses specific Greek terminology for ethics and aesthetics here, he does not thereby baptize Greco-Roman virtues as consonant with "Christian values" or attempt to embrace the good in Greco-Roman culture, as is commonly supposed (taking 4:8 out of context). Rather, Paul is inviting careful scrutiny about what counts for matters of virtue. In this sense, the notion is similar to his opening prayer in the letter: that they, through growing knowledge and insight, become better able to test and discern *those things that distinguish* (1:10).

4:9a Practicing in Accordance with Paul's Teaching and Modeling

Paul follows the call to audit claims of virtue and commendation in the surrounding society with a final reminder of the framework by which these matters should be assessed and thus practiced for messianic citizenship (4:9a). He provides a counterpart enumeration, using a format similar to what is in the previous verse: *the things that you have learned, received, heard, and seen in me—these things you must practice.* This command, in effect, summarizes the exhortation of the letter. It reminds them of their history in the faith and their history with Paul (e.g., 1:3-8). It reinforces the specific teaching in this letter and before this letter (3:18). It especially recalls the model of messianic citizenship (2:5-11) that Paul exemplifies (3:2-17; cf. 1:12-26; 2:16-17; 4:10-13). Ethical reflection and practice appropriate to Messiah do not operate with ethical and aesthetic generality that simply mirrors public attitudes (4:8). Instead, they properly function as the Philippian believers give careful attention to the tradition, teaching, and models provided through Messiah, as mediated by *slaves of Messiah*, such as Paul (1:1).

4:9b Assurance: The God of Peace Will Be with You

As a climaxing punctuation to his exhortation, Paul provides further assurance while directly challenging Roman peace propaganda: *And the God of peace will be with you* (see TBC below, "God of Peace, Peace of God").

THE TEXT IN BIBLICAL CONTEXT

Women Leaders and Coworkers in Paul's Assemblies

Besides the two women leaders and coworkers named here, Paul's letters reveal a long list of women with similar roles in Paul's assemblies. Phoebe (Rom 16:1-2) is called a *diakonos* ("minister," not just "deacon") and *prostatis* ("patron" and/or "leader," not "helper"). Introduced with an affirming recommendation, Phoebe probably served as Paul's patron and spokesperson accompanying his letter to Rome. Prisca ("coworker," Rom 16:3-5; 1 Cor 16:19; as Priscilla, Acts 18:2, 18, 26) is often named first before her husband, Aquila, and was clearly an important leader, regarded well by a number of congregations. Junia, along with her husband, Andronicus, is called an "envoy" ("apostle"). She and her husband, both Jews by birth, were adherents of Messiah even before Paul (Rom 16:7). Nympha was host for a house assembly and no doubt also the head of a household (Col 4:15). In the same category we can place Lydia (Acts 16:13-15, 40). These names correspond to the witness of Acts that many "leading [high-ranking] women" were joining Paul's assemblies in Macedonia and Greece (Acts 17:4, 12, 34). Apphia (Philem 2) is only identified as "our sister," but quite clearly has some leadership role, based on the way she is included in the address of Paul's letter to Philemon. Finally, Mary is identified as one "who has labored among you" (Rom 16:6 AT), Tryphena and Tryphosa "have labored in the Lord" (Rom 16:12 AT), and the "beloved Persis . . . has labored in the Lord" (Rom 16:12 AT; on women in the Greco-Roman world, see Lefkowitz and Fant; E. Stegemann and W. Stegemann).

God of Peace, Peace of God

In Paul's writings, *peace* is the most frequent epithet for God next to that of *Father*, occurring frequently in stereotyped form at letter closings. This title has often been neglected as one of Paul's most important designations for God's character and saving mission (Swartley 2006: 208–11). In a few places, the phrase seems part of a generic liturgical closing:

> The God of peace be with you all. Amen. (Rom 15:33)
>
> Finally, brothers and sisters: rejoice, put things in order, heed my appeal, agree with one another, live in peace; and the God of love and peace will be with you. (2 Cor 13:11 AT)

Highlighting this aspect of God's character in relation to the community's peace, we also have the phrase in 1 Corinthians 14:33: "*for God is not a God of disorder but of peace.*" (Also, closely associated with the final grace wish: Rom 16:20; 2 Cor 13:11, 13/14; Phil 4:9, 23; 1 Thess 5: 23-24, 28; 2 Thess 3:16, 18; for the "peace of Christ," cf. Col 3:15; Eph 2:14.)

In 1 Thessalonians, Romans, and Philippians, however, Paul's reference to "the peace of God" has a strong theopolitical edge (Reasoner; Swartley 2006: 245–51; Crossan and Reed: 74):

> May the God of peace himself sanctify you entirely;
> and may your spirit and soul and body be kept sound and blameless
> at the coming of our Lord Jesus Christ. (1 Thess 5:23)
>
> The God of peace will shortly crush Satan under your feet. (Rom 16:20a)

While the phrase "God of peace" does not occur in the LXX and occurs rarely in other early Jewish writings (notably in Testament of Dan 5:2), this theology of Paul derives its inspiration from the Scriptures (e.g., Isa 9:5-6; 32:17; 45:7-8 KJV, NET; 60:17; Jer 6:14; 14:13-16). At the same time, the phrase "God of peace" in 1 Thessalonians, Romans, and Philippians is framed in response to Paul's exposure to Roman political propaganda celebrating Roman peace. The declaration in 1 Thessalonians 5:23, for instance, plays on the notion of soundness of body and soul that function as part of the Roman propaganda of victory and security. Earlier, Paul has parodied Roman declarations of "peace and security" (1 Thess 5:1-9; Koester).

The ideology of a Roman worldwide peace was disseminated during the Augustan period (31 BCE–14 CE), thanks to the propagandist poets Ovid, Tibullus, and Virgil (Wengst 1987: 46–51). The "peace of Augustus" was solemnized by the Roman Senate in 13 BCE. In the same year, Augustus's Altar of Peace was dedicated on the grounds of Campus Martius (Field of Mars), where there were also altars to Mars (god of war) and Apollo. Just outside the formal city limits of Rome, the Campus Martius was the primary location of Roman military activities, both as an exercise ground and for parades and games. Coins minted in the year of Claudius's accession (41 CE) proclaim "the peace of Augustus." Under Nero (54–68), the rhetoric of the peace of Augustus was renewed vigorously. During the entire first century, the Roman goddess Peace (Pax) was universally preached as part of Roman "gospel" propaganda, even though perhaps not quite as extensively as the goddesses Victoria and Fortuna, and Concordia and Salus (Fears 1981b, 1981c).

The Roman historian Tacitus, writing in 98 CE, acknowledges that conquered populations resisted Roman peace propaganda. He puts the following words into the mouth of the British leader Calgacus as he tries to rouse his thirty thousand troops for war against the conquering Romans at the start of the Battle of Mons Graupius in 84 CE:

> But today the uttermost parts of Britain are laid bare; there are no other tribes to come [to our assistance]; nothing but sea and cliffs and these more deadly Romans, whose arrogance you shun in vain by obedience and self-restraint. Harriers of the world, now that earth fails their all-devastating hands, they probe even the sea: if their enemy have wealth, they have greed; if he be poor, they are ambitious; East nor West has glutted them; alone of humankind they behold with the same passion of concupiscence waste alike and want. To plunder, butcher, steal, these things they misname empire: *they make a desolation and they call it peace.* Children and kin are by the law of nature each man's dearest possessions; they are swept away from us by conscription to be slaves in other lands: our wives and sisters, even when they escape a soldier's lust, are debauched by self-styled friends and guests; our goods and chattels go for tribute; our land and harvests in requisitions of grain; life and limb themselves are used up in leveling marsh and forest to the accompaniment of gibes and blows. (Tacitus, *Agricola* 30–31, emphasis added)

Inward Peace, Outward Peace

Paul does not choose between inward and outward peace: instead, he stresses that the inward disposition is vital to the outward experience of peace. Paul was not the only one resisting Roman peace propaganda. Here Paul's rhetoric is surprisingly similar to that of the Stoic philosopher Epictetus (55–135 CE) when he contrasts the "peace proclaimed by God through reason" and the kind of peace proclaimed by Caesar:

> Caesar seems to provide us with profound peace: there are no wars any longer, nor battles, no brigandage on a large scale, or piracy. . . . Can he, then, at all provide us with peace from fever too, and from shipwreck too, and from fire, or earthquake, or lightning? Come, can he give us peace from love? He cannot. From sorrow? From envy? He cannot—from absolutely none of these things. But the doctrine of the

> philosophers promises to give us peace from these troubles too. And what does it say? "People, if you need me, wherever you may be, whatever you may be doing, you will feel no pain, no anger, no compulsion, no hindrance, but you will pass your lives in tranquillity and in freedom from every disturbance." When people have this kind of peace proclaimed to them, not by Caesar—why, how could he possibly proclaim it?—but proclaimed by God through reason, are they not satisfied, when they are alone? When they contemplate, . . . everything is full of peace. (Epictetus, *Discourses* 3.13.9-13; following Reasoner)

The big difference between Epictetus and Paul is that this Stoic grounds inner peace in a mental transformation through rational contemplation, while Paul grounds it ultimately in God's character and the assured arrival of God's reign of justice and peace (e.g., Rom 14:17). For Paul, the battle for God's reign is also a battle for hearts and minds (cf. 2 Cor 10:3-5).

Echoes of the Sermon on the Mount

At a number of places, Paul's moral exhortation echoes the teachings of Jesus, even though Paul does not cite his sources (TBC on 2:1-5, "Status Inversion"). In this passage, the following topics have close parallels in the Sermon on the Mount (and other gospel texts): (1) the theme of nonretaliation and kindness to adversaries (Matt 5:38-48; Luke 6:27-32); (2) the necessity of petition and asking, and God's promise to respond Matt 6:7-13 // Luke 11:2-4; and Matt 7:7-11 // Luke 11:9-13; (3) the theme letting go of "anxiety" or "cares": having no cares // anxieties about anything, but seeking first God's reign (Matt 6:25-34 // Luke 12:22-32); the danger of the "cares of this age" smothering new sprouts of seed (Mark 4:19 // Matt 13:22 // Luke 8:14; similarly Luke 21:34); having no "anxiety" about what words to use before persecuting authorities (Mark 13:11 // Matt 10:19 // Luke 12:11); Martha's fastidious "anxiety" (Luke 10:41).

THE TEXT IN THE LIFE OF THE CHURCH

Mediators in the Church

Paul's letters show significant interest in the work of mediators. Indeed, it appears that the required competencies for those chosen to be in Paul's inner circle of coworkers included wisdom and skill in interpersonal dynamics, not just theological understanding. Paul's exhortations on resolving conflicts internal to congregations, for instance, show considerable concern for the conflict-transformation process (Col 3:12-15; 1 Cor 13:5, 7; Phil 4:5; 1 Thess 5:14-15; Rom

12:12-21; Zerbe 1992). Besides Philippians 4:2-3, one can point to the crucial role of Titus in mediating Paul's complex disputes with the Corinthian congregations, both with the congregation as a whole and with a particular individual in the Corinthian church who insulted (probably defamed) Paul himself (2 Cor 1:23–2:13; 7:2-16; 8:6, 16-24). Indeed, without the mediating work of Titus, Paul's own conflict with the Corinthian assembly might never have been resolved. The importance of community mediation is also emphasized in 1 Corinthians 6:1-8, where Paul confronts certain members not only for having lawsuits with each other, but especially for taking these disputes to the civic ("unjust") law courts. He implicitly invites them not to let their grievances (6:1) escalate into lawsuits (6:7), rhetorically questioning:

> When you constitute a tribunal for matters of livelihood, [why do] you appoint (as judges) those who are despised in the assembly? I say this to your shame. Can it be that there is no one among you that is wise enough to adjudicate between one brother and another? (6:4-5 AT)

In this light we can also appreciate Paul's advice:

> And let the peace of Christ function as arbitrator among your hearts, to which indeed you were called in the one body. (Col 3:15 AT)

Another case is the complex dynamic between Philemon and Onesimus, in which Paul himself is implicated. Paul seeks to mediate a resolution between them, even as he also hopes for a transformation in their relationship. Finally, we could consider Paul's careful attempt to mediate the protracted dispute between the "strong" and the "weak" sectors among the network of house assemblies in Rome (Rom 14:1–15:13).

Nearness and Agency: Engaging Paul's Visionary Passion

Paul's brief words in Philippians 4:5 encapsulate and raise classic issues with which the church continues to wrestle: (1) Does not the continued nonevent of the full messianic *parousia* (presence, arrival; Lat. *adventus*) cause us to question our urgent commitment to this vision of universal reconciliation? (2) Does Paulinism give too much over to messianic agency, letting the redeemed community sit back and wait, preoccupied with its own purity and distinctiveness? (3) Can Paul's "kyriarchalism" (explicit "lordship," hierarchical, sovereignty language) be made relevant to those who find it problematic? These are matters for continued engagement with Paul and his letters.

In places of protracted tyranny and injustice, some Christians have concluded that Paul's words require contemporary updating. For instance, in the Filipino "theology of struggle," what was once left entirely in the hands of Christ is now a mandate for active Christian involvement in the struggle for peace and justice (Zerbe 2005). North American interpreters have also energetically raised the issue of "agency" in Paul's theology, wondering whether it is adequate for the church's agency as it faces the challenges of today's world (Elliott: 152–66). This interest in "nearness" and "agency" has nothing to do with the concerns of end-time, chart-making speculation. Rather, it is a matter of coming to terms with Paul's hope for the concrete and imminent realization of God's goal of redeeming the world as a place of justice, peace, and the integrity of creation. This visionary hope is not to be treated as mere "enthusiasm" that gets the best of Paul's more sober interests, nor is it separate from the core of his theology (supposedly) about personal, individualized, or heavenly redemption.

Paul's "apocalyptic" (world-transforming, divinely achieved) vision is paradoxically both revolutionary and conservative in potential. It is potentially revolutionary by creating liminal (in-between) spaces that unplug from the prevailing structures and norms. But it is also potentially conservative in that it invites people to wait, to defer in matters pertaining to the world as a whole. The problem of the legacy of Paul's voice is that once apocalyptic urgency is removed, what remains is often a conformist affirmation of the status quo. The imperative for the church today is either to recover the urgency of radical, world-transforming destabilization (what scholars call apocalyptic or eschatological hope), or to rethink agency. In other words, Paul puts the emphasis entirely on messianic agency in the imminent conclusion of God's world-transforming plan (e.g., 1 Cor 15:24-28; Rom 11:26). The church must now wrestle with the ways it takes on a greater risk of agency and urgency in the world (not just in its own midst) in light of a different eschatological situation in which "nearness" seems persistently deferred and synergistic "urgency" practically neutralized.

Our sense of nearness may be different in perspective from that of Paul. But the need for urgency in working and living in alignment with God's purposes for the world has not changed. While Paul indeed does put great emphasis on messianic agency in the work of God's renewal of the world, there is also a decisive, synergistic role for the messianic community, as the body of Christ. Paul's emphasis on the ongoing and future agency of Christ is a continued and crucial reminder that the work and outcome are not ultimately our own.

Philippians 4:10-20

Celebrating the Mutuality of Partnership and God's Rich Provision

PREVIEW

Paul has saved the best for the last: formally acknowledging the assistance that he recently received from the Philippian congregation. He already alluded to their service on his behalf (1:5, 7; 2:25-30). In conclusion, he now expresses himself more fully and carefully. The passage is surprisingly marked by both commendation and reticence, ecstatic joy and qualification. Complicating it all are prevailing customs surrounding giving and receiving and the kinds of social relations that the mutual giving and receiving both express and shape. Paul's apparent ambivalence is best understood as a resistance to the pattern of prevailing patron-client norms of giving and receiving that reinscribes a social hierarchy. Paul emphasizes that the assistance he has just enjoyed both illustrates and solidifies a relationship of partnership, one of mutuality, with God affirmed as the ultimate provider. Following three acknowledgments of their recent service, each carefully clarified, Paul concludes with a reverberating word of assurance and doxology, bringing the letter to a fitting close.

OUTLINE

First Acknowledgment: Joy in Their Mindfulness, 4:10-13
- 4:10b Clarification from Their Side: "Lack of Opportunity"
- 4:11-13 Clarification from Paul's Side: "Not That I Speak according to Lack"

Second Acknowledgment: The Blessing of Partnership, 4:14-17
- 4:15-17 Commendation and Clarification

Third Acknowledgment: A Commercial Receipt for Receiving an Abundance, 4:18
- 4:18b Clarification: The Fragrant Aroma of a Sacrifice Pleasing to God

Concluding Promise and Doxology, 4:19-20
- 4:19 Assurance: God the Ultimate Provider
- 4:20 Doxology

EXPLANATORY NOTES

What astonishes many readers are a number of peculiarities about this passage: (1) it takes so long for Paul to get to this topic; (2) he avoids referring to their assistance as a "gift" (though regularly supplied in English translations of 4:17-18); (3) he never specifically says thank you; and (4) he hints that he never needed or solicited the support (4:11-13, 17). Why is Paul so cautious, reticent, perhaps even censuring, where we would expect him (according to our cultural assumptions) to flood his readers with gushing thanks?

The delay of this topic until the end has bewildered many Western interpreters into thinking that this passage can only be a fragment of a letter written well before the rest of the letter, or parts of the letter *[Literary Integrity, p. 298]*. The assumption is that something as important as this can hardly have been left till the end. But there are many good reasons why Paul reserved a most crucial piece for last while referring to the matter right from the beginning (1:5-7) and along the way (2:12, 25-30). By saving this topic for the end, Paul is able to conclude with a crowning celebration of their partnership with him and the gospel, the theme with which the letter began. This passage is hardly a postponed afterthought, but a strategically planned conclusion showing masterful rhetorical design: 1:3-11 and 4:10-20 provide a carefully crafted frame enclosing the main body of the letter. Moreover, through a theological interpretation of their assistance, Paul concludes with striking words of assurance (4:19) and doxology (4:20), which would have reverberated with the hearers as the congregational reading ended. Paul may not have wanted this matter to cloud his sustained exhortation on the rigorous path of messianic citizenship (1:27–4:1). Instead, he has kept them on their seats, waiting for how he will formally acknowledge their assistance.

Critical to appreciating this text is an understanding of the prevailing Greco-Roman cultural patterns of giving and receiving and the social relations assumed or generated by such activity (see Saller; Peterman; Barclay).

1. Giving and receiving entails significant social implications. Giving a gift or favor is typically designed to establish a relationship, whether between individuals, between an individual and a group, or between groups. To make a false move in word or deed in relation to established conventions of giving and receiving could have significant consequences (Saller: 1–29). A lasting relationship is established when a gift is accepted and acknowledged appropriately. But enmity may result if a gift is rejected, since that reflects negatively on the generosity of the giver. This helps explain why some rich Corinthians felt especially slighted when Paul refused their offer of financial support (see 1 Cor 9; 2 Cor 11:7-11; 12:13-18).

2. Giving and receiving was tied to status and honor. Ability to exceed in giving establishes oneself as the superior member of the relationship, unless parity in giving and receiving can be maintained. To grow in status, one must exceed in giving. Thus the practice of benefaction and munificence was pursued energetically among the elite. For the elite, "it is more blessed to give than to receive" because it displays one's personal virtue and social power (the motive is different in the saying of Jesus recorded in Acts 20:35). The wealthy powerful, therefore, are regarded as the "benefactors" (cf. Luke 22:25): "The most basic premise from which the Romans started was that honour and prestige derived from the power to give others what they needed or wanted" (Saller: 126).

3. Receiving a gift or favor obligates the receiver to reciprocate appropriately with a countering gift or favor and/or an acknowledgment of the ongoing indebtedness inherent in the benefactor-client relationship. Appropriate reciprocation on the part of the inferior party in an exchange relationship includes heaping praise, honor, and thanksgiving on the benefactor, especially if the person is unable to offer a material equivalent to the benefactor. On the contrary, it is a sign of mutuality and friendship *not* to engage in excessive displays of thanksgiving. A letter dating to 58 CE between two physicians illustrates this well as the letter writer acknowledges the receipt of some requested supplies: "I may dispense with writing

to you with a great show of thanks [*megalas eucharistias*]; for it is for those who are not friends that we must give thanks in words. I trust that I may maintain myself in some degree of serenity and be able, if not to give you an equivalent, at least to show some small return for your affection toward me" (cited in Peterman: 74–75). The "gift" is simply a sign of mutual affection.

4. The language of commercial exchange often figures in depictions of social relationships of giving and receiving, due apparently to the typically transactional nature of social relationships.

5. Finally, the Scriptures of the Judean world (our OT) make it clear that God is the one who ultimately rewards benefactors who give to those in need (or God himself is the benefactor who takes care of the needy). Comparable statements cannot be found in Greco-Roman sources.

Once this cultural framework is understood, Paul's closing words become more comprehensible, since they apparently are delicately designed to counter prevailing patterns of benefaction and patronage. In this case, giving and receiving are not what establishes or determines the relationship. Giving and receiving are not simply for utilitarian ends (whether as friends, partners, or patron-clients). Paul and this congregation do not have a conventional relationship of reciprocity and patron-client benefaction. Rather, their mutual partnership in the gospel (1:5, 7; cf. 1 Cor 9:23), their mutuality in Messiah, establishes and governs their practices of giving and receiving. Paul wishes to ward off any misunderstanding of the nature of their relationship through their assistance and his receipt of it. The lack of a specific thank-you thus also becomes comprehensible. In Paul's view, generous giving should result in thanksgiving to God (see esp. 2 Cor 9:11-15; also TBC below, "Patterns of Economic Mutualism").

Paul thus explains their assistance to him in the following main ways: (1) On the negative side, it is not that Paul is a needy dependent seeking this kind of contribution, nor has Paul made excess comment on his need (4:11-13, 17). On the positive side, (2) it is an expression of a longer and deeper partnership in which there is mutual giving and receiving. Consistent with the framework of a partnership, (a) it represents their continued *mindfulness* of him (4:10), which they may have had all along, but did not always have a chance to demonstrate; (b) it represents the *fruit* that accrues to their dividends in the larger project of the gospel (4:17); and (c) it represents their prior *arrears* (2:30) of duty and obligation in terms of their mutual arrangement as partners. (3) Their assistance is ultimately a sacrifice made in honor of God's goodness (4:18b). (4) The partnership is framed by God's ultimate ability to supply need; God is the ultimate provider who will take care of appropriate reciprocation (4:19-20).

While Paul deftly avoids saying a specific thank-you, he clearly expresses gratitude for the contribution he received in three acknowledgments (4:10a, 14, 18a). These are interrupted by clarifications (vv. 10b, 11-13, 17) and a commendation through recollection (vv. 15-16), and extended by theological interpretation (vv. 18), words of assurance (v. 19), and doxology (v. 20). Perhaps the most important (indirect) thank-you comes in the early mention of their close relational tie: *I have you in my heart, for both in my chains and in the defense and confirmation of the gospel, you are all copartners with me in generosity* (*charis*, 1:7). Gratitude is expressed (as culturally appropriate) by a comment on how their emotional bond has been deepened through mutual assistance!

First Acknowledgment: Joy in Their Mindfulness 4:10-13

The first formal acknowledgment of their assistance explains their act and his response in terms of the theme of joy that has traveled through the letter: *I rejoiced in the Lord greatly that now at last you revived your mindfulness of me; indeed, you were thinking of me, but had no opportunity to show it.* He has already hinted of this joy in 1:3 (in fact, in retrospect, we now know that his expression of joy in 1:3, something otherwise absent in his thanksgivings, was designed to allude to this exchange). And Paul's words in 2:2 (*Make my joy complete*) and 4:1 (*my joy and victor's wreath*) also become more intelligible: he already experiences much joy from them. In the context of their current distress, the incentive for them to heed his exhortation on solidarity for the gospel is based on that presence of joy and the possibility that it could indeed grow even more.

Paul claims that this joy is because they *now at last* have *revived* (lit. *blossomed again*) their mindfulness of his circumstances, taking up again the themes running through the letter of mental disposition toward the other (Phil 2:2-5, 20-21; 3:15) and of their mutual circumstances (1:12, 27; 2:17-18). He means this in a complimentary way. To ward off any misunderstanding that the words *now at last* might imply some indirect censure, he offers that their earlier inaction was not for lack of mental disposition toward him but for lack of opportunity. What this means is somewhat unclear, but it does indicate that there has been some time gap between their earlier support and this recent support.

The next clarification refers to his own circumstances and disposition through the first of two disclaimers ("not that" clauses, Phil 4:11-13, 17; cf. 3:12). His joy in their assistance is not simply to be explained by reference to *his* problems: *Not that I speak according to lack* (*hysterēsis*, lit. "behindness," thus "need, want, deficiency, poverty"). The ISV renders the sense well: *I am not saying this because I am in any need.* Instead, we will learn that his joy has to do with what their assistance reveals about *their* commitment and partnership in the gospel (4:14-18; cf. 2 Cor 9:11-13). As for himself, again as exemplary model, Paul highlights his own response to deficiency in two parallel clauses. First, he has learned to be *self-sufficient* (or *content*) in whatever state he finds himself in, whether in abject poverty or in material abundance (Phil 4:11-12a). This involves knowing what it means both *to be lowered* (recalling the imagery of 2:3, 8; 3:21) and *to exceed*. The readers also recall his language earlier of *gains* and *losses* (3:7-11). Second, drawing on the language from formal initiation into religious mysteries, he claims in each and every circumstances to have *been ushered into the mysteries* or *learned the secret*—both of being well fed and being hungry, both of abundance (*exceeding*) and of lack, or deficiency.

This is not some ordinary self-sufficiency or emotional detachment from material realities. Nor is this some special religious discipline. Rather, the source for *self-sufficient contentment* comes from *the one who strengthens me*. Paul designs this personal confession as another indirect reassurance of divine benefaction for his partners in suffering. The point is not that he or others in need should not receive assistance. Rather, the point for his readers is that contentment and joy can also be found in circumstances of relative "lack" and "lowering," an issue that Paul considers particularly relevant for the Philippians (cf. 2:3-4; 3:18-19).

Second Acknowledgment: The Blessing of Partnership 4:14-17

Following these clarifications (vv. 10b-13), Paul moves to a second acknowledgment, which more explicitly commends the congregation (v. 14). He now puts their aid in the context of their earlier established partnership (1:5, 7). Apparently Paul has recognized that one way out of the patron-client system of benefaction, with its status-creating and debt-obligating giving, is by reframing relationships in terms of a *partnership* (similarly 1 Cor 9:23, where Paul wishes to get out of the trap of having his work characterized in relation to particular returns, proposing that he would rather act as the "fellow partner," that is, a "shareholder of the gospel," who is interested more in equity than in wages). The partnership is not generated—nor are obligations expected—by the giving and receiving of its members. Rather, the partnership, and thus its obligations, has a deeper foundation and motivation: the *good message of Messiah*, a *partnership of grace-generosity* (1:5, 7; 2:1; 3:10-11).

Paul therefore says, *You did well by partnering together with me [synkoinōneō] in my tribulation*, recalling his words in 1:7, where he also names them as *copartners* (*synkoinōnoi*). In using the colloquial phrase *You did well*, Paul carefully avoids the technical terms for Greco-Roman benefaction and patronage (*euergeteō*, "to provide benefaction, do good deeds"; cf. *euergetēma*, "an act of patronage/benefaction"; *euergesia*, "benefaction"; cf. *euergetēs*, "benefactor," Luke 22:25), as he also does elsewhere in his letters when discussing financial assistance and partnerships (Rom 15:22-33; 2 Cor 8–9; Philem 15-22).

Paul continues with a commendation that recollects their partnership with him *in the beginning of the gospel*, referring to when the congregation was established (cf. 1:5, *partnership in the gospel from the first day until now*). His partnership with the Philippians took the form of *the accounting [logos] of giving and receiving*, namely, mutual support for a common cause (cf. 2 Cor 11:8-9).

At first Paul mentions that the partnership was initiated (or activated?) after he departed from Macedonia, recalling their assistance when he was in Corinth (2 Cor 11:9). But then Paul backtracks in space and time, clarifying that even before he left Macedonia, the Philippians had *sent [assistance] for his need* not just once but twice, when he was in Thessalonica. Interestingly, Paul tells the Corinthians that he was no burden to them via needing to "rob" other churches, receiving support from believers in Macedonia (2 Cor 11:7-9); and he reminds the Thessalonians that he was not a burden because he worked for his own livelihood (1 Thess 2:9; 2 Thess 3:8), failing to mention the assistance from the Philippians. We can infer that the assistance from Philippi was not substantial enough to cover all his living expenses and those of his coworkers.

Paul emphasizes that this special relationship was unique: no other congregation experienced the same kind of partnership with Paul. We do not know why Paul entered into this kind of partnership only with the congregation in Philippi. It certainly was not his common pattern: he sought to avoid a reputation as a "peddler/retailer" (2 Cor 2:17) motivated by a "pretext for greed" (1 Thess 2:5; cf. 1 Cor

9:1-18, 23; 1 Thess 2:9; 2 Thess 3:7-12). His reason for refusing financial aid from the Corinthians was explicit: so that they would not be his patron or employer in the work of the gospel, somehow obligating him to the rich elite among them (1 Cor 9:1-18, 23), a refusal that strained his relationship with many of them (2 Cor 11–12). Perhaps it was the relative poverty of the Philippians (2 Cor 8:1-5) that made their contribution less onerous, imbalanced, or implicitly demanding.

We do not know if and when this partnership was formalized (for a formal partnership, cf. Gal 2:10 AT: "the right hand of partnership"). Was it formally established when Paul was still with them (cf. Sampley: 51–77: they formed a contractual partnership according to the current business model, the Roman consensual *societas*)? Was it formally established when he was with them on the agreement that it would only be activated later (Capper)? Or was it rather informally established, before or after his first departure?

On the one hand, it is possible that the congregation established forms of economic mutualism among themselves and with Paul when he was still with them. This might have resulted from their enthusiasm for Paul's vision of radical social transformations dawning in the world through the work of Messiah (e.g., Gal 2:9-10; 3:26-28; 2 Cor 8:13-14; Rom 12:13, 16). On the other hand, it is possible that their earlier assistance to him was unsolicited and outside the scope of any prior agreement. Perhaps the first contribution came as somewhat of a surprise, and it was through Paul's acceptance of the assistance that the partnership of giving and receiving was established, after Paul decided that he could not refuse them without jeopardizing his relationship with them. Or perhaps the Philippians were originally only seeking to reciprocate according to established conventions as an expected response of gratitude for his initial work on their behalf.

Whatever the origins, what matters to Paul now is that they enjoy a mutual partnership in the work of Messiah's gospel. The partnership itself is what now creates the obligations, responsibilities, and debts through an attitude of mutual commitment and interest, not particular acts of giving or receiving, which could put one party at an advantage or disadvantage.

Paul hopes that they will not consider their assistance to be a response to his solicitation or desire, which would entail attendant problems of direct reciprocation. Instead, he hopes that they simply consider their assistance as the expression of the established partnership. Thus he offers his second "not that" clause: *Not that I seek what is given; but I seek the fruit that accrues to your account* (4:17). To paraphrase: *I seek neither a handout nor a payment, but I am interested in an investment that gains dividends or equity for you* toward the shared enterprise of the gospel (1:5; cf. Philem 17-19 on commercial imagery of a "partnership"; similarly 1 Cor 9:14-18, 23 on Paul's desire for the dividends of a "shareholder," not the wages of a laborer). What might Paul mean by using this commercial metaphor? While it recalls language of "storing up treasures in heaven" by giving to the poor (Mark 10:21 // Matt 19:21 // Luke 18:22; Matt 6:19-21; Luke 12:21, 33-34), Paul is probably alluding to their *progress in loyalty* (1:25), the flowering of *the fruit of justice through Jesus Messiah* (1:11). (For the "fruit" [gain, income] stemming from generosity, see also 2 Cor 9:8-12.)

The word that is frequently translated *gift* (NRSV; NIV) in Philippians 4:17 is more neutrally *what is given* (*doma*), a *contribution* or *remittance* (LSJ), explained as a contribution toward their shared equity. To speak of a gift in the sense of unsolicited, free, or undeserved gift, Paul uses different words (*dōrea, dōrean*).

Third Acknowledgment: A Commercial Receipt for Receiving an Abundance 4:18

Lest there be any misunderstanding that Paul remains unimpressed or ungrateful, in quite expressive language he declares his third acknowledgment of their assistance, using the standard language of commercial receipts (v. 18a): *But I have been paid in full.* Even more: *and I am in excess*, that is, you have overdone it! Reaching the climax, he concludes, *I am filled to the full* (NRSV: *fully satisfied*; NIV: *amply supplied*), *having received from Epaphroditus the things from you*. Even as Paul again avoids using the word *gift* (but added by NRSV, NIV), one cannot imagine a more effusive set of compliments for their assistance.

Then Paul dramatically shifts into the language of sacrifice to finally clinch the true character of their act: it is *an aroma of fragrance, a sacrifice acceptable and pleasing to God*. Paul had earlier likened both their ministry in relation to Paul and that of Epaphroditus on their behalf as *public service*, which sometimes means priestly service (2:17, 30). Their actions through Epaphroditus are now even more explicitly presented in terms of a sacrificial offering. In the OT, the *aroma of fragrance* is always used to describe a "burnt offering/ sacrifice." The combination occurs elsewhere in the NT in Ephesians 5:2, while both words separately also occur in 2 Corinthians 2:14-16 to describe the aroma and fragrance of burnt flesh in sacrifice in reference to the sacrifice of bulls during a Roman triumphal celebration. (For the language of sacrifice/offering *acceptable* or *pleasing to God*, see, e.g., Rom 12:1-2; 15:16, 31.) This is the ultimate, if indirect, thank-you for their partnership with Paul and more precisely the ultimate "thanksgiving to God" generated by acts of mutual aid (see 2 Cor 9:11-13).

Concluding Promise and Doxology 4:19-20

Paul concludes by pointing to the ultimate benefactor and provider. Paul in effect calls on his conviction that his own (*my*) patron will provide for them all, more than adequately, as a kind of response to their generous act: *And my God will fill every need of yours according to his abundance* (wealth, riches) *in glory* (brilliant renown) *in Messiah.* Just as Paul is *filled* (v. 18) and his own needs are met (v. 16), now Paul exclaims that *God will fill every need of yours.* While their own generosity has exceeded (v. 18), it will be even further exceeded in keeping with the supply from *God's abundance.*

The phrase *in glory* here does not specify a location, such as meaning "in heaven." Paul consistently uses the word *doxa* to refer to (1) renown, honor, praise, and (2) brilliant splendor. It is a synonym with "honor" (Rom 2:7) and "praise" (Phil 1:11) and an antonym to "dishonor" (1 Cor 15:43) and "lowliness" (Phil 3:21). *In glory* (that is, *in brilliant renown*) thus describes the majestic quality and extent of God's abundant wealth. God's grand *wealth in glory/renown* thus poses a direct counterpoint to the lavish and sparkling wealth and power demonstrated by Roman power in Philippi, in accordance with Paul's consistent claims throughout the letter. In Philippians, then, God in Messiah is not only the true source of all cosmic-political power (2:9-11) and the proper framework for social honor and status (3:19-21), but also now the source and supply of all economic wealth, the very things that Rome claims to own and display through its "globalized" system. This supply of wealth is secure, activated, and available specifically *in Messiah Jesus* (through his agency, within the sphere of his renewing work), reemphasizing another consistent theme of the letter (cf. 1:26; 2:9-11; 3:8-11, 13-14, 20-21). This promise of unlimited wealth and status in Messiah provides the final answer to loss and divestment in the present order of time for the sake of Messiah (cf. 3:4-11).

We find a similarly remarkable promise of God's rich provision in the context of inviting mutual aid for the needy in 2 Corinthians 9:8-15: "God is able to cause every generosity [*charis*] to exceed unto you, so that by always having every self-sufficiency [*autarcheia*, or contentment], you will [in turn] exceed in every good work [of generosity]" (9:8 AT).

Paul's confident declaration of God's ultimate supply leads directly to doxological acclamation: *To our God and Father be glory [renown] into the ages of the ages.* This is the third assertion in Philippians that all praise goes back to God (1:11; 2:11). The whole letter is now caught up in this outburst. That is, generosity in giving and receiving leads directly and ultimately to doxology: giving glory to whom glory is due (cf. 2 Cor 9:11b, 14b, 15). This is the ultimate thank-you.

And so Paul can end with the final coda: *Amen*, a Hebrew loanword meaning "truly" or "let it be so." Paul's closing *amen* reflects the persistence of Hebrew (and Aramaic) liturgical patterns from his synagogue heritage, just as the opening grace and peace blessing does (see on 1:2; for other liturgical uses of Aramaic in Paul's Greek-speaking assemblies, see *maranatha* [1 Cor 16:22] and *abba* [Rom 8:15; Gal 4:6]).

THE TEXT IN BIBLICAL CONTEXT

Patterns of Economic Mutualism in Paul's Assemblies

Paul's coherent theology and practice of economic mutualism can be observed in three kinds of contexts: (1) between Paul and an individual congregation (Philippians; Philemon); (2) within individual congregations; and (3) between assemblies in different regions, a kind of global partnership between richer and poorer communities.

Most striking and best documented is Paul's tireless commitment to an international partnership, sealed in Jerusalem "with the right hand" when he promised to "remember the poor" (Gal 2:1-10). Paul spent a large portion of his waking energy undertaking a relief fund for his fellow messianic compatriots of Judea, impoverished by food shortages caused by both famine and the Roman Empire's tributary system of economic extraction from conquered territories. When raising funds among richer urban assemblies in the Greco-Roman world, he consistently claims to promote not just charity and benevolence, but also the concrete goal of partnership and equality with the lowly and poor (1 Cor 16:1-4; 2 Cor 8–9; Rom 15:25-32; Acts 24:17). He is careful to explain that any participation in this generosity (*charis*; 1 Cor 16:3; 2 Cor 8:4, 6, 7, 9, 19; 9:8) is founded on God's prior generosity (2 Cor 8:1, 9: 9:14), is voluntary

(8:3; 9:5), and is an expression of love (8:8, 24). He also emphasizes that it represents an "obedience to your oath of loyalty (confession) to the gospel of Messiah" (2 Cor 9:13 AT; cf. 8:8; 9:8-10) and demonstrates the obligation and public service (*leitourgia*; 2 Cor 9:12; Rom 15:27) appropriate to a reciprocal partnership (*koinōnia*; Rom 15:26-27; 2 Cor 8:4, 23; 9:13):

> They [the Macedonians and Greeks] were well-pleased [to contribute], but they are also obligated [in debt] to them: for if the nations came to be copartners with them in spiritual things [cf. Rom 11:17], they are [in turn] obligated [indebted] to offer public service [perform benefactions] in fleshly [material] things. (Rom 15:27 AT)

Indeed, this project aims to fulfill God's vision of a manna economy of equality (2 Cor 8:13-14) in which there is no "having more" nor "having less" (2 Cor 8:15, citing Exod 16:18). There is a striking parallel between the language and theology of these texts (esp. 2 Cor 8–9) and Paul's reflections and affirmations in Philippians (e.g., adequacy, contentment [*autarkeia/autarkēs*], 2 Cor 9:8; Phil 4:11; God's reward and provision, 2 Cor 9:10-11; Phil 4:13, 19; "public service," 2 Cor 9:12; Phil 2:25, 30; thanksgiving to God, 2 Cor 9:12; Phil 1:3; partnership, 2 Cor 9:13; Phil 1:5; 4:15; *generosity* [*charis*] defined by *mutualism*, Phil 1:7; 2 Cor 8:4). (See also TBC on 1:3-11, "Paul's Reconstruction of *Charis*.")

Evidence for practices of mutualism in local assemblies is limited, but not entirely lacking. Paul exhorts the Thessalonians to excel even more in the practice of mutual aid to support the poor (1 Thess 4:9-10; 5:14; 2 Thess 3:13), despite some irregularity of behavior (1 Thess 4:11-12; 2 Thess 3:6-12). Paul reminds the Romans to practice concrete "friendship love," expressed in "partnering with the needs of the saints," "love of the stranger" (hospitality), "associating with the lowly," and "regarding each other according to the same rank" (Rom 12:10, 13, 15-16). Paul's letter to the Galatians stresses the pattern of economic mutualism in support of teachers (6:6) and refers to doing "good" and "sowing" in the sense of providing economic assistance (6:7-11; cf. 2 Cor 9:6-11). The Corinthian letters confront extreme economic disparity and elite arrogance (1 Cor 1:26-31; 4:8-13; 11:17-34). It is likely that the weekly collection was designed not just for the needy far away (1 Cor 16:1-4), but also for the destitute locally. A few generations later (ca. 110s), this practice persisted. We learn about a common fund (*to koinon*) to support the needy (Ignatius, *To Polycarp* 4.3; cf. the evidence for communal welfare in the later pastoral epistles, 1 Tim 5:3-16; Justin

Martyr, *First Apology* 66–67). (For a lengthier treatment of this topic, see Meggitt; Zerbe 2012: 75–92.)

Partnership Parallels between Philippians and Philemon

Paul's carefully crafted commercial language pertaining to a business partnership in Philippians has a striking parallel to his letter to Philemon. In many ways these letters appear as twins. Both letters are sent from prison (most likely around the same time). Both include a promise for an imminent visit from Paul (Phil 1:25-26; 2:24; Philem 22). Both involve delicate communication about an emissary sent to provide service to Paul in prison and now being returned (Epaphroditus, Phil 2:25-30; 4:15-18; Onesimus, Philem 8-21). Both include a reference to a *fellow soldier* to Paul (Phil 2:25; Philem 2). And both request intercessory prayer for Paul's deliverance (Phil 1:19; Philem 22). Most impressively, both articulate a framework of partnership that frames issues of mutual giving and receiving and possible indebtedness or obligations around the possibility of "doing good" (Phil 1:6; Philem 6). In both, Paul's language is highly indirect (in modern Western perspective), appropriate to prevailing cultural expectations for matters of giving and receiving (see EN above).

What is apparent is that Paul has just received a substantial contribution from Philemon (the actual patron), to which Paul offers an indirect thank-you, as he does in Philippians. He congratulates Philemon for "the love and loyalty" that Philemon has demonstrated both to Lord Jesus Messiah *and* to the community ("saints"; Philem 5 AT). Paul hopes that Philemon's demonstrated "partnership of loyalty" might become even further effective or enabling in connection with the potential for "all the good [that may be accomplished] among us for the cause of Messiah" (v. 6 AT). Most English translations wrongly give the impression that Paul congratulates Philemon on having shared in the verbal communication of the gospel (NRSV: "the sharing of your faith"; CEV: "as you share your faith with others"). Instead, Paul is drawing attention to the social and economic shape of his "partnership of loyalty" (v. 6 NLT is better: "put into action the generosity that comes from your faith"). Using the language of relational bonds as a way to acknowledge assistance among those who are social equals, as Paul does in Philippians, he adds, "I have received much joy and consolation by your love" (as concretely demonstrated by Philemon's assistance). Indeed,

Philemon's assistance means that the "bowels (inner life) of the saints have been refreshed through you" (v. 7 AT).

Thus in a way analogous to his letter to Philippi, Paul in this context highlights that he and Philemon are, in effect, commercial partners (v. 17). Accordingly, in both Philippians and Philemon, Paul articulates mutual assistance with the language of mutual indebtedness or obligation (Phil 2:30; Philem 18-19). In both cases, envoys (Epaphroditus, Onesimus) have provided service to Paul on behalf of the other partner (Phil 2:25-20; Philem 13). In both relationships, Paul thus appeals to the "account ledger" of the partnership (Phil 4:17; Philem 18), though it is clear that Paul is referring to this somewhat metaphorically and certainly understands in-kind contributions to be as valid and valuable as direct financial contributions for the shared undertaking (the cause of the gospel/Messiah, Phil 1:5; Philem 6).

The major difference between Philippians and Philemon is that in the latter case, Paul is asking for even more, drawing attention to his own in-kind contributions that balance the account (Philem 17-21). Obliquely but clearly, Paul is asking Philemon to give Onesimus his legal freedom so that he can be more effective in service of the gospel (vv. 15-16, 21). Paul knows that he asking a lot financially. His costs would include the commercial value of Onesimus as a slave plus any adjustments to that value ("if he has defrauded or owes you," AT). Thus Paul promises to pay up in the future while reminding Philemon of the magnitude that he has already contributed in the partnership, ensuring Philemon's very "life" (vv. 18-19). In commercial terms, Paul accordingly asks that he "might receive some profit [interim payout, benefit, dividend] in the Lord" so that in interpersonal terms his own "bowels [inner being] might be refreshed in Messiah" (v. 20).

THE TEXT IN THE LIFE OF THE CHURCH

Economic Mutuality as Partnership, Duty, and Obligation

Seeking to take Paul's exhortation seriously, the *Confession of Faith in a Mennonite Perspective* (1995) advises: "As stewards of money and possessions, we are to live simply, practice mutual aid within the church, uphold economic justice, and give generously and cheerfully" (Article 21, citing Phil 4:11-12; 2 Cor 8:13-14; 9:7; James 5:4).

Stephen Fowl reflects on the pitfalls of the most common form of aid today among Christians: "suppliant-donor patronizing" (Fowl

2005: 139–41). Generosity, whether in the form of financial assistance or in the form of sending human resources, is typically motivated by pleas from the "needy" (or their advocates) to the generosity of "donors," invoking some sense of responsibility on the basis of pity and sympathy. Relief organizations often rely on what has been called a kind of "poverty porn" as a means of raising money. Meanwhile, following any donation based on a plea, the needy must also acknowledge their dependency by offering an appropriate thank-you. All this reinscribes the mental and social divide between the "needy" and the "donors." While Christian development organizations regularly use the language of partnership, the framework of these arrangements is usually at the whim of the more powerful (resource-rich) side of the relationship and often terminated unilaterally. The question to be repeatedly raised, then, is whether the rich and poor, the privileged and the oppressed, can truly ever be partners. *Partnership* is a word that we use too glibly.

Paul's perspective poses a direct contrast and challenge to these arrangements. Instead of suppliant-donor patronizing, he seeks to promote a sense of mutuality, interdependence, and solidarity, such that any response to need is but a reflection of true partnership, and thus duty and obligation, that never demeans the needy and in fact blurs the boundaries between the "needy" and the "donors." This mentality and activity, he claims, is included in what it means to practice (global) messianic citizenship.

Philippians 4:21-23

Final Greetings and Grace Blessing

PREVIEW

Hoping that the final crescendo of Philippians 4:19-20 is what will remain resounding in the ears of the gathered assembly in Philippi, Paul quickly brings the letter to its formal close with brief words of standard greetings and the final grace blessing. One greeting takes them by surprise and confirms the message of his deeply felt and forcefully argued letter: *especially those of Caesar's household* send greetings. The gospel has infiltrated even into the Roman imperial bureaucracy.

OUTLINE

Greetings to All Those in Philippi, 4:21a
Greetings from All Those with Paul, 4:21b-22
Grace Blessing, 4:23

EXPLANATORY NOTES

Greetings and some kind of grace wish constitute the most consistent features of Paul's letter closings. This regular practice reminds us that Paul is always in the business of personal and social networking—maintaining and extending connections among the faithful. Paul's success as an apostolic envoy is probably not to be attributed, in human terms, to some grand public oratory, which he actually denies that he has (2 Cor 10:10; 11:6), but to his relational ability, strength of personality, zealous passion, intellectual acumen, and strategic insight.

While Paul regularly asks the hearers to greet various people in the vicinity of a letter's destination, nowhere else does Paul enjoin, as he does here, *Greet every consecrated person [saint] in Messiah.* Paul elsewhere asks that particular individuals or house churches be greeted (Rom 16:3-15; Col 4:15), that readers-hearers "greet one another with a holy kiss" (Rom 16:16; 1 Cor 16:20; 2 Cor 13:12), or that they "greet all the brothers and sisters with a holy kiss" (1 Thess 5:26). In this case Paul's stress on *every saint* is meant to bolster his sustained desire to include and unify *all* his beloved in Philippi (1:1, 4, 7, 8, 25; 2:17, 26; *every* and *all* translate the same Greek word *pas*).

Next, Paul mentions those who send greetings. Elsewhere when he does this, he identifies individuals (Rom 16:21-23; 1 Cor 16:19b; Col 4:10-14; Philem 23-24) yet also groups who send greetings (cf. Rom 16:16b, "all the assemblies of Messiah"; 1 Cor 16:19-20a, "the assemblies of Asia," "all the brothers"; 2 Cor 13:13, "all the consecrated"). He also sometimes writes his own signature greeting (1 Cor 16:21; Col 4:18; 2 Thess 3:17; cf. Gal 6:11). Here Paul passes on greetings first from *the brothers and sisters with me*, which in this case probably refers to his circle of immediate coworkers (see EN on 2:25). The phrase *with me* seems to refer to those who are supporting him in his imprisonment, as has Epaphroditus (2:25-30). In this case it is unclear why Paul does not refer to anyone in particular (as in Col 4:10-14 and Philem 23-24, which might have been dictated from the same imprisonment), especially since some of these persons are likely known also to them (e.g., Luke [Col 4:14] and Aristarchus [Col 4:10; Philem 24], who is apparently from Thessalonica [Acts 20:4]). We can surmise that this lack of names is either because more specific personal greetings can be passed on by Epaphroditus orally, or because of caution, as a way to shield identities from prying imperial eyes should the letter be intercepted.

Next, Paul passes on greetings from *all the consecrated (saints)*, presumably from his immediate vicinity or within the scope of his geographical network in and around Ephesus. In this way, the two entire groups of *saints* in both Philippi (1:1; 4:21, *every saint*) and Ephesus (4:22) are mutually related in one grand movement of God's redemptive work in Messiah. Such words also offer a measure of encouragement: just as Paul stresses that he and his Philippian friends are inseparably bonded (1:3-8, 24-27, 30; 2:17-18), so also he emphasizes that all God's people are united together (cf. 1 Cor 1:2; 16:20; 2 Cor 13:12).

A startling specification comes next: greetings come from *especially those of Caesar's household*. This does not refer to the actual physical household (palace) of Nero (contra Fee), or to Caesar's relatives, or to the imperial court in Rome. Rather, the phrase *Caesar's household* regularly indicates more narrowly the imperial bureaucracy (civil service), whether in Rome or scattered throughout the empire and staffed especially by imperial slaves and freedmen (Weaver), and more generally those who are clients in the emperor's service, perhaps with access to the imperial court (Hollingshead). *Caesar's household* is thus roughly synonymous with Paul's earlier reference to *the whole praetorium and all the rest* (1:13), presumably referring to the group of imperial officials and servants in the Roman provincial headquarters in Ephesus.

While Paul earlier stresses that the knowledge of Messiah and his cause had pervaded *the whole praetorium and all the rest*, Paul now indicates that there are messianic sympathizers and adherents precisely in the ranks of the imperial civil service, perhaps not unlike the figure of the Philippian jailer (Acts 16:16-40). We do not know whether this was a result of Paul's own ministry or that of the assemblies or coworkers within his network (cf. 1:14-18). The crucial implication is that this is crowning proof of the gospel's growing triumph, precisely in the heart of the Roman power grid, which is largely hostile to Messiah and his people. As such, this would have been heard as a final expression of solidarity with others who are also experiencing pressure and hostility from those who are proclaiming Caesar as Lord and Savior.

Grace Blessing 4:23

Undoubtedly reflecting leave-taking practices of actual gathered assemblies, the grace benediction is the most consistent feature of Paul's closing words in his letters. It is found with a few variations: "the grace of [our] Lord Jesus [Messiah]" is pronounced as being or going either "with you" (using plural *you*; Rom 16:20; 1 Cor 16:23; Col 4:18; 1 Thess 5:28; cf. 1 Tim 6:21; 2 Tim 4:22), "with you all" (2 Cor 13:13/14; 2 Thess 3:18; cf. Eph 6:24; Titus 3:15), or "with your spirit" (using plural *your*; Gal 6:18; Phil 4:23; Philem 25). Paul puts the word *spirit* in the singular (as in Gal 6:18; Philem 25), modified by the plural *your*. This seems to be a way to emphasize the singularity of their one spirit as a community (see on Phil 1:27; 2:1; cf. 1 Cor 12:4, 11, 13; Eph 4:2-7).

Paul opens his conversations, therefore, with a pronouncement of the *grace and peace* (favor and wellness) that comes *from* God and Christ *to* his partners. Here Paul closes with the same combination. He has just declared that *The peace of God . . . will guard* them, and that *the God of peace will be with* them (4:7, 9). Now Paul bids farewell with a pronouncement that Christ's own *grace* (generosity) be *with* them. Grace and peace make a biblical hendiadys (a two-in-one).

As in the salutation and in crucial places in between, Paul closes with the threefold combination of name plus titles: *Lord Jesus Messiah* is the source of gracious blessing and favor in the broadest of senses (see TBC below).

TEXT IN BIBLICAL CONTEXT

Words for *Grace* in the Bible

Paul's language of grace (Gk. *charis*) draws on a rich biblical tradition. Unfortunately, modern English translations do not show this consistently. When the translators of the Septuagint (LXX: the Greek translation of the Hebrew Bible, in the 2nd c. BCE) came across the Hebrew word *ḥen*, they always translated with the Greek word *charis*, even though the two words do not always overlap completely in meaning. And when the translators of the King James Bible (1611) came across both the Hebrew word *ḥen* and the Greek word *charis*, they almost always translated with *grace*, regardless of the nuance. But because our English usage of *grace* has narrowed just to the "spiritual," modern translations regularly use different words to translate the range of senses of these words (e.g., kindness, approval, friendliness, charm, beauty, adornment, warm reception, favor, generosity, gratitude).

In the Hebrew Bible, we find *ḥen* mostly in expressions "to bestow or grant grace/favor" to someone, or "to find or win grace/favor" in someone's eyes. When it comes to the first idiom, it is God primarily who grants or shows grace/favor to someone (e.g., Ps 84:11), often undeservedly or unexpectedly. For this meaning, the verb form is also used (*ḥanan*, show compassion, favor; be gracious; e.g., Num 6:25). The second idiom may be used for a person finding grace/favor in God's eyes (e.g., Noah or Moses), but also for people finding grace (in a range of senses) before someone else (Jacob before Esau, Joseph before Pharaoh, Israel before the Egyptians, a wife before her husband, Ruth with Boaz, David with Saul, David with Jonathan, a righteous person before God and all humans, Esther before all people but especially the king).

The case of Esther is an example of how the word *ḥen* can refer both to moral or verbal loveliness and to physical beauty and charm, even adornment (*grace* in this sense can also be deceitful, Prov 31:30). But the word can also refer to "acts of generosity," especially to the poor or weaker (see EN on Phil 1:7). Closest to Paul's usage in this closing benediction is the use of *ḥen* in liturgical pronouncements for blessing, prosperity, and success (Zech 4:7; see also EN on 1:2).

While the Greek word *charis* has a similar range of meaning, it is used most especially for the radical "generosity" now demonstrated in and through Jesus. The importance of this notion throughout the NT can hardly be overstated. The word *charis* is absent from Matthew and Mark (yet the concept is there), but Luke highlights the theme in Jesus' opening sermon in Nazareth. He stresses the "words of grace" that proceeded from Jesus' lips, drawing attention to his proclamation of the "the year of the Lord's favor" (Luke 4:19-22 AT; *charis* occurs 25x in Luke-Acts). John's gospel does not use the term frequently, but draws attention to its major significance in the opening poem (1:14-17, using the word 4x).

Paul can be considered the theologian of grace in the NT (100 of the 155 occurrences of the word in the NT). *Grace* (generosity) is in fact the name of the new world-transforming regime that is now inaugurated in Christ (Rom 5–6). Moreover, grace is not only at the core of God's character (2 Cor 6:1); it is also at the motivating core of Christ's own character as a model to his followers (8:9). This grace is in turn bestowed on people (1 Cor 1:4). Paul knows himself to be entirely dependent on God's transforming grace, which also energizes his own vigorous striving (15:10). Indeed, all of life is a grace: "What do you have that you did not receive?" (as a grace; 1 Cor 4:7). Paul and his friends are "partners in grace" (Phil 1:7) in the deepest of senses. (See also TBC on 1:3-11, "Paul's Reconstruction of *Charis*.")

TEXT IN THE LIFE OF THE CHURCH

The Citizen Community of Christ: Concluding Reflections

In Philippians, Paul draws heavily on the image of the new community of Christ as a citizen community. In contrast to other nation-states, it has its own distinctive constitution and government, and its own unique sense of citizenship, territory, peace, and security. This powerful metaphor offers an invitation to the church today to explore the various ways in which it has or enacts a "politics," whether self-consciously or not. Although this notion in Paul was articulated in the context of the prevailing theopolitical framework of the ancient world (where religion and politics were not separated), careful reflection is needed on how this notion of a messianic citizenship is relevant for those of us who live in the context of the secular politics of the modern democratic state. Still, we should grant that in many parts of the world today, the political and the religious continue to be intertwined, not separated. In what ways, then, is the practice of messianic citizenship today undertaken in a socially and politically meaningful way, not just in a private, religious, or spiritual manner?

The following questions need to be faced as we reflect on the contemporary relevance of this theme, and as we consider what is unique about the character of Christian citizenship, in contrast to other claimants on our identities and loyalties.

1. What is the distinctive foundational narrative (salvation epic) of this commonwealth, embracing the past, present, and future (Phil 2:6-11; 3:20-21)? How can this community be both confident and humble in declaring its originating story? Who are its founding heroes, and what values do those heroes promote? Most sovereignties (nation-states) are based on some sort of founding violence: in what ways is violence embraced or rejected in this case? How do the founding events and story shape its continued social reality and formation? What assurances of security and victory can it give its citizens? What benefits or opportunities can it promise its citizens, current and prospective?

2. What kind of constitution does this citizen community have? What fundamental social values and aspirations are enshrined in it? Does it have a charter of rights that projects a vision for a new society? How does its constitutional charter seek to ensure that this citizen community can avoid turning into another power-hungry, oppressive system?

3. What kind of government (regime) does this people have? What does it mean in practice that it is truly set up as a Christocracy, constituted by the rule/lordship of Christ? How is supreme power practically mediated and manifested in a way different from other polities? What kind of on-site, middle-level administrators (servant leaders) should it have? How are these put into place? How does it balance the vision of welcome, mutuality, partnership, and equality with a framework for leadership, as it seeks to avoid the pitfalls of institutionalized power?

4. Who is welcome to join, to enjoy and take advantage of the benefits of this Christian commonwealth, while also shouldering the

burden of its responsibilities? How does one join? In what ways is this citizenship community distinctive as a voluntary, invitational society? In what way is its sense of "nationality" expressed? What implications does that framework have for how Christians today might approach prevailing notions of nationality or nationalism?

5. What are the demands or voluntary expectations of allegiance and loyalty that go along with enjoying the benefits of this regime of Christ? What kinds of service or sacrifices might it require of its citizens in the name of patriotic loyalty to Christ?

6. What kind of identity does this commonwealth nurture as a citizen community? Does it offer a new identity (held as a "dual citizenship") alongside other identities? Does it foster a counter-identity or ultimate identity (that always trumps other identities)? Or does it entail a kind of nonidentity that hollows out other identities and calls into question normal identity constructions (Agamben 2005: 19–43)? Can one truly and fully be a dual citizen of this Christian community and of another regime or nation at the same time? In what ways might this commitment supersede other commitments or claims to loyalty? What do you do when multiple identities conflict?

7. Does this citizen body have a specific territory or make territorial claims? What is the meaning of its claim on the whole of creation (Phil 2:11; 3:21)? Does this promote an imperialist crusader mentality, or does it actually subvert territorial sovereignty as usual, while promoting a global citizenship that reaches beyond loyalty to a particular nation-state? What implications does this have for assessing the usual claims to territorial sovereignties by modern states? What are the implications of the fact that its central regime/government is now waiting in exile (3:19) and its members are scattered in diverse earthly territories and states?

8. How does the citizen community of Christ handle the questions of diversity, marginalization, or inequality? What kind of hierarchies can it tolerate or does it reject? How does it wrestle with challenges to its internal coherence and unity? Is the unity of global Christianity a merely aspirational or spiritual concept, or is it something that is realizable? How does it wrestle with pluralism in the context of its global, universal claims?

9. What security issues does this community face, especially from other political formations in the middle of which it might exist? What kinds of pressures are experienced by those committed to this government-in-waiting experience? What kind of adversaries does it have? Can it really have enemies? How does it explain why

others might be hostile to it? What kind of warfare or defensive resistance does it endorse? What kind of soldiers does it honor? Will its members go to war for earthly sovereignties?

What can we conclude, then, about the politics of this community? For Paul, there is no separation of the personal, relational, religious, and political. Paul's primary practical and political undertaking is focused on drawing people into and nurturing communities that celebrate (rejoice in) an alternative citizenship through Christ, a citizenship in anticipation, a citizenship in exile—a citizenship with a nurtured mental disposition and a corresponding practice. Paul's politics is not one of direct assault on powers such as Rome. But Paul's politics is also not one of mere detachment and idle waiting. As J. C. Beker puts it, in Paul there is a crucial combination of eschatological (visionary, future-oriented) passion and practical sobriety (Beker: 135–81, 303–49). Paul's vision of a world in the process of transformation through Christ is the very driving force of his political work in establishing and nurturing alternative assemblies as the beachhead of God's reign.

Paul's messianic politics is decidedly "patriotic." That is, Paul expects those welcomed into the saving sphere of Christ to be fervently loyal to it, to the point of death. As a result, loyalty to Christ cannot coexist with an equivalent zealous loyalty to any other dominion, human or spiritual. The notion of a coexisting dual citizenship is foreign to Paul's thinking. For Paul, there is only citizenship oriented to God's secure regime in heaven, which means that its members, those from Israel and all the nations, can only be world citizens (Phil 2:9-11; 3:20-21). The claims of Christ override all other claims of political identity and sovereignty.

Despite the palpable counterimperial rhetoric in Philippians and the rest of Paul (esp. 1 Thessalonians, 1 Corinthians, Romans, Colossians), it cannot be said that Rome is the chief or sole enemy to be overcome in Paul's theological rhetoric. Paul perceives the unredeemed powers at work in the universe to be far more subtle and pervasive than we can easily pinpoint by referencing only one obvious exemplar such as Rome. Nor is it true that Paul is motivated by some kind of built-up resentment focused on Rome and the glories of the Greco-Roman cultural world more generally. Paul is not simply hostile to or envious of Rome. Rather, the point is that the gospel of Christ—when experienced, articulated, and proclaimed by its own inner reality and logic—simply runs against alternative totalizing allegiances and polities, whether public or private, political or religious.

Paul is hesitant to give Rome too much credit; it is merely one face of a much deeper crisis of a world out of control. Nor does he wish assemblies committed to Christ to simplistically find an easy focus to their own resentment or fears; the powers cannot be so easily particularized. Paul's move, rather, is to place even Rome under the ultimate sovereignty of God (Phil 2:9-11; 3:20-21).

Outline of Philippians[1]

I. Opening — **1:1-11**

- A. Address and Grace-Peace Blessing — 1:1-2
  - 1. Sender and Addressee — 1:1
  - 2. Grace and Peace Blessing — 1:2
- B. Thanksgiving and Prayer — 1:3-11
  - 1. Thanksgiving to God — 1:3-6
  - 2. Explanation of Paul's Disposition — 1:7-8
  - 3. Prayer — 1:9-11

II. Disclosure: The Gospel's Advance and Paul's Confidence despite Adversity — **1:12-26**

- A. Retrospective: Messiah Is Being Proclaimed—The Advance of the Gospel, despite Adversity and Rivalry — 1:12-18a
- B. Prospective: Messiah Will Be Magnified—The Advance of Loyalty-Faith, in Deliverance and Reunion — 1:18b-26

III. Exhortation — **1:27–4:9**

- A. Practicing Messianic Citizenship, Part 1 — 1:27–2:18
  - 1. Being a Citizen Body Worthy of the Gospel of Messiah — 1:27-30
    - a. The Singular Imperative of Messianic Citizenship — 1:27a
    - b. The Unified Alignment of the Citizen Community under Siege — 1:27b-28a
    - c. Clarifying the Nature and Outcome of the Struggle — 1:28b-30

[1] See also p. 35 for a slightly different way of presenting the structure and flow of Philippians.

(1) Facing Destruction or Deliverance 1:28b

(2) The Graces of Both Loyal Devotion and Suffering 1:29

(3) A Shared Struggle 1:30

2. A Citizen Body Marked by Unity and Status Inversion 2:1-5

a. Premises: Resources and Virtues in the Context of Suffering 2:1

b. The Soul and Mind-Set of Messianic Communal Politics 2:2-5

(1) Common Bond and Purpose 2:2

(2) Common Status: Striving for the Other 2:3-4

(3) Embracing the Mentality of Messiah 2:5

3. Tribute to Messiah: Self-Emptied Divinity and Exalted Slave 2:6-11

a. Humiliation 2:6-8

(1) A Divine Being Who Rejects Upward Striving 2:6

(2) Two Stages of Messianic Humiliation 2:7-8

(a) A Divine Being Who Takes the Form of a Slave 2:7a-c

(b) A Human Being Who Lowers Himself to Death on a Cross 2:7d-8

b. Exaltation 2:9-11

(1) God Responds to Hyperelevate Messiah 2:9

(2) Goal: The Final Universal Acclaim of Messiah, to the Glory of God 2:10-11

4. The Citizen Community's Agency in the Drama of Salvation 2:12-18

a. Active Participation in the Drama of Salvation 2:12-13

b. A Community of Character and Mission 2:14-16

c. Mutual Rejoicing in the Midst of Suffering 2:17-18

B. Travel-Talk Interlude: Timothy and Epaphroditus as Models of Messianic Citizenship 2:19-30

1. Plans for Sending Timothy Soon 2:19-23

a. The Hope for Timothy's Imminent Visit and Its Purpose 2:19

b. Recommendation of Timothy as Model Messianic Envoy 2:20-22

c. Timing Contingency: Paul's Own Circumstance 2:23

2. Confidence in Paul's Own Imminent Visit 2:24

3. Commendation of Epaphroditus as Model Messianic "Soldier" 2:25-30

a. The Necessity of Sending Epaphroditus 2:25
b. The Reasons for Sending Epaphroditus 2:26-28
c. Receiving and Honoring Epaphroditus 2:29-30
C. Practicing Messianic Citizenship, Part 2 3:1–4:9
1. Israelite-Messianic Citizenship Contrasted with (Roman) Adversaries 3:1-3
a. Transition and Resumption of Exhortation 3:1a
b. Hesitation Formula 3:1b
c. Israelite-Messianic Citizenship Contrasted with Roman Polity 3:2-3
(1) Coded Caricature of Roman Polity 3:2
(2) Israelite-Messianic Citizenship Claimed and Reframed 3:3
2. Demonstrating Messianic Citizenship: The Model of Paul 3:4-17
a. Being Confident in the Flesh: Paul's Israelite Cursus Honorum 3:4-6
b. Boasting in Messiah 3:7-14
(1) The Balance Sheet: A Reassessment 3:7-8
(2) The Social Register: A Resocialization 3:9-11
(3) The Racetrack: Intense Pursuit toward the Ultimate Prize 3:12-14
c. Practicing the Mind-Set 3:15-17
3. Contrasting Regimes and Destinies 3:18–4:1
a. Enemies of the Cross: Their Walk, Mind-Set, and Destiny 3:18-19
b. Messiah's People: Their Awaited Deliverer and Destiny 3:20-21
c. Concluding Exhortation: Stand Firm 4:1
4. Closing Exhortations 4:2-9
a. Reconciliation of Euodia and Syntyche 4:2-3
b. Consolation and Encouragement in Suffering 4:4-7
(1) Rejoice in the Lord Always 4:4
(2) Clemency toward All People 4:5a
(3) Assurance: The Lord Is Near 4:5b
(4) No Anxiety, Dedication to Prayer with Thanksgiving 4:6
(5) Assurance: The Peace of God Will Guard Hearts and Minds 4:7
c. Ethical Discernment and Models 4:8-9
(1) Auditing Civic Virtues and Public Commendations 4:8

(2) Practicing in Accordance with Paul's Teaching and Modeling 4:9a
(3) Assurance: The God of Peace Will Be with You 4:9b

IV. Celebrating the Mutuality of Partnership and God's Rich Provisions 4:10-20

A. First Acknowledgment: Joy in Their Mindfulness 4:10-13
B. Second Acknowledgment: The Blessing of Partnership 4:14-17
C. Third Acknowledgment: A Commercial Receipt for Receiving an Abundance 4:18
D. Concluding Promise and Doxology 4:19-20

V. Final Greetings and Grace Blessing 4:21-23

A. Greetings to All Those in Philippi 4:21a
B. Greetings from All Those with Paul 4:21b-22
C. Grace Blessing 4:23

Essays

CIRCUMSTANCES OF THE MESSIANIC ASSEMBLY (CHURCH) IN PHILIPPI On the basis of Paul's consoling words and his direct exhortation, we can infer that he understands the assembly of Messiah loyalists in Philippi to be facing a twofold crisis: pressure from the outside and disintegration on the inside. Indeed, these issues are probably interrelated, given the way Paul addresses them.

External Pressure Paul makes no reference to the external problem until 1:27-30, when we learn that they are engaged in a *struggle* (*agōn*, fight, ordeal, 1:30). It is a struggle before particular *adversaries* that involves *suffering* and is generating *fear* (*intimidation*). The adversaries think the assembly should come to *destruction*. A few months later, Paul says that the Macedonian loyalists, presumably including those in Philippi, have encountered a "severe testing of affliction" (2 Cor 8:2 AT).

The themes of suffering and social alienation run through the letter, both explicitly and implicitly, involving Messiah, Paul, and the assembly in a three-way mutual dynamic (Bloomquist; Jewett). It is a suffering shared with both Paul (1:30; 2:16-18; 3:10-11) and Messiah (2:5-11; 3:10-11). This situation explains the core exhortation to "stand firm" (1:27; 4:1; cf. 1 Thess 3:8, from a similar circumstance), the consolation (1:28–2:1; 4:4-9, 19-20), the exhortation to see suffering as a grace (1:30), the exhortation to rejoice precisely in suffering (2:17-18), the acknowledgment of endangerment as a threatened minority in relation to cultural surroundings (2:15-16), the imagery of the assembly as a beleaguered city-state (1:27), and the persistent eschatological orientation and reassurance (1:6, 10; 1:21-24; 2:9-11, 16; 3:4-14; 3:20-21; 4:1, 4-9, 19-20).

Clues regarding the nature of this adversity and its perpetrators come from a variety of sources. First, Paul indicates that it is a struggle of the *same* sort that he earlier experienced in Philippi and continues to experience in his imprisonment (1:30). This suggests that the ordeal has primarily to do with opposition from Roman imperial authority and from the Roman social elite generally (cf. Acts 16:11-40; 1 Thess 2:2). The particular character of Roman Philippi, especially its history as a Roman military colony, seems to have much to do with this. The book of Acts reports that Paul was earlier accused of "destabilizing the city and advocating practices unlawful for us Romans to accept or practice" (Acts 16:20-21 AT), something neither he nor the author of Acts denies. In a similar way, Paul is accused shortly thereafter in Thessalonica of "defying Caesar's decrees and saying that there is another king, one called Jesus" (17:7 AT). On "Roman soil," it is illegal to preach new divinities and to make converts. Just as important was promoting practices perceived to undermine the Roman social and political order. Any sign of disloyalty to the Roman Empire—its way of life, its gods, and its emperors—was a serious matter for the civic authorities. Moreover, Philippians hints that the struggle involves particular legal issues and possibly imprisonment. The nature of the thinly veiled counterimperial rhetoric through the letter seems to confirm this (1:27; 2:6-11, 15-16; 3:2, 18-21; 4:7, 9, 23).

The messianic assembly was not among the associations approved by the civic and imperial authorities. The Roman authorities closely monitored the activities and presence of any nonregistered "associations" or "organizations" (*collegia*; Gk. *hetairai*), sometimes prohibiting them (e.g., Pliny the Younger, *Letters to Trajan* 10.96), for fear that some might foment organized disloyalty, even while looking innocuous from the outside (Arnaoutoglou; Cotter 1996). At stake for the Romans was the *pax decorum*, the harmonious relationship between humans and gods, maintained by means of appropriate ceremonies and practices, including oaths of loyalty.

The hostility, therefore, should not be thought of as merely involving negative reactions to "godly lives" or as general mob violence in response to presumed instigation by a Jewish element (contra O'Brien). Specific circumstances that have precipitated the reaction more likely include (1) the act of proclamation and deliberate proselytizing, in connection with the content of the gospel, focusing on an alternative Lord, alternative kingdom, and alternative moral code (cf. Acts 16:20-21; 17:6-7; Oakes 2001: 91); (2) the perception that the assembly was constituted by subversive Judeans (Acts 16:20-21); (3) deliberate disengagement from the cult of Rome and Caesar, along with other cults (de Vos: 264; Fee: 31, 172; Tellbe 1994, 2001); (4) disengagement from some guilds and associations devoted to pagan gods or imperial symbols (Oakes 2001: 89–91); (5) tensions within families and reactions by elite men, as a result of women being attracted to the assembly (Portefaix); and/or (6) the somewhat in-house, secretive activities of the assembly, creating suspicion.

As for the nature of the suffering, one can only conjecture that it involved legal proceedings in some cases, general social harassment from neighbors, public shaming in some form, and economic loss, since many who refused to offer devotion to Roman virtues and gods were alienated from labor associations and artisan guilds (Oakes 2001: 89–92). The economic reality of financial ruin could explain Paul's economic metaphor of loss, gains, and equity in offering his own story as an example (3:4-11;

4:11-13, 16-19; cf. also Rev 13:17), and the image of embracing slavery (1:1; 2:6-8).

Internal Disintegration Paul does not characterize the internal dynamics of the assembly at Philippi in any direct manner (in contrast to, e.g., 1 Cor 1:10-13; 4:6, 18; 11:18; 2 Cor 12:20), except in one case, where he advises that a dispute between two individuals be mediated (Phil 4:2-3). Otherwise, we must infer these dynamics from indirect references embedded in Paul's exhortation. The first calls to exhibit unity come in 1:27 (that they *stand firm in one spirit, strive together with one soul*) and 2:1-2 (that they display a *partnership* in the spirit, love, and compassion for one another, display one and the *same mind-set*, show the *same love*, being *joined in soul*). Paul also warns them against *grumbling and disputing* (2:14). His exhortation that they seek the interests of the other member and rank others higher than oneself and his warning against seeking selfish ambition and empty glory suggest some level of internal fracture (2:3-4; cf. 4:2-3). Moreover, the repeated emphasis on including *all* the members in his exhortation and consolation (1:1, 7 [2x], 8, 25; 2:17; 4:21) implies some level of factionalism.

The dispute between Euodia and Syntyche suggests some level of internal disunity (4:2-3), especially since Paul's exhortation to them uses the same terminology as when the entire assembly is addressed (2:2). The significance of this dispute for internal relationships is especially great if Euodia and Syntyche were part of the leadership team of the assembly (as is likely; see the EN), perhaps as heads of different house assemblies within the larger group of Messiah loyalists in Philippi. At the same time, however, there is no evidence of serious strife and division (of the sort, say, experienced in Corinth). And there is no evidence of any resident "false teachers" *[Opponents in Philippians, p. 300]*.

The internal conflict does not seem to be merely a matter of (horizontal) interpersonal conflict or theological-ethical disputes. Paul's exhortation (2:2-11; 3:4-14) suggests that it has to do with status-and-rank hierarchies, which we can surmise are based on socioeconomic factors of status and/or on ethnopolitical identities. Moreover, it appears likely that the internal problem is in some way tied to the external threat, which may have exacerbated latent conflictual dynamics. It is probable that (1) some sectors of the assembly were more affected by the persecution than others, based on their social status (citizenship, legal order, wealth), with perhaps some wealthier members not being willing to help the weaker and more vulnerable members (Oakes 2001); and (2) that the disputes involved different views on how to respond to the pressure—that is, in what ways to conform and assimilate and in what ways to stand firm and apart (see, e.g., Carter 2006: 61; de Vos: 265–67; Fee: 33, 366; Geoffrion: 26–27; Krentz; Peterlin; Tellbe 1994, 2001).

CITIZENSHIP, ANCIENT AND MODERN Ancient concepts and practices of citizenship (political identity) differ substantially from modern concepts and practices.

Modern Citizenship The modern notion of citizenship is understood primarily as an aspect of nationality and, more precisely, as membership (with its privileges and obligations) in a politically sovereign state, a "country." This framework is largely a product of the Westphalian model of states and citizenship that emerged at the end of the Eighty Years' War (1568–1648) between Spain and the Dutch Republic and the Thirty Years' War (1618–1648), which brought an end to the Holy Roman Empire in Europe. According to the Peace of Westphalia (1648), the ideal state was to be a nation-state, where ethnolinguistic identity (one's "nation," by virtue of "birth," *natio*) correlated with political sovereignty and self-determination (the "state"): thus, France for the French, Germany for the Germans, Spain for the Spanish, and so forth. Many countries still recognize citizenship along genealogical lines (for instance, until recently becoming a Japanese meant joining a Japanese genealogy). Still, not all modern states are ideal nation-states (some are explicitly plurinational states [Bolivia]; some ethnolinguistic nations are split into two [Korea]; and some "nations" do not enjoy statehood [Kurdistan; Palestine]).

Ancient Citizenship Citizenship in the Greco-Roman world was very different from today, when it pertains to "nationality," however defined.

1. Originally the formal and legal language of citizenship applied to membership in a city-based citizen community. The Roman Empire was technically the empire of a particular city. Roman citizenship, therefore, was not a matter of national identity, but of privileged membership in the city that ruled the Mediterranean region. Our English terminology of citizenship has evolved from city-based concepts, in particular from Anglo-Norman *citesein* (resident of a city; from the Old French *cité*, city), from the Latin *cives* (citizen) and *civitas* (city), and from the Greek *politēs* (citizen) and *polis* (city, citizen community).

The terminology and formal legal concepts of "citizenship" were first developed in the context of the Greek city-state system. A citizen (*politēs*) was a member of a city (*polis*, citizen community) organized around a particular constitution (*politeia*) and governing institutions (*politeuma*). It thus enjoyed and practiced a particular citizenship (*politeia*, manner of life). Greeks shared a broader pan-Hellenic ethnolinguistic identity as Greeks (perceived in contrast to "barbarian" nations). But more important from the archaic period (800 BCE) to the Macedonian conquest of greater Greece in 338 BCE was formal membership in a sovereign and autonomous city-state constituted as a citizen community (*polis*). In that context, "citizenship" was thus originally a way of defining urban privilege. In its more limited meaning, a citizen was an adult male (a) who as "free" enjoyed privileges of membership in an urban community (as opposed to slaves or dependent and taxed farmers in the surrounding region under a city's jurisdiction), and (b) who as a member of the citizen "assembly" (*ekklēsia*) was eligible to participate in some manner in the governance of a city (though this varied, based on whether the city governance was autocratic, oligarchic, or democratic). More broadly, citizenship pertained to a city-based citizen community and could informally include the dependent women and children of an adult male citizen. After the conquests of the Macedonian Alexander the Great (334–323 BCE), numerous cities of the Hellenistic kingdoms that followed (from Asia Minor to Egypt and Mesopotamia) were founded according to this Greek model.

For many other peoples of the ancient world, however, political identity (with ethnic, religious, linguistic, genealogical, and geographical dimensions united into one) was primarily a function of being a member of an ethnolinguistic "nation" (Gk. *genos, ethnos*). This was true of the Israelite nation and many others. By the first century, city-based citizenship terminology (*politeia*) could thus be appropriated informally to refer to membership in or identity as an ethnic people-nation (e.g., Eph 2:12).

2. In modern liberal-democratic states, citizenship is generally held by the vast majority of those who reside in the country (usually only excluding immigrants and aliens). In contrast, citizenship in the Greco-Roman world demarcated a privilege that excluded many residents of a city or region—not only the migrants (metics), but also the poor (urban poor and peasant farmers) and slave classes, and technically women and children. Thus the population of any city and its surrounding dependent regions was comprised of citizens and noncitizens, with the relative percentage of each varying from place to place. As Athens slowly absorbed all of Attica, Athenian citizenship was enjoyed by the majority. By contrast, Sparta annexed conquered populations, retaining them as second-class state-serfs (Helots), while granting citizenship only to the privileged elite in the conquered territories.

In first century, only 10 percent of the Roman Empire's population of around 60 million enjoyed Roman citizenship, most of those residing in Italy. Only after the special privileges pertaining to Roman citizenship were significantly reduced in value was Roman citizenship granted to almost all adult males in 212 by the emperor Caracalla. By then, other social categories had become routinely used to ensure legal, political, and economic privilege.

3. Citizenship was conceptualized genealogically (often with particular tribes or clans holding greater or lesser status). Roman citizens held the coveted three names (*tria nomina*), and the middle name always designated a person's tribal name (*gens*). To become a Roman citizen legally, one needed to formally join a Roman tribal genealogy. Roman citizenship included the right of *connubium*—marriage with full-blooded Romans and citizenship for offspring. As Republican Rome slowly achieved ascendancy throughout Italy and beyond (3rd c. to 1st c. BCE), a persistent struggle was whether or not to grant its closest "allies" citizenship in Rome proper. Part of the debate was whether to absorb these new citizens into existing Roman tribes or whether to create new tribes (presumably with lesser status). In the early Principate (beginning in 27 BCE), many new citizens in the provinces were granted a Julian or Claudian tribal identity at the behest of their imperial patrons (the Julio-Claudian dynasty, 27 BCE–68 CE). Meanwhile, in the 30s CE, the city of Alexandria requested the creation of a new Roman tribe into which their worthy elite could be inducted.

4. In modern liberal-democratic states, all citizens are formally equal in status and privilege (as was the case in the ideal covenant community of Israel). This principle did not generally hold in the ancient world. Most cities required a minimum level of wealth or income for citizenship eligibility, and financial levels determined the level of office one might hold. For instance, in the city of Tarsus, the constitution was rewritten in 30 BCE after a certain Athenodorus was able to take power and set up a pro-Roman oligarchy. Those not granted citizenship were permitted to purchase citizenship for the price of 500 drachmae (around two years' gross income for a laborer). As in other ancient cities, Roman citizens were strictly ranked according to their legal "order": from aristocratic patricians (senators, equestrians, decurions [magistrates in the provinces]) to plebeians (commoners), with privileges and opportunities pertaining to those statuses. Requests for obtaining Roman citizenship from aliens included a *census* (financial) rating. Some aliens were granted partial Roman citizenship rather than full citizenship.

5. During the Roman Empire, various levels of citizenship existed (depending on the relative status, privileges, and power of the city in which one might have been a citizen). An individual could hold multiple citizenship memberships at the same time. For instance, the "free" population of the city of Alexandria was graded according to the following levels of citizenship (levels of legal status and rights), from top to bottom: Roman, Latin (an intermediate status), Alexandrian (Greek), Judean (who were allowed some level of internal governance as a "political body" [*politeuma*] led by a ruling "council" [*boulē*]), and finally native Egyptian. Paul could claim citizenship in the city of Rome (the highest citizenship available), the city of Tarsus (Acts 21:39), and in the polity of the nation Israel (Rom 9:4; 2 Cor 11:22; Phil 3:5). Some provincial cities (certain groups of individuals within cities) were granted Roman citizenship as *municipia* or *colonia* of Rome, while other communities (or individuals) were granted "Latin rights" (based on the earlier framework of the Rome-led Latin League).

6. For many provincials (residents of the conquered, occupied territories) who somehow gained it, Roman citizenship provided a legal framework for status and privilege and was not celebrated as a primary "national" identity. That status was often treated as a practical benefit, not as a statement of identity, allegiance, or culture. Nevertheless, Romans expected a certain loyalty of those granted citizenship. Oaths of loyalty were a key part of the citizenship ceremony. Officeholders (magistrates) in cities ranked as "Roman municipalities" were required to take oaths of citizenship, including oaths of allegiance to Roman gods and (divinized) rulers. In one surviving text from the regime of Domitian (81–96 CE), the order is that incumbent officers (*duovirs, aediles, quastors*)

> shall in a public meeting take oath by Jupiter, by the deified Augustus, by the deified Claudius, by the deified Vespasian Augustus, by the deified Titus Augustus, by the *genius* [guardian spirit] of Domitian Augustus, and the [municipal] tutelary gods, that they will properly

> perform whatsoever they believe to be in accordance with this charter and in the public interest of the [Roman, Latin] citizens of the municipality. (Lewis and Reinhold: 322)

Privileges of Roman Citizenship The legal protections, privileges, exemptions, and social distinctions that accompanied Roman citizenship in a typical city of the empire were considerable. These included protection from the arbitrary power of ruling magistrates and governors, intermarriage with Romans, exemption from torture or corporal punishment without trial, freedom to conduct legal business in Rome, portability of the status as a migrant away from Rome or Italy, the right of appeal to Caesar in court cases, and some immunity from some of the laws (e.g., taxes and civic obligations) of individual cities in the empire.

Obtaining Roman Citizenship Roman citizenship could be obtained (1) by birth, (2) by manumission from a Roman slave owner (with some limits to this), and (3) by citizenship grants to noncitizens and aliens. Because Roman citizenship was a marker or means of social, political, or economic status and success, access to it was carefully guarded, and attempts to gain it were energetic. Serious penalties were attached to false claims of Roman citizenship or to taking fraudulent steps for procuring Roman citizenship for oneself or one's children. Birth from a single Roman parent did not make one a Roman. Generally, the status of a child followed the legal status of the "inferior" parent. Of course, the many children sired by Roman soldiers serving away from home had no claim to Roman citizenship.

Roman citizenship was regularly and extensively granted to the political and economic urban elite in pacified regions as a way to ensure their devotion and loyalty to Rome while serving as the empire's ruling class. Romans often judged an alien's display of loyalty (or lack thereof) to be far more critical than the person's legal standing as a Roman, as demonstrated by the case of Paul, who languished for years in Roman prisons, and was finally executed (according to early Christian tradition; e.g., 1 Clement 5.1–6; Ignatius, *To the Ephesians* 12.1–2), probably on suspicion of treason.

Grants of citizenship during the period of the Roman Empire were controlled by the emperor, to whom requests were directed (usually by a provincial governor on behalf of someone deemed worthy). Grants of citizenship to provincials were commonly granted but often restricted to urban elites (municipal officeholders) as a way to ensure their loyalty and to bring them into the empire's ruling class. Citizenship could also be obtained as a reward for services rendered to the Roman state, for instance, in commercial undertakings to supply grain to Rome or (most commonly) through military service. The prospect of obtaining citizenship at the conclusion of loyal and able military service became a crucial recruitment mechanism to staff the empire's legions. Successful athletes were also regularly considered for citizenship. Since requests for citizenship were usually directed to the emperor from provincial governors or the emperor's influential friends, citizenship could also be obtained through cash donations (bribery). (For Paul's case, see Acts 16:22-24,

35-39; 22:25-29.) Sometimes a city might appeal to the emperor for a new Roman tribe to be inaugurated as a vehicle for some of their elite citizens to obtain Roman citizenship.

Registration and Proof of Citizenship For those born Romans, citizenship records were presumably stored in city archives, and perhaps a certified copy could be kept in one's possession when traveling. For those granted citizenship after birth, lists of inductees were sometimes listed on bronze plaques in the city where the status was formally granted. While some might have carried certified papyrus or vellum diplomas, numerous bronze or wooden plaques of Roman citizenship have also been discovered. See Bruce; Cohen: 81, 125–27; Doughty; Garnsey and Saller: 15, 35, 87–88, 111, 115–16, 124; Goodman: 51–52, 78, 165–66, 219–20; Lefkowitz and Fant: 110, 114, 119, 121; Lewis and Reinhold: 52–55, 129–35, 134–35, 233, 321–23, 521–27; Kelly: 49–50, 60, 73, 130; Schürer: 134–37; Sherwin-White 1973, 1978.

CRITICAL QUESTIONS REGARDING PHILIPPIANS 2:6-11 More ink has been spilled on the discussion of Philippians 2:6-11 than almost any other text in Paul. Ever since the groundbreaking work of Ernst Lohmeyer in 1928, it has become a part of received wisdom among biblical scholars that 2:6-11 in some way represents a pre-Pauline hymn that Paul quoted or adapted to the present context. Recent scholarship, however, has shown increasing skepticism of the notion that these verses are both a hymn and essentially pre-Pauline (e.g., Brucker: 17, 21–22, 349–50; Fee: 193–94; Fowl 1990; Wright 1991; Hellerman: 155–56, 202–3, 211; Oakes 2001).

The following interrelated issues have become the focus of the discussion and debate: (1) genre: poetry or prose; hymn, confession, or other; (2) authorship: Pauline or pre-Pauline; (3) stanza structure as a hymn, including source reconstruction relative to alterations by Paul; (4) the Christology of the hymn: its primary conceptual background and rhetorical resonances.

1. Genre. How should these verses be regarded? In what genre should they be cast? In particular, do they represent poetry, and is this best deemed a hymn (song of praise) to God? Or are these verses a confessional formulation? The main arguments for these verses as a hymn are: (a) the initial relative pronoun (*hos*, who; cf. Col 1:15; 1 Tim 3:16); (b) the rhythmic character and exalted language of these verses in contrast to the surrounding verses; (c) the structured parallelism similar to other examples of Semitic (Hebrew) poetry; and (d) the internal, self-standing coherence of the verses relative to the immediate context.

But these arguments are not decisive: (a) The opening *hos* in 2:6 is unlike other alleged hymns (Col 1:15, 18b; 1 Tim 3:16); in 2:6 the transition is natural and smooth, beginning a new sentence. (b) Exalted, declarative prose or poetry does not necessarily indicate a hymn. While Paul's language is exalted and rhythmic, the sentences flow according to natural prose in a manner not unlike other passages in Paul. (c) The form and syntax of these verses is unlike any Greek hymnody or poetry. The text is also unlike any known Hebrew psalmody. Many of the alleged lines or stanzas are irregular. Indeed, theories of its stanza structure are multiple, some requiring complex redaction scenarios—in other words, the form is not transparent. Verses 9-11 are especially nonpoetic in formulation. Furthermore, Fowl has demonstrated that *hymnos* refers to songs of praise in honor of a deity or honored person and has the form of an ascription of praise followed by the reasons for it (Fowl 1990: 31–45). The form and structure of 2:6-11 is quite different. (d) All aspects of these verses—both the paradigmatic aspects (2:6-8) and the kerygmatic aspects (2:9-11)—are intimately tied to the rhetoric of the immediate context and Paul's broader concerns evident in the letter. Nothing in these verses goes beyond what would be required in the immediate context (see EN on 2:6-11).

In the explanatory notes to 2:6-11, I suggest that the genre of public tribute or encomium might be more apt as an analogy (cf. Brucker). According to Aristotle (*Rhetoric* 1367b; 1.9.33-41), the panegyric (Gk. *panēgyrikos*, lit. a speech for the public assembly) and the encomium (*egkōmion*) represent subsets of tribute and praise (or blame) oratory in epideictic rhetoric. A panegyric, offered on the occasion of civic festivals or athletic games, involves a public oration designed to honor a living or deceased hero. It highlights the virtues and deeds of the hero, in the hopes of arousing citizens to emulate the glorious deeds and noble virtues of the hero. In general, the encomium is smaller in scale, offered to honor a worthy citizen, perhaps at the dedication of a statue or at the investiture into public office. According to Aristotle, pure praise focuses simply on virtue, whereas encomium additionally stresses accomplishments and rewards. Other rhetoricians suggest that the encomium may highlight matters of pedigree, upbringing, achievements, or comparisons with others to demonstrate special worthiness and calls to emulate.

The declaration of Messiah's full career—with particular reference to his pedigree, virtue, accomplishments, and reward—points to the encomium as a suitable analogy of oratorical form.

More particularly, these verses are closest to the form of an abbreviated curriculum vitae (course of life) or cursus honorum (course of honors [tracing the rise through the ranks of public office])—a career summary of the sort enshrined in inscriptions and epitaphs. (Our word *career* comes from the Latin word *cursus* [running, course, progress, advance], which is closely related to the verb *curro* [to run, move quickly], and the nouns *currus* [chariot, vehicle] and *curriculum* [running, course, race, career].) That Paul has in mind the image of a career as an advance and race is evident from the way this theme comes up in the context (1:25; 2:16; 3:12-14). Paul's own career (2:16; 3:4-14) will be modeled on that of Messiah.

While the text here is rhythmic (Hooker) and employs thought rhythms, it is certainly not poetic in a narrower sense (for instance, in the manner hymnic songs might have been constructed in a Greek-speaking environment). The passage uses the same kind of extended prose structure that Paul uses on other occasions and in the immediate context where Paul heaps up parallel images in 2:1-4.

2. Source: Not Pre-Pauline. A prevailing opinion among contemporary scholars is that the entirety or core of these verses derives from a pre-Pauline hymn in honor of Messiah, which Paul quotes and edits. Some suppose that Paul composed these verses as a self-standing hymn (a song that lauds) before its inclusion in this letter.

The theory that these verses stem from a pre-Pauline hymn emerged during the heyday of source and form criticism, which was dominated by the search for traditions behind or embedded in biblical texts as a way to get behind the texts to uncover a social reality earlier than the texts themselves. The quest for an account of the evolution of Christology especially drove this pursuit (see Martin and Dodd).

The arguments for non-Pauline authorship are as follows (e.g., Hansen: 127–30). (a) Its character as a hymn, in contrast to the pastoral concerns of the immediate context. (b) Its completeness: once started, Paul had to continue with the entirety, even though much of it was irrelevant to his immediate purposes. It is "so complete in itself and so much more majestic than its context" (Hansen: 128). (c) Its style (e.g., its rhythmic cadence and bipartite structure) is significantly different from the rest of Paul's writing. (d) Rare words and word usage are most easily explained on the basis of Paul's quotation of source material. Four terms appear only here in Paul's writings (*harpagmon*, seizing, or what is seized; *katachthonion*, that which is under the earth; *hyperypsosen*, highly exalted; *morphē*, form). Phrases not found elsewhere in Paul include *to einai isa theō (being equal to God)*, *the name of Jesus*, and the combination *under the earth* with *in heaven and on earth*. Words used with supposed unique senses include *emptied, schema, form, appearance,* and *obedient*. (e) Finally, the theological content of the hymn varies from what one might otherwise expect from Paul. It includes unusual formulations (Christ as a *slave*; the *name above every name*; a three-story cosmology; the notion of Christ's exaltation instead of the more usual resurrection; the confession that *Jesus Messiah is Lord* as a universal, cosmic acclamation, not just as an ecclesial, Spirit-inspired confession). And favorite Pauline themes are absent (Christ's death as atoning "for us"; resurrection from the dead).

But these arguments are not convincing: (a) As an encomium, these verses fit naturally into Paul's immediate pastoral exhortation. The words and images of 2:6-8 correspond closely with the exhortation in 2:3-4. Even the stylistic parallelism between 2:3-4 and 2:6-7 (the use of not/but clauses) suggests a close correlation with the immediate context. (b) Its entirety, including the "kerygmatic" portion (2:9-11), is intimately tied to Paul's rhetorical purposes in the letter as a whole. To suppose that Paul somehow had to continue with 2:9-11, since these verses go on to the declarative mode beyond the paradigmatic mode necessary to his argument started in 2:5, misses the obvious pastoral agenda of Paul throughout the letter (cf. 3:20-21). (c) Paul is quite capable of shifting into this sort of rhythmic, declarative mode in his letters (e.g., 1 Cor 1:22-25, 26-28; 6:12-13; 9:19-22; 13:1-13; see Fee: 39–45, 191–94). (d) The rare words are easily explained as motivated by Paul's special rhetorical interests and the letter's particular circumstances, as with the other rare words elsewhere in the letter. Of the total 438 words used, 42 occur only here in the NT, and another 34 occur only here in Paul (for the listing, see Fee: 18–19). (e) All of the themes found in these verses have parallels in other passages in Paul, though they are framed differently (e.g., self-lowering, 2 Cor 8:9; obedience even to death, Rom 5:19; resurrection as exaltation, 1 Cor 15:24). Paul highlights the imagery of exaltation instead of resurrection because the issue of status and honor is at stake for the Philippians. He stresses the universal acclamation of Messiah's lordship because of the theopolitical agenda of the letter (cf. 3:21). And he pictures the universe (cf. *all things* in 3:21) in three storeys perhaps because of the familiarity of the three-storey universe in popular understanding. To require Paul always to refer to Christ's death as an atoning death puts a theological straitjacket on Paul and betrays the interpreter's prior theological convictions. And to expect Paul to refer to all aspects of his christological understanding in this short span disregards the many other confessional formulations in Paul that use a variety of expressions and include those aspects of Messiah's person or work appropriate to the contextual argument.

The simplest and most compelling solution is to suppose that Paul composed these verses specifically for this context, carefully and deliberately choosing words and themes for maximal relevance and impact for his immediate hearers-readers, while drawing on words and themes from the tradition bequeathed to him and from his own christological reflection (similarly Fee: 193; Oakes 2001: 208–10; Hellerman). Crossan and Reed observe that Philippians 2:6-11 "could just as well be Paul's own creation integrating the deep horror of his Ephesian near-execution organically and mystically with the execution on the cross of Christ himself" (Crossan and Reed: 288–89).

3. Structure and Source/Redaction. If this is a hymn in some sense, how should one understand its structure? Into what kind of stanzas should it be divided? Those who favor the theory of a pre-Pauline hymn have offered various proposals for the stanza structure of 2:6-11, looking for evidence of poetic symmetry (e.g., Hansen: 125-26). Ernst Lohmeyer (1928), the first proponent of the hymn theory, presented its structure in six stanzas of three lines each. Joachim Jeremias (1953) presented the hymn in three stanzas of four lines each. But to achieve his desired symmetry, he had to excise three phrases from the reconstructed text of the original hymn as Pauline additions: even death on the cross, in heaven and on earth and under the earth; to the glory of God the Father. Martin presents the hymn as a series of couplets in six pairs that could be chanted antiphonally (1980, 1997). His neat structure also requires the same deletions offered by Jeremias.

The most questionable aspect of the pre-Pauline hymn theory is that these words, apart from Paul's supposed additions, should not be used as evidence for Paul's own theology (e.g., Kreitzer 1987: 115: "We should not necessarily presuppose that the Christology of the hymn is identical to that of Paul"). A similar approach is to suppose that the original, reconstructed form of the text should somehow determine its meaning as incorporated into Paul's dictation, not the other way around. But as Fee observes, even if these words are quoted or drawn from tradition, they are fully chosen and affirmed by Paul and thus constitute evidence for Paul's own theology (see discussion in Fee: 45, 193).

4. The Conceptual Framework. Finally, how should the conceptual context of the hymn-encomium be regarded? In earliest Christianity, the significance of Messiah was articulated in terms of the titles, paradigms, and roles available from contemporary theological reflection and tradition, inspired both from Scripture and beyond (e.g., Martin and Dodd). Debates about the meaning of particular words or phrases have raised the issue of the primary inspirational background that gives coherence to these verses (for a summary of the most influential proposals, see O'Brien: 193–98). (a) Is Messiah playing out a kind of human paradigm (as the second Adam)? In this case, Christ, made *in the form of God* in the sense of being "in the image of God" (cf. Col 1:15; 2 Cor 3:18), rejects the quest to be *equal to God* in the sense of being "like God" (Gen 3:5), but accepts his status as a human. In this case, Messiah is not necessarily endowed with preexistent divine status and is adopted into divinity by virtue of completing his messianic mission (cf. Rom 1:3-4). (b) Or is Messiah cast in the role of divine Wisdom (Prov 8:22-31) or divine Word, who, although the firstborn of creation is also God's creative agent and the one who pervades creation (Col 1:15-17), has become incarnate in the world (cf. John 1:1-18), a career well-known in Jewish theological texts? And is "obedient Wisdom" presented in contrast to the "son of Dawn" (Lucifer) of Isaiah 14:12-15, who seeks to be "like the Most High" and who by the first century had become understood in some circles as the fallen angel cast out of heaven (1 Enoch 6–11; Matt 11:23; Luke 10:18; Rev 12:9)? (c) Or is Paul drawing primarily on the theme of the suffering servant from Isaiah? (d) Or is Paul drawing on one or more of these known patterns, but telling Messiah's career in way that deliberately parodies Roman imperial propaganda about the divinity of its emperors, their "empty glory," or their apotheosis (divinization after death) to a status "equal to the gods"? (The redeemer myth of Gnosticism has also appealed to many: the descent and ascent of the primal man-savior of later gnostic texts.)

As we shall see, Paul draws primarily on the pattern of divine Wisdom, but in a way that draws out specific counter-Roman resonances.

Divine Wisdom Christology On the basis of the figure of Wisdom (Heb. *ḥoqmah*; Gk. *sophia*) in Proverbs 3 and 8 and other scriptural references to the role of God's Wisdom in the act of creation (e.g., Psalm 104:24), later Jewish sages and writers during the later period of Second Temple Judaism developed a diverse and rich understanding of Wisdom as a "hypostasis" of God himself, somewhere between being a personification of God and an independent divine being (Sirach 24; 1 Enoch 42; Bar 3–4; Wisd of Sol 7; for further texts, see Dunn: 269). Subsequently, various aspects of this reflection shaped early christological reflection and proclamation (e.g., John 1:1-18). This wisdom reflection persisted in the theology of the "two powers of heaven" among Jewish thinkers well into the Christian era (ultimately deemed heretical by the rabbis of the 3rd c. and

4th c.; see Boyarin 2004: 134–45). The influence of the figure of divine Wisdom in the present text is evident especially in the themes of preexistence as a hypostasis of God and taking on material form (incarnation) as part of a mission to humanity.

Second-Adam Christology The figure of Messiah as second Adam appears significantly in the writings of Paul. For Paul, Messiah is both the model human and the progenitor of a new humanity, the one in whom the image of God is being restored (see EN on Phil 3:21). In articulating this notion, Paul regularly poses a parallel contrast between Adam and Messiah, the second or last Adam (Rom 5:12-21; 8:29; 1 Cor 15:21-22, 44-49; 2 Cor 3:17-18; 4:4; Gal 4:9; Phil 3:21; Col 1:15; 3:9-11). Paul's second-Adam Christology draws especially from Genesis 1–3 and Psalms 2, 8, and 110 as mediated through later Second Temple Jewish theological reflection (e.g., Wisd of Sol 2). Those who highlight the imagery of second-Adam Christology in Philippians 2:6-11 tend to argue that the text does not carry the notions of preexistence and incarnation. Instead, the text plays out an Adamic narrative: Messiah is like Adam in being originally in the "image of God" (Gen 1:27; cf. 1 Cor 11:7; Col 1:15; 2 Cor 4:4) and in this sense is *in the form of God* (Phil 2:6). But in contrast to Adam, Messiah refused to quest for divinity ("to be like God," Gen 3:5). Rather, Messiah as second Adam voluntarily accepted the form of corruptible humanity (e.g., Rom 8:3; Gal 4:3-4) as part of his messianic mission to be the one in whom the image of God is being restored (exaltation). In this way, it is argued, the Christology of 2:6-11 is adoptionist: Jesus is a human who by virtue of fulfilling his messianic calling was exalted to God's right hand (cf. Rom 1:3-4; Acts 2:22-36; 3:13-26).

Suffering-Servant Christology The figure of the suffering servant (Isa 52:13–53:12) is paralleled in the imagery of being emptied (poured out) and in the themes of humiliation, obedience, servanthood (slavery), and subsequent exaltation. Those who emphasize this model argue that the notions of vicarious atonement should also be read into Paul's declaration. In my view, the vicarious element of self-lowering "for others" is evident from the surrounding context (2:3-4, 20; 3:4-11) and does not hinge on whether or not the text is alluding specifically to Isaiah's suffering servant.

Scholars typically favor one of these christological paradigms to the exclusion of the other two. My own view is that all three of these figures of Messiah—divine Wisdom, second Adam, and suffering servant—coalesce in the narrative of the present text. None of these figures by itself can explain all aspects of Paul's images. We should not assume that ancient authors used our sometimes straitjacketed modern categories in articulating their Christology. Rather, we should assume that biblical authors drew on and integrated a number of available paradigms, whether consciously or unconsciously, to help explain various dimensions of the person and work of Jesus, in effect constructing a new figure from earlier paradigms.

Paul did not need to choose between imagery for second Adam and imagery for divine Wisdom. In current biblical scholarship, second-Adam interpreters of 2:6-11 typically claim that it carries an adoptionist Christology, whereas interpreters favoring divine Wisdom posit the pre-existence (though not necessarily the full status of Deity) and incarnation of Wisdom in Messiah. Typically the two paradigms are considered mutually exclusive in this text. While Paul does seem to imply some dimension of the second-Adam theme in this text (esp. Messiah as prototypical, paradigmatic human, 2:7c-8; cf. 3:10-11; see also EN on 3:20-21), Paul certainly does not associate second-Adam Christology with adoptionism. This is clearest in 1 Corinthians 15:21-22, 44-49, where Paul draws on the Adam-Messiah contrast in a way that stresses the heavenly Messiah versus the earthly Adam (for a both-and approach, see Yoder Neufeld 2007: 321–23).

A Counterimperial Christology Attention to these three paradigms alone has resulted in narrow theological readings of the text in the interest of clarifying a precise doctrine of Christ (Christology) while overlooking the theopolitical valences of the text. While the three christological figures of divine Wisdom, second Adam, and suffering servant operate in the deeper background, the particulars by which the encomium is constructed show that Paul has composed this declaration to directly counter Roman imperial propaganda. As a result, Paul's readers surely caught the obvious insinuation that Messiah Jesus is the reality, while Imperator Caesar is the parody. (See the EN to 2:6-11.) For detailed discussion, see Eastman; Fowl 1990; Hurtado; Koperski; Martin 1997; Martin and Dodd; Nebreda.

DATE AND PLACE OF WRITING Paul most likely wrote Philippians while he was imprisoned by Roman imperial authorities in Ephesus, the leading city and capital of the Roman province of Asia, just before his departure for Macedonia (Acts 20:1-2) in the mid-50s (perhaps July–October 55 or 56). He was detained for at least a month before his dispatch of the letter to Philippi, the minimum duration for the requisite travel time noted in Philippians.

Time Frame On the premise of an imprisonment at the end of Paul's three-year ministry centered in Ephesus, the yearly frame of 55 or 56 is deduced by what is known about Paul before and after the end of his Ephesian ministry, especially from Acts, a reasonably reliable source for the general schema of Paul's travels. On the one hand, it must permit a three-year ministry in Ephesus (Acts 20:31; cf. 19:8-10), which cannot have begun before the year 52 or 53, allowing an eighteen-month ministry in Corinth during the datable proconsulship of Gallio (51–52, attested by the Delphi Inscription; Acts 18:12-17), and a return voyage to Jerusalem and Antioch (Acts 18:22-23) before his overland trek to Ephesus. On the other hand, the key subsequent event is a two-year detention in Caesarea (Acts 24:27), beginning at least a half year after his departure from Ephesus. This detention overlapped with the uncertain date of the transition between Felix (52–ca. 58) and Festus (ca. 58–62) as procurators in Judea (Acts 23–25).

The monthly frame of July to October is derived by backtracking from other events (Acts 20:1-6): Passover in Philippi (Acts 20:5-6: March 18 of 56, or April 5 of 57); travel and three months in Corinth (Acts 20:2-3: December–February); travel and ministry in Macedonia (Acts 20:1-2; 2 Cor 2, 7: October–November); and departure from Ephesus (sometime in October–November).

On this premise, the following probable sequence of Paul's letters results: 1 and 2 Thessalonians (ca. 50), 1 Corinthians and Galatians (ca. 53–54), Philippians (55 or 56; perhaps also Colossians and Philemon), 2 Corinthians (late 55 or 56), Romans (spring 56 or 57).

Location The traditional view, which prevailed by the end of second century, is that Paul wrote Philippians while in Rome, during the two-year period indicated by the narrative in Acts 28 (esp. vv. 30-31), presumably sometime around 60–62 CE. The main alternative view is that Paul is writing while in prison in Ephesus (first articulated in 1900 and growing in acceptance). Less compelling alternative proposals have included Caesarea (first propounded in 1799) and Corinth (first suggested in 1731, but not seriously proposed until 1973).

What we know from the letter is that (a) Paul is imprisoned *in chains* (Phil 1:7, 13, 14, 17), (b) this imprisonment is in the context of the *praetorium* (1:13), (c) in the city were members of *Caesar's household* (4:22), (d) Paul is embroiled in a judicial charge that might lead to a sentence of death (1:18-26), and (e) the imprisonment was long enough to allow considerable time for communication by multiple trips between Philippi and the location of imprisonment.

The main arguments in favor of an Ephesian imprisonment are as follows:

1. Ephesus as the location of a severe, life-threatening imprisonment is not easy to refute. The usual argument is that Paul cannot have been imprisoned there because Acts does not refer to such an imprisonment. But Paul's own words suggest that he was imprisoned on more occasions than narrated in Acts. Writing soon after his departure from Ephesus (Acts 20:1-2; 2 Cor 2:13; 7:5), Paul refers to multiple imprisonments in 2 Corinthians (6:5; 11:23), whereas to that point in his life Acts narrates only one imprisonment. An Ephesian imprisonment involving the threat of death is likely at or toward the end of his three-year ministry there.

Such an incarceration with accompanying torture and threat of execution seems required by references in 2 Corinthians, written in the few weeks or months after his departure from Ephesus. He refers to the "tribulation" he had just experienced "in Asia," an ordeal in which "we were so utterly, unbearably crushed that we despaired of life itself" because "we [felt that we] had upon us the judicial sentence [*apokrima*] of death" (2 Cor 1:8-10 AT). These words easily match the judicial nature and severity of the situation presupposed in Philippians 1:7, 18-26 and 2:17. While Paul does not refer specially to Ephesus in that text, it is clear that

Ephesus is the prime location when he refers to his ministry "in Asia" (e.g., 1 Cor 16:8, 19). Similarly, Acts refers generically to Paul's ministry in Asia, while in fact meaning one centered in Ephesus (Acts 20:18; cf. 19:10).

A recent experience of extreme suffering involving the prospect of death is also attested in 2 Corinthians 2:14-16, where Paul describes his prison ordeal as a Roman military "triumph," a victory parade, on the way to his ritual execution (4:7-12; 4:16–5:10; 6:3-10; 11:23-30). While these reflections could include the experience of ordeal in Macedonia (7:5), the experience in Asia appears to be the main subject of Paul's reflections on suffering in 2 Corinthians.

In Romans (written less than a half year after he left Ephesus), Paul's references to Andronicus and Junia as his "fellow prisoners" (Rom 16:7) and to Prisca and Aquila as those "who risked their necks for my life" (16:3-4) best suit a recent Ephesian imprisonment. Paul's specific retrospective reference to terrific trials, including formal charges brought to the authorities (8:31-39) and more general allusions to the necessary pathway of suffering on the road to glory (Rom 5:1-5; 8:17-30), correlate with the particular circumstances of an Ephesian imprisonment and resonate with the experiential concerns of both Philippians and 2 Corinthians.

2. Paul's stated plans in Philippians, namely his hope to visit Philippi *soon* after his release from prison (Phil 2:24), do not work well with a presumed first incarceration in Rome. Paul's hope was that Rome would be a springboard for heading to Spain (Rom 15:24, 28). This notation in Philippians works perfectly, however, with an Ephesian incarceration before his departure from Ephesus.

3. The communication and necessary journeys between Paul and the Philippians are far more plausible in relation an imprisonment in Ephesus instead of Rome. One-way travel from Rome to Philippi would require seven to eight weeks (730 land miles [1,175 km] in addition to a one- to two-day voyage across the Adriatic), whereas travel from Ephesus to Philippi could be completed in close to one week (under ideal conditions): a sea voyage of 300 miles (480 km), plus one day for land trip of 8 miles (13 km) from Neapolis to Philippi (Osiek: 30).

Since his imprisonment, at least two trips have occurred: (a) Paul sent a message to Philippi that he is in prison and in need (Phil 4:14); (b) Epaphroditus came with assistance to Paul's place of imprisonment (2:25; 4:18). Many commentators add two more intervening trips on the assumption that Epaphroditus learned of the Philippians' response to his sickness (a message to Philippi about Epaphroditus's sickness; a message to Paul expressing sorrow over Epaphroditus's sickness). But 2:26 may just as likely indicate that Epaphroditus simply knows the news has been sent to the Philippians of his sickness.

Moreover, Paul envisions that another trip to Philippi and back could take place, presumably before his release. He expects to dispatch Timothy as his personal envoy soon, to travel to Philippi, provide support, and bring back news (Phil 2:19-22). Involving distances similar to that between Ephesus and Philippi, Timothy had earlier been dispatched to Thessalonica from Corinth (ca. 50; 1 Thess 3:2, 6) and to Corinth from Ephesus (ca.

53–54; 1 Cor 4:17; 16:10). But such a lengthy return visit from Rome to Philippi is difficult to imagine as the premise for travel envisioned in Philippians 2:19-22.

4. References to the *praetorium* (Phil 1:13) and to *house(hold) of Caesar* (4:22) suit an Ephesian setting as well as a Roman setting, contrary to the argument of the traditional view that these only suit Rome as the location. The word *praetorium* originally denoted "the general's tent" or a military camp "headquarters," then evolved to denote also the "palace" of a provincial imperial governor and the emperor's own elite troops, stationed in Rome. The word appears to have a wide range of reference in the middle of the first century: it is not limited to the elite imperial special forces or to a governor's residence or military headquarters; it is even used to refer to a large house or palace of royalty or of an important person. Generally speaking, a *praetorium* is the name given to the headquarters, and perhaps also residence, of the Roman imperial official who resided as the supreme administrator, judge, and military commander of a region (*provincia*). It can also be used to refer to the building that houses the military headquarters in a Roman imperial fortification. In the NT, we find Pilate's "praetorium" in Jerusalem (Mark 15:16; Matt 27:27; John 18:28, 33; 19:9), probably part of the originally Herodian royal complex. We find "Herod's praetorium" in Caesarea Maritima (Acts 23:35), the palace constructed there by Herod the Great. As the seat of the imperial proconsul in Asia, Ephesus undoubtedly also had a praetorium (even though there is no documented reference to such a particular place in Ephesus). In Philippians, the term *praetorium* most likely refers to the entire headquarters of the provincial imperial administration.

Caesar's household does not mean members of the Caesar's immediate family and does not need be limited to members of the imperial court in Rome. Even Herod Agrippa (who appears in Acts 12) is called a "member of Caesar's household" (Philo, *Against Flaccus* 35). Rather, the designation can refer more generally to those in the imperial bureaucracy and administrative service, whether as freedmen or as slaves, and found in any major urban center. The designation might even mean the imperial fiscal staff who took charge of the imperial bank in Asia (*fiscus asiaticus*), with headquarters in that city. There is inscriptional evidence that in Ephesus members of the civil service, both freedmen and slaves, formed themselves into *collegia* (guilds) of the emperor (Martin 1980: 170).

For further discussion, see others who argue for an Ephesian setting (Agosto 2007: 285; Osiek: 27–30, 200; Perkins: 343; Hansen), those who argue for a Roman setting (Silva: 5–7; Fee: 34–37; O'Brien: 19–26; Witherington: 24–26; Cassidy 2001a: 124–43; 2001b: 84–103; Peterman: 19–20), or those refraining from taking a position (Fowl 2005: 9; Gorman 2001: 417–18; Martin 1980: 36–57).

HARPAGMOS The meaning of the word *harpagmos* (Phil 2:6, *harpagmon*) has been a matter of debate since the christological controversies of the third and fourth centuries. The difficulty is that the word most commonly refers to what is seized and not already possessed (or to the act of seizing), often through greed or violence (LSJ). Arian adoptionists claimed that this prevailing meaning proves that Christ was indeed a human being adopted as Son of God through his resurrection (such that his striving for full divinity with God, which he at first did not have as a human, was theoretically possible), while orthodox trinitarians gave the word a different connotation, equating being *in the form of God* to being *equal to God*.

In the last hundred years of biblical scholarship, some interpreters have sought to resolve the debate by attention to precise philological analysis, while others have tried to resolve the question by examining the theological premises or narrative frame of the broader passage in which it is found. Thus some have argued that the word signals the imagery of a potential "robbery of Godlikeness," which directly contrasts with Christ's actual decision. Others have concluded that the word refers to the possibility of retaining what one already has (NIV 1984: *something to be grasped*). In contrast to both of these suggestions, the view apparently prevailing today is that the word means to *exploit* (potentially use for self-advantage) what one already has, in sharp contrast with what Christ actually decided (Hoover; Wright 1991; NRSV, NIV 2011).

Philological evidence alone cannot establish the exact nuance of the word in the present context. The problem can be explained by the ambiguity of the English word *seize*. While the term most commonly refers to taking what one does not already have, in some contexts it can imply taking advantage of what one might already possess or have access to (as in "Seize the day" or "Seize the time").

The view taken in this commentary is that a number of factors come together to suggest that the word can be understood in Philippians 2:6 in its robust sense, referring to what is seized (as prey, robbery, or booty), especially through greed or violence. (1) This is the sense of the word in its overwhelming number of occurrences. (2) Cognates of the word confirm that the word root consistently has this sense (see below). (3) The hortatory context and intent contrasts upward striving to downward movement (2:3-11; 3:2-21). (4) Paul holds to some kind of subordinationist Christology. He avoids speaking of Messiah Son of God as in the very same status with the one Father and Creator of all things (e.g. 1 Cor 8:6; 11:3; 15:24-28). Thus even as a divine being who shares identity with God, Christ had potential room for further seizing to usurp the role and status of God himself.

Cognates to the word *harpagmos* confirm that its basic sense has to do with seizing something not already possessed. A *harpagos* is literally a "hook." It is the root of the English word *harpoon*. Accordingly, a *harpagmos* can be thought of as "that which is harpooned." A *harpē* is a greedy, cruel, grasping person, and the name for a bird of prey in Greek and Roman mythology, a monster with a woman's head and body and with bird's wings and claws, from which is derived our "harpy eagle." *Harpax* denotes "robbing, rapacious, robber, grappling iron, flesh hook, wolf" (see Matt 7:15; Luke 18:11; 1 Cor 5:10, 11; 6:10). *Harpagē* means "seizure, robbery, rape, thing seized, booty, prey, greediness" (e.g., LXX: Lev 5:21 [6:2 NRSV]; Eccl 5:7 [5:8]; Isa 3:14; 10:2; Nah 2:13; Jth 2:11; Tob 3:4 [Sinaiticus];

1 Macc 13:34; 4 Macc 4:10; NT: Matt 23:25; Luke 11:39; Heb 10:34). *Harpagma* is "booty, prey" (Job 29:17 LXX). The verb *harpazō* is used for snatching and plunder, never for retaining or exploiting for oneself (Matt 11:12; 13:19; John 6:15; 10:12; 2 Cor 12:2; 1 Thess 4:17). *Harpalagos* denotes a hunting implement. *Harpaxandros* is "man-snatching" (see LSJ).

HISTORY OF THE MESSIANIC ASSEMBLY IN PHILIPPI

Founding of the Congregation (ca. 50 CE) The book of Acts indicates that the assembly was founded during Paul's "second missionary journey" (Acts 15:36–18:22). Following the Macedonian call (16:6-10), Paul arrived in Europe by ship via the port Neapolis (modern Kavala), then made the ten-mile (sixteen-km) trek to Philippi (near modern Krenides) on foot (16:10-12).

According to Acts (16:11-40), Paul looked for a Jewish meeting place for prayer outside the city boundaries by the river (Gangites/Ganga), a short distance west of the city proper. Paul met a group of women who apparently become key leaders in the congregation (Lydia, Acts 16:13-15, 40; probably Euodia and Syntyche, Phil 4:2-3) *[Profile of the Assembly, p. 305]*. Paul's stay was relatively brief, perhaps a few months; but a warm relationship was established.

Conflict with the Roman Imperial Authorities In the narrative of Acts, Philippi was the first place where Paul got into serious trouble with the Roman imperial authorities. His announcement of Messiah Jesus created quite a stir since it was perceived as a subversive threat to many in the privileged ruling class. In contrast to the practices and beliefs of the Roman social elite of Philippi, Paul preached Jesus as the one and only Lord and his worldwide dominion in the coming reign of God. As Acts attests, the conflict that emerged had to do with the character of Philippi as a specially designated Roman *colonia*: Paul was accused of "destabilizing the city and advocating practices unlawful for us Romans to accept or practice" (Acts 16:20-21 AT). In a similar way shortly thereafter in Thessalonica, Paul was accused of "defying Caesar's decrees, saying that there is another king, one called Jesus" (17:7 NIV). Promoting practices perceived to undermine the Roman social and political order was a cause for suspicion. Any sign of disloyalty to the Roman Empire—its way of life, its gods, and its emperors—was a serious matter for the civic-imperial authorities. The Roman authorities closely monitored the activities and presence of any nonregistered "associations" or "organizations" (*collegia*; Gk. *hetairai*), sometimes prohibiting them (e.g., Pliny the Younger, *Letters to Trajan* 10.96) for fear that they might foment disloyalty, however innocuous they may have looked from the outside (Arnaoutoglou; Cotter 1996).

The book of Acts dramatizes the ensuing conflict and suggests that the healing of a slave girl from spiritual and economic bondage put the brewing conflict out into the open. Paul was "seized" by the owners of a fortune-telling slave girl whom Paul had freed from her bondage to "a pythonic [oracular] spirit." He was "dragged into the forum" to be indicted before the magistrates and was publically attacked by a crowd (Acts

16:19-21). The attack seems to have drawn on anti-Jewish sentiments: Paul and his companions were slandered for simply being "Judeans" and were thus under suspicion for disloyalty (16:20).

Paul's departure was under duress. He was detained, tortured (cf. 1 Thess 2:2: "violently and shamefully treated"; the congregation witnessed his "suffering" and "struggle," Phil 1:29-30), and then he was expelled from the city, though not before some miraculous events of deliverance. Through this crisis a prison warden or guard (probably a low-ranking servant in the imperial system) and his household joined the community of Jesus (Acts 16:25-34). According to Acts, Paul seems to have been reticent to pull out his Roman citizenship card until the aftermath (16:22-39). Perhaps he considered it more a burden than a blessing, or perhaps Acts hints that the Roman authorities did not follow the laws protecting Roman citizens when it came to dealing with certain individuals profiled to be undesirables.

Ongoing Communication over the Next Five Years, Including Their Support of His Ministry After leaving Philippi, Paul proceeded to Thessalonica, where he also declared the gospel of God in the face of great opposition and founded another assembly (Acts 17:1-10; 1 Thess 2:2-3). While Paul was in Thessalonica, the Philippian assembly sent him financial support more than once as an expression of partnership (Phil 4:15-16). Later, Paul had brief visits in Berea and Athens, but then stayed eighteen months in Corinth (50–51). When in Corinth, he received financial support from "the brothers and sisters coming from Macedonia," most likely from Philippi (2 Cor 11:8-9 AT). After a trip back to his home-base congregation in Antioch (in Syria; Acts 18:19-22) and mission work in Phrygia and Galatia, Paul found his way to Ephesus, where he stayed for around three years (likely in the years 52–55; Acts 18:23–19:41).

Paul probably kept up the relationship with the Philippians through letter writing (perhaps evident in Phil 3:18, *I have told you often*) and through his coworker Timothy (perhaps on Timothy's way to Corinth, 1 Cor 4:17; 16:10; Acts 19:22). Then followed a gap in time when there was no exchange of mutual assistance (Phil 4:10, 15). Still, Paul claims that the Messiah loyalists there were *dear to him*, despite the separation (Phil 1:6-7).

Torture and Despair in Ephesus (Summer 55) At the end of Paul's three years in Ephesus, he was detained on a capital charge and tortured by the civic and Roman imperial authorities (probably on grounds of suspicion of treason and anti-imperial agitation) *[Date and Place of Writing, p. 290]*. He was awaiting trial on what appears to be a capital charge (Phil 1:7, 18-20; 2:17)—probably treason.

A series of exchanges between Paul and the congregation resulted: (1) they heard that he was imprisoned; (2) they sent Epaphroditus to Paul with financial assistance (Phil 2:25-30; 4:10-20), such that Paul calls him *their envoy [apostle] for his need* (2:25); (3) a report was sent to Philippi that Epaphroditus was sick (2:26). Some interpreters propose that Paul received a receipt for this report and thus learned of their distress over this news about Epaphroditus. While this is a possible interpretation of 2:26, it is not a necessary one.

Opposition and Distress in Philippi Meanwhile, the Philippians themselves were under attack from various sectors (Phil 1:27-30; 2:14-18; 3:2, 18-19; 4:4-7; 2 Cor 8:1-3). Paul says that their struggle was the same as the one he experienced in Philippi and the one he was now experiencing (Phil 1:29-30)—hinting that it involved conflict with the Roman imperial authorities *[Circumstances of the Messianic Assembly, p. 277]*.

Letter from Prison While Awaiting Trial (Philippians) Paul decided to send Epaphroditus back to Philippi with a letter after Epaphroditus recovered from a life-threatening illness (2:25-30). Meanwhile, Paul expected a decision on his case before the imperial authorities to be imminent (2:19-23). He was unsure of the outcome. Paul was resigned to life or death but hoped for release and further service (1:18-26; 2:17-18, 24). He also set the stage for Timothy's imminent visit and return (2:19-20) and indicated his own hopes to visit them as soon as he was released (2:22-24).

Paul's Second Visit (Fall/Winter 55) After his release, Paul traveled through Macedonia, including Philippi (Acts 20:1-2; 2 Cor 2:13), on his way to a three-month stay in Corinth (Acts 20:2-3), where he wrote Romans (Rom 16:1-2, 21-23). He had sought to meet Titus in Troas but had to move ahead, meeting him finally in Macedonia (2 Cor 2:12-13; 7:5-7). Titus was on his return from Corinth, bringing good news, the cause of great comfort and joy.

In Macedonia (presumably including Philippi), Paul continued to encounter affliction (2 Cor 7:5-15) along with the suffering of the church there (8:1-5) while nursing his own wounds, both physical and mental (esp. anguish over the problems in Corinth). The Macedonians (presumably including Philippians), despite their relative poverty (according to Paul), contributed significantly to the relief fund that Paul was collecting for the famine-impoverished believers in Judea (2 Cor 8:1-7; Rom 15:26), leading Paul to brag about them as he tried to obtain the more wealthy Corinthians' support for the same relief fund (2 Cor 9:1-5).

Paul's Third Visit to Philippi (March/April 56) According to Acts, Paul stopped by Philippi and celebrated the Festival of Passover/Unleavened Bread there (ca. March–April 56) on his trip to Jerusalem with an entourage carrying the relief fund to Jerusalem (Acts 20:3-14).

The Church in Philippi after Paul Later evidence is sketchy, but it is certain that a struggling assembly survived. Apparently the Philippians provided assistance to Ignatius, bishop of Antioch, as he stopped there on his journey as a prisoner from Antioch to his martyrdom in Rome, around 110 CE. Ignatius, *To Polycarp*, a cover letter for collection of Ignatian letters, attests to his travel from Troas to Neapolis, the port of Philippi.

Polycarp later praises them for "assisting on their way those bound in chains" (*To the Philippians* 1.1), alluding to Ignatius, and implies that they have special information on Ignatius to share (ch. 13).

Polycarp (bishop of Smyrna, north of Ephesus) writes *To the Philippians* (date uncertain, 120–160?) in response to their request for his assistance in collecting the letters of Ignatius and as his cover letter for Ignatius's writings to which he had access. In his letter he warns the Philippians of certain disorders and of apostasy. He refers to letters (plural!) of Paul written to Philippians (ch. 3) "from the study of which you will be able to build yourselves up in faith." Polycarp quotes Philippians several times (along with some gospels and letters). For instance, he refers to "enemies of the cross" in connection with list of persecutors and those outside the church worthy of prayer (ch. 12; Phil 3:18). His letter includes an emphasis on "witness of the cross" as central to Christian identity and practice and a general exhortation on steadfast faith and virtue under persecution. It refers to Christian "citizenship" practice and identity, alluding to Philippians 1:27. Polycarp also mentions a former elder Valens, now under discipline for covetousness and idolatry (*To the Philippians*, ch. 11).

In the next centuries, Philippi became a major Christian center of Pauline martyrology. After the Christianization of the Roman Empire under Constantine and his successors, seven different magnificent church structures were built in the fourth to sixth centuries, replacing earlier Roman monumental buildings in the downtown center, so that Philippi rivaled the architectural splendor of Thessalonica and Constantinople.

The city of Philippi was devastated by an earthquake in 619 CE and never recovered, even though it remained a military outpost in the continuing conflicts among the Byzantine Greeks, Slavic Ostragoths, Bulgars, and eventually Turks. A nearby Greek (Orthodox Christian) village continued to name itself Philippi and has survived.

LITERARY INTEGRITY OF PHILIPPIANS The theory that Philippians represents a conflation of two or three letters authored on separate occasions has prevailed in many circles, even though its status as an assured result of biblical scholarship has waned in recent years (Watson). Conflation theories identify the following features of Philippians as evidence.

First, the rupture in thought and tone at 3:1-2: (a) the supposed change in tone from warm to warning; (b) the *finally* in 3:1 seems to indicate a letter closing; (c) travel-talk (2:19-30) is often found at the close of Paul's letters; (d) 3:2 abruptly begins a completely new topic, addressing a new threat, and there is no reference to Paul's *chains* in 3:2-21; (e) the explanation for writing the *same things* in 3:1b is ambiguous and rough.

Second, some questions pertain to 4:10-20: (a) one would expect a response on such an important item to come earlier in the letter; (b) one would expect that Paul would not have taken so long to respond; (c) phrases such as *I rejoiced greatly* are often found at the beginning of ancient letters.

Third, supporting evidence is sometimes found in the reference in Polycarp's *To the Philippians* to more than one letter from Paul to the Philippians.

Fourth, 2 Corinthians may set a precedent: most scholars think it has various levels of editing and comprises at least two separate letters.

To explain these features of Philippians, some scholars support a two-letter hypothesis (e.g., one theory identifies letter 1 as Phil 1:1-3:1a; 4:2-7, 10-23; letter 2 as 3:1b–4:1, 8-9) or a three-letter hypothesis (e.g., letter 1 as 4:10-20; letter 2 as 1:1–3:1; 4:2-9; 4:21-23; letter 3 as 3:2–4:1; for more variations, see below). Others suggest an interruption theory: something distracted Paul as he penned 3:1. Then, after hearing distressing news about a new threat to the community, he continued his letter with a new topic in 3:2.

Arguments in favor of the letter's integrity in its current form are the following:

First, the closing section, 4:10-20, is perfectly comprehensible in its current location once Paul's rhetorical purpose is comprehended: Paul is careful to reframe what might be perceived as a debt-producing gift and pose it as a duty appropriate to a partnership. Moreover, major expressions of gratitude are sometimes reserved for the close of ancient letters (Peterman); Paul has alluded to their assistance more than once as the letter unfolds (1:5, 7; 2:29-30). Finally, the time gap in Paul's formal response is often overestimated. There is no need to think that the contents of 4:10-20 could have been communicated any earlier than with the rest of the letter.

Second, while the transition at 3:1 is indeed rough (cf. Fee), a crucial argument for integrity is the remarkable thematic unity not only between 3:2-21 and 1:27–2:18, but also linking the opening and closing of the letter (Engberg-Pederson; Fee: 21–23; Hanson: 15–19). More important, there is no evidence that 3:2 focuses on a new threat to the community.

Third, the diversity of conflation theories exposes a high level of subjectivity in the letter's methods and evidence. The third letter is variously proposed: according to one theory, it includes 3:2–4:3, 8-9; according to another it includes 3:1–4:9; and according to another it consists of 3:1b–4:1, 8-9 (see further proposals in Garland; Klauck: 318). Moreover, conflation theorists have failed to offer convincing explanations for the methodology and purposes of the final editor.

LOVE OF HONOR IN ROMAN SOCIETY Roman society was deeply stratified, as typical of advanced agrarian empires. The empire as a whole and local regions within were essentially divided into two classes: the few elite lording it over the nonelite majority. Roman law and custom enshrined these divisions in a variety of ways, most notably in the arrangement of the "orders" into which one was born. The nonelite Romans were divided by law into free citizens, freed persons, and slaves. Laws pertaining to marriage and inheritance were designed to maintain the purity of these orders and the distinctions among Romans first, Latins second, Greeks third, and finally the lower nationalities: children of mixed marriages went to the level of the lower-status partner. The elite of the empire were divided into three aristocratic orders of Roman citizens: senators, equestrians, and decurions (the leading citizens of cities in the "provinces," conquered territories). Even those at the elite level were preoccupied with graded status and honor within these categories.

Far more important for Romans than economic class and status was the matter of social (public) honor, glory, and fame. Honor was the key cultural value and preeminent public commodity. As the historian Dio Chrysostom (ca. 40–ca. 120 CE) put it, when it came to the matter of questing for public service and office-seeking in both Rome and the provinces, Romans were driven by "the struggle for reputation" (*doxa*, glory; Dio Chrysostom, *Orations* 66.18). Similarly, the Roman historian Tacitus (ca. 56–ca. 120 CE) referred to the "passion for glory" (*cupido gloriae*; *Histories* 4.6). The Roman senator Cicero (106–43 BCE) remarked, "Rank must be preserved" (*Pro Plancio* 15). Cicero expresses these core values well: "To be equal to others in liberty, and first in honor" (*Philippics* 1.34). "By nature we yearn and hunger for honor, and once we have glimpsed, as it were, some part of its radiance, there is nothing we are not prepared to bear and suffer in order to secure it" (*Tusculanae disputationes* 2.24.58). "Ambition [*gloria*] is a universal factor of life, and the nobler a man is, the more susceptible is he to the sweets of fame. We should not disclaim this human weakness, which indeed is patent to all; we should rather admit it unabashed" (*Pro Archia* 26; for these references, see Hellerman: 3, 34–35, 44–45).

Given the region's collectivist cultural framework, "one's honor was almost exclusively dependent upon the affirmation of the claim to honor by the larger social group to which the individual belonged" (Hellerman: 35). In this specific sense, honor was the preeminent public commodity. Accordingly, "loss of reputation [*adoxia*]" is worse than "financial reverse" (Dio Chrysostom, *Orations* 16.3; Hellerman: 38). As MacMullen summarizes: "The Romans indeed acknowledged a goddess called Money (*pecunia*); but . . . her cult was tributary to another, Status (*philotimia*)" (MacMullen: 118). For the elites at least, wealth was a vehicle for something more desirable: public honor. While those who hoarded their wealth (spending it only on themselves) were deemed dishonorable, those who spent lavishly on municipal edifices, temples, streets, aqueducts, or public baths were accorded supreme honor for their benefactions. Indeed, public munificence, including food handouts during civic festivals, was motivated primarily by the quest for honor and status, not for the service of others. A system of urban patronage emerged as a way to foster one's own honor and to confirm the established hierarchy of status and class (this system of "benefaction" was sharply challenged in Luke 22:24-27).

OPPONENTS IN PHILIPPIANS The scholarly study of Philippians has seen a massive output of work on the subject of who (or what faulty teaching or practice) Paul might be referring to in a number of oblique passages. Whether or not these groups (or practices) should be identified as opponents is itself a disputed point. The debates have focused especially on Paul's reference to (1) *the dogs, evildoers, and butchery* in 3:2; and (2) the *many who walk as enemies of the cross of Messiah* in 3:18. In addition, some posit the presence of some specific false teaching (or teachers) that Paul indirectly confronts in 3:12-15.

Other references or implicit allusions to adversaries or rivals in Philippians are less obscure. First, there are rival preachers in the location of Paul's imprisonment (1:15-18). Some interpreters suggest that Paul's reference to *everyone* in contrast to Timothy (2:21) may refer to the same sort of group. But this is certainly a rhetorical hyperbole designed to commend Timothy's impressive moral fiber (see TBC on 1:12-26, "Factionalism and Rivalry"). Second, there are the authorities and accusers responsible for Paul's imprisonment (1:12-14, 19-20; see TBC on 1:12-26, "Paul's Imprisonment"). Third, there are the *adversaries* of the assembly in Philippi who desire the community's destruction and generate *terror* for Messiah loyalists (1:28). Paul is here referring to the Roman imperial authorities and Roman citizens. He says that this struggle is of the same sort that he earlier experienced in Philippi (1 Thess 2:2; cf. Acts 16:11-40) and is now experiencing during his imprisonment, probably in Ephesus (Phil 1:30). These specific adversaries should be seen as a subset of the *crooked and perverse nation* in which the saints in Philippi find themselves (2:15-16).

Whether or not the references in 3:2 and 3:18 should be correlated with one or more of these other references, however, is a matter of debate. Most interpreters put them into a completely different category of opponents. The best interpretation of 3:18 is that it alludes to the pattern of life (*walk*) championed by the persecuting adversaries of the saints in Philippi (group 3 above); indeed, even the rival preachers of 1:15-18 (group 1 above) display aspects of this pattern (*eritheia, rivalry/partisanship* [Phil 1:17; Gal 5:20; 2 Cor 12:20]; *selfish ambition* [Phil 2:3]).

The Many Enemies of the Cross of Messiah Scholarly interpretations of those *many who walk as enemies of the cross of Messiah* (3:18) fall into the following categories (for overviews, see, e.g., Fee; Hansen; D. Williams):

A. Those who are outside the Christian community:
   1. nonbelieving Jews (usually correlated with the referents of 3:2)
   2. Roman citizens of Philippi, perhaps associated with the adversaries of 1:28 and the *perverse nation* of 2:15
B. Those who self-identify within the Christian community (but not valid, from Paul's perspective), whether
   1. Judaizing Christians (correlated with a similar interpretation of 3:2; e.g., Marshall 1991, 1993)
   2. triumphalist, morally lax, antinomian (Gentile) Christians (the majority view among scholars)
      a. evident in the Philippian church and elsewhere (Martin 1980; similar to the antinomians of Corinth, 1 Cor 1–4)
      b. not part of the Philippian church (Bruce; Hawthorne); itinerants, but not personal rivals to Paul (Fee)

   c. lapsed believers who had left the church, perhaps some also in Philippi, and/or
   d. associated with (gnostic-like) "spiritual perfectionism" (cf. 3:12-14)

C. Those marked by a certain practice, both non-Christian (A.2 above) and Christian (B.2 above; thus Fee)

Although it is true that Paul explicitly names a *walk* (a social pattern and value system), not a specific grouping (C), he does so in a way that seems to refer especially to Roman adversaries of the community (A.2) without excluding Messiah loyalists who are drawn to that same *walk* (B.2). The profile presented in 3:18-19 appears closely correlated with the adversaries of 1:28, which is a further subset of the general Roman context of Philippi in 2:15-16, the *crooked and twisted nation.*

The Dogs, Evildoers, and Butchery We turn, then, to the final reference to a group or tendency that Paul confronts. Since this commentary takes a minority position on this matter, it is necessary to address it in greater detail (see also EN on 3:2-3). This is a complex matter, involving the question of the rhetorical coherence and focus of all of 3:1–4:1 and its correlation with the argument of 1:27–2:18. Some scholars find three separate groups or perspectives that Paul challenges in Philippians 3: Judaizing Jewish Christians (3:2), some sort of spiritual perfectionists (3:12-15), and Gentile Christian antinomianism (3:18-19). Other scholars find only two distinct trends or groups: Judaizing Jewish Christians or nonbelieving Jews (3:2) and Gentile Christian antinomians (3:18-19). Others find just one group or perspective targeted, usually Judaizing Jewish Christians or nonbelieving Jews (3:2, 18-19).

The simplest and most compelling solution is that Paul has one general challenge in view and that it correlates closely with the adversaries (1:28) and the corrupt environment (2:15-16) noted earlier. The problem for modern readers is that in the case of 3:2, Paul seems to be using coded language understood by his readers but obscure to us. In that verse, Paul refers more specifically to both the hostile, violent action (*dogs, butchery* [those who cut up, hack, slaughter]) and the moral corruption (*evildoers*) of the adversaries in particular, whereas in 3:18-19 Paul critiques the general practices of the broader Roman sociopolitical environment in which these adversaries can be found (represented by these adversaries), practices that constitute a significant temptation for the struggling assembly of Messiah. To put it another way, 3:2 (*dogs, evildoers, butchery*) seems to correspond specifically to 1:28 (*adversaries* who project terror and desire *destruction*), with both as a subset of 2:15-16 (*corrupt and perverse nation*) in correlation with 3:18-19 (*many walking as enemies of the cross of Messiah*).

In recent years, scholars have increasingly recognized several things about these opponents: (1) The rhetoric of Philippians 3:2-11 is paradigmatic, not specifically polemical or apologetic. That is, Paul does not contest the theology of supposed Judaizers here but highlights issues pertaining to his own citizenship experience. (2) There is probably no immediate "Christian Judaizing" threat in the immediate environment of Philippi. (3) The repeated imagery of *confidence in the flesh* is not narrowly targeting Jewish or "Jewish-Christian" perspectives or rivals (it does not narrowly refer to physical circumcision). (4) The structure of Paul's *cursus honorum* in 3:5-6 draws on the *cursus* pattern common in Roman Philippi (see EN on 3:2).

Nevertheless, the notion that Paul is in some way referring to "Christian Judaizers" in 3:2 has largely remained unquestioned. Mark Nanos (2009) has now demonstrated the lack of evidence for "dogs" as common out-group rhetoric by Jews and Paul's use of it therefore as reverse invective. The remaining arguments in favor of the Judaizing thesis can also be questioned: namely, that the *katatomē-peritomē* contrast requires it, that Galatians 5:12 provides the best analogy, and that the argument in Philippians 3:2-11 is specifically designed to undermine the Judaic identity markers claimed in 3:5-6.

The word *katatomē* (butchery, slaughtering) does not specifically mean mutilation (in the sense of a violent disfiguring to render imperfect), but refers to any general violent and intensive "cutting up" of flesh or meat, the human body, landscape, or leather. It can refer to (1) a cutting into (incision, laceration), cutting down, cutting up, hacking, or butchering of flesh, as in personal assault or in a butcher shop; (2) slaughter and butchery in war; (3) cutting into leather to make strips; (4) an excavation in the ground, such as a mine, quarry, harbor, or theater (or part of a theater: orchestra or corridor); (5) an inscription in stone; or (5) the cutting of a grid plan into a preexisting city (LSJ).

The image of *those who violently cut flesh*, along with *dogs* and *evil workers*, is inspired especially from the Hebrew and Greek versions of Psalm 22:16 ("They have gouged my hands and feet," 21:17 LXX), where the reference is to oppressors (see EN on 3:2). Paul chose the word *katatomē* (1) to provide a dramatic *k* alliteration in Philippians 3:2 (see EN on 3:2-3); (2) to provide a synonym to the verb for *digging/gouging* in the Hebrew (DSS text, *krh*; see ISV mg.; Flint: 43) and Greek versions of Psalm 22:16 (Gk. *oryssō*), a word that can refer to cutting flesh as much as to cutting into ground or landscape; and (3) to anticipate a wordplay (paronomasia) on *peritomē* ("cutting around," circumcision), not necessarily to mock and malign circumcision but to contrast a violent and intensive cutting of flesh with a refined, surgical cutting as a marker of character and identity.

In the earliest extant interpretations of Philippians 3:2, the threefold reference to *dogs*, *evildoers*, and *butchery* was applied to various kinds of "schismatics" (based on the image of "cutting up"). The Judaizing interpretation is not attested until the anti-Jewish rhetoric of Augustine and John Chrysostom (Augustine, *Against the Two Letters of the Pelagians*, ch. 22; John Chrysostom, *Homily on the Epistle to the Philippians* 10) in the emerging Christian imperial situation, when the church's attacks on the synagogue were mounting. This view was popularized in the English-speaking world through a marginal note in the Geneva Bible (1560: "He alludeth to Circumcision, of the name whereof while they boasted, they cut asunder the Church") and by the heading in the KJV (1611: "He warneth them to beware of the false teachers of the Circumcision"). Only in the last hundred years has the English translation *mutilation* prevailed (Wycliffe [1382–98]: *dyuysioun [division]*; Tyndale [1525–26] and Coverdale [1535]: *dissencion*; Geneva Bible [1560], Bishops' Bible [1568], KJV [1611], ASV [1901]: *concision*; NABRE: *the mutilation*; NET, NRSV: *those who mutilate the flesh*; TNIV: *those mutilators of the flesh*; TEV: *those who insist on cutting the body*; ISV: *the mutilators*; NJB: *self-mutilators*; NASB: *false circumcision*; the most neutral translation is the JB: *the cutters*).

Instead, the evidence seems to indicate that in 3:2 Paul negatively caricatures Roman culture and authority, and in 3:3 Paul positively appropriates circumcision as a Judaic-messianic citizenship symbol (similarly Nanos 2013). This is suggested especially by (1) the range of meanings and associations possible with *katatomē* against the received wisdom that it must refer to mutilation; (2) the intertextual correlations between Philippians 3:2 and Psalm 22:16 (following the LXX and DSS text tradition, where the threefold images refer to oppressors), indicating that the threefold reference identifies persecutors of the community; (3) the coherence of the argument in 3:2-4:1, suggesting that the agenda of 3:2-3 corresponds to that of 3:18-21; and (4) the close correspondence between the themes and argument of 3:1–4:1 in relation to 1:27–2:18, which applies also to the various references and allusions to opponents or faulty perspectives *[Literary Integrity, p. 298]*.

This interpretation is similar to that of N. T. Wright (2000), who argues that in Philippians 3 Paul is not at all interested in confronting Judaism or Judaizing Jewish Christianity (even though 3:2 does allude to Jews in general), but simply appropriates this citizenship language of Judaism as a way to set up Paul's real interest in discussing the matter of Roman citizenship and Caesar's rule, warning believers in Philippi of the temptation to assimilate to this seductive environment. The interpretation of this commentary goes further in doubting that even in 3:2 Paul is seeking to evoke (negative) images of Judaism.

Problems arise with the traditional interpretation. First, it assumes that Galatians defines Paul (the Protestant bias; comments by Fee [294] are telling):

> That Paul does not mention them ["Judaizers"] again would seem to indicate that they are not present—although they surely will have tried their wares in Philippi in times past—and that a present threat of "Judaizing" does not seriously exist. The reason for the invective lies with Paul. Such people have been "dogging" him for over a decade, and as the strong language of Gal 5:12 and 2 Cor 11:13-15 makes clear, he has long ago had it to the bellyful with these "servants of Satan" who think of themselves as "servants of Christ" (2 Cor 11:15, 24).

Second, it takes for granted that if opponents of Paul are to be found, they must naturally be Jews of some kind (either outside Messiah's body or [worse] insider "Judaizing" traitors—the legacy of Christian interpreters, once Christianity is absorbed by the imperial power and coexists with it). Third, it overlooks the evidence that in Macedonia (both Philippi and Thessalonica) the adversaries of the messianic assembly are fellow countrymen, not Jews (cf. 1 Thess 2:14). Indeed, Acts paints a picture of the key lines of hostility in Philippi as being between Jews (of the messianic variety) and Romans (Acts 16:20-21). (For further on Phil 3:2, see also Zerbe 2012: 171–73.)

PROFILE OF THE ASSEMBLY IN PHILIPPI Various attempts have been made to develop a profile of the Philippian assembly in regard to its size, ethnic-political identity, and socioeconomic rank. Reconstructions of the profile have been significant for interpretations of (1) the distress experienced by the assembly, (2) the internal difficulty evident within the community, and (3) Paul's rhetoric in promoting a particular messianic identity and loyalty.

The traditional view is that the community is composed primarily or entirely of Roman citizens. Many are descendants of original veteran colonists and proud of their Roman identity and status. Some are wealthier, even if none are from the elite class of decurions (the order from which the magistrates come). The scenario posits that Paul invites them to develop a proper understanding of their dual Roman-Christian citizenship, balancing their religious and their political identities and responsibilities insofar as they pertain to different spheres of life. As Christians, they can remain patriotic Romans as long as their Roman loyalty does not cause them to transgress the way of life appropriate for Christians.

One alternative to this view accepts this basic profile of the community but argues that Paul's exhortation boldly calls the members, both free citizens and public slaves, to relinquish their proud identity and loyalty as Romans. For those few without the cherished Roman citizenship, Paul's call is to desist from their quest to gain Roman citizenship as the supreme guarantee of security and happiness (Cassidy 2001b: 163, 189, 191, 194–95; de Vos).

A leading second alternative, and the view taken in this commentary, argues for the following profile:

1. *Ethnopolitical Identities.* The assembly probably includes a range of ethnic backgrounds, political identities, and social-legal ranks. It appears that a sizable core group are Judean (Jewish) citizens by birth, proselytes, or Judean adherents or sympathizers ("God-fearers," e.g., Lydia, Acts 16:14; Crossan and Reed; Fee: 17–18). Evidence in favor of this includes the following: the beginnings of the community in a Jewish place of prayer, the lack of evidence of conflict with the Jewish community (see EN on Phil 3:2-3 and 3:4-11), the presence of scriptural allusions in the letter, Paul's positive appropriation of Jewish identity markers (Phil 3:3a, *We are the circumcision*), and Paul's decision to celebrate the Feast of Unleavened Bread in Philippi (Acts 20:16).

Linguistically, most are probably at home in Greek culture, and some might hold citizenship in a Greek city, such as migrants from Asia (e.g., Lydia). Others might be Greek-speaking migrants who lack formal citizenship in a Greek city (the majority, according to Portefaix: 117), members of other ethnic groups (perhaps some indigenous Thracians).

Those who hold Roman citizenship are perhaps a strong minority, perhaps 25–40 percent (Oakes 2001), but probably not the majority. Among those residing in urban Philippi, Roman citizens were likely no more than 50 percent, so the percentage of Roman citizens in the messianic congregation can hardly have been higher than this.

Issues of ethno-political identity likely contributed to internal tensions in the community. In Philippians, those without Roman citizenship are called to desist from questing for citizenship status and the privileges that go with it. Meanwhile, those who enjoy Roman citizenship are invited to dissociate themselves from any pride of rank or zealous loyalty as Romans and are instead invited to place their hopes, security, and identity solely in relation to Lord Messiah Jesus (Oakes 2001, 2002, 2005). Those with a primarily Israelite identity are invited to celebrate that status, but also to reframe it in light of Messiah (3:4-14).

2. *The Community's Size.* Estimates range from around 30 individuals (de Vos: 250–61), to around 50–100 (Oakes 2001: 55–70), or over 100 (Portefaix: 137). The higher estimate is argued on the basis of the presence of multiple leaders (Phil 1:1; 4:2-3), which may mean the possibility of more than one household assembly (Portefaix: 137).

3. *Socioeconomic Status.* Based on general evidence about Paul and his communities, the most likely candidates for membership would be those from lower or middling ranks, although those with high "status inconsistency" must also have been present (e.g., women from elite/wealthy families; Acts 17:4, 12). Most members probably came from a social status similar to Paul himself: primarily subsistence-level artisans and small merchants, with a few of more comfortable status, but far from the wealth of the elite Roman classes (Meggitt). If the core of the group consisted of artisans or small-time merchants, the community may have met in small houses, *insulae* (apartment buildings), or workshops (de Vos: 250–61). Alternatively, meetings could be held in the larger homes of wealthier individuals (for instance, Lydia, who was head of a household and host to Paul and Silas; Acts 16:15), who might also have enjoyed Roman citizenship. It also appears that there is considerable variation in status and rank, contributing to internal disunity and rivalry (Oakes 2011). Though not as wealthy overall compared to the Corinthians (2 Cor 8:2; 11:9), the community had resources sufficient to support Paul in prison (Epaphroditus; financial aid). The use of commercial imagery in Philippians (3:4-9; 4:10-20) assumes a level of familiarity with small-business practices.

4. *Gender Dynamics.* Evidence suggests that a good portion of those in leadership were women (Lydia, Acts 16; Euodia, Syntyche, Phil 4:2-3), continuing the original core group of mainly women (Acts 16:13-16, 40). Some of these may have come from families with relatively high status compared to some other members. This may reflect the general sociocultural context of Roman Macedonia, where women appear to have been in more significant positions of civic leadership compared to some other locations.

ROMAN IMPERIAL CULT The term *imperial cult* refers to the wide variety of ways in which a living emperor, a deceased divinized emperor, or divinized members of the emperor's family were venerated (revered, honored, given homage, worshiped) during the imperial period of Rome. Generally speaking, in Italy and the West, the imperial cult involved devotion to the *genius* (divine spirit) of the living emperor and devotion to a divinized emperor (as a god, divinity) after his death or to divinized members of the imperial family after their deaths (e.g., Livia, the wife of Augustus). In the Greek-speaking East, however, the imperial cult sometimes included devotion to the living emperor as divine (Lewis and Reinhold: 61–67). Living emperors, even if not honored as divine, could be regarded as manifestations of the divine (*deus praesens*, divine presence) or as agents/sons of the god(s). In many places the imperial cult was closely integrated with, or coexisted with, established local cults, possible because of the syncretistic-polytheistic environment. For instance, the sacred precincts devoted to Augustus in Ephesus were part of the larger complex of the temple to Artemis-Diana.

The imperial cult essentially involved a codependent symbiotic relationship between Roman imperial powers and local provincial elites. The imperial cult was not orchestrated and controlled centrally from Rome, though certainly Rome monitored the ways in which veneration of the emperors and Roman gods was practiced. Local provincial elites promoted the imperial cult for the honor to the city that the cult offered and to ensure the continued receipt of imperial benefactions from Rome. Furthermore, cities vied for the status of being a center of the imperial cult because of the economic advantages that it would bring. Beneficial for both Rome and its elite subjects (who benefited from Roman rule), the imperial cult became a focal point for displaying and promoting general loyalty to Rome, especially in the form of personal loyalty to the emperor (and his divinized ancestors, notably Julius Caesar and Augustus Caesar). Veneration of this sort was public and communal, integrally sociopolitical in character and purpose, but no less "real" (and personally felt) for the vast majority of participants. Insofar as success in general was deemed to be a sign of divine favor and patronage in the Greco-Roman world, its significance went far beyond its political function. In sum, as Garnsey and Saller put it, the imperial cult was "a conveyor of imperial ideology, a focus of loyalty for many, and a mechanism for the social advancement of a few" (167).

The imperial cult incorporated a wide array of material and cultural productions, institutions, and activities.

1. It involved the erection of temples, shrines, altars, porticoes, statues, along with imagery (iconography) and inscriptions on buildings, gates, arches, or walls. In the region of Asia Minor, at least two hundred different installations of temples or altars serving the imperial cult have been documented. In some case, there was considerable competition among cities in a region for the status of erecting a temple in honor of a living or divinized emperor. Requests to erect major imperial temple complexes were sent to Rome, and emperors then awarded the special privilege to cities they chose.

2. The imperial cult included public festivals and games, many of which included sacred communal meals, a distribution of food (grain, meat, or wine), or some other gifts from local benefactors. (These ritual meals provide the background to Paul's remarks in 1 Cor 10:1-22.) At the heart of these festivals were public processions (sometimes led by dancing young men and women), which snaked through a city and culminated with a grand liturgy at an imperial temple. Busts of living or divinized emperors—sometimes with thrones, along with images of patron gods—were typically carried in the procession. Records of festal calendars indicate that some cites boasted up to ten annual festivals or ceremonies in honor of the emperor or emperor's family (beginning with Julius Caesar and Augustus): these public festivals commemorated an emperor's birthday, accession, military victory, divinization (apotheosis, deification), or other major event. Processions were organized according to social rank, thus displaying and routinizing (reinforcing) the sociopolitical hierarchy of the city or region.

3. The imperial cult was built around various rituals, including making sacrifices, expressing thanksgivings, burning incense, and offering prayers, whether (in the case of a living emperor) "for" the emperor, or "to" the emperor (in some locations), or to the *genius* (guardian spirit) of the emperor.

4. The imperial cult generated a considerable number of priestly offices, titles, and roles as part of the organization and practice of events in honor of the emperor or the emperor's family. These priestly roles were highly sought after by regional provincial elites, and they were usually distributed among the highest ranks of the decurial elite in the major urban centers.

5. Public ritual events became opportunities to show (or demand) oaths of loyalty to Rome and the emperor. This was especially so for conquered populations.

6. The imperial cult, along with other propaganda vehicles, proclaimed a theopolitical gospel (imperial ideology) focused on the benefits derived from the virtuous deeds of the emperor and Rome more generally. Despite variations in how this was coded (across time and place), we can call this "Roman imperial theology" or "the gospel of Augustus," given its basic coherence. This ideology includes the granting of honorific titulature to the emperor (living or divinized)—son of God, savior of the world, lord of the earth, bringer of world peace, high priest, *augustus* (exalted one, manifest one), father of the fatherland, god (usually after divinization), and so on. A core part of this was the granting of honors "equal to the gods." The formal granting of the title *augusta* to women of the imperial family by the Senate was usually the stepping-stone to receiving the status of divinity after their death and having a formal cult (system of worship, including temples, priesthood, and sacrifices) established in their honor *[Roman Imperial Propaganda, p. 312]*.

7. The imperial cult generated a range of literary and liturgical productions, including hymns, epic poems, and dramas.

8. The imperial cult could be expressed unofficially as artisan guilds or other associations dedicated themselves to patron Augusti (deified

members of the imperial family). Such commitments helped these associations achieve formal recognition by civic and/or imperial authorities.

The Imperial Cult in Philippi Archaeological evidence indicates that in the period of Claudius (41–54) and Nero (54–68), the imperial cult had special prominence in Philippi, being at the center of civic and religious life. While it is unlikely that the living emperors were honored as divine in Philippi, devotion to the cult of Augustus and to his wife, Livia, was well established. For emperors like Claudius and Nero, it was sufficient to be honored as Augustus, thus to be manifestations of the divine, or sons of deified ancestors.

The imperial cult in Philippi was significant in part because of its military history as a colony of Augustan veterans and loyalists. The deified Augustus was revered as the colony's founder and divine patron. Philippi seems to have had special regard for the deified Julius Caesar. Popular tradition had it that the divinized Julius Caesar appeared at the battle of Philippi in 42 BCE and that Cassius (the assassin of Caesar) had actually failed in his attempt to kill Caesar, since his divinity guaranteed his immortality (Hellerman: 188).

At least two temples in the downtown forum focused on the Augusti (the first Augustus and his family members and descendants, even by adoption, also declared Augustus/Augusta by the Senate). With its own priesthood, the cult of deified Livia, for instance, is evident by the second half of the first century CE. At least two priesthoods existed for organizing and promoting the various festivals and ceremonies associated with the Roman state cult. The main honorary priesthoods were available to those of the decurial class. As elsewhere, the imperial cult reinforced the colony's social, economic, and political hierarchy and promoted loyal devotion to Rome.

Beginnings of the Imperial Cult The Roman imperial cult in the first century reflected the aura surrounding Augustus Caesar after he gained supremacy over his rivals and promoted state worship. As a state cult, its beginnings can be associated with the divinization of Julius Caesar posthumously, by act of Senate (Jan. 1, 44 BCE). At that time a major priestly order (*flamen maior*) was established in his honor, with Mark Antony as the head *flamen*. Caesar's divinization was associated with the appearance of a comet after his death, interpreted as the soul of the deified Caesar joining the ranks of the gods (Pliny the Elder, *Natural History* 2.93–94). After this, Octavian, the sole heir of Julius Caesar as his adopted son (45 BCE), regularly used the title *divi filius* (son of the deified) as part of his aura, broadcasting that title in a variety of ways (e.g., on coins and on mile markers throughout the empire). In 42 BCE, Octavian (then taking the name Caesar), with approval from the Senate, began construction of the Temple of the Divine (Deified) Julius, also known as the Temple of the Comet Star (lit. long-haired star), the only temple in Rome where a comet was the object of veneration. This is the first example of a resident of Rome being both deified and honored with a temple and cult (with priesthood and liturgy). Caesar is portrayed by some as descending from one of several gods, most commonly Venus and Jupiter. This cult and its ideology served Octavian's quests for sole supremacy over Rome and its territories (42–30 BCE).

Deeper antecedents can also be identified. Octavian had styled himself as a new Alexander the Great and drew inspiration from Alexander's history. In his midtwenties, Alexander had portrayed himself as a "son of Zeus." Encouraged by Persian and Egyptian practices, including ritual prostration (*proskynēsis*; its cognate verb is often translated "worship" in the NT) of all subjects, Alexander promoted similar veneration of himself in Greece and Rome. After his death, a vibrant cult to Alexander emerged among his local subjects (in Greece and Macedonia) that lasted well into the Roman era, providing both a model and inspiration for the Roman imperial cult three centuries later (Hellerman: 188).

In the year 31 BCE, Octavian (Caesar) defeated his last rival at the Battle of Actium (western Greece), and he offered sacrifices to Apollo, his patron deity. This victory secured his political supremacy in Rome. Shortly thereafter, he consolidated Rome's geographical control over the lands of the Mediterranean (absorbing Egypt and securing the borders with Parthia [the empire in the East, centered in Persia]). This victory brought to an end the devastating wars among powerful senator-generals (and their legions and their clans) that had raged since 49 BCE in the provinces, where the suffering was greatest.

In anticipation of his return to Rome in 29 BCE, the Senate of Rome made the following decrees: (1) Octavian would be granted a military "triumph," a distinctively Roman victory parade and ceremony; (2) he would wear a triumphant crown at all subsequent festivals; (3) the entire city should go out to meet him; (4) the day of his return to Rome should be honored with sacrifices and held sacred forever; (5) "his name should be included in their hymns equally with those of the gods"; and (6) he could choose priests of any number for presiding over sacred festivities (Dio Cassius, *Roman History* 51.20). Later that year, Caesar (the former Octavian) dedicated the "temple of the divine Julius" on August 18, 29 BCE.

Subsequently, in 27 BCE, the Senate honored Caesar by granting him the title "Augustus" (implying a divine aura as *deus praesens*). Various propagandists and poets began to extol the blessings of the new era that had come through Augustus. In 17 BCE, Augustus reinstituted the "saeculum games," marking the dawn of a new "age" (*saeculum*) in a three-day religious festival that included athletic events, sacrifices and offerings, theatrical productions, and hymnic contests. Later, after Augustus was declared *Pontifex Maximus* (high priest) in 13 or 12 BCE, he was able to organize more deliberately the imperial cult (both in Rome and in the provinces) as part of the state worship. In accordance with Roman scruples, Augustus did not promote the veneration of himself as divine in Rome in state festivals (starting a precedent). He did allow (and expect) the lower orders to venerate his genius at the Lares Compitales, shrines of the city wards renamed Lares Augusti.

The imperial cult in the provinces (lit. military "charges," conquered territories outside Italy) began soon after Caesar's victory at Actium in 31 BCE. In 29 BCE he "gave permission for" (i.e., instituted) the establishment of "sacred precincts" (temples) dedicated to the goddess Roma and [Julius] Caesar in Ephesus (for the province of Asia) and in Nicaea (for the province of Bithynia). He commanded that the Romans resident in these cities pay honor to these two divinities. In addition to the Temple of Dea Roma and Divus Julius, more imperial temples were erected during the reign of Augustus or shortly thereafter, including the Temple of Augustus in proximity to (or incorporated within) the Temple of Artemis, the Temple of Augustus in the city itself, and a Royal Portico (with imperial statues) in the upper city square (Price: 254–55).

The crucial innovation, however, was his decree at the same time that in Pergamum (Asia) and Nicomedia (Bithynia) there would be sacred precincts built and consecrated to himself, to receive "divine honors." At these sites, he would receive devotion from the "Greeks" and other aliens who were "subject to the Romans." In other words, offering "divine honors" to a living emperor was expected only of subject non-Romans, a practice that would continue with later emperors. In addition, Pergamum received the authority to hold sacred games (defined as those which included food distributions) in honor of [Augustus] Caesar's temple. These were to be presided over by a "high priest" (Dio Cassius, *Roman History* 51.20.6; Tacitus, *Annals* 4.37–38).

In 29 BCE, the provincial "assembly of Asia" inaugurated a competition to offer a crown "for the person who devised the greatest honor for the god [Caesar Augustus]." The proposal suggests that this attempt to honor was a modest repayment for the great benefactions that had accrued through Caesar's virtuous deeds. The crown was finally awarded to the Roman proconsul of Asia in 9 BCE, who had proposed that the birthday of Augustus be regarded as the province's New Year's Day. It was decreed that copies of the proconsul's proposal and the resulting decree would be inscribed in white marble and placed in the sacred precincts of temples in honor of Rome and Augustus throughout Asia. (Fragments from five locations have been discovered; the most complete copy was in Priene). The decree of 9 BCE claims that "Caesar [Augustus] when he appeared exceeded the hopes of all who had anticipated good tidings [*euangelia*], not only by surpassing the benefactors born before him, but not even leaving those to come any hope of surpassing him"; that "the birthday of a god marked for the world the beginning of good tidings [*euangelia*] through his coming"; and that his coming was "divinely ordained for the benefaction of all humankind." As "most divine Caesar," he was proclaimed not only as lord and savior of the empire and of the earth, the one who has brought wars to an end, but also as lord of the calendar and time (Crossan and Reed; Price).

In 26 CE, during reign of Tiberius, Ephesus competed with ten other cities for the privilege of constructing a temple dedicated to Tiberius as living emperor. Only in 89 CE did Ephesus receive the formal honor of being a *neōkoros* (temple warden) of the Sebastoi (Augusti, "divine venerables," referring to the imperial family). When applied to a city, the honor of being *neōkoros* implied that the whole urban area was at the service of the Augustan gods (including then the living Domitian). The city in return enjoyed special favor of the Augustan gods, enhancing its status as a city.

Following the divinization of Augustus after his death in 14 CE, cults in his divine honor and in honor of his divinized wife, Augusta Livia, proliferated in various locations in the provinces, along with cults of goddess Roma. Tiberius (ruled 14–37 CE) permitted only one temple to be erected in his honor (in Smyrna). Later, Claudius (ruled 41–54 CE) allowed only one temple in his honor to be erected (in Britain; refusing requests from elsewhere, such as Alexandria). Both thereby followed the lead of Augustus. By contrast, Caligula (37–41 CE) vigorously promoted devotion to himself as a god throughout the empire. After his death, the Senate officially damned his memory, requiring that temples and statues dedicated to him be destroyed and that his name be chiseled out wherever had been inscribed throughout the empire.

A local placard proclaimed the accession of Nero in 54 CE. Discovered in Egypt, it illustrates the theopolitical claims of the Roman Empire as promoted in the imperial cult:

> The one who was owed to the ancestors, and god-made-manifest, Caesar [Claudius], has gone to join them [that is, has become deified]. And the Autokrator [*Imperator*: supreme commander, thus emperor] whom the world anticipated and hoped for has been proclaimed—the good spirit [Gk. *daimōn*; Lat. *genius*] of the inhabited world [*oikoumenē*] and source of all goodness [blessings], Nero Caesar, has been proclaimed. Consequently, we should all wear garlands and with sacrifices of oxen give thanks to all the gods. [Year] one of Nero Claudius Caesar Augustus Germanicus, the twenty-first of the month New Augustus [the earlier renamed Egyptian month Hathor, in honor of Tiberius].

See Brodd and Reed; Crossan and Reed; Elliott; Fears 1988; Heen; Garnsey and Saller; Gradel; Hellerman: 78, 80–87, 160, 188; Kelly; Lewis and Reinhold; Price. On Roman Philippi in general, see Alcock; Bormann; Hendrix; Oakes 2009.

ROMAN IMPERIAL PROPAGANDA: THE GOSPEL OF AUGUSTUS The ancient world knew no fundamental separation of what we call religion and politics. Religion was embedded in kinship (ethnicity) and in politics and was not thought to be a private matter in contrast to a public one. On the other hand, politics was oriented around kinship, while framed and legitimized (supported, reinforced) through religion. The ideology (propaganda) promoted by the Roman imperium and its beneficiaries, therefore, was inevitably and thoroughly theopolitical (or religiopolitical).

Roman imperial propaganda focused on the victories and benefits that came through the virtuous deeds of the emperor and Rome more generally. Despite variations in how this was coded (across time and place) and despite the lack of official control on how Rome or the emperors were presented, a basic coherence to Roman imperial ideology (theology) can be discerned. Insofar as this ideology focused on or drew inspiration from Caesar Augustus, we can call this the "gospel of Augustus."

The core claims of Roman imperial ideology were that (1) the gods have chosen Rome as a way to bring blessings to the world, and that Rome will remain forever; (2) Rome and its emperors are agents of divine will and rule, or manifestations of the divine presence among human beings, and so are entitled to direct the world and to shape human history and society; (3) Roman rule through the emperor manifests blessings from the gods—security, peace, justice, and fertility—especially among those that submit to Rome's rule and so offers "good tidings" (*euangelia*; Carter: 83–84).

This ideology-gospel was disseminated or promoted through a multitude of media: the imperial cult *[Roman Imperial Cult, p. 307]*; imperial proclamations posted or announced in cities; coins; literature (poems, odes, epics); images (statues, panel representations, etc.); inscriptions on buildings and in public spaces (forums); mile markers always displaying IMP CAESAR DIVI F (Imperator Caesar, Son of God), along with distances to the "golden milestone" set up in the Roman Forum beside Saturn's temple (in 20 BCE); athletic games, civic festivals, and more.

A core part of this ideology was rehearsing the deeds and virtues of the emperors, especially Augustus, extolling the blessings of peace and well-being that had come through their reign. It included a variety of ways of giving divine or semidivine titles or characterizations to a living or divinized emperor, notably Augustus: son of God (*divi filius*), savior of the world, benefactor of the whole human race, lord of the earth, bringer of world peace, *augustus* (exalted one, manifest one), good guardian spirit (Lat. *genius*; Gk. *daimōn*) of the world, father of the fatherland, the divine father among humans who bears the same name as his heavenly father, the marvelous star of the Greek world shining with the brilliance of the great heavenly Savior, ruler of oceans and continents, vicar of the gods, heaven's shining light, divine presence (*praesens divus*), arbiter of life and death for the nations, god of god, god (usually after divinization), and so on. A key part of this was the granting of honors (or being declared) "equal to the gods" (Heen; Crossan and Reed; Price).

Beginning with Augustus, the emperors were regarded as the embodiment of the personified and deified virtues (which were already the objects of Roman "cults of virtues"; see Fears 1980, 1981a, 1981b, 1981c). Already in his own lifetime, and in his own posthumously broadcasted Acts of the Divine Augustus, inscribed in imperial temples throughout the empire, Augustus was extolled in Latin and in Greek as the one who embodied and modeled the cardinal virtues of valor (*virtus*, Gk. *arētē*), clemency (*clementia*, Gk. *epieikeia*), justice-righteousness (*iustitia*, Gk. *dikaiosynē*), and piety (*pietas*, Gk. *eusebeia*, dutiful and devoted conduct toward the gods, one's family, and country; Res gestae divi Augusti 34). Even fidelity (*fides*, Gk. *pistis*) was routinely heralded as a key hallmark of beneficent Roman rule (Elliott 2008: 38–40).

Even during his lifetime, Augustus was hailed by Roman hymnic authors as god incarnate, who can atone for the past guilt of the race. The poet Horace (20s BCE) extols the living Augustus as follows:

> You, winged son [Hermes-Mercury] of benign Maia, if changing your form, you assume on earth the guise of man, right ready to be called the avenger of [Julius] Caesar; late may you return to the skies and long may you be pleased to dwell amid Quirinus's [Roman] folk; and may no untimely gale waft you from us angered at our sins. Here rather may you love glorious triumphs, the name of "Father" (*Pater*) and "Chief" (*Princeps*); nor allow the Medes to ride on their raids unpunished; while you are our leader, O Caesar. (*Odes* 1.2, 21, 29-30; Crossan and Reed: 41–42)

Elsewhere Horace declares: "We believe that Jupiter is king in heaven because we hear his thunders peal; Augustus shall be deemed a god on earth (*praesens divus*, divine presence) for adding to our empire the Britons and dread Parthians" (*Odes* 3.5). In another place he offers that Augustus is different from earlier posthumous divinities: "Upon you, however, while still among us, we bestow [divine] honors already, set up altars to swear by in your name, and confess that nothing like you will hereafter arise or has arisen before now" (*Epistles* 2.1.12–17).

The emperor Tiberius was reticent to receive divine honors in his own lifetime, so as to avoid negative repercussions in elite circles in Rome, but was keen to promote the divine honors of his father, Augustus, as "equal to God" when he responded in 19 CE to a request from the East that he (Tiberius) receive divine honors:

> Your goodwill, which you display on all occasions when you see me, I welcome, but your acclamations, which for me are invidious and such as are addressed to gods [lit. equal to the gods, *isotheous*], I altogether deprecate. For they are appropriate only to him who is actually the saviour and benefactor of the whole human race, my father [Augustus]. (Heen: 145)

See Crossan and Reed; Carter; Elliott and Reasoner, ch. 3 (with more bibliography); Fears 1980, 1981a, 1981b, 1981c, 1988; Zanker. For the imperial context of Paul's gospel, Horsley 1997, 2000, 2004.

SYZYGOS Numerous issues arise when we try to interpret the words Paul uses to identify a mediator in a dispute (4:2). Paul presents the masculine vocative form of the adjective and compound noun: *gnēsie syzyge*, most neutrally, *genuine conjoin*(er/ed). He uses the noun form (*syzygos*) of the verb "to join together" (*syzeugnymi*; as in Mark 10:9, for marriage). The noun can have either a passive sense "what/who is joined together" (conjoined) or an active sense "what/who joins together" (conjoiner). From this Greek root *zygos*, *yoke*, we get the biological term *zygote*, the "joining" of two gametes (the Sanskrit *yoga*, *yoke*, is a synonym). The direct Latin equivalent of *syzygos* is *conjux*, from the verb *conjungere*, from which come words such as *conjugate*, *conjunction*, *conjugal*, and by extension *conjoin*, *conjoined*. In Paul's world, this word *syzygos* (or its feminine form, *syzygē*) was used most commonly in a passive sense to designate a close friend, brother, spouse, or even fellow contestant (BDAG). Indeed, its regular use to designate one's spouse (as still in Modern Greek) caused some early interpreters to suppose that Paul was here referring to his wife (Clement of Alexandria, *Stromata* 3.6.52).

How does Paul use the term here? (1) Most English translations take the word *syzygos* in a passive sense to designate a relationship with Paul (NRSV: *my loyal companion*; NIV: *my true companion*; NIV 1984: *loyal yokefellow*; TEV: *my faithful partner*). But the term *my* is not in Paul's Greek, and the translation *loyal* is not quite the nuance of the adjective *gnēsios*, which more narrowly means true in the sense of "genuine, legitimate, real." (2) Alternatively, many modern translations supply a marginal note that Paul could be using a male name or nickname Syzygos. While *syzygos* is not found anywhere in ancient literature or inscriptions as a name, the possibility that it is used here as a name or nickname cannot be ruled out. Similarly constructed forms are attested as names (e.g., Sympherus, lit. "bear-together-with," another metaphor of companionship; O'Brien). If Paul is identifying someone by name or nickname, the adjective *genuine* (*gnēsios*; used adverbially of Timothy in 2:20) highlights the person's true character: "truly named Syzygos." (Paul similarly plays on the meaning of a name in Philem 10-11: Onesimus as "useful").

In this context the most likely scenario is that Paul is addressing a recognized but unnamed conciliator in the congregation, employing a term that dramatizes a role and capability, that of "joining together," taking *syzygos* in its active sense (Fee: 392–93). The translation *conciliator* is perfectly apt. Its original Latin root can have the sense of "combining," even "matchmaking" (of spouses). (Similarly in Latin, a *concilium* [council] is an "assembly," that which is "brought together.") The use of the adjective *gnēsios* (in the sense of "true-to-character") is suggestive of the active meaning of *syzygos*, along with the play on words that immediately follows, using again a compound with the prefix *syn* (with, together) and meant in an active sense of "co-mingling," that is, "reconciling" the two named women.

Speculation as to whom Paul might be referring has left no firm results. The most compelling suggestion is Lydia (Acts 16:14-15, 40). She could easily fit either sense of *syzygos*: both as endearing words of companionship ("true conjoined" partner) in that she was close to Paul's struggle during the early days of the Philippian assembly, and as "true conciliator" of a community, given her role as leading patron of the congregation. The formal and courteous *I request* (*erōtaō*) would suit the leadership role of Lydia. Though Paul uses the grammatical gender expected of a male addressee, even fluent speakers of Koine Greek in subsequent years did not think it impossible that Paul was addressing a female (e.g., Clement of Alexandria, ca. 150–215 CE, *Stromata* 3.6.52).

The New Testament
World
COLONY OF PHILPPI
Philippi
Neapolis
Amphipois
BLACK SEA
ITALY
Rome
ADRIATIC SEA
ILLYRICUM
OR
DALMATIA
MOESIA
THRACE
MACEDONIA
Philippi
Neapolis
Amphipois
Thessalonica
Beroea
Appollonia
SAMO-
THRACE
Puteoli
Neapolis
ACHAIA
Nicopolis
SICILY
Rhegium
Syracuse
Athens
Corinth
Cenchreae
AEGEAN SEA
Mysia
Troas
Assos
Mitylene
Pergamum
Thyatira
Sardis
Philadelphia
Smyrna
Ephesus
Hierapolis
Colossae
Laodicea
SAMOS
Trogyllium
Miletus
PATMOS
Cos
COS
Cnidus
Rhodes
RHODES
ASIA
Phrygia
Pisidia
Antioch
Iconium
Lystra
Derbe
LYCIA
Patara
Myra
PAMPHYLIA
Perga
Attalia
CILICIA
TRACHEA
BITHYNIA and PONTUS
Ancyra
Tavium
Pessinus
GALATIA
CAPPADOCIA
Lycaonia
Cilician Gates
Tarsus
Seleucia
Antioch
CILICIA and SYRIA
MELITA
MELITINE
N
W
E
S
CRETE
Phoenix
Salmone
Fair Havens
CAUDA
CLAUDA
CYPRUS
Salamis
Paphos
MEDITERRANEAN SEA
Sidon
Damascus
Tyre
Ptolemais
Caesarea
Joppa
Jerusalem
Gaza
Cyrene
LIBYA
Alexandria
EGYPT

Bibliography

Abrahamsen, V. A.

1995 *Women and Worship at Philippi: Diana/Artemis and Other Cults in the Early Christian Era*. Portland, ME: Astarte Shell.

Agamben, Giorgio

2005 *The Time That Remains: A Commentary on the Letter to the Romans*. Translated by Patricia Dailey. Stanford, CA: Stanford University Press.

2011 *The Sacrament of Language: An Archaeology of the Oath*. Translated by Adam Kotsko. Stanford, CA: Stanford University Press.

Agosto, Efrain

2004 "Patronage and Commendation, Imperial and Anti-Imperial." In *Paul and the Roman Imperial Order*, edited by Richard Horsley, 103–24. Harrisburg: Trinity Press International.

2007 "The Letter to the Philippians." In *A Postcolonial Commentary on the New Testament Writings*, edited by F. Segovia and R. W. Sugirtharajah, 281–93. London: T&T Clark.

Alcock, S. E.

1993 *Graecia Capta: The Landscapes of Roman Greece*. Cambridge: Cambridge University Press.

Alexander, P. S.

1984 "Epistolary Literature." In *Jewish Writings of the Second Temple Period*, edited by M. E. Stone, 578–96. Assen: Van Gorcum; Philadelphia: Fortress.

Apilado, Mariano C.

2000 *The Dream Need Not Die*. Vol. 2 of *Revolutionary Spirituality*. Quezon City: New Day Publishers.

Arnaoutoglou, Ilias N.

2002 "Roman Law and *Collegia* in Asia Minor." *Revue Internationale des droits de l'Antiquité* 49:27–44.

Baraheni, Reza
1976 *God's Shadow: Prison Poems*. Bloomington: Indiana University Press.

Barclay, John M. G.
2015 *Paul and the Gift*. Grand Rapids: Eerdmans.

Barth, Markus
1974 *Ephesians: Introduction, Translation, and Commentary*. 2 vols. New York: Doubleday.

Beker, J. Christiaan
1980 *Paul the Apostle: The Triumph of God in Life and Thought*. Philadelphia: Fortress.

Black, D. A.
1995 "The Discourse Structure of Philippians: A Study in Text-Linguistics." *Novum Testamentum* 37:16–49.

Bloomquist, L. G.
1993 *The Function of Suffering in Philippians*. Journal for the Study of the New Testament Supplement Series 78. Sheffield: JSOT Press.

Bockmuehl, Markus
1998 *The Epistle to the Philippians*. Black's New Testament Commentary 11. Peabody, MA: Hendrickson.

Boer, Martinus C. de
2011 *Galatians: A Commentary*. Louisville: Westminster John Knox.

Bonhoeffer, Dietrich
1972 *Letters and Papers from Prison*. New York: Macmillan.

Borg, Marcus, and John Crossan
2009 *The First Paul: Reclaiming the Radical Visionary behind the Church's Conservative Icon*. New York: HarperOne.

Bormann, L.
1995 *Philippi: Stadt und Christengemeinde zur Zeit des Paulus*. Supplements to Novum Testamentum 78. Leiden: Brill.

Boyarin, Daniel
1994 *A Radical Jew: Paul and the Politics of Identity*. Berkeley: University of California Press.
2004 *Border Lines: The Partition of Judeo-Christianity*. Philadelphia: University of Pennsylvania Press.

Brewer, R.
1952 "The Meaning of *Politeuesthe* in Philippians 1:27." *Journal of Biblical Literature* 71:227–31.

Brodd, Jeffrey, and Jonathan L. Reed
2011 *Rome and Religion: A Cross-Disciplinary Dialogue on the Imperial Cult*. Atlanta: Society of Biblical Literature.

Bruce, F. F.
1992 "Citizenship." *Anchor Bible Dictionary* 1:1048–49.

Brucker, R.
1997 *"Christushymnen" oder "epideiktische Passagen"? Studien zum Stilwechsel im Neuen Testament und seiner Umwelt*. Forschungen zur Religion und Literatur des Alten und Neuen Testaments 176. Göttingen: Vandenhoeck & Ruprecht.

Brunk, George R., III
2015 *Galatians*. Believers Church Bible Commentary. Scottdale, PA: Herald Press.

Campbell, Douglas
2005 *The Quest for Paul's Gospel: A Suggested Strategy*. New York: T&T Clark.

Capper, B.
1993 "Paul's Dispute with Philippi." *Theologische Literaturzeitung* 49:193–214.

Carter, Warren
2006 *The Roman Empire and the New Testament: An Essential Guide*. Nashville: Abingdon.

Cassidy, Richard
2001a *Paul in Chains: Roman Imprisonment and the Letters of Paul*. New York: Crossroad.
2001b *Christians and Roman Rule in the New Testament: New Perspectives*. New York: Crossroad.

Cohen, Shaye H. D.
1999 *The Beginnings of Jewishness: Boundaries, Varieties, Uncertainties*. Berkeley: University of California Press.

Collins, John J.
1997 *Apocalypticism in the Dead Sea Scrolls*. London: Routledge.

Collins, Raymond
2008 *The Power of Images in Paul*. Collegeville, MN: Liturgical Press.

Confession of Faith in a Mennonite Perspective
1995 Scottdale, PA: Herald Press. Available at http://www.mennonitechurch.ca/about/cof/.

Confession of Faith of the General Conference of Mennonite Brethren Churches
1999 Winnipeg, MB: General Conference of Mennonite Brethren Churches. Available online at http://www.mennonitebrethren.ca/resource/the-mb-confession-of-faith-detailed-edition/.

Cotter, W.
1993 "Our *Politeuma* Is in Heaven: The Meaning of Philippians 3:17-21." In *Origins and Method: Towards a New Understanding of Judaism and Christianity*, edited by B. H. McLean, 92–104. Journal for the Study of the New Testament Supplement Series 86. Sheffield: JSOT Press.
1996 "The Collegia and Roman Law: State Restrictions on Voluntary Associations, 64 BCE–200 CE." In *Voluntary Associations in the Graeco-Roman World*, edited by J. S. Kloppenborg and S. Wilson, 74–89. London: Routledge.

Craddock, Fred
1984 *Philippians*. Interpretation: A Bible Commentary for Teaching and Preaching. Atlanta: John Knox.

Crossan, John Dominic
1999 *The Birth of Christianity: Discovering What Happened in the Years Immediately after the Execution of Jesus*. New York: HarperOne.

Crossan, John Dominic, and Jonathan Reed
2004 *In Search of Paul: How Jesus's Apostle Opposed Rome's Empire with God's Kingdom*. New York: HarperSanFrancisco.
Dahl, N. A.
1995 "Euodia and Syntyche and Paul's Letter to the Philippians." In *The Social World of the First Christians: Essays in Honor of Wayne A. Meeks*, edited by L. M. White and O. L. Yarbrough, 3–15. Minneapolis: Fortress.
Davies, Ioan
1990 *Writers in Prison*. Cambridge, MA: Blackwell, 1990.
de Vos, Craig Steven
1999 *Church and Community Conflicts: The Relationships of the Thessalonian, Corinthian, and Philippian Churches to Their Wider Civic Communities*. Society of Biblical Literature Dissertation Series 168. Atlanta: Scholars Press.
Donaldson, Terence L.
2010 *Jews and Anti-Judaism in the New Testament: Decision Points and Divergent Interpretations*. Waco: Baylor University Press.
Doughty, D. J.
1995 "Citizens of Heaven: Philippians 3:2-21." *New Testament Studies* 41:102–22.
Dunn, James D. G.
1998 *The Theology of Paul*. Grand Rapids: Eerdmans.
Eastman, Susan Grove
2010 "Philippians 2:6-11: Incarnation as Mimetic Participation." *Journal for the Study of Paul and His Letters* 1:1–22.
Eisenbaum, Pamela
2009 *Paul Was Not a Christian: The Original Message of a Misunderstood Apostle*. San Francisco: HarperOne.
Elliott, Neil
2008 *The Arrogance of the Nations: Reading Romans in the Shadow of Empire*. Minneapolis: Fortress.
Elliott, Neil, and Mark Reasoner, eds.
2011 *Documents and Images for the Study of Paul*. Minneapolis, Fortress.
Engberg-Pedersen, Troels
2000 *Paul and the Stoics*. Louisville: Westminster John Knox.
Fears, J. Rufus
1980 "Rome: The Ideology of Imperial Power." *Thought* 55:98–109.
1981a "The Cult of Jupiter and Roman Imperial Ideology." *Aufstieg und Niedergang der römischen Welt* II.17.1:1–141.
1981b "The Cult of Virtues and Roman Imperial Ideology." *Aufstieg und Niedergang der römischen Welt* II.17.2:827–948.
1981c "The Theology of Victory at Rome: Approaches and Problems." *Aufstieg und Niedergang der römischen Welt* II.17.2:736–826.
1988 "Ruler Worship." In *Civilization of the Ancient Mediterranean*, edited by Michael Grant and Rachel Kitzinger, 2:1009–25. New York: Scribner's.

Fee, Gordon D.
1995 *Paul's Letter to the Philippians.* New International Commentary on the New Testament. Grand Rapids: Eerdmans.

Fernandez, Eleazar S.
1996 *Toward a Theology of Struggle.* Maryknoll, NY: Orbis Books.

Flemming, Dean
2009 *Philippians: A Commentary in the Wesleyan Tradition.* New Beacon Bible Commentary. Kansas City, MO: Beacon Hill.

Flint, Peter W.
1997 *The Dead Sea Psalms Scrolls and the Book of Psalms.* Leiden: Brill.

Forester, W.
1995 "*sōtēr.*" *Theological Dictionary of the New Testament* 7:1010–12.

Fowl, Stephen E.
1990 *The Story of Christ in the Ethics of Paul: An Analysis of the Function of Hymnic Material in the Pauline Corpus.* Journal for the Study of the New Testament Supplement Series 36. Sheffield: JSOT Press.
2005 *Philippians.* The Two Horizons New Testament Commentary. Grand Rapids: Eerdmans.

Garland, David
1985 "The Composition and Unity of Philippians: Some Neglected Literary Features." *Novum Testamentum* 27:141–73.

Garnsey, Peter, and Richard Saller
1987 *The Roman Empire: Economy, Society, and Culture.* Berkeley: University of California Press.

Geoffrion, Timothy C.
1993 *The Rhetorical Purpose and the Political and Military Character of Philippians: A Call to Stand Firm.* Lewiston, NY: Mellen.

Georgi, D.
1991 *Theocracy in Paul's Praxis and Theology.* Minneapolis: Fortress.

Gilpin, W. Clark.
2003 "Testimony: The Letter from Prison in Christian History and Theology." https://divinity.uchicago.edu/sites/default/files/imce/pdfs/webforum/012003/Gilpin_Commentary2.pdf.

Goodman, Martin
2008 *Rome and Jerusalem: The Clash of Ancient Civilizations.* London & New York: Penguin.

Gorman, Michael J.
2001 *Cruciformity: Paul's Narrative Spirituality of the Cross.* Grand Rapids: Eerdmans.
2004 *Apostle of the Crucified Lord: A Theological Introduction to Paul and His Letters.* Grand Rapids: Eerdmans.
2009 *Inhabiting the Cruciform God: Kenosis, Justification, and Theosis in Paul's Narrative Theology.* Grand Rapids: Eerdmans.
2015 *Becoming the Gospel: Paul, Participation, and Mission.* Grand Rapids: Eerdmans.

Gradel, Ittai
2004 *Emperor Worship and Roman Religion.* Oxford: Oxford University Press.

Greenleaf, Robert K.
2002 *Servant Leadership: A Journey into the Nature of Legitimate Power and Greatness*. 25th anniversary ed. New York: Paulist Press.
Hansen, G. Walter
2009 *The Letter to the Philippians*. Pillar New Testament Commentary. Grand Rapids: Eerdmans.
Harrill, James Albert
1998 *The Manumission of Slaves in Early Christianity*. Tübingen: Mohr Siebeck.
Hawthorne, Gerald
1983 *Philippians*. Word Biblical Commentary 43. Waco, TX: Word.
Hays, Richard B.
1993 *Echoes of Scripture in the Letters of Paul*. New Haven: Yale University Press.
Heen, Erik M.
2004 "Phil 2:6-11 and Resistance to Local Timocratic Rule: *Isa theō* and the Cult of the Emperor in the East." In *Paul and the Roman Imperial Order*, edited by Richard Horsley, 125–54. Harrisburg: Trinity Press International.
Heil, John Paul
2010 *Philippians: Let Us Rejoice in Being Conformed to Christ*. Early Christianity and Its Literature. Leiden: Brill.
2011 *The Letters of Paul as Rituals of Worship*. Eugene, OR: Cascade.
Hellerman, Joseph H.
2005 *Reconstructing Honor in Roman Philippi: Carmen Christi as Cursus Pudorum*. Society for New Testament Studies Monograph Series 132. Cambridge: Cambridge University Press.
Hendrix, H. L.
1992 "Philippi." *Anchor Bible Dictionary* 5:313–17.
Hollingshead, James R.
1998 *The Household of Caesar and the Body of Christ: A Political Interpretation of the Letters from Paul*. Lanham, MD: University Press of America.
Holloway, P. A.
2001 *Consolation in Philippians: Philosophical Sources and Rhetorical Strategy*. Society for New Testament Studies Monograph Series 112. Cambridge: Cambridge University Press.
Hooker, Morna D.
2000 "The Letter to the Philippians: Introduction, Commentary, and Reflections." In *The New Interpreter's Bible* 11:469–549.
Hoover, Roy
1971 "The *Harpagmos* Enigma: A Philological Solution." *Harvard Theological Review* 64:95–119.
Horsley, Richard
2003 *Jesus and Empire: The Kingdom of God and the New World Disorder*. Minneapolis: Fortress.
Horsley, Richard, ed.
1997 *Paul and Empire: Religion and Power in Roman Imperial Society*. Harrisburg, PA: Trinity Press International.

2000 *Paul and Politics: Ekklēsia, Israel, Imperium, Interpretation.* Harrisburg, PA: Trinity Press International.

2004 *Paul and the Roman Imperial Order.* Harrisburg: Trinity Press International.

Hubmaier, Balthasar (d. 1528)

1989 *Balthasar Hubmaier: Theologian of Anabaptism.* Translated and edited by H. Wayne Pipkin and John H. Yoder. Scottdale, PA: Herald Press.

Hurtado, L. W.

1984 "Jesus as Lordly Example in Philippians 2:5-11." In *From Jesus to Paul: Studies in Honour of Francis Wright Beare,* edited by P. Richardson and J. C. Hurd, 113–26. Waterloo, ON: Wilfrid Laurier University Press.

Ileto, Reynaldo C.

1979 *Pasyon and Revolution: Popular Movements in the Philippines, 1840–1910.* Quezon City: Ateneo de Manila Press.

Jeremias, Joachim

1953 "Zur Gedankenführung in den paulinischen Briefen." In *Studia Paulina in Honorem J. de Zwaan,* edited by J. N. Sevenster and W. C. van Unnik, 146–54. Haarlem: E. Bonn.

Jewett, Robert

1970 "Conflicting Movements in the Early Church as Reflected in Philippians." *Novum Testamentum* 12:362–90.

Jonge, Marinus de

1992 "Christ." *Anchor Bible Dictionary* 2:914–21.

Johns, Loren

2003 *The Lamb Christology of the Apocalypse of John: An Investigation into Its Origins and Rhetorical Force.* Tübingen: Mohr Siebeck.

Kelly, Christopher

2006 *The Roman Empire: A Very Short Introduction.* Oxford: Oxford University Press.

King, Martin Luther Jr.

1963 "Letter from a Birmingham Jail." Available at http://www.africa.upenn.edu/Articles_Gen/Letter_Birmingham.html (text) or http://okra.stanford.edu/transcription/document_images/undecided/630416-019.pdf (pdf of transcription).

Kittredge, Cynthia Briggs

1998 *Community and Authority: The Rhetoric of Obedience in the Pauline Tradition.* Harvard Theological Studies. Harrisburg, PA: Trinity Press International.

Klaassen, Walter

1981 *Anabaptism in Outline: Selected Primary Sources.* Scottdale, PA: Herald Press.

2001 *Anabaptism: Neither Catholic nor Protestant.* 3rd ed. Kitchener, ON: Pandora Press.

Klauck, Hans-Joseph

2006 *Ancient Letters and the New Testament: A Guide to Context and Exegesis.* Waco: Baylor University Press.

Koester, Helmut
1997 "Imperial Ideology and Paul's Eschatology in 1 Thessalonians." In *Paul and Empire*, edited by R. Horsley, 158–66.

Koperski, Veronica
1996 *Knowledge of Christ Jesus My Lord: The High Christology of Philippians 3:7-11*. Kampen: Kok Pharos.

Koukouli-Chrysantaki, Chaido
1998 "Colonia Iulia Augusta Philippensis." In *Philippi at the Time of Paul and after His Death*, edited by Charalambos Bakirtzis and Helmut Koester, 5–35. Harrisburg, PA: Trinity Press International.

Kreitzer, L. J.
1987 *Jesus and God in Paul's Eschatology*. Sheffield: Sheffield Academic Press.

Krentz, E. M.
1993 "Military Language and Metaphors in Philippians." In *Origins and Method*, edited by B. H. McLean, 105–27. Journal for the Study of the New Testament Supplement Series 86. Sheffield: JSOT Press.

Larson, Doran
2010 "Toward a Prison Poetics," *College Literature* 37/3. http://www.freepatentsonline.com/article/College-Literature/234570864.html.

Lefkowitz, Mary R., and Maureen B. Fant
2005 *Women's Life in Greece and Rome: A Source Book in Translation*. 3rd ed. Baltimore: Johns Hopkins University Press.

Lewis, Naphtali, and Meyer Reinhold, eds.
1955 *Roman Civilization: Selected Readings*. Vol. 2, *The Empire*. New York: Harper & Row.

Lincoln, Andrew
1981 *Paradise Now and Not Yet: Studies in the Role of the Heavenly Dimension in Paul's Thought with Special Reference to His Eschatology*. Society for New Testament Studies Monograph Series 43. Cambridge: Cambridge University Press.

Lintott, Andrew
1999 *Violence in Republican Rome*. 2nd ed. Oxford: Oxford University Press.

Lohmeyer, Ernst
1928 *Kyrios Jesus: Eine Untersuchung zu Phil. 2,5-11*. Heidelberg: Carl Winters.

Longenecker, Bruce W.
2009 "Socio-Economic Profiling of the First Urban Christians." In *After the First Urban Christians: The Social-Scientific Study of Pauline Christianity Twenty-Five Years Later*, edited by Todd D. Still and David G. Horrell, 36–59. London: T&T Clark.
2010 *Remember the Poor: Paul, Poverty, and the Greco-Roman World*. Grand Rapids: Eerdmans.

MacMullen, Ramsay
1974 *Roman Social Relations: 50 B.C. to A.D. 284*. New Haven: Yale University Press.

Marchal, Joseph A.

2006 *Hierarchy, Unity, and Imitation: A Feminist Rhetorical Analysis of Power Dynamics in Paul's Letter to the Philippians.* Atlanta: Society of Biblical Literature.

2008 *The Politics of Heaven: Women, Gender, and Empire in the Study of Paul.* Minneapolis: Fortress.

2011 "Imperial Intersections and Initial Inquiries: Toward a Feminist, Postcolonial Analysis of Philippians." In *The Colonized Paul: Paul through Postcolonial Eyes*, edited by Christopher Stanley, 146–60. Minneapolis: Fortress.

Marshall, I. Howard

1991 *The Epistle to the Philippians.* Epworth Commentaries. London: Epworth.

1993 "The Theology of Philippians." In *The Theology of the Shorter Pauline Letters*, edited by K. P. Donfried and I. H. Marshall, 115–74. Cambridge: Cambridge University Press.

Martens, Elmer

2009 "Intertext Messaging: Echoes of the Aaronic Blessing (Numbers 6:24-26)." *Direction* 38/2:163–78.

Martin, Ralph P.

1980 *Philippians.* New Century Bible. Grand Rapids: Eerdmans.

1997 *A Hymn of Christ: Philippians 2:5-11 in Recent Interpretation and in the Setting of Early Christian Worship.* Rev. ed. Downers Grove, IL: InterVarsity.

Martin, Ralph P., and Brian J. Dodd, eds.

1998 *Where Christology Began: Essays on Philippians 2.* Louisville: Westminster John Knox.

Meeks, Wayne

1983 *First Urban Christians: The Social World of the Apostle Paul.* New Haven: Yale University Press.

Meggitt, Justin J.

1998 *Paul, Poverty, and Survival.* Studies of the New Testament and Its World. Edinburgh: T&T Clark.

Murphy-O'Connor, Jerome

2008 *St. Paul's Ephesus: Texts and Archaeology.* Collegeville, MN: Liturgical Press.

Naficy, Majid [Nafīcī, Majīd]

1996 *Poetry and Politics and Twenty-Four Other Essays.* [In Persian.] Spånga, Sweden: Baran.

Nanos, Mark D.

2009 "Paul's Reversal of Jews Calling Gentiles 'Dogs' (Philippians 3:2): 1600 Years of an Ideological Tale Wagging an Exegetical Dog?" *Biblical Interpretation* 17:448–82.

2011 "Paul and Judaism." In *The Jewish Annotated New Testament. New Revised Standard Version Bible Translations*, edited by Amy-Jill Levine and Marc Zvi Brettler, 551–54. Oxford: Oxford University Press.

2012 "A Jewish View." In *Four Views on the Apostle Paul*, edited by Michael F. Bird. Grand Rapids: Zondervan.

2013 "Paul's Polemic in Philippians 3 as Jewish-Subgroup Vilification of Local Non-Jewish Cultic and Philosophical Alternatives." *Journal for the Study of Paul and His Letters* 3.1:47–92.

Nanos, Mark and Magnus Zetterholm, eds.

2015 *Paul within Judaism: Restoring the First-Century Context to the Apostle*. Minneapolis: Fortress.

Nebreda, Serio Rosell

2011 *Christ Identity: A Social-Scientific Reading of Philippians 2.5-11*. Göttingen: Vandenhoeck & Ruprecht.

Neville, David

2013 *A Peaceable Hope: Contesting Violent Eschatology in New Testament Narratives*. Grand Rapids: Baker Academic.

Novenson, Matthew V.

2012 *Christ among the Messiahs: Christ Language in Paul and Messiah Language in Ancient Judaism*. New York: Oxford University Press.

Oakes, Peter

2001 *Philippians: From People to Letter*. Society for New Testament Studies Monograph Series 110. Cambridge: Cambridge University Press.

2002 "God's Sovereignty over Roman Authorities: A Theme in Philippians." In *Rome in the Bible and the Early Church*, edited by Peter Oakes, 126–41. Grand Rapids: Baker Academic.

2005 "Re-mapping the Universe: Paul and the Emperor in 1 Thessalonians and Philippians." *Journal for the Study of the New Testament* 27:301–22.

2009 "Contours of the Urban Environment." In *After the First Urban Christians: The Social-Scientific Study of Pauline Christianity Twenty-Five Years Later*, edited by Todd D. Still and David G. Horrell, 21–35. London: T&T Clark.

O'Brien, Peter T.

1991 *The Epistle to the Philippians: A Commentary on the Greek Text*. New International Greek Testament Commentary. Grand Rapids: Eerdmans.

Osiek, Carolyn

2000 *Philippians, Philemon*. Abingdon New Testament Commentaries. Nashville: Abingdon.

Perkins, Pheme

1992 "Philippians." In *The Women's Bible Commentary*, edited by Carol Newsom and Sharon Ringe, 343–46. Louisville: Westminster/ John Knox.

Peterlin, Davorin

1995 *Paul's Letter to the Philippians in the Light of Disunity in the Church*. Supplements to Novum Testamentum 79. Leiden: Brill.

Peterman, G. W.

1997 *Paul's Gift from Philippi: Conventions of Gift-Exchange and Christian Giving*. Society for New Testament Studies Monograph Series 92. Cambridge: Cambridge University Press.

Pfitzner, V. C.
1967 *Paul and the Agon Motif: Traditional Athletic Imagery in the Pauline Literature.* Supplements to Novum Testamentum 79. Leiden: Brill.

Portefaix, L.
1988 *Sisters Rejoice: Paul's Letter to the Philippians and Luke-Acts as Seen by First-Century Philippian Women.* Coniectanea Biblica: New Testament Series 20. Stockholm: Almqvist & Wiksell.

Portier-Young, Anathea E.
2011 *Apocalypse against Empire: Theologies of Resistance in Early Judaism.* Grand Rapids: Eerdmans.

Price, S. R. F.
1984 *Rituals and Power: The Roman Imperial Cult in Asia Minor.* Cambridge: Cambridge University Press.

Reasoner, Mark
2014 "Paul's God of Peace in Canonical and Political Perspective." In *The History of Religions School Today: Essays on the New Testament and Related Ancient Mediterranean Texts,* edited by Thomas R. Blanton IV, Robert M. Calhoun, and Clare K. Rothschild, 13–26. Tübingen: Mohr Siebeck.

Reed, Jeffrey
1997 *A Discourse Analysis of Philippians: Method and Practice in the Debate over Literary Integrity.* Journal for the Study of the New Testament Supplement Series 136. Sheffield: Sheffield Academic Press.

Reider, Aasgard
2004 *My Beloved Brothers and Sisters: Christian Siblinghood in Paul.* London: T&T Clark.

Reimer, Raymond H.
1997 *"Our Citizenship Is in Heaven": Philippians 1:27-30 and 3:20-21 as Part of the Apostle Paul's Political Theology.* PhD diss., Princeton Theological Seminary.

Saller, Richard P.
1982 *Personal Patronage under the Early Empire.* Cambridge: Cambridge University Press.

Sampley, J. Paul
1980 *Pauline Partnership in Christ: Christian Community and Commitment in Light of Roman Law.* Philadelphia: Fortress.

Sattler, Michael
1973 *The Legacy of Michael Sattler.* Translated and edited by John H. Yoder. Scottdale, PA: Herald Press.

Schellenberg, Ryan
2013 *Rethinking Paul's Rhetorical Education: Comparative Rhetoric and 2 Corinthians 10–13.* Early Christianity and Its Literature. Atlanta: Society of Biblical Literature.

Schoberg, Gerry
2013 *Perspectives of Jesus in the Writings of Paul: A Historical Examination of Shared Core Commitments with a View to Determining the Extent of Paul's Dependence on Jesus.* Cambridge, UK: James Clarke & Co.

Schürer, Emil

1986 *The History of the Jewish People in the Age of Jesus Christ*. Vol. 3.1. Revised and edited by G. Vermès et al. Edinburgh: T&T Clark.

Sherwin-White, Adrian N.

1973 *The Roman Citizenship*. Oxford : Clarendon Press.

1978 *Roman Society and Roman Law in the New Testament*. Grand Rapids: Baker.

Shillington, V. George

1998 *2 Corinthians*. Believers Church Bible Commentary. Scottdale, PA: Herald Press.

2011 *Jesus and Paul before Christianity: Their World and Work in Retrospect*. Eugene, OR: Cascade.

Silva, Moisés

2005 *Philippians*. 2nd ed. Baker Exegetical Commentary on the New Testament. Grand Rapids: Baker Academic.

Smith, James A.

2005 *Marks of an Apostle: Deconstruction, Philippians, and Problematizing Pauline Theology*. Semeia Studies. Atlanta: Society of Biblical Literature.

Stanley, D.

1984 "Imitation in Paul's Letters: Its Significance for His Relationship to Jesus and to His Own Christian Foundations." In *From Jesus to Paul: Studies in Honour of Francis Wright Beare*, edited by P. Richardson and J. C. Hurd, 127–41. Waterloo, ON: Wilfrid Laurier University Press.

Stegemann, Ekkehard W., and Wolfgang Stegemann

1999 *The Jesus Movement: A Social History of Its First Century*. Minneapolis: Fortress.

Stowers, Stanley

1986 *Letter-Writing in Graeco-Roman Antiquity*. Philadelphia: Fortress.

Swartley, Willard M.

1996 "War and Peace in the New Testament." *Aufstieg und Niedergang der römischen Welt* II.26.3:2298–2408.

2006 *Covenant of Peace: The Missing Peace in New Testament Theology and Ethics*. Grand Rapids: Eerdmans.

Tellbe, Mikael

1994 "The Sociological Factors behind Philippians 3.1-11 and the Conflict at Philippi." *Journal for the Study of the New Testament* 55:97–121.

2001 *Paul between Synagogue and State: Christians, Jews, and Civic Authorities in 1 Thessalonians, Romans and Philippians*. Coniectanea Biblica: New Testament Series 34. Stockholm: Almqvist & Wiksell.

Toews, John E.

2004 *Romans*. Believers Church Bible Commentary. Scottdale, PA: Herald Press.

2009 "The Politics of Confession." *Direction* 38/1:5–16.

Ward, Allen M., Fritz Heichelheim, and Cedric Yeo

2010 *A History of the Roman People*. 5th ed. Boston: Prentice-Hall.

Ware, James P.
2011 *Paul and the Mission of the Church: Philippians in Ancient Jewish Context*. Grand Rapids: Baker Academic.

Watson, Duane F.
1988 "A Rhetorical Analysis of Philippians and Its Implications for the Unity Problem." *Novum Testamentum* 30:57–88.

Weaver, P. R. C.
1972 *Familia Caesaris: A Social Study of the Emperor's Freedmen and Slaves*. Cambridge: Cambridge University Press.

Wengst, Klaus
1987 *Pax Romana and the Peace of Jesus Christ*. Translated by J. Bowden. Philadelphia: Fortress.
1989 *Humility: Solidarity of the Humiliated; The Transformation of an Attitude and Its Social Relevance in Graeco-Roman, Old Testament-Jewish, and Early Christian Tradition*. Minneapolis: Fortress.

White, L. M.
1990 "Morality between Two Worlds: A Paradigm of Friendship in Philippians." In *Greeks, Romans, and Christians*, edited by D. L. Balch, E. Ferguson, and W. A. Meeks, 201–15. Minneapolis: Fortress.

Williams, Demetrius
2002 *Enemies of the Cross: The Terminology of the Cross and Conflict in Philippians*. Sheffield: Sheffield Academic Press.

Williams, Jarvis
2010 *Maccabean Martyr Traditions in Paul's Theology of Atonement: Did Martyr Theology Shape Paul's Conception of Jesus' Death?* Eugene, OR: Wipf & Stock.

Winter, Bruce
1994 *Seek the Welfare of the City: Christians as Benefactors and Citizens*. Grand Rapids: Eerdmans.

Wistrand, Magnus
1992 *Entertainment and Violence in Ancient Rome: The Attitudes of Roman Writers of the First Century A.D.* Studia Graeca et Latina Gothoburgensia 56. Göteborg, Sweden: Acta Universitatis Gothoburgensis.

Witherington, Ben, III
1994 *Friendship and Finances in Philippi: The Letter of Paul to the Philippians*. The New Testament in Context. Valley Forge, PA: Trinity Press International.

Wright, N. T.
1991 *The Climax of the Covenant: Christ and the Law in Pauline Theology*. London: T&T Clark.
2000 "Paul's Gospel and Caesar's Empire." In *Paul and Politics: Ekklesia, Imperium, Interpretation*, edited by Richard Horsley, 160–83. Harrisburg, PA: Trinity Press International.
2003 *The Resurrection of the Son of God*. Minneapolis: Fortress.

Yinger, Kent
2009 "Paul and Evangelism: A Missiological Challenge from New Testament Specialists." *Missiology* 37:385–96.

Yoder Neufeld, Thomas R.
2002 *Ephesians*. Believers Church Bible Commentary. Waterloo, ON: Herald Press.
2007 *Recovering Jesus: The Witness of the New Testament*. Grand Rapids: Brazos.

Zanker, Paul
1990 *The Power of Images in the Age of Augustus*. Ann Arbor: University of Michigan Press.

Zerbe, Gordon
1992 "Paul's Ethic of Nonretaliation and Peace." In *The Love of Enemy and Nonretaliation in the New Testament*, edited by Willard Swartley, 177–222. Grand Rapids: Eerdmans.
1993 "'Pacifism' and 'Passive Resistance' in Apocalyptic Writings: A Critical Evaluation." In *The Pseudepigrapha and Early Biblical Interpretation*, edited by James H. Charlesworth and Craig A. Evans, 65-95. Sheffield: Sheffield Academic Press.
2003 "The Politics of Paul: His Supposed Social Conservatism and the Impact of Postcolonial Readings." *Conrad Grebel Review* 21/1:82–103. Reprinted with minor revisions in *The Colonized Paul: Paul through Postcolonial Eyes*, edited by C. Stanley, 62–73. Minneapolis: Fortress, 2011.
2005 "Constructions of Paul in Filipino Theology of Struggle." *Asia Journal of Theology* 19/1:188–220. Reprinted with minor revisions in *The Colonized Paul: Paul through Postcolonial Eyes*, edited by C. Stanley, 236–55. Minneapolis: Fortress, 2011.
2008 "Paul on the Human Being as a 'Psychic Body': Neither Dualist nor Monist." *Direction* 37/2:168–84. Reprinted in Zerbe 2012: 183–94.
2012 *Citizenship: Paul on Peace and Politics*. Winnipeg: Canadian Mennonite University Press.
2015 "From Retributive to Restorative Justice in Romans." *Direction* 44/1: 43-58.

Žižek, Slavoy
2000 *The Fragile Absolute, or, Why Is the Christian Legacy Worth Fighting For?* London: Verso.

Selected Resources

Bockmuehl, Markus. *The Epistle to the Philippians.* Black's New Testament Commentary 11. Peabody, MA: Hendrickson, 1998. Valuable in this commentary designed for a broad readership is the author's own fresh translation, along with his attention to the social and political setting of Paul's letter and to the concerns of Christian practice and theology.

Flemming, Dean. *Philippians: A Commentary in the Wesleyan Tradition.* Kansas City, MO: Beacon Hill, 2009. This readable commentary, also based on the author's own translation, has a particular interest in the missional significance of Paul's letter. Flemming provides plenty of insightful and relevant detail while never losing sight of the overall meaning of the entire letter.

Fowl, Stephen E. *Philippians.* The Two Horizons New Testament Commentary. Grand Rapids: Eerdmans, 2005. Fowl provides a rich interpretation of Philippians by deliberately approaching the text in its literary shape and its historical context from a robust theological perspective that draws the contemporary reader concerned with Christian practice into conversation with premodern commentators.

Gorman, Michael J. *Inhabiting the Cruciform God: Kenosis, Justification, and Theosis in Paul's Narrative Theology*. Grand Rapids: Eerdmans, 2009.

———. *Becoming the Gospel: Paul, Participation, and Mission*. Grand Rapids: Eerdmans, 2009. These highly regarded synthetic works on Paul's gospel and mission are based on careful exegetical treatments of Paul's letters and are therefore valuable resources for understanding specific letters.

Hellerman, Joseph H. *Reconstructing Honor in Roman Philippi: Carmen Christi as Cursus Pudorum*. Society for New Testament Studies Monograph Series 132. Cambridge: Cambridge University Press, 2005. Hellerman's monograph is one of the best resources for understanding the cultural and social context of Paul's letter. By careful attention to surviving inscriptions discovered through archaeology, the book provides an insightful walk through the streets of Philippi in the time of Paul.

Oakes, Peter. *Philippians: From People to Letter*. Society for New Testament Studies Monograph Series 110. Cambridge: Cambridge University Press, 2001. This significant study effectively explains the social makeup and dynamics of life in Philippi and takes us into the actual lives of people. The book especially highlights Paul's call to unity in the context of economic suffering and exclusion through maintaining loyalty to Christ instead of devotion to Caesar.

Peterman, G. W. *Paul's Gift from Philippi: Conventions of Gift-Exchange and Christian Giving*. Society for New Testament Studies Monograph Series 92. Cambridge: Cambridge University Press, 1997. This study explains Paul's comments on the generous contribution he received from Philippi, through careful attention to prevailing patterns of gift exchange in the Greco-Roman world that perpetuated social hierarchies. Peterman's treatment draws attention to Paul's desire to introduce an alternative vision of true mutualism and partnership that contrasts with Roman Philippi's rank-oriented society.

Wright, N. T. *Paul for Everyone: The Prison Letters, Ephesians, Philippians, Colossians, and Philemon*. 2nd ed. Louisville: Westminster John Knox, 2004.

———. *Philippians: 8 Studies for Individuals and Groups*. Downers Grove, IL: IVP Connect, 2009. These shorter treatments of Philippians come from a prolific writer on Paul and his letters. Despite their accessible and abbreviated format, they are full of depth and insight and are designed for study, reflection, and discussion by those seeking to follow Christ authentically in the present.

Index of Ancient Sources

Mark

Luke

John

Acts

1 Corinthians

2 Corinthians

Galatians

Ephesians

Philippians

Colossians

1 Thessalonians

2 Thessalonians

1 Timothy

2 Timothy

Titus

Philemon

The Author

Gordon Zerbe was born in Tokyo, Japan, and spent the first fifteen years of his life in that country, with a few interludes in the United States. Over the years, he has lived in three Canadian provinces and six U.S. states. He and his wife, Wendy Kroeker, moved to Winnipeg in 1988. He has been at Canadian Mennonite University since 1990 and currently serves as vice president academic.

He has a diploma in biblical studies from Columbia Bible College (B.C.), a BA in social work from Tabor College (Kans.), an MA in biblical studies from Mennonite Brethren Biblical Seminary (Calif.), an MA in cultural anthropology from Western Washington University, and a PhD from Princeton Theological Seminary (N.J.).

A highlight in his career was a series of years in the Philippines as visiting professor at the Silliman University Divinity School (1996–98, 2002–4), under the auspices of Mennonite Central Committee.

"Here is a theopolitical reading of Philippians that addresses the church's urgent need for crosscultural, socially challenging interpretations of Paul's beloved letter. Zerbe's commentary is a gift to Christians seeking a deeper understanding of Paul's call to radical discipleship in the life of the church." *—Susan Grove Eastman, associate research professor of New Testament, Duke Divinity School*

"Zerbe brilliantly brings alive the cultural and political air Paul and the Philippians breathed. In startlingly fresh language, Paul's theopolitical vision of the church as a partnership of 'Messiah Jesus loyalists' emerges as a radical alternative citizenship to that of Rome and confronts us about our own loyalties. This outstanding commentary will give readers fresh ears with which to hear Paul all over again." *—Thomas R. Yoder Neufeld, professor emeritus, Conrad Grebel University College*

"After reading this commentary, you will never view Philippians the same way again! We meet a prisoner in chains writing to a suffering assembly whose citizenship under Messiah Jesus contrasts with Roman citizenship of the day. Combining 'empire-critical' and rhetorical analysis with a fresh translation, Zerbe takes readers on a crosscultural trip that pours profound new meanings into this letter for believers today." *—Reta Halteman Finger, author of* Creating a Scene in Corinth

"This is a superb commentary from a mature scholar. Zerbe combines historical and exegetical expertise with lived missional experience in circumstances of oppression, to impressive effect. Every page contests an easy 'spiritual' reading of Philippians. Zerbe immerses his readers in the first-century drama of staying loyal to a Messiah in the face of imperial ideology and challenges them, judiciously and compellingly, to discern their own responsibilities today." *—Neil Elliott, author of* Liberating Paul *and* The Arrogance of Nations

"Rich in analysis of citizenship in the Roman Empire, compelling in argumentation for a contrasting citizenship in transformational communities of Jesus loyalists, and fresh with insights into debated issues of translation and theology, Zerbe's commentary on Paul's letter to the Philippians sparkles with usable material for preaching, teaching, and personal Bible study."
—Jon Isaak, director of the Centre for Mennonite Brethren Studies

"Zerbe's engaging commentary on Philippians as a theopolitical summons to the practice of 'kingdom allegiance and messianic citizenship' represents the best of Anabaptist New Testament scholarship. It also reflects Zerbe's deep involvement with the church in the Philippines. At the same time, this insightful—and occasionally provocative—interpretation can challenge Christians of every tradition and culture to wrestle with the gospel's call to live worthily of the crucified and resurrected Lord." *—Michael J. Gorman, Raymond E. Brown Professor of Biblical Studies and Theology, St. Mary's Seminary and University*

"An excellent resource by an excellent scholar for anyone—teacher, pastor, scholar, student, lay, clergy—wanting to learn more about the ancient world of Paul, his letter to the Philippians, and its relevance for today. It will be at the top of the reading list for my courses about Paul."*—Laura L. Brenneman, New Testament editor of the Studies in Peace and Scripture series*

CPSIA information can be obtained
at www.ICGtesting.com
Printed in the USA
LVHW011325170222
711211LV00004B/167